CONTACT STRATEGIES

Contact Strategies

Histories of Native Autonomy in Brazil

HEATHER F. ROLLER

STANFORD UNIVERSITY PRESS
Stanford, California

STANFORD UNIVERSITY PRESS
Stanford, California

©2021 by the Board of Trustees of the Leland Stanford Junior University. All rights reserved.

No part of this book may be reproduced or transmitted in any form or by any means, electronic or mechanical, including photocopying and recording, or in any information storage or retrieval system without the prior written permission of Stanford University Press.

Printed in the United States of America on acid-free, archival-quality paper

Library of Congress Cataloging-in-Publication Data
Names: Roller, Heather F., author.
Title: Contact strategies : histories of native autonomy in Brazil / Heather F. Roller.
Description: Stanford, California : Stanford University Press, 2021. | Includes bibliographical references and index.
Identifiers: LCCN 2020044691 (print) | LCCN 2020044692 (ebook) | ISBN 9781503628106 (cloth) | ISBN 9781503628113 (paperback) | ISBN 9781503628120 (ebook)
Subjects: LCSH: Whites—Brazil—Relations with Indians—History. | Indians of South America—Wars—Brazil. | Indians, Treatment of—Brazil—History. | Autonomy. | Brazil—Ethnic relations—History.
Classification: LCC F2520 .R64 2021 (print) | LCC F2520 (ebook) | DDC 305.800981--dc23
LC record available at https://lccn.loc.gov/2020044691
LC ebook record available at https://lccn.loc.gov/2020044692

Cover design: Heather F. Roller

Cover photo: Munduruku anklet (Johann Natterer Collection), c. 1830, KHM-Museumsverband, Weltmuseum Vienna.

Text design: Kevin Barrett Kane

Typeset at Stanford University Press in 10/14.4 New Baskerville

For my father, Michael Flynn

Contents

Illustrations ix
Acknowledgments xi
Abbreviations xv
Reference Maps xvi–xvii

	Introduction	1
1	Facing Empire	23
2	Why Embrace the Whites?	58
3	Practices of Peace	89
4	A Return to War Is Always Possible	120
5	Against Extinction	160
	Conclusion	188

Appendix: Indigenous Groups Discussed in the Text 201
Notes 207
Bibliography 293
Index 325

Illustrations

Maps

1	Territories of the Mbayá-Guaikurú in the Paraguay River Basin	xvi
2	Territories of the Mura in the Amazon River Basin	xvii

Figures

I.1	Native Visitors at a Plantation, 1835	12
1.1	"Waterfalls of the Cuñaré River," c. 1780s	27
1.2	Map of Goiás, c. 1750	35
1.3	Aerial photograph of the Pantanal	40
2.1	Portrait of the Guaikurú chief Caimá and his wife in 1791	70
2.2	Portrait of a Mura, 1787	84
3.1	Muras hunting turtles, c. 1800	101
3.2	Kadiwéu necklace, early twentieth century	111
3.3	Indian expenses at Coimbra, early 1800s	112
4.1	Party of visiting Bororos, 1827	127
4.2	Portrait of a Guaikurú, 1845	147
4.3	"Encampment of Guaycuru Indians" near Albuquerque, 1845	149
4.4	Portrait of a Munduruká on the Tapajós River, 1828	156
5.1	"Caduveo (Mbayá) Indian Woman, Nabileque River," c. 1897	163
5.2	"Mura Indian woman from the village of Jauary-Autaz," 1926	167

5.3	"Caduveo (Mbayá) Indian, 'Capitancinho,' Nabileque River," c. 1897	170
C.1	Kadiwéu Reserve boundary marker 19	195
C.2	First march of the Mura Indigenous people, 2019	197

Acknowledgments

To begin, I want to recognize the historical and present-day efforts of Indigenous peoples in Brazil to preserve their traditions, protect their communities, and keep their forests and rivers alive in the face of great adversity. This care work is heroic; it is so much easier to turn away. We must hope that the rest of the world, afflicted by a frightening new virus, will begin to listen to the warnings that Native peoples have been sounding for a long time: that our alienation from nature and heedless pursuit of profit carry grave consequences for our collective survival.

I acknowledge, too, the work of Brazilian archive, library, and museum staff who look after the historical patrimony of the people despite the disgraceful neglect and austerity that has been imposed on cultural institutions across Brazil. The 2018 burning of the National Museum in Rio de Janeiro epitomizes the tragic result of this neglect, as tens of thousands of Native artifacts and millions of other records turned to ash. That loss is still keenly felt, in different ways, by staff, scholars, and especially Native communities across Brazil.

I have been able to complete this book only because so many people, near and far, supported my work. When I was in the earliest stages of imagining what it might look like, the late John Monteiro read my proposal and urged me to think more broadly about how Native peoples nurtured their autonomy through the centuries. Rather than advising me to scale down the project, he encouraged me to go big, which was exactly what I needed to hear at that moment. His generous engagement with other scholars' work will always be remembered.

I am also tremendously grateful to Mark Harris. From reviewing this book in the most constructive terms possible to sharing precious archival documents with me, his collegiality is unmatched. Along with Silvia Espelt-Bombin, Mark also brought me to the University of St Andrews at a key moment in the development of my ideas.

A number of other scholars in the United States and Brazil have directly aided my research and writing. Cynthia Radding and Danna Levin Rojo believed in the originality of my work and brought me into fruitful dialogue with people working on other parts of the Iberian borderlands. Hal Langfur, George Reid Andrews, and Zephyr Frank wrote important letters of support and always offered me sage advice. Rafael Chambouleyron has shared rich research materials over the years, including the most beautiful map I've ever seen, from the library at Évora, Portugal; he also offered valuable feedback on a chapter of the manuscript. Vanda da Silva helped me navigate the state archive in Cuiabá, shared key transcriptions of documents there, and took me on a trip to the Chapada dos Guimarães that I will never forget. Also memorable was spending a few days at an Amazonian Studies workshop with Marta Rosa Amoroso, where we pored over eighteenth-century documents together. I'm especially grateful to Neil Safier for facilitating so many generative conversations about Indigenous history and Amazonia at the John Carter Brown Library. I first met Amy Turner Bushnell there, and her interest in broad patterns of Native autonomy across the hemisphere helped inspire my own.

I received references and copies of important research materials from Adriana Athila, Mary Karasch, David Mead, Tamar Herzog, Fabrício Prado, Oscar de la Torre, Mônica Pechincha, Ian Read, Francismar Lopes de Carvalho, Danilo Bandini Ribeiro, and Mark Harris. For sharing their insights about Indigenous histories and politics with me, I thank Jeff Erbig, Laura Zanotti, Carlos Fausto, Eduardo Neves, Camila Dias, Lucia Sá, Silvia Espelt-Bombin, Yuko Miki, Maria Regina Celestino de Almeida, Karl Heinz, Alexandre Cardoso,

Elizabeth Ewart, Seth Garfield, Sean McEnroe, Ray Craib, Matthew Restall, Camilla Townsend, Coll Thrush, Marcy Norton, Dana Graef, and Yanna Yannakakis.

My colleagues in the History Department and the Native American Studies Program at Colgate University are the sorts of people you really miss seeing when everyone is working remotely. Dan Bouk, my most trusted reader, offered insightful comments on the introduction and conclusion. David Robinson, Andrew Rotter, Robert Nemes, Ray Douglas, Jill Harsin, and Graham Hodges have given wise counsel on everything from fellowship applications to publishing, while Antonio Barrera and Ryan Hall shared books and ideas about Indigenous history in other parts of the Americas. I thank two of my former students: Haley Allen, who pushed me to articulate the stakes of this project; and Matthew Kato, who assisted me with a particularly daunting research task. The students of History 358 also deserve credit for collectively helping me think through some of the big questions that animate the book.

I have been sustained by the friendship, laughter, and support of Marie Antonelli, Sylvia Sellers-García, Maura Tumulty, Ana Jimenez, Kerri Hudson, Brenton Sullivan, Daniella Doron, Dan Bouk, Marta Perez-Carbonell, Ryan Hall, Becca Loomis, Dionne Bailey, Thaís Rezende da Silva de Sant'ana, Jen McGee, Xan Karn, Geoff Shamos, Sean Burns, Teresa Cribelli, and Jyoti Balachandran.

A fellowship from the American Council of Learned Societies, in partnership with the National Endowment for the Humanities and the Social Sciences Research Council, supported a year of research trips to Brazil in 2013–14. An intense year of writing was made possible in 2017–18 by a National Endowment for the Humanities Fellowship. (I must add that any views, findings, conclusions, or recommendations expressed in this book do not necessarily represent those of the National Endowment for the Humanities.) Colgate University also provided several grants to support research in Brazil and Portugal, as well as crucial time away from teaching and service. I have treasured this time to think, dig in archives, and write, and I do not take it for granted.

At Stanford University Press, Margo Irvin, Cindy Lim, and Emily Smith gracefully shepherded the manuscript through the publication process. An anonymous reviewer joined Mark Harris in providing crucial feedback. Kaylie Patacca and Dai Yamamoto provided maps assistance along the way, and Erin Greb produced the complex reference maps that appear in the book. At the copyediting stage, Barbara Armentrout combed through the manuscript with care.

Permission from Oxford University Press and Duke University Press to reprint material is gratefully acknowledged. Parts of chapters 2 and 3 were originally published as "Autonomous Indian Nations and Peacemaking in Colonial Brazil," in *The Oxford Handbook of Borderlands of the Iberian World*, ed. Cynthia Radding and Danna Levin Rojo (Oxford University Press, 2019), 641–66. A portion of chapter 5 was published as "On the Verge of Total Extinction? From Guaikurú to Kadiwéu in Nineteenth-Century Brazil," *Ethnohistory* 65, no. 4 (2018): 647–70.

John and Clare, thank you for giving me the time I needed to finish this book, especially during our quarantine in the spring and summer of 2020. This book is dedicated to my father, Michael. Thank you for all the essential help—the care you gave to my daughter, the rides to wherever I needed to be, the welcoming space of your home by the sea. You are a pillar of support and unconditional love.

Abbreviations

The following archive abbreviations are used in the notes:

ACBM	Arquivo da Casa Barão de Melgaço (Cuiabá, Brazil)
AIHGB	Arquivo do Instituto Histórico e Geográfico Brasileiro (Rio de Janeiro, Brazil)
AHE	Arquivo Histórico do Exército (Rio de Janeiro, Brazil)
AHI	Arquivo Histórico do Itamaraty (Rio de Janeiro, Brazil)
AHEG	Arquivo Histórico Estadual de Goiás (Goiânia, Brazil)
AHU	Arquivo Histórico Ultramarino (Lisbon, Portugal)
ANRJ	Arquivo Nacional (Rio de Janeiro, Brazil)
APMT	Arquivo Público do Estado de Mato Grosso (Cuiabá, Brazil)
APEP	Arquivo Público do Estado do Pará (Belém, Brazil)
BNRJ	Biblioteca Nacional (Rio de Janeiro, Brazil)
BPE	Biblioteca Pública de Évora (Évora, Portugal)

Abbreviations in the document citations refer to Caixa (Cx.), Documento (Doc.), Códice (Cod.), and fólio (fl.).

MAP 1 Territories of the Mbayá-Guaikurú in the Paraguay River Basin.
Erin Greb Cartography.

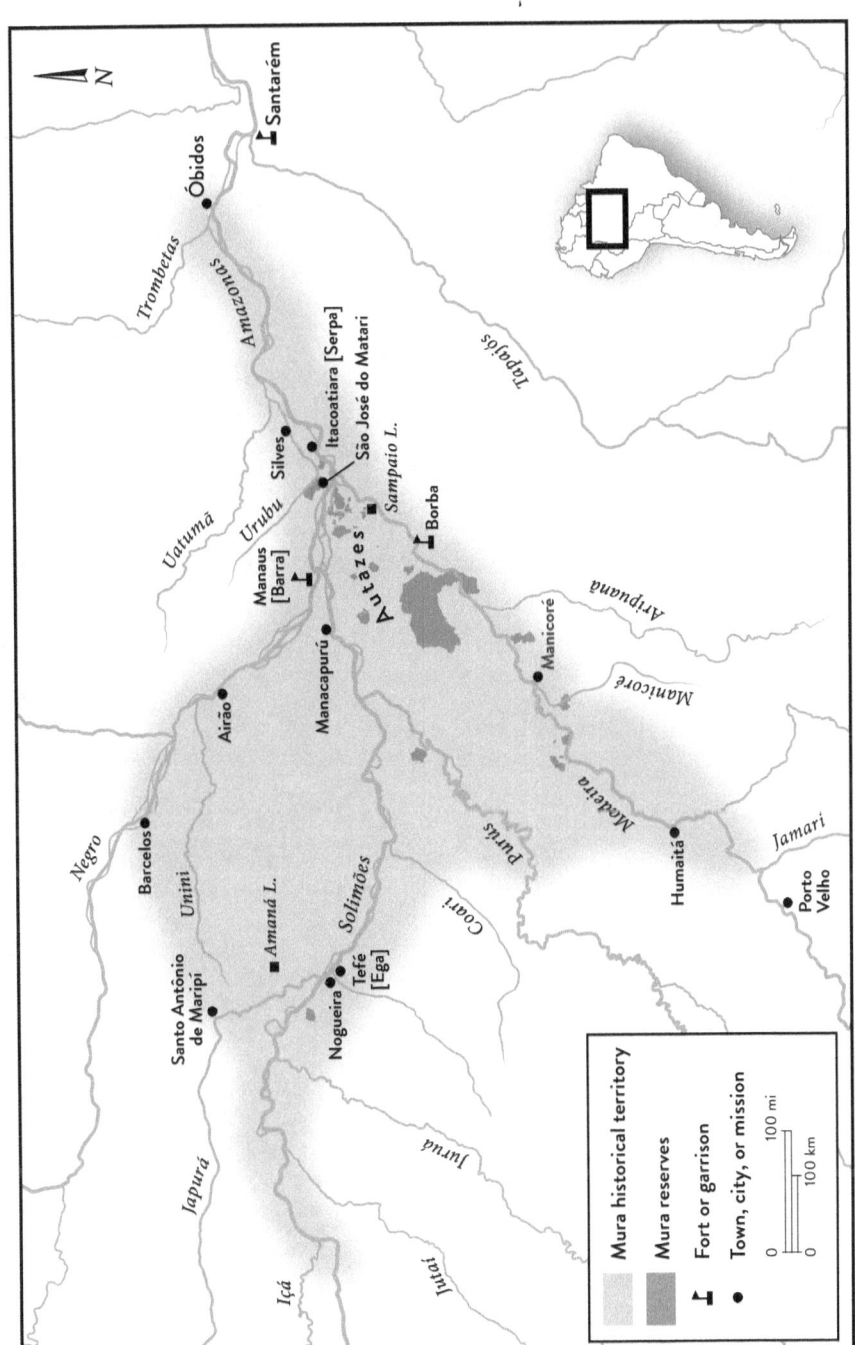

MAP 2 Territories of the Mura in the Amazon River Basin.
Erin Greb Cartography.

# CONTACT STRATEGIES

Introduction

THE XAVANTE BOYS would never forget their first impressions of the city. Trucks roared and spewed exhaust, sirens blared, and people yelled in a strange tongue. The boys' home village—with its savannas, forests, and streams—was hundreds of miles away. In the city, they would live with middle-class foster families, learn another language, and attend school. Over the years, each would become familiar with the cultural codes of the *warazu*, the whites. Most would even enjoy life in the city, with its soccer games and afternoons watching cartoons, but they constantly felt the pull of home.[1]

There had been eight boys in all, handpicked by their chief, Apoena, in the late 1970s and early 1980s. "It is to Ribeirão Preto that they will be sent," the chief had said, referring to a city in the state of São Paulo, Brazil. "They go with a mission: to study, to learn, to enter the heart of warazu culture." The chief's decision was part of a much longer process of moving closer to whites and seeking to dictate the pace and forms of that contact. Apoena himself was legendary among his people and among Brazilians for making peace back in the 1940s. As the Xavante described it, they had "tamed the whites," ending a long period of bloodshed and successfully channeling a flow of gifts and other material benefits into Xavante hands. But waves of ranchers and other settlers had come, too. They moved deeper into Native territories, felled forests, and strung up barbed wire to contain vast herds of cattle. By the 1970s, the situation had become dire. As one Xavante elder remembered, Apoena "thought a lot about the future and the survival of the community. That's how he came up with the strategy against the non-Indians." He would send the Xavante children, some of whom were his own grandsons, "to learn the language of the warazu to defend our people."[2]

The Xavante were not ignorant or naïve about contact. Since the eighteenth century, Xavante groups had engaged in cycles of violence and revenge with white interlopers, but they also had interacted peacefully with traders, missionaries, and officials. Some Xavantes even agreed to live in state-run settlements or missions, until epidemics and abuse drove them to migrate farther into the interior.[3] With these collective memories of trauma and loss, the boys' mothers cried for them when it was time to bid farewell for what they feared was the last time. But they consented to Apoena's plan, for they agreed that the boys had important roles to play in the history of their people. They called it the Xavante Strategy.[4]

Seven of the eight boys returned home as grown men. They became leaders of Xavante villages and were key figures in the struggle to reclaim their lands in the state of Mato Grosso—a struggle in which Portuguese language skills and other forms of intercultural fluency were essential.[5] The eighth stayed in São Paulo, working as a Xavante representative in the world of the whites and promoting knowledge of Xavante culture. He even helped produce a documentary film about the boys' experiences in the city, as they carried out the visionary plan of Apoena.[6]

This book is about the ingenuity and complexity of Native contact strategies, used and adapted by a wide range of Indigenous groups in Brazil as they sought to maintain their autonomy over about two centuries. It aims to bring the reader into a world distant from the Atlantic coast, yet connected to it by flows of people, objects, and ideas. The inhabitants of this world almost never put pen to paper, but their actions and occasionally their words filled the pages of missionary chronicles, official reports, and the accounts of explorers and would-be settlers in their territories. They also passed down their own oral histories, which were occasionally collected by travelers and ethnographers. Such records, though fragmentary, tell us a great deal about the dynamics of contact. They also remind us of an essential fact, one that is often obscured by our knowledge of how things turned out: for a very long time, large numbers of people managed to live outside the structures of colonial or national rule.

Brazil was not the only place. Around 1800, over half of the habitable territory of the Western Hemisphere—from the American Southwest to the Caribbean coast of Central America to the vast grasslands of Argentina and Chile—was under effective Native control.[7] Scholars have recognized the social and political implications of this situation but have generally analyzed it from the Euro-American side, from the perspective of state societies that wanted to assert stronger claims over borderlands and nonstate peoples. We are only just beginning to consider what it looked at it from the other side, from the perspective of autonomous Indians who saw those "borderlands" as the edges of their homelands. This shift in perspective has been framed as "facing east" or, more broadly, as "facing empire." It is an effort—always incomplete, given our source material—to understand how the processes of state and settler expansion looked from the vantage point of still-autonomous peoples.[8]

My previous book focused on how Native Amazonians built enduring communities under Portuguese colonialism.[9] In my initial research for that project, I made a rather rigid distinction between Indigenous peoples who were incorporated into the colonial system (the focus of that research) and those who were not; I assumed that autonomous groups *stayed that way* by rejecting or avoiding contact with colonial society. They had, I thought, chosen the opposite path—the path of no engagement. But soon I began finding sources that described autonomous Native peoples initiating contacts, stipulating their conditions, and directing their course. I realized that this deeper history of engagement needed to be told. It is not simply a flight story nor an incorporation story—these being the traditional framings for Indigenous history in Brazil. Instead, it is a story of how independent Native groups sought access to new products, knowledge, and people, for their own purposes and, whenever possible, on their own terms.[10]

The central argument developed in these pages is that autonomous Native peoples often took the initiative in their contacts with Brazilian society. Rather than fleeing or permanently withdrawing from that society, many groups sought to appropriate what was useful and powerful from the world of the whites. (In this context, *white* had little to do with skin color and was instead defined as non-Indigenous.) At the same time, Indigenous people chose not to live like whites.[11] They refused fixed settlement, rejected formal religious conversion, and continued to move and gain their subsistence in the old ways—even as they visited capital cities, acquired new, useful things like axes, guns, and horses, and incorporated non-Indigenous people into their bands. They also sought to control the pace and extent of contact: they might open up to outsiders for a period of time and then decide to limit interactions for as long as was collectively deemed necessary.

Stories of Native agency and power are important, especially when they overturn old narratives of defeat, passivity, or irrelevance. We discover that in some times and places, Indigenous peoples felt that they had the upper hand: they considered Euro-Americans to be weak opponents and sought, often successfully, to manipulate them for their own gain. It would be a mistake, however, to idealize these initiatives. Many Indigenous groups across the hemisphere grew fiercely divided over questions of strategy. They argued and even shed blood over disagreements about how to position themselves defensively or opportunistically before the invaders, and if these internal conflicts could not be reconciled, Native groups might splinter, sometimes permanently. Some turned on neighboring Indigenous societies, brutalizing those who could not (or would not) play by the new rules of engagement. As an example of a divisive strategy, we might think of the extensive trafficking in Native children that occurred in Brazil, peaking in the nineteenth century. That trade was mediated by a rising cohort of Native leaders whose power and authority derived from their success at controlling such exchange relations with Europeans and their descendants. Other leaders and peoples wanted no part of human trafficking, and some became victims of it. We can see echoes of such divergences among and between Native groups today, often revolving around the question of whether to allow extractive industries like logging or mining on their lands.

With the goal of understanding the full range of Native strategies in situations of contact, the book is framed broadly. It bridges two major periods of Brazilian history as traditionally defined. Most scholars who acknowledge the power and persistence of Native peoples in colonial Brazil have seen independence from Portugal in 1822 as the beginning of a new era of Native decline and disappearance. Without discounting the hardships that they faced with the violent expansion of settler enterprises and new forms of state repression, the book aims to highlight the processes by which many Native groups endured as autonomous peoples. Even late in the nineteenth century, Brazilian authorities admitted among themselves that some two-thirds of the empire's territory was "inaccessible to the civilized man" and that many settlements in the interior were surrounded by "wild Indians" who threatened them with "formidable hostilities."[12] Behind this rhetoric of loathing are histories of Native autonomy and resistance that no longer can be relegated to a distant past. At the same time, it is clear that colonialism, as a set of practices and ideologies, continued to structure the interactions of the state, settlers, and Native peoples long after the birth of the Brazilian empire and republic.[13] Throughout the centuries considered in this book, Native peoples' historical roles and contemporary rights to resources and land were denied according to a persistent colonial logic. The reader will therefore see the adjective *colonial* attached to the conventionally defined era of Portuguese rule in Brazil and its associated institutions, while terms like *colonial, colonization,* and *colonialism* are used in their broader sense.

Whereas most Indigenous histories focus on a single group or region, this one weaves together stories from across Native Brazil (see the appendix). It also tracks changes in strategies over time and space by accompanying the trajectories of two powerful groups: the Mura and the Mbayá-Guaikurú (or simply Guaikurú).[14] With homelands in the two major river basins of South America—the Amazonian and the

Paraguayan—these two peoples were at the center of some of the continent's fiercest battles over routes and territory. Through their labor, they each created immense landscapes of seasonal bounty: in the case of the Guaikurú, groves of fruiting palms and lush grazing lands that emerged from the annual floodwaters; and in the homelands of the Mura, rivers and lakes that teemed with aquatic life.[15] Though there was no known contact between the Mura and the Guaikurú, I think of them as connected by vast, intricate networks of water. They were also linked in the writings of state officials, who came to see them as common threats—or as valuable allies. Some of these authors were known to have encountered both groups in the field.[16]

Like many of those labeled "indomitable" around the hemisphere, the Mura and the Guaikurú were peoples skilled in the use of canoes or horses, which made them fast and formidable in warfare.[17] For a half century or more, they successfully fought colonial expansion in their respective regions, using a devastatingly effective combination of old and new techniques of warfare. Each group also forged long-lasting (though still fragile) peace agreements with the Portuguese in the late eighteenth century, which brought both Native peoples into regular, often close interaction with a range of colonial actors. But the story did not end with their supposed "pacification." In the nineteenth century, they made themselves indispensable to the Brazilians as allies and impossible to ignore as enemies. And over the course of the last century, they have revealed—through their words, actions, and claims—the hollowness of narratives that proclaim them to be extinct.

The Guaikurú and the Mura are among the few Native groups in Brazil for which we have a rich, long-term register of historical documents.[18] Anthropologists and a handful of historians have already written about each group, but this book presents new evidence from the neglected collections of regional archives in Brazil. The paper trail on the Guaikurú extends into Spanish America, too, beginning in the late sixteenth century and intensifying as they positioned themselves at the center of the Spanish-Portuguese imperial rivalry of the eighteenth century.[19] Though I decided to limit my archival research to Brazil and Portugal, mindful of the fact that the project already sprawled across regions and time periods, I have looked past colonial and national borders in my search for relevant scholarship on the strategies of autonomous Native groups. I have also relied on the fieldwork of anthropologists engaged with descendant communities of Guaikurú (who are known as the Kadiwéu) and Mura peoples and have looked to Native oral histories and interviews to understand how contact has been lived and interpreted in the modern period.

We tend to assume that very few autonomous Native groups affected processes of colonization and state formation in the Americas. The handful of groups that feature prominently in the literature—such as the Comanche and the Mapuche—are usually described as exceptional cases. Much distinguished these Native societies from others, but I will argue that within the Brazilian context, the Guaikurú and Mura were more *emblematic* than exceptional.[20] Similar strategies of engagement were used by many Native peoples in different regions and periods, as the sources make clear. If some Indigenous groups' interactions with state societies were better documented, it was often because they occurred on a larger scale, for a longer period of time, or in regions of greater geopolitical importance.

Contact strategies shifted over time, often dramatically. In some historical contexts, openness to outside people and things made sense and brought real advantages. At other times, the same group might decide that it was better to reject and withdraw. These were strategies not necessarily in the mode of conscious, rational calculation (though sometimes they were that), but more in the sense of practical decision-making and improvisation in response to ever-changing situations.[21] It has to be acknowledged, of course, that many Native societies did not survive long enough to pursue such strategies. But those that did left their mark on colonial and national societies—imposing upon them, rejecting them, or even offering an alternative to them.[22]

Homelands and Borderlands

In an agricultural treatise about the northwest Amazon in the eighteenth century, one finds an entry on the *urucum*, or annatto, tree. Removed from their spiky pods, the urucum seeds could be boiled down and made into a brilliantly red dye, and the author of the treatise noted that "nearly all of the heathens paint themselves with the beautiful finery of this color." For colonists, urucum was a potential export product, and some began to cultivate the tree. But it was also seen as a kind of indicator species for independent Indians in the interior: "Only where there are no heathens are there no urucum trees; in fact, if one is found out in the forest, it is a sign that there were, or still are, some heathens in those parts."[23] Because there was no indelible frontier line separating colonial territories from Indigenous ones, colonists depended on features of the landscape to identify spaces that were more or less secure, closer or farther from the corridors and enclaves of colonial power.[24] Not only particular tree species but also trails through the jungle, fishing weirs in remote waterways, burned or cleared areas, columns of smoke in the distance, or—more ominously—arrows embedded in footpaths might indicate that one was in Native territory. Colonial maps also depicted these interior spaces, leaving them disconcertingly empty or filling them with symbolically dense tree cover. Sometimes the mapmaker added a club-wielding Indian to remind European audiences of what such spaces represented, but local settlers knew intuitively, through the daily practice of deciding where they could land their canoes, pasture their animals, or hunt.[25]

One of Brazil's first historians described the early Portuguese colony as a crab civilization, its settlers clinging to the Atlantic coast.[26] But by the early eighteenth century, armed adventurers had begun moving aggressively west in search of mineral wealth and Native slaves. Over the course of decades, they set up mining operations and trading camps in the *sertão*, the remote interior lands or "wilderness." Collaborating with these settlers, the Crown established forts and strategic settlements as a means of staking Portuguese claims to the lands and resources (including human ones) of the interior. But rather than the sovereign imperial realm imagined by distant Europeans, these were outposts—as any colonist unlucky enough to be stationed at an upriver garrison knew. The urucum trees were all around.

The spaces in proximity to these outposts and routes of expansion but not under state control have been conceptualized by anthropologists of South America as the *tribal zone*. The arrival of Europeans, along with their germs and technology, fundamentally altered social relations and ecological conditions in Indigenous core areas; at the same time, Native groups sought to adapt their strategies of trade, warfare, and survival to the new context. Processes of structural change, from increased militarization to political centralization, played out across this zone, even among those groups not in direct contact with Europeans.[27] In other words, there was no world apart for independent Native peoples. For all of their internal complexity and deep history, they were never cordoned off from the developments at the coasts, along the colonial highways, or at the outposts of empire. This autonomous and interconnected Indigenous realm was a "Native New World."[28]

Historians of this hemisphere often refer to the spaces where different peoples came into contact, but where no single group could claim absolute control, as *borderlands*. More specifically, borderlands could be zones between rival European empires—say, the Portuguese and the Spanish—where the balance of power was shifting and uncertain.[29] But what if Indigenous initiatives were just as important as, or even more important than, imperial rivalries in shaping the borderlands over time? What if borderlands formed around or between Indigenous homelands? How might emerging colonial societies have been shaped by the social, cultural, and political dynamics of Indigenous spaces? In the words of historians Pekka Hämäläinen and Samuel Truett: "Instead of merely asking what Indians did when Europeans grappled for power, we must take a larger view. We must ask how Indians created the conditions for borderlands history rather than simply looking at how they acted within it."[30]

Long-lived stereotypes about unconquered Indians stand in the way of more nuanced understandings of Native historical agency in the borderlands and interior spaces of Brazil. Consider, for example, what I have identified as the first detailed description of the Mura, written by a Jesuit missionary in the early years of the eighteenth century. He characterized the "heathen corsairs" (*gentio de corso*) of the Madeira River region as follows: "Truly wild beasts of the forest, they are only human in the form of their bodies. They do not have houses, nor villages; they wander ceaselessly through the forest, sleeping wherever they are at nightfall; and they eat only fruits, game, and wild honey.... Everything they eat is more raw than roasted or cooked." Although they were said to be friendly with two other Native groups, with whom they visited and shared food, the author said that the Mura would turn on these friends violently if they did not receive everything they wanted on these visits—in what was likely a reference to the feasts and ritual combats that the Mura still practice to this day with neighboring groups.[31] In such descriptions, independent Indians were associated with nature and savagery, harkening back to medieval European images of the wild man and representing the antithesis of all that was civilized.[32]

In calling the Mura *gentio* (heathens), the Jesuit author used the standard term for unconverted Indians. Originally referring to those who were neither Christian nor Muslim, by the sixteenth century the term was being applied to the Native peoples encountered by the Portuguese in South America and Africa, who were thought to practice no religion at all. According to the old proverb, the Brazilian Indians were "sem fé, sem lei, sem rei" (without faith, without law, without king). In another version, they were "sem barba, sem honra, sem vergonha" (without beard, without honor, without shame). For centuries, Native peoples would be defined in terms of what they supposedly lacked.[33]

Unconquered Native polities were also seen as instinctively hostile, a trait that was almost always linked in colonial texts to their mobile way of life. According to the same Jesuit author, the Mura "attack the whites wherever they come across them . . . and they are greatly feared by the rest of the heathens. They go about in groups of eighty, ninety, or one hundred, and anywhere they go, they soon make war, without any other cause than taking women from one another."[34] By the eighteenth century, the Mura had become, along with the Guaikurú, the "archetype of ferocious nomads." These narratives of "an 'errant' and 'pillaging' people forever wandering the *sertões*," or wilderness, shaped anti-Indigenous policies and justified wars against a wide range of independent Native groups.[35] The same peoples were often accused of cannibalism, typically without any direct evidence. Instead, authors recycled older images of roasting human flesh, which had appeared in famous sixteenth-century accounts of Native peoples.[36] The threat of hostile "barbarians" also had a certain convenience. Local power brokers might, for example, invoke such threats as a means of justifying armed expansion into new territories or protecting their own interests and privileges in moments of political change. For the Crown, hostile Native groups might serve in a different but equally useful role: they effectively blocked unauthorized people—smugglers, prospectors, or rival Europeans—from entering particular territories.[37]

Savage, wild, heathen, cruel, barbarous, errant, and *wandering*: this is how writers most commonly described independent Indians, well into the modern period. They often compared them to pests like ants (which destroyed crops) and mosquitoes (which plagued humans), and they wrote about their presence as a kind of "infestation" of lands and rivers.[38] When settlers took Native captives, they referred to them as "pieces"—selling them, renting them out, and bequeathing them to their heirs as human property.[39] Jarring as all these words and images are, historians know how to read around and between them. With the awareness that autonomous people have been vilified throughout global history by those who have failed to exert social, economic, and political control over them, we can question or reject outright the negative traits that have been ascribed to independent Indians. At the same time, we can highlight evidence of Native initiative and strategy. Take, for example, the many historical descriptions of Native mobility. Instead of the aimless nomadism that has been criminalized for centuries, it is possible to detect a capacity for territorial expansion, nimble practices of subsistence, and purposeful engagement with the outside world.[40] Likewise, denunciations of Native raiding as senseless cruelty often contain evidence of purposeful targets, and they can be cross-examined with other sources that describe how Indians responded to the provocations of settlers and soldiers and took advantage of their tactical weaknesses. Historical documents, in other words, can be read in ways that their authors never intended.

Admittedly, the source limitations for the study of nonstate people's histories are daunting even within ethnohistory—a field that formed around the method of bringing ethnological insights to the interpretation of documents produced in situations of contact or conflict.[41] Native peoples of the Americas who were incorporated as colonial subjects at least "shared some common discursive terrain with Europeans," such as a basic understanding of colonial law and Christianity. Some of these Native subjects even produced their own written sources in a European language or in an alphabetized version of their mother tongue.[42] But for autonomous Native groups during the era of Portuguese colonization, the most direct statements we have were filtered ones, usually communicated through interpreters. To my dismay as I was doing the research for this book, even the names of important leaders usually went unrecorded in the sources. Native cosmologies and prophecies, if recounted at all, tended to be described in a fragmentary, muddled, or condescending way, making them impossible to reconstruct as they existed centuries ago. But many autonomous Native peoples quickly acquired facility with Euro-American conventions and symbols when it served their interests to do so and when there were political or economic openings available to them. They might cross a border to visit a frontier fort, show up on the outskirts of a colonial town, or make friendly overtures at a plantation, seeking an audience with local power brokers or an opportunity to trade (figure I.1). They sometimes interacted with travelers who passed through their territories, or hosted visitors in their villages. These actions and choices left traces in the documentary record that we can mine for insights into Native motivations and aims.

FIGURE I.1 Native Visitors at a Plantation, 1835.
Source: Johann Moritz Rugendas, *Malerische Reise in Brasilien* (Paris: Engelmann & Cie, 1835).

The historical sources for this book have had to be eclectic and far-ranging. They include official correspondence, military reports, missionary chronicles, legislative or policy documents, travelers' accounts, natural histories, maps, portraits, ethnographies, and oral histories. Moving from the early eighteenth century into the twentieth century, the sources change dramatically in quantity and quality. On the one hand, documentation became more decentralized and fragmentary with the end of Portuguese rule; even the thick rag paper was replaced by brittle domestic sheets after independence. On the other hand, one finds more individual voices and a greater quantity of culturally important motifs and stories. Many of these were collected by amateur ethnographers, who felt a sense of urgency to preserve bits and pieces of Native cultures that they assumed were on their way to extinction.

In the 1890s, one such traveler-ethnographer in Western Brazil described an elderly Kadiwéu woman, squatting in the sun, preparing urucum seeds to make paint. "The operation was long and patient," he wrote. "And because her hands were the principle instruments used, it happened that her fingers were ever more dyed with the beautiful red color in preparation. Instead of cleaning them with a rag or washing them, she simply rubbed them off on her body, which, with the passing of time, turned completely red, so much so that the old woman looked like an ancient statue of terra cotta." The Kadiwéu and their Guaikurú ancestors once collected urucum in the wild, but by the late nineteenth century, they were growing their own and trading it with neighboring Native groups. For many Indigenous peoples in South America, including the Kadiwéu, painting with urucum and other natural dyes remains central to their ritual life, aesthetics, and identity.[43] The sight of an urucum tree means that one is close to home.

Indigenous Histories of Contact

For the nearly three hundred Native groups now living in Brazil, contact is a process that plays out every day. As the Indigenous leader Ailton Krenak reminds us, it cannot be reduced to an initial encounter between Europeans and Native peoples back in 1500 or 1800.[44] Historically, contact has taken many forms, not all of which involve face-to-face encounters. We know, for example, that European pathogens could arrive among Indigenous peoples long before Europeans themselves and that trade goods could pass through Native intermediaries to reach even very remote groups. These forms of indirect contact have had profound effects on Native societies over time. Access to metal blades—even old, used fragments—could lead to more slash-and-burn farming and less permanent horticulture. Internal power dynamics could shift as some villages developed better access to trade goods. Epidemic diseases might decimate some groups while permitting others to expand into depopulated territories. Thus, seemingly isolated Indigenous groups were thoroughly transformed by contact even before their first direct encounters with explorers, slave traders, missionaries, or government officials.[45]

Contact and isolation have often been cyclical, characterized by periods of expansion and retraction. Scholars have described "tidal" patterns of contact: "The nineteenth-century rubber economy drew back into the system peoples who had been subjected to missionary influences more than a century before. Twentieth-century state agents contacted 'pristine' peoples already attacked by seventeenth- and eighteenth-century *bandeirantes* [armed explorers]. Native groups also enacted the 'discovery' of whites and commodities more than once."[46] The tidal metaphor, however, suggests a kind of unstoppable outside force acting upon these groups, when in fact these patterns of contact were very much shaped by their own agency. Previous experiences of contact shaped later ones, as Indigenous peoples tried to pursue or evade different kinds of interactions with outsiders.

The anthropologist Glenn Shepard has coined the term *voluntary isolation* to describe the situation of contemporary groups that have purposely isolated themselves, having lived through (or heard their elders' stories about) the dangers of contact in the past. Rather than being understood as "uncontacted" in a primordial or fetishized sense, their isolation should be recognized as the outcome of historical processes and their own collective decision-making.[47] It is also a time-tested strategy against disease, especially in the case of sicknesses transmitted through human contact. As one Xokleng man explained to a state administrator in the early twentieth century, "he was going into the forest, never to return—not to the camps around the Indian Post, not even close to us. . . . Asked why he would do such a thing, he declared that all the white people were enemies to the Indians, and if the *civilizados* did not exterminate [his people] by fire and sword, they would do it by means of sicknesses."[48] Native peoples have long been aware of the disproportionate impacts of disease on their communities, as well as the way in which disease has been weaponized by settlers. They see the past and present connections between the coming of sickness, the establishment of illegal "man camps" (of miners, loggers, soldiers) in their territories, and colonialist attitudes among those charged with upholding the law.[49] This awareness has shaped Native responses to the coronavirus pandemic as it sweeps across Brazil and Amazonia in 2020. Many Indigenous communities have attempted to close their borders or regulate contact with outsiders, and they have denounced the land invasions and illegal extractive activities that are accelerating in a context of social disruption and governmental neglect.[50]

Indigenous peoples are—and always have been—engaged in a process of interpreting and reinterpreting their own histories of contact.[51] To this day, for example, the Mura reject the use of the word *pacification* to describe their turn toward peaceful relations with whites.[52] Colonial Portuguese sources would date this shift to 1784–1786, but from a Mura perspective, it would likely be seen as a long-term process, one that would not make sense to limit to the late eighteenth century. Rather than a top-down effort of the state, peacemaking was driven by the yearnings, initiatives, and long-term goals of various Mura groups, and it did not entail surrendering their political and social autonomy. In recent decades, Mura leaders have tried to recover earlier histories of ferocity and indomitability. The leader Barreto Mura described coming across an epic poem by a colonial official, which chronicled the hostility of the Mura to the Portuguese (and framed the subsequent peace agreement as an act of divine providence): "It was in this book"—a reprint of the 1785 *Muhuraida* poem—"that I saw that our Mura people were fierce!" Barreto hoped that his fellow Muras would draw strength from this historical path of action and from the defiance shown by other Native peoples of Amazonia: "the courage to go before the authorities, to come together, to paint themselves [as warriors], and say: We are going to fight! We are going to show our faces!"[53]

Contact does not inevitably or uniformly weaken cultural integrity. For scholars, this insight has come out of paying attention to Indigenous perspectives, especially those that have emerged within the Indian rights movement in Brazil, and putting contemporary processes into dialogue with earlier, colonial histories of contact.[54] In doing this work, historians and anthropologists have identified important continuities in Indigenous ways of interacting with powerful or menacing outsiders. In the early nineteenth century, for example, we find the Guaikurú formally at peace with the Portuguese and living seasonally near the colonial fort on the upper Paraguay River. There, according to the Portuguese fort commander, the Guaikurú went around "boasting daily that even though we are very fierce, they know how to tame us."[55] The Indians had, in effect, reversed the mirror on the colonists: *they* were the fierce ones in need of domestication. Anthropologists of lowland South American cultures have identified similar narratives of Native groups situating whites in a subordinate position within their own vision of the world and seeking to capture what was new and different from the invaders. This Indigenous "openness to the Other," originally formulated by Claude Lévi-Strauss, has been theorized as a logic of "predation." The idea is that Indigenous groups assimilate—and even consume—foreign elements and enemy people, as part of a process of social reproduction.[56] The important book *Pacificando o branco* (Pacifying the whites) frames this as "the phenomenon of 'cannibalizing' the colonial encounter." Going beyond the old dichotomy of cultural defeat or unyielding resistance, it is possible to see an alternative path—one in which contact with outsiders was actively sought, for Native peoples' own ends.[57]

Of course, as anthropologists themselves have recognized, there is the danger of overgeneralizing and idealizing this process. We might come to view every Indigenous group as always engaged in some sort of predation, "capable of transforming itself continually, cannibalizing historical situations, in order to remain the same." But the concept, I think, remains useful. It keeps us questioning colonial narratives of "pacified" Indians, and it challenges the traditional scholarship that treats contact, conquest, and assimilation as proceeding in only one direction.[58]

Using the language of *contact strategies* admittedly requires some epistemological caution. Western categories of historical agency—like the notion of the free, rational individual seeking to maximize opportunity—do not map neatly onto Indigenous peoples of the past. (And it is worth pointing out that such categories flatten the aims and actions of non-Indigenous people, too.) At the same time, it is clear that the denial of Native peoples' roles in the making of their own histories and in the shaping of the modern world has been fundamental to attacks on their autonomy.[59]

Nowhere is this clearer than in the ongoing attempts to deny the legitimacy of Native claims to land. Beginning in the nineteenth century, the territories of independent Indians were legislatively treated as "vacant" or "unused," on the basis of the argument that they could not be owned or used by people who were seasonally mobile ("nomadic"). Reserves were eventually demarcated for some Indigenous groups, with the rationale that Indians—defined legally as minors—needed state protection, oversight, and a firm push down the path to acculturation. In the context of rampant land-grabbing and violent conflict between Native groups and settlers, the reserves were better than nothing. But they were often too small, too easily invaded by settlers, and too vulnerable to reduction or division by the state.[60] Davi Kopenawa, shaman and spokesman of the Yanomami people, has denounced this as a stance of willful oblivion: "The white people's thought remains full of forgetting. . . . [They] only think about covering over the land with their drawings so they can carve it into sections and only give us a few pieces encircled by their mines and plantations. After that, they will be satisfied and they will tell us: 'This is your land. We give it to you!'"[61] Other Native groups found that they were no longer seen as "true Indians" and were not considered eligible for any land rights at all. These judgments, promoted by local landowners and authorities in Brazil, were backed by global convictions about the inevitability of Native disappearance in the modern era. As an ideological move, it offered the convenience of erasing Native identities and historical claims to territory at the same time. Such efforts continue in the present, in Brazil and elsewhere in the world, but they are challenged at every step by scholars, activists, and especially Native peoples—many of whom are activists and scholars themselves.[62]

Identities Imposed, Invented, and (Re)claimed

It is a paradox that narratives of Native disappearance coexist with a dizzying number of ethnonyms, or ethnic-group names, in the historical record of the Americas. One stumbles through a thicket of different spellings, alternate names, subgroup designations, names of possibly extinct groups, pejorative nicknames, umbrella terms, and autodenominations.[63] The terms were not only the products of Euro-American confusion or fantasy, though these certainly played a part in their formation. The Portuguese, like the Spaniards, classified Indigenous "nations" using a mix of territorial, linguistic, sociopolitical, and phenotypic criteria.[64] Sometimes they relied on the assessments of Indigenous guides or mercenaries, who were asked to identify other groups on the basis of the distinctive weapons found at an abandoned village or the physical appearance of a fallen warrior.[65] In many cases, colonial authors lumped groups together and ignored autodenominations. In a recent interview, Ondino Casimiro—a teacher, church leader, and famed musician among the Magüta (Ticuna) people of the upper Solimões River region—described the historical imposition of the Ticuna ethnonym in the following terms: "I've always said that I don't like this word that they use, Ticuna. When the Portuguese came to Brazil, they saw the Magüta Indians, with their faces painted and their noses black, and that just meant Ticuna to them. That's why I don't like this word. The actual name of this people is Magüta, which means 'fished by Y'oi'"—referring to one of the main culture heroes of his people, said to have pulled the first Magüta out of a creek.[66] Even warring or rival Indigenous factions might be categorized by colonial authors as a single, cohesive nation. There were clear geopolitical motives behind doing so: border disputes sometimes turned on an imperial power's ability to claim large blocks of Indigenous allies. It was also a situation in which authors attempted to write about extra-colonial people and places about which they had little direct or reliable knowledge.[67]

Ethnonyms also reflected the ways that Native peoples characterized one another, often going back to the precolonial era. Sometimes these were full of disdain: the name Guaikurú, for example, meant "wicked and dirty people" in the language of the Guarani, who applied it to many neighboring groups in the Chaco before the arrival of Europeans.[68] Terms shifted rapidly according to the political realignments or ethnic regroupings that occurred as a result of contact between Native groups or with colonial societies. Scholars have noted, for example, that ethnonyms multiplied at moments of intense interethnic negotiation and conflict. Many were subsequently lost, and those that persisted in the historical record often belonged to groups that were more successful in exerting control over others.[69] The Kadiwéu are a case in point. During the eighteenth and nineteenth centuries, they were just one Mbayá-Guaikurú subgroup among about a half a dozen mentioned in the sources, but from the 1890s onward, only the Kadiwéu remained.

None of this was predictable. As a result of the historical and cultural process known as *ethnogenesis*—the opposite of ethnocide—new groups of people emerged throughout the borderlands. These included powerful raiding and trading societies that came to dominate weaker Native groups and threaten the security of settler communities, often on horseback, wielding guns or metal-tipped lances. Others were composite groups formed of people fleeing violence and slavery—escaped African slaves, runaway mission Indians, or deserting soldiers—who were then incorporated into Indigenous communities.[70] The Mura and Guaikurú (including the Kadiwéu) shared features of both types of emergent societies during the eighteenth century. Over their many years of contact with Brazilian society, they came to identify themselves with a particular territory: the wetlands and hills to the east of the Paraguay River in the case of the Guaikurú/Kadiwéu, and the maze of rivers and lakes known as the Autazes in the case of the Mura. This process of identification—described by scholars as *territorialization*—was a historical one, shaped by state efforts of boundary making and confinement as well as Native peoples' ongoing and changing relationships with the land they inhabited.[71]

Ethnogenesis did not end with national independence but rather continued in new forms and to new collective ends. When the Brazilian state set aside special funds in the middle decades of the nineteenth century for the "civilization" of "wild Indians," some Native groups began dressing and acting the part when they appeared before provincial authorities. They painted their bodies and claimed not to speak Portuguese, even though they were suspected of being longtime residents of the missions.[72] Government officials depicted this as simple subterfuge, but it also speaks to the flexibility of those identities and the blurry lines between incorporated and unincorporated Native peoples in that period.

In the last decades of the twentieth century, many rural communities in Brazil mobilized as Indigenous groups because it was a viable alternative to more traditional forms of political mobilization and also because they valued the rituals, myths, histories, and solidarities (including ties to the land) associated with that ethnic identity. In other words, it was both an effective strategy *and* a meaningful move for the community. Whether by asserting a direct connection to an Indigenous group assumed to be "extinct," incorporating culturally and territorially with an already recognized group, or forming a composite Indigenous identity, communities have obtained state recognition and rights to land and other resources.[73] Part of that process of reclamation has involved language, but it has played out in surprising ways. In Amazonia, for example, some Native groups have revived Nheengatu, the *língua geral*, or hybrid "general language" developed by the Jesuits for their missionary enterprise. The historian Márcia Mura explains that "with the passing of time, it went from being a language of colonization to become a language of resistance" for communities that had lost their mother tongue and saw Nheengatu as an important marker of difference with non-Indigenous language and culture.[74] Ethnic reclamation and revitalization movements continue in Brazil to this day, though they confront hostility from their non-Indigenous neighbors and from Brazilian society more broadly, as well as from the state as it has embraced the interests of the mining and agribusiness sectors.

The sources rarely allow historians to distinguish between imposed ethnonyms, deliberately claimed ones, and those that carried real meaning for the peoples to whom they were attached. We are left tracing inconsistencies and contradictions among the fragmentary sources at our disposal.[75] But once in a while, it is possible to glimpse Indigenous people making active assertions about their identities. A Mura group refused to tell colonial officials which among their group were subservient allies and captives from other ethnic groups, claiming a united identity: "The Muras do not want to say where they are from, and they say only that they are all Muras."[76] More than a century later, a Kadiwéu informant explained to a visiting foreigner that before wealthy ranchers came to take their land, "the Guaycurús were already fixed, established, rooted, and occupied in the raising of cattle and horses. Their 'NATION'—for that is how they designate their tribe—had been the first to occupy and settle all of the fields of this region and to possess cattle and horses, and they had always been livestock farmers and ranchers."[77] In these cases, the interlocutors may have been skeptical, but Indigenous strategies still shine through.

Each of the following chapters begins with a brief reconstruction of how autonomous Native groups might have approached different moments of contact. These are composite sketches, meant to remind the reader that the book is not framed as a series of discrete case studies; instead, the aim is to identify deep and broad patterns across Native Brazil. At the same time, I do not want to lose the texture of what real people were doing, saying, and (possibly) thinking in the past. To that end, the histories of the Mura and Guaikurú (Kadiwéu) run through every chapter, interwoven with one another and with the experiences of other independent Native groups.

Long portrayed as either reactive or passive, Indigenous peoples appear in these pages as creative and resourceful in navigating their rapidly transforming world. The first chapter finds them spying, scouting, traveling great distances, and temporarily immersing themselves in colonial contact situations, so as to obtain more information about the colonial world and its shifting mosaic of threats and opportunities. By the late eighteenth century, some of the most powerful Native groups in Brazil had decided to forge more peaceful relationships with the Portuguese. That many did so without submitting to colonial governance suggests that we need to look far beyond stories of "pacification" to understand why and how these peace processes unfolded. Chapter 2 reconstructs the peacemaking initiatives of the Mura and the Guaikurú, showing how each of these aimed to open up new social, political, and economic possibilities. Chapter 3 centers on peace talks and gift exchanges—two arenas of close interaction and tension during this era—and considers how these were shaped by Native cultural dynamics and political agendas.

The transition to national states and borders has been called the "most enduring divide" in the field of borderlands history because it is seen as breaking all the molds and precedents of what we conventionally call the colonial period. But if new nations (or a new empire, in the case of Brazil) brought the narrowing of diplomatic channels and of political opportunities for many Native peoples in the borderlands—now framed as "bordered lands"—independent Indians did not disappear.[78] Chapter 4 focuses on how, in the nineteenth century, autonomous Native groups in Brazil fought to defend what they had gained in their previous alliances with whites. Indigenous cultural persistence is explored in Chapter 5, which shows that Native groups drew on time-honed ways of dealing with outsiders and with rising pressures on land and resources in the late nineteenth century and early decades of the twentieth century. The Conclusion turns to descendant communities to consider how historical strategies for initiating and controlling contact have informed struggles for survival and self-determination in the present.

1 Facing Empire

▶ FROM BEHIND THE TREES, the spies watched the cargo canoes move slowly upriver. Each boat was bulky and awkward as it pushed through the narrows of the river, where the current ran fast. They could see that the rowers were brown-skinned like themselves but wore cloth trousers and took orders from the white men on board. Where canopies of wild cacao trees grew thick along the river banks, the canoes stopped. The newcomers set up camp on the shore, opening up a space for themselves, hacking at the greenery with their machetes. Once this was done, they could be seen splitting up into work teams. Some of them made small canoes that they took up the creeks, heading deeper into the forest to gather cacao pods. Others, just skinny boys, stayed behind to fish and cook for the whites and to dry the harvest as it arrived, load after load. Those at the camp always looked up and down the river, searching the trees on the water's edge, as if they knew they were being watched. The cacao men who circulated in the groves were even more wary, always keeping their guns within reach and posting guard at night.

Weeks later, when the canoes sat low and heavy in the water, the cacao men could be seen preparing for the trip downriver with their cargo. When they were finally gone, the Indians went to inspect what had been left behind. They had seen these things before: the still-smoldering fires; the drying mats for the cacao seeds, sticky and buzzing with insects; and the scars of metal blades on trees. They stood under the thatched-roof shelter where the white men had swung in their hammocks, smoked their pipes, and cleaned their guns. If they looked carefully, the Indians could find traces of manioc meal near the cooking area, and perhaps a stray fishhook, shiny and sharp to the touch.[1]

Indigenous spies left no written records of what they discovered. But we can reconstruct, however imperfectly, what the colonial world would have looked like from the perspective of those who were still living (mostly) outside of it, several centuries after the arrival of the first European colonists. What did autonomous Indians see, facing empire?[2] They were not innately or instinctively resistant peoples, though many groups still had strong warrior cultures. Nor were they, at the other end of the spectrum, unsuspecting future victims, unaware of the dangers surrounding them. In fact, Indigenous groups had acquired a great deal of information about the colonial world and the risks and possibilities that it offered. Many had sought to experience parts of that world—often at a distance, but sometimes up close—through reconnaissance, raids or violent encounters, and visits to trade or work. They passed the stories of what they saw down to their children and grandchildren, making sure to prepare them for what might come. Autonomous Indians were also plugged into vast and varied networks of information.[3] Among them lived many captives, including members of powerful settler families in major cities like Cuiabá and Asunción, who could answer their questions and perhaps convey a deeper understanding of European ways. Indians also crossed paths with people who had, against the odds, escaped from colonial captivity: the Indigenous prisoners who had managed to return home and the fugitive slaves and runaway mission Indians whom they sometimes incorporated into their groups. And as they had always done, independent Indians exchanged stories, rumors, and warnings with other Native groups—though many of these interethnic networks had been severed by European conquest.

This chapter considers what still-autonomous Native groups in the eighteenth-century borderlands likely knew about Europeans, colonialism, and life in the colonial sphere. It then goes a step further and asks how Indigenous peoples used this knowledge to shape the form and pace of contact. We can begin with a basic caveat: different Native groups pursued and had access to very different kinds of information over time, as colonial processes played out in different ways and on varied time scales throughout Brazil. The chapter is the first of five that revolve around the Guaikurú and Mura—again, not because they were exceptional cases, but because they were emblematic of the experiences and choices that many Indigenous groups made in different regions and eras.

Questions and Answers

Even those in very sporadic contact with the colonial world had some inkling of its diversity. Depending on the region, Indigenous groups in the Brazilian borderlands of the eighteenth century might encounter or hear stories about the Portuguese as well as the Spanish, French, Dutch, or English. These peoples had distinct languages, settlements, and leaders, but they also had much in common. They were clearly in competition with each other for land, resources, and allies, and they told Indians unflattering things about one another. One elderly Peracota chief, whom the Portuguese met on a reconnaissance expedition along a tributary of the upper Rio Branco, reported that the Spaniards at a nearby border town had spoken of the Portuguese in disparaging terms: they were said to be few in number and bad in character (*poquitos* and *malos*), in contrast to the multitude of good Spaniards (*muchitos* and *buenos*). The chief seemed undaunted by such contrasts and agreed to serve as a short-term guide and geographical informant to the Portuguese on their expedition. He would decide for himself whether what the Spaniards had said about their rivals was true.[4]

It had long been obvious that there were different kinds of leaders and intermediaries among each group of whites: missionaries, government officials, landowners, traders, and explorers. Native peoples aimed to figure out which of these might serve as advantageous contacts in their efforts to obtain metal tools, for example, or to negotiate the exchange of captives. These different types of people had distinct interests and concerns, and to deal with them productively, Indians needed to gain an understanding of what made them tick. Missionaries, they learned, tended to be concerned with Indians' willingness to listen, watch, and emulate, while government officials and military men often looked for displays of friendship and loyalty. Frontier landowners liked to make deals but sought assurances about the security of their families and livestock, whereas traders were keen to make a profit, even at some personal risk. Explorers, mapmakers, and scientists could be engaged in trade as well, exchanging gifts for information about the names of rivers or mountains, the proximity of dangerous rapids, or the location of particular people or products. The task was to identify patterns, to place these newcomers into meaningful categories and subcategories, so that their behavior could be predicted and their moves anticipated.[5]

But misunderstandings and ruptures seemed to occur whenever independent Indians interacted with whites; one might go so far as to say that this was the most predictable element. Indigenous groups in contact situations quickly learned that negotiation and mediation were crucial. To this end, they often turned to liminal figures who had one foot in the colonial world and the other foot in the Indigenous world—people who did not easily fit into the emerging categories, in other words.[6] These included *cunhamenas*, the white or mixed-race entrepreneurs who often accepted Indigenous wives as a means of forging profitable slave-trading relationships with autonomous Native groups. Indians saw that cunhamenas seemed to act independently of the other whites and often played by Indigenous rules of exchange. But sometimes this got the cunhamenas in trouble; when they returned to the city, they might be punished and forbidden to go back to the Indians.[7] The reverse could happen to the Blacks who first came among Native groups as fugitives, fleeing from their masters. Their fortunes could improve quite suddenly, if the fugitives had something useful to offer the whites, and they might be employed as guides and translators in Native territories (figure 1.1).[8]

Indigenous people who worked with such cross-cultural informants in the eighteenth century saw that the categories they had constructed to make sense of the colonial world were sometimes inadequate. They had to account for fissures within colonial society, which opened up room for maneuvering, and they began to see how rivals could be played off against one another in advantageous ways. (Europeans had

FIGURE 1.1 "Waterfalls of the Cuñaré River," c. 1780s. The members of the Portuguese border demarcation commission stand on the spit of land in the center of the painting. The Spanish commissioner who painted the watercolor, Francisco Requena, appears on the right side, consulting with an Umáua informant (mistakenly labeled "Omagua"). The Black man standing behind Requena, described as the "Negro interprete," is either Juan de Silva or Fernando Rojas, the famous intermediaries (and former fugitives) of the Upper Amazon region.

Courtesy of the Oliveira Lima Library at the Catholic University of America.

similar revelations about the wide range of Native groups and leaders that they encountered in the Americas and made legislation that was specific to different kinds of Indians.[9]) But potentially useful as it was, colonial diversity—the multiplying and shifting subcategories—came to be seen as disconcerting, too. Which groups and individuals posed the gravest threats at any given moment? And to what extent, if at all, could any of these people be trusted to act in humane ways?

With these questions always lingering in the background, Native groups collected insights into the characters, motives, and methods of colonial peoples. As Guaikurú leaders constantly pressed a Jesuit missionary, José Sánchez Labrador, who worked among them in the 1760s, "What are the Spaniards trying to do? What are their intentions?"[10] This was during a period of heightened suspicions, as the Spanish authorities in

Asunción had not fulfilled their promise to send herds of cattle to the new mission at Belén, near the Paraguay River. In this context, the Guaikurús at the mission told and retold stories of Spanish treacheries from eras past. Perhaps their oral histories stretched as far back as the beginning of the 1600s, when a group of Guaikurú men, women, and children had entered Asunción to trade for wine that they later discovered had been poisoned by residents of the city. The governor at the time, fearing that the Indians would exact revenge for the poisoning of the trading party, sent an expedition to attack them in their villages, killing some eighty Guaikurús.[11] The Indians also remembered how, in the late seventeenth century, the Spanish had suspected a Guaikurú plot to invade Asunción and had come up with a ruse: a military official had invited Guaikurú noblemen to a party at his residence, got them all drunk, and then had some three hundred of them killed. Sánchez Labrador described the Indians as "full of feeling" as they recounted the story of the massacre of their ancestors, "telling us that the Spaniards had broken the friendship that they had professed to them, and that they would never trust men who had so many words—that is, who lied."[12]

Events in 1764 confirmed this centuries-old distrust of Spaniards once again. As Guaikurú warriors marched through the streets of Asunción, having accepted an invitation to serve as military auxiliaries for a Spanish offensive against another Native group, rumors of an anti-Spanish plot began to circulate among residents of the city. Panicked, or perhaps opportunistically exploiting popular fears, the governor sought to drive the Guaikurú auxiliaries out of Asunción. After several failed attempts to do so, he deliberately sent people infected with smallpox to mingle with the Indians. This led to an epidemic that killed hundreds of Guaikurús over the following months and spread to neighboring groups like the Guaraní.[13] This extreme act of biological warfare was not unprecedented. Smallpox, with its distinctive symptoms and clear paths of contagion (first- or secondhand contact with an infected person), was the preferred weapon for such warfare in the eighteenth century. Indigenous peoples in the Ohio Valley had been betrayed by the British just the year before, in 1763, in the infamous "smallpox blanket" episode at Fort Pitt.[14]

The missionary had to work hard to prove to the Guaikurú that he and his fellow Jesuits were different—that they fit into a different category of men. For a brief time in the 1760s, Sánchez Labrador seems to have succeeded where previous missionaries had failed. During an important visit to Asunción in 1760, Guaikurú leaders were hosted at the Jesuit college (where they feasted on honey, a favorite treat), and they were afterwards persistent in asking the governor for Jesuit missionaries, saying that they "only wanted those from the big house"— referring to the college—"who wore black," referring to the Jesuits' robes. Two Guaikurú subgroups ended up residing seasonally at the mission of Belén, and other subgroups visited or engaged in dialogues with Sánchez Labrador.[15] We can imagine, based on the missionary's description of their councils, how they might have decided on such an important matter: the men would have sat in a circle, passing around a tobacco pipe, with the chief present but not dominating the discussion, and the women would have stood behind them, "speaking more than the men."[16]

When they learned that the Jesuits would be expelled from the Spanish realm (in 1767), these Guaikurú groups were confused and then angry to discover that Sánchez Labrador would not be returning to the mission. Before his final departure from Asunción, two chiefs came to exhort him to stay. One chief—an old man who had led the first group to establish themselves, at least seasonally, in the mission—asked why the missionary's replacement had put up a fortified wall around his residence and surrounded himself with soldiers. The chief also requested that the Spanish king be informed of the Guaikurús' wish for Sánchez Labrador to return, for he had cared for them in their sicknesses and learned their language. The other chief, who had stayed at the mission for a shorter time, was blunter in his disillusionment: "They are no good, the ways of the Spaniards," he allegedly told Sánchez Labrador, before withdrawing in disgust with the rest of his people.[17]

During the middle decades of the eighteenth century, the Guaikurú also learned important lessons about the Portuguese interlopers who traveled in growing numbers through their territories. An episode in 1731 on the Taquari River proved that these were not men who acted honorably. Settlers on a punitive expedition from Cuiabá had put a

Guaikurú chief in chains after he came to the Portuguese in peace and had accepted the settlers' invitation to ride in their boats upriver to where the expedition commander was waiting. This commander set the chief free but then failed to punish his men for such an offense; the move angered the chief further and created a volatile situation. The chief managed to leave the scene on a fast horse, but several of his family members, including his mother and sister, were packed off to Cuiabá in the settlers' boats.[18] About a decade later, in 1740, it was the Portuguese who offered peace to the Guaikurú, presenting trade goods and friendly messages through an interpreter. The Guaikurú took precautions, however, refusing to hold talks on the river island where the Portuguese were camped, and insisting that the delegation come to the shore instead. At first, the talks went smoothly: promises to fight mutual enemies (Native and Spanish) were sealed by the collaborative raising of a cross on the riverbank, complete with loud *Vivas!* to the king of Portugal. But the next day, when a group of Portuguese soldiers went onshore "unguardedly" to trade with the Guaikurú, fifty of them were slaughtered. It is impossible to know whether the attack had been provoked by something the soldiers said or did, or whether it was premeditated treachery, as the Portuguese assumed, but it may have been done in retribution for previous Portuguese actions against the same group—and perhaps even the same chief.[19] (No individual Guaikurú chiefs were named in the Portuguese sources until the 1770s, as far as I know.) Either way, for the next six decades the Guaikurú joined their on-again, off-again allies, the Payaguá, in making a bloodbath of portions of the Paraguay River and its tributaries.[20]

Colonial betrayal made an indelible impression on the Mura, too, according to the Jesuit João Daniel. Like many writers of the period, Daniel noted that the Mura had a "profound hatred of the whites" but added that they "had given them much cause."[21] Going beyond the typical description of the Mura as indiscriminately and instinctively violent—"truly wild animals of the forest, only human in the form of their bodies," making war on anyone they met[22]—Daniel offered a backstory that helped explain the targets and the intensity of the attacks. Referring to events that dated from the early eighteenth century, he recounted how a missionary had convinced a group of Muras to resettle in the mission, promising to transport them downriver as soon as he had set aside sufficient supplies of food, cloth, and tools. As the Indians waited for him to return, a Portuguese settler showed up, invoking the missionary's plans and claiming to act in his stead. Deceived by his promises, dozens of Mura men, women, and children packed themselves into the settler's large canoe and accompanied him downriver. As soon as they were out of sight of their village, the settler had them bound as captives; later he sold them into (illegal) slavery in the suburbs of Belém. The Muras who remained behind "waited anxiously to find out how their relatives had been received in the mission. . . . As soon as they discovered the ruse and enslavement, instead of the Christian liberty promised at the mission, they conceived this hatred against the whites, and perhaps against the missionaries as well, since they were persuaded that he"—referring to the missionary—"originally had come with the aim of enslaving them." From that time onward, Daniel asserted, not a year had passed without Mura attacks on the settler canoes that went up the Madeira River in search of cacao, as well as on the handful of missions that the Jesuits had founded along the river and at its mouth. "In truth," Daniel lamented, "they have avenged that ruse well, and vented their rage, in so many deaths."[23]

The story of the fraudulent settler and deceived Indians may have been apocryphal, holding a certain appeal for missionaries who sought to make sense of the ongoing attacks on the missions and their own failures to make overtures to the Mura. But even if the particulars of this story are untrue, other sources confirm the lesson at its heart: the arrival of whites in Native territories brought dangers, even mortal ones. The Mura took note as the newcomers established fortified outposts at strategic points along the Madeira, conducted armed expeditions up and down the river, competed for turtles, and returned every year for the cacao that grew along the banks of the Madeira and its tributaries. Private parties were involved in this enterprise, as were Jesuit missionaries, beginning in the second half of the seventeenth century: "On the Madeira, the Jesuits sowed missions and harvested cacao."[24] Portuguese settlers raided Mura and other Native villages for slaves—either spontaneously, when they found them on their collecting trips, or with premeditation, when they mounted armed expeditions into

Indigenous territories.²⁵ Settlers brought as many as forty Mura slaves at a time to be sold in Belém, having killed many more.²⁶ The middle of the eighteenth century was especially brutal for the Indigenous peoples of the Madeira Valley. In 1749–1750, measles ravaged the missions and caused many of their Native residents to flee into the forest, spreading the disease to untold numbers of Indians.²⁷

Mura leaders and warriors would have been on high alert when, in 1749, the Portuguese mounted a major expedition up the Madeira River, with the goals of strengthening Portuguese claims to territory contested by Spain and of opening a regular supply route to the gold mines of Mato Grosso. Composed of 150 heavily armed men, the expedition passed locations of recent Mura attacks and exchanged gunfire for volleys of arrows on several occasions. The Mura were described as occupying an immense stretch of the Madeira River. Evidence of their presence or proximity was recorded from the mission of Trocano (later, Borba) all the way to the first rapids near the Jamari River, several hundred miles upriver, where an earlier mission site had been abandoned. The expedition apparently felt under constant and unrelenting surveillance. Its chronicler described how the Portuguese shot at Mura spies, who melted into the forest; the next day, they found an arrow embedded in the sand of a river beach, which the experienced crewmen translated as a dare or challenge. The Mura were said to ambush them at night or at places where the expedition canoes had to navigate through difficult currents, and the Portuguese had to set up heavily guarded camps wherever they stopped along the way.²⁸ Along one stretch, the expedition passed a series of lookout structures—which the chronicler described as similar to watchtowers (*guaritas*), with thatched roofs—that the Indians were thought to have built on the high banks above the river.²⁹ The level of vigilance and caution exercised by various groups of Mura during the 1749 expedition is significant, even if we account for the colonial tendency to exaggerate the threat posed by "hostile Indians." The evidence suggests that autonomous Native groups saw the expedition for what it was: a pivotal step in Portuguese imperial consolidation. As we will see, they made a series of decisive moves when the pace and scope of that consolidation became even clearer during the 1750s.

Caution, however, could give way to curiosity in other contexts. In the early years of his evangelizing among the Guaikurú, Sánchez Labrador described how difficult it was to convince the Indians to visit his fledgling mission. He had even less success in persuading them to go to Asunción, because they already knew so much about its dangers. But it helped that the Guaikurú were intensely curious about European goods and technology: "They look at everything and ask about it all, like people who seek to discover the causes and circumstances of anything new that is put before their eyes." Sánchez Labrador seemed to have kept a cabinet of curiosities with which to dazzle the Guaikurús who came to the mission. A prism cast rainbows onto the trees and other objects. A magnetic lodestone "was a mystery so strange to them, that the wonders of its attraction and other effects spread through all of the encampments. No heathen from upriver came without soon asking us to show them the stone that *lived and ate iron*." A windup clock with a bell that rang on the hour drew Indians from far and wide to examine its movements, and those already in residence at the mission played the role of "astronomers," explaining to their eager listeners how the clock kept time with the movements of the sun.[30] Other groups of Guaikurú came to the mission to see the images of the saints and to touch the sacred objects of Christian ritual. Sánchez Labrador, with a keen sense of spectacle, set up an altar in the field where he had received some visiting Native dignitaries and outfitted the son of a chief and another boy from the mission as impromptu assistants for the Mass. He then sent the opulently dressed boys to walk from village to village with ceremonial formality, spreading the word of the kind and generous (and perhaps powerful) padre. A procession formed behind the boys, who then received more gifts upon their return to the mission, while the chief and his wife looked on approvingly—though their group never agreed to stay at the mission for any significant length of time.[31]

This, then, was the other side of the coin—and the source of much ambivalence, internal disagreement, and lived contradictions for Indigenous peoples over time. Decorative manufactured items, metal tools, and firearms had come to occupy a central place in Guaikurú culture after centuries of contact. The cutlasses that the Guaikurú received from the Portuguese and even from the Spanish ("for their own throat-cutting," as some critics noted dryly) in exchange for their horses are a good example of how colonial objects might become indispensable to Indians. The Guaikurú used cutlasses for all manner of cutting tasks; they decorated their sheaths with crimped metal pieces and beads; and they cleaned and sharpened the blades frequently. Men rarely left home without a cutlass in hand, and these short swords were a marker of status.[32] An anthropologist's statement that "Western goods provided new and increased opportunities for both technological and symbolic innovation" among Native peoples seems as true for the eighteenth century as it is for the modern era.[33] From their earliest direct or indirect contacts, Indians learned that Europeans were dangerous but that they had novel and interesting things that could be appropriated for Indians' own purposes. The pressing question was *how*?

Knowledge and Territoriality

Around 1750, an unknown cartographer created a remarkable map. It shows the interior of South America as a colorful patchwork quilt of colonial and extracolonial populations (figure 1.2). The map depicts the Captaincy of Goiás, in Central Brazil, along with parts of neighboring captaincies. Predictably, the mapmaker labeled bishoprics, administrative boundaries, towns, and colonial travel routes, as well as major geographical features like rivers and mountain ranges. The mining settlements cluster at the center of the map, contained by a ring of mountains and the upper Tocantins River. But unlike many of his contemporaries, the mapmaker did not depict the rest of the territory as empty of inhabitants or as securely within imperial control. Instead, he labeled some areas as *sertão*—a term for the backlands that connotes danger, impenetrability, and hidden riches—and others as specific Indigenous territories.[34] In the spaces between rivers or on the far side of mountain ranges, we see labels for the Land of the Caiapó Heathens, the Land of the Akroá Heathens, and the Village of the Xavante. In all, eight different polities appear on the map with their respective territories and villages, and although they represent only a small fraction of the Native peoples in this part of the continent, their inclusion on the map is

FIGURE 1.2 Map of Goiás, c. 1750.

Source: Biblioteca Pública de Évora, Gaveta 4, no. 24. I am grateful to Rafael Chambouleyron for sharing this map with me.

still significant. It shows a mid-eighteenth-century recognition of a formidable and even expanding autonomous Indigenous world that lay beyond (and between) the river highways, mining enclaves, and bustling cities of the colony.[35]

A picture at the bottom of the map emphasizes that this Indigenous world was armed and dangerous—though it depicts a Xavante man aiming an arrow at an Akroá, who wields a club and hatchet (a metal trade item). These Native groups did make war upon one another in eighteenth-century Brazil, but they posed threats to colonial society, too. Perhaps the mapmaker chose to represent them in this way so as to suggest that they would not always stand in the way of colonial expansion. They were, he probably thought, barbaric peoples whose days were numbered. Yet the map hints at a few of the ways in which independent Indians successfully used the knowledge they had gained over years—centuries, even—of direct and indirect contacts with whites. The outcomes of the struggle for power and territory were not preordained.

Some Indigenous groups withdrew into long-term territorial isolation as colonial enterprises encroached, but this was not the only or even the most common strategy. What many autonomous Native groups did—in Brazil as in other parts of the Americas—was more dynamic. They expanded into geographically strategic places, often major river systems or borderlands contested by European powers.[36] At the same time, Indigenous peoples found safe places from which they could easily come and go, so as to take advantage of seasonal resources and trading or raiding opportunities in more risky areas. One historian has described how three formidable Indigenous polities in North America—the Iroquois, Comanche, and Lakota—"built what might be called kinetic regimes, which were networks of power and support that revolved around mobile activities" and crisscrossed colonial and extracolonial spaces. These groups were "geographically privileged" in the sense that they occupied, or came to occupy, regions where they could access European horses, tools, and guns yet might be able to avoid contact with Europeans and their sicknesses when necessary.[37]

As far back as we can trace them as a distinct ethnic category in the documents, the Mura appear as a people engaged in this kind of strategic movement. It helped that they were expert canoemen, whose lightweight bark canoes could travel faster and with greater dexterity than wood dugouts or the larger cargo canoes used by colonial expeditions. Documents from the first half of the eighteenth century describe the Mura as occupying the lower to middle Madeira River, up to the first rapids. An early missionary report from around 1714 said that the Mura were hostile to whites and many other Indigenous groups, but that they were friendly with two groups living on tributaries of the Marmelos River, which intersects the Madeira several hundred miles upriver. Interestingly, that same report described the area around the mouth of the Madeira as being inhabited by a completely different mosaic of Native peoples, among them agriculturalists—evidence that is supported by archaeological findings and the existence of large plots of *terra preta*, the anthropogenic black soil linked to pre-Columbian sites of habitation.[38] Sometime later, a territorial shift occurred: sources from the second half of the century described that same area near the Madeira River's mouth, called the Autazes, as the principal base of the Mura.[39] The Autazes offered many attractions: a complex network of seasonally flooded channels and islands, forests rich in useful wood and fruit, lakes stocked with fish, and beaches crawling with turtles, all with easy access to the main river highway of the Amazon-Solimões.

It was only around the middle years of the eighteenth century that unknown but significant numbers of Muras made this watery maze their own, after it had been depopulated by earlier waves of disease, slaving expeditions, and Indigenous warfare. If they had ever practiced swidden agriculture on the banks of the Madeira—and the 1749 expedition chronicle contains a snippet of evidence to suggest that they had—the Muras who moved to the Autazes seemed to have given it up. In their new home, they fished, hunted, planted short-term crops on the exposed mud flats, and gathered edible fruit, nuts, and honey. In other words, they adapted to the area's seasonal regime of flooding.[40] They also took advantage of the Autazes as a secure base from which to launch raids on the colonial villages and cargo canoes of the Amazon-Solimões, Japurá, and Negro Rivers. The fact that those villages had just gone through a major transition—from missions to secularized, state-sponsored villages, in the late 1750s—may have played a role in the

Muras' decision to move downriver and closer to those hubs of activity.[41] The Muras who stayed behind on the lower to middle stretches of the Madeira River probably devoted more of their time to nonagricultural subsistence and raiding, too, after that river was officially opened (in 1753) to commercial fleets loaded with trade goods and African slaves. These relatively slow-moving boats could be detected far in advance by Mura scouts and were easy targets for ambush.[42]

The Mura seemed to the Portuguese to have grown to "gigantic" dimensions, in terms of territory as well as population, by the 1760s and 1770s. Colonial administrators across the Portuguese Amazon constantly invoked the Mura threat in those years—assuming any unfriendly Indians to be Muras—and sounded the alarm whenever they were thought to have attacked for the first time in an area.[43] Soon the Mura were rumored to be circulating as far east as the Trombetas River and as far west as the Juruá River, a distance that would have taken around fifty days to travel by canoe (see map 2).[44] Other reports indicated that some Mura groups had moved their base of operations to the northern side of the Solimões River, closer to areas contested by the Spanish Crown. As one traveling magistrate noted with displeasure, one could go over a hundred leagues on the Amazon-Solimões River between the Madeira and Coari Rivers "without seeing anything more than water, earth, and irrational beings"—referring to independent Indians. "All of this made us long to arrive in the settlements, since there was not a single one in that vast interval where we could make landing"—a situation that "could only be remedied by the complete destruction of the Mura heathens."[45] It seems likely that the Mura *did* expand the range and intensity of their attacks in this period, and later sources would confirm their presence on all of the abovementioned rivers. But the claim that the Mura were more numerous than all of the people in the Rio Negro captaincy was surely inaccurate.[46] It supported the excuses made by village directors for the poor progress of state-sponsored agriculture, the failures of forest collecting expeditions, the lateness or incompleteness of annual reports to the governor, and so on. They also could justify requests for extra supplies and military support. In this sense, the war with the Mura offered a certain convenience—at least, for village administrators not in the direct line of fire.[47] Later, after they had initiated peaceful relations with the Portuguese, the Mura attempted to set the record straight: many of the thefts of manioc meal and tools, they said, had been carried out not by the Mura, but by Indians deserting from the state-sponsored villages.[48]

"White men with tender feet are useless" in the fight against the Mura, grumbled one frontier official, who proposed mobilizing troops of Native villagers instead.[49] Indeed, many of the armed expeditions sent against the Mura in the 1760s through the early 1780s failed at what one governor described as a frustrating "Bush War" (*Guerra do Mato*). Even after "making the rounds of all the riverbanks and lakes of that River, where the heathens usually go," the troops might not encounter a single person. One reason was that in the flood season, the Mura withdrew to higher ground in the interior forests, where colonial troops could not find them.[50] Then, in the low-water season, the Mura fanned out along four major rivers, whenever possible traveling along the hidden channels that ran parallel to the main waterway or connected them to other river systems, and staged surprise attacks on nearly every colonial settlement in the region.[51] The evidence from this period shows that the territorial repositioning of the Mura was not driven by a desire to evade contact; if anything, many Mura groups moved into closer proximity. This was an annexation of strategic riverine spaces that had been depopulated of other Indigenous groups and colonists and that offered a combination of safe refuges and easy access routes for poaching the human and material resources of the colony—though probably not as many as colonial officials claimed.

The Guaikurú positioned themselves even more centrally between the Spanish and the Portuguese in the violent borderlands of the Paraguay River valley. Over the course of the seventeenth and eighteenth centuries, various Guaikurú groups expanded northward and eastward to occupy the territory that came to be called Mbayánica or Mbaiânica (from Mbayá, the ethnonym used by the Spaniards for the Guaikurú). Said to be three hundred leagues long and almost as many wide, it extended from the Jejuí River in the south to the Taquari River in the north, encompassing both sides of the Paraguay River (see map 1).[52] Like the Mura, the Guaikurú moved into areas that had been depopulated, such as the abandoned Jesuit missions of Itatim (1631–1659) on the eastern side of the Paraguay River. They also contributed to that depopulation in the first place.[53]

Horses and floodwaters shaped Guaikurú territoriality over time. Accumulating ever-larger herds of horses since their first contacts with Spanish conquistadores in the sixteenth century, the Guaikurú came to dominate the Pantanal—a massive wetlands whose name comes from the word *pântano*, or swamp—and to control the thoroughfare of the upper Paraguay River, which marked the effective dividing line between Spanish- and Portuguese-claimed territories (figure 1.3).[54] The Portuguese had once assumed that the Pantanal was a single lake, rather than an interconnected system of rivers, channels, and depressions that filled and brimmed over for five to six months each year. One Portuguese explorer complained, "Many times the best guides have found themselves disoriented and lost without ever finding their route" in this watery maze.[55] Several mountain ranges, especially the lush Serra da Bodoquena, provided higher ground during the flood season—as well as safe haven from the open grasslands in times of war. In this resource-rich region, the Guaikurú caught fish and alligators; hunted deer, wild boar, and feral cattle; collected palm fruits, nuts, and fibers; and moved in search of seasonal pastures for their large herds of horses and sheep.[56]

FIGURE 1.3 Aerial photograph of the Pantanal.
Photograph courtesy of Markus Mauthe/Laif/Redux.

Like the Autazes for the Mura, the location and physical characteristics of the Pantanal and the Paraguay River gave the Guaikurú maximum advantage in their trading and raiding ventures. In the eighteenth century, Guaikurú parties could travel downriver to the city of Asunción to trade with Spaniards, steal livestock from Spanish ranches on the way back, and then find refuge (and perhaps even some willing trade partners) on the Portuguese-claimed side of the border. At the peripheries of colonial settlements and in the surrounding hills and mountains, they could find abundant feral cattle for meat and hides.[57] The missions of Sánchez Labrador (1760–1767) and his successor Mendes (1769–1774) attracted the Guaikurú groups living farther to the south, who found that they could obtain desirable gifts and food at the price of a temporary stay under missionary tutelage. To replenish their supplies of Indigenous captives, Guaikurú warriors could head north to raid Jesuit missions in the province of Chiquitos (modern Bolivia), or they could make war against other autonomous Native groups in the Chaco region (Paraguay) and in Mato Grosso (Brazil). New opportunities for looting and captive-taking came with the Portuguese gold-seekers and explorers who in the 1720s began to ply the route between São Paulo and the gold mines of Mato Grosso—a route that brought them along the Taquari River at the northern edge of Guaikurú territory.[58] For decades, the Portuguese attributed most of these devastating attacks to the Payaguá, famous river corsairs of the Paraguay. It was only much later that they realized their error: at least one of the Guaikurú subgroups had adopted the canoe and become adept at riverine warfare.[59] In the 1790s, one Portuguese fort commander reviewed the historical records to calculate that the Guaikurú had killed some four thousand of his countrymen and extracted a fortune in gold and other loot.[60]

Because of their longer history of documented contacts with Europeans, we know more about these various Guaikurú subgroups (imprecisely categorized as *parcialidades* by the Spanish and then the Portuguese) and their respective territories than we do about the Mura. Six Guaikurú parcialidades appear in the records from the eighteenth and early nineteenth centuries.[61] Each occupied a distinct territory, some closer to Spanish centers and others to Portuguese outposts;

each also maintained its own herds of horses and sheep and its own hunting, fishing, and foraging grounds. Although connected by kinship ties, language, and customs, and occasionally involved in joint military ventures or exchanges of captives and trade goods, the various parcialidades operated mostly independently of one another, under the leadership of their own chiefs. They were further divided into smaller, kin-based groups, each headed by a subordinate "captain" and living as many as ten leagues apart.[62] One scholar has argued that these various subgroups did not even use the ethnonym Mbayá in their dealings with Spaniards (or Guaikurú with Portuguese), except when they wanted to seem more threatening or formidable. They considered raids and other military attacks to be the responsibility of the specific subgroup that had sent warriors, rather than that of the "nation" as a whole—a perception not shared by the colonists who mounted punitive expeditions against any and all who might be called Mbayá-Guaikurú.[63]

A careful reading of later sources confirms that the Guaikurú did not act as a united "ethnic block" as they positioned themselves territorially and in relation to colonial powers.[64] The same was true of the Mura, Caiapó do Sul, Munduruku, Xavante, and other powerful Native peoples who often appear as generic "heathens" (*gentio*) in the written documents. Any analysis of Native warfare and resistance strategies has to take these multifaceted contact histories into account.[65]

What colonial authors (and some scholars) have depicted as instinctual, spontaneous, or unprovoked violence on the part of Native peoples was almost always more complex, linked to their specific circumstances and past experiences with the colonial world.[66] Indians sometimes tried to explain this, and occasionally their explanations made it into the historical record. When a Native group (likely Guaraníes) in the southern borderlands confronted a Spanish-Portuguese demarcation party in 1753, their envoys told the colonial interlopers that "the lands they have audaciously come to demarcate do not belong to the dominion of Portugal, nor to the conquests of Spain." Rather, Native peoples "have remained in the peaceful possession of these vast lands not only for years, but for centuries; and although they are considered barbarians for their lack of civilized manners, they should not be judged novices in the exercise of arms." The Indians went on to threaten the demarcation party with the "ruin of war" if they did not peacefully withdraw from the territory. In the distance, some six hundred Native warriors waited on horseback, their guns and lances glittering in the sun.[67]

Knowledge and Resistance

Indigenous groups resisted and attacked more effectively, as they came to know more about the nature of the threats that faced them and began to adopt some of the weapons and combat techniques of their enemies. This adoption likely took a generation or two. "In the beginning these heathens were ignorant of our powers," lamented a mid-eighteenth-century council in Goiás after the violent desertion of a group of Akroás from a Jesuit mission, in which the missionary and eighteen settlers were killed. "But today one finds them knowing and using our tactics and our weapons." The Akroás had been trained to use guns by the very man who had coerced them to settle in the mission in the first place; they then turned their acquired skills and technology to new ends, in a pattern that can be seen in other parts of the Brazilian borderlands.[68] Like the Guaikurú—and the Mapuche, the Chichimeca, and the Comanche, to name just a few—the Akroá had learned how to make war on horseback, and soon their raids focused on obtaining more of these useful animals.[69] As the eighteenth century progressed, hard metals like bronze and iron also began to glint on the tips of Indigenous lances and arrows. Knives, cutlasses, hatchets, and even guns quickly made their way through Native trade circuits, leading some colonial authorities to complain that the Indians were even better armed than the Spanish or Portuguese.[70]

Although there were royal prohibitions against giving Indians firearms, going back to the sixteenth century in Brazil, these were often overlooked in the case of Native allies who served (or might serve in the future) as military auxiliaries. Indeed, the Guaikurú acquired many guns through alliance as well as trade.[71] In the Amazon, authorities grew concerned about an illicit trade conducted by soldiers and river merchants that put guns and ammunition in the hands of independent Indians. The government repeatedly prohibited any person from "bringing arms, gunpowder, and lead shot to the heathens, because of the harm that can result." But these orders were often disregarded—for example, settlers from one town in the middle Amazon allegedly "set up a warehouse of guns, gunpowder, and lead shot in the Land of the Mawé Heathens."[72]

Indigenous groups who did not have guns (or who preferred not to use them) did what they could to render the technology less effective and to diminish its fearsome power. The Payaguá—described as "amphibious Indians" for their skills on and in the water—overturned Portuguese canoes so as to soak their enemies' guns and gunpowder and retreated under their own canoes when fired upon.[73] In the lower Amazon, a group of Juruna was led by a renegade Indian from a colonial village, who, during an ambush of an expedition canoe from that village, urged the Juruna warriors "not to fear the [expedition's] guns, for these were of fire and took time to discharge, and in these intervals they could kill everyone with their arrows." Emboldened, the Juruna "got right in the muzzles of our guns," according to the expedition members who survived to tell the tale.[74]

As this example suggests, many autonomous Native groups became more audacious in their attacks over time, but they also became more careful to engage in the kinds of fights with colonists that they could win. Independent Native groups watched as the Portuguese and their Spanish rivals set up forts and militarized towns along the frontiers of their colonies. They took note, too, of the heavily armed escorts that accompanied river expeditions through their territories, and the punitive expeditions sent to put bullets in their men and to enslave their women and children. They went to collect the bodies of their warriors, killed in skirmishes with the Portuguese, and found that their corpses had been mutilated.[75] These were signs of escalation, and they demanded an effective response.

Many Native peoples honed techniques of guerrilla warfare—or *guerra volante*, as it was called in the early modern period. One Brazilian dictionary of the era defined this term as "what the Indians do, attacking and escaping without engaging in formal battle" and referenced a 1660 letter from the Jesuit António Vieira.[76] In that letter, the famous missionary described the Nheengaíba of the Amazon delta region, an area of early European penetration, as occupying "a chaotic and intricate labyrinth of rivers and thick forests, the former with infinite inlets and outlets, the latter without any entry or exit; where it is not possible to encircle, nor find, nor follow, nor even see the enemy."[77]

From the early to mid eighteenth century, as they learned from their contacts with colonists who ventured up the Madeira River, the Mura shifted from face-to-face combat to ambush-style attacks on colonial canoes and hit-and-run raids on settlements.[78] They certainly were using guerrilla warfare techniques by the time of the 1749 expedition. Its chronicler described Muras showering a colonial canoe with arrows and then withdrawing at the sound of return gunfire; over the following days and weeks, as the expedition made its way upriver, the Indians staged ambushes that took advantage of forest cover, nighttime, and places where the colonial canoes were especially vulnerable to attack.[79] By 1760, Mura groups had grown so bold as to attack people close to the fort at the junction of the Negro and Solimões Rivers; by the mid-1770s, they were said to terrorize colonial settlements and travelers across a vast area and to prevent many colonial Indians from going to work on their homestead gardens or participating in forest collecting expeditions—although, as mentioned earlier, some of these attacks were likely carried out by other Native groups and conveniently blamed on the Mura.[80] In 1765 and then again in 1779, large colonial expeditions targeted the Mura. The latter expedition claimed to have killed nearly eight hundred Muras in what may have been the deadliest rampage against their people by the Portuguese.[81]

If it was meant to be a deterrent of future warfare against the colony, the killing spree had the opposite effect.[82] In the years that immediately followed, the Mura attacked with even more ferocity and precision. They went after the large transport canoes and even the fishermen supplying the border demarcation headquarters of Ega, on the Solimões River, where Spanish and Portuguese dignitaries gathered in large numbers. One officer at Ega fretted that the Muras' "daily insults" were reaching new extremes in the early 1780s, and that they "no longer showed any fear of the beating of the war drums, which they hear daily, or of the gunshots fired from the canoes" that patrolled the waters around the town.[83] That same year, 1782, thirty canoes of Muras surrounded the strategic frontier village of Maripí for three days, threatening to burn it to the ground, though the Muras still withdrew at the sound of gunfire.[84]

Some of the differences between Native guerrilla tactics and conventional European warfare became clear during the later period of Portuguese-Guaikurú alliance. Portuguese officers denounced the "cowardice" of allied Guaikurú warriors during a joint military expedition against the Spaniards in the early 1800s, the Indians having refused to confront Spanish firepower in the invasion of a fort. One commander accused them of playing the role of "useless spectators" to the main event and engaging only when the fort was ready for looting.[85] Another commander who knew the Guaikurú well summarized their irritatingly pragmatic approach: "They see the Spanish and Portuguese way of making war as stupid: giving and receiving blows, and even killing face to face, to gain advantage at such great cost. Only fools do such things. The Guaikurú way of making war is safer and more prudent, for they inflict damage without receiving harm . . . succeeding in their aims without any risk at all." Could the Guaikurú possibly think of anything more vexing to say in framing the distinction for their Portuguese (or Spanish) allies? Indeed, they could: "And so they conclude . . . that since the Portuguese and Spaniards say they will go to heaven when they die, they do well in wanting to die early. But since they also say that the Guaikurú will go to hell after death, in that case the Guaikurú want to delay death for as long as possible."[86] Ridicule aside, it is clear that Native warfare had adapted over time to the mix of threats and opportunities that Indians faced.[87]

Some Indigenous groups mastered the use of deception and trickery in war. But on this topic, the colonial sources are tricky, too, for their authors were keen to see deception behind every encounter gone wrong. After several decades of familiarity with the Guaikurú, a Portuguese fort commander wrote that "they appear as friends, asking for peace and reconciliation, committing to buy some livestock and cloth, and even offering the companionship of their women, who, instructed in their perfidy, make themselves appear easy and sweet."[88] (They were not the only Indigenous group that allegedly used women as enticements; the Apinajé, too, were said to "cleverly instruct their women and girls to pretend to submit to the will of the Portuguese and to entangle them until hidden Indians run up and kill them with their clubs."[89]) The same commander claimed that if the Guaikurú sensed vulnerability on the part of their opponents, they would seize the opportunity to attack; otherwise, they just went on posing as innocuous visitors or traders. This may have been an accurate assessment of Guaikurú tactics of dissimulation, but it also attests to what one scholar of Indian-settler relations has characterized as the "ambiguity of threat and exchange."[90] We know from many other times and places that autonomous Native peoples engaged in limited, brief contacts with whites, with the aim of gathering information or obtaining material goods. "Fear, suspicion, and bravado formed the dominant tone of such interactions," because they were not seen as being embedded in longer-term social relationships.[91] Colonial authors, for their part, could not be sure whether such visits were preludes to a planned attack or the beginning of more friendly relations. Only hindsight made them certain of the former.

The Guaikurú encountered the Portuguese under exactly these kinds of ambiguous circumstances in the mid-1770s. Those were years of heightened vigilance for Native peoples, who found themselves hemmed in by two new forts: the Spanish constructed Concepción (1773) toward the southern end of Guaikurú territory, and the Portuguese built Coimbra (1775) near the northern end. In 1776, the Portuguese commander at Coimbra led an expedition down the Paraguay River to explore an area known as the Fecho dos Morros, which consisted of a large island in the middle of the river. After several days of mutual surveillance with a large group of Guaikurús—who strategically split up into parties in canoes and on horseback—the Portuguese managed to convince the Guaikurús to exchange some gifts and promise to visit Coimbra Fort. The Guaikurús, for their part, sought to make several things clear in this interaction: that they had a productive relationship with Spain (indeed, some of them spoke Spanish and knew something of Christianity); that they did not trust the "useless" Portuguese at all; but that they had livestock to trade and were eager to obtain metal tools and weapons, especially cutlasses and knives. (The commander gently suggested, in his report to the governor, that if axes were sent from the capital as gifts for the Guaikurú, "it would be best if these were smaller than ours"). For the first time, Guaikurú leaders were named in the Portuguese sources: the elderly chief was called Lourenço (or Lorenzo in Spanish sources), and those who spoke on his behalf were three "captains," identified as Felipe, Manoel, and José.[92] The same Chief Lourenço and one of the captains showed up at Coimbra in late 1777, for their first visit at the new fort; they received gifts of food, tobacco, and trinkets without incident, though they surely noticed that the commander met them outside the fort under armed guard, with two pistols in his belt—a decision for which he was criticized by his men at the time.[93]

We know that two of the same Guaikurú captains, Felipe and José, returned to the fort in the dry season of early 1778, accompanied by a "multitude" of men, women, and children.[94] The Indians approached the fort slowly, some from upriver and some from downriver, burning fires whose smoke signals served as a form of long-distance communication among Guaikurú subgroups.[95] At first, the fort commander was not too concerned about the fires, which he was used to seeing in the distance, but after a few days, he began to feel a mounting sense of dread. With the fort encircled by growing numbers of Guaikurús, an invasion seemed imminent, and the commander sounded an alarm to make the soldiers take up their posts. An officer under armed guard went out to meet the arriving Indians and their captains. These affirmed their peaceful intent, pointing to all the women and children in their company, as well as the horses, cattle, and sheep they had brought to trade. Several Guaikurú representatives agreed to enter the fort to receive gifts from the commander, while the rest of the Indians (some three hundred of them) mingled with Portuguese soldiers a few hundred paces beyond the fort's walls.[96] The Indians at that point told the Portuguese officer that their women were afraid of his soldiers' firearms and asked that these be withdrawn and put away. He agreed to do so, hiding the guns under some kind of cloth or cloak. Then "the Indians then began to come closer to the Portuguese and invited some of them to rest in the laps of the women, which they did; after that, the trading began."[97] The fort commander would later claim that "the desire to buy the goods that the heathens brought had stupefied the judgment" of the soldiers. Fifty-four of them would soon meet their death.[98]

This is where the written sources diverge. The fort commander, our only eyewitness account, claimed that the Guaikurús outside the fort attacked the soldiers just after he rang the chapel bells to signal to his men that it was time to come back from consorting with the Indians.[99] A summary by the city council of Cuiabá, based on an investigation conducted later that year, described the attack as beginning the moment the Guaikurú representatives emerged from the fort, after their visit with the commander.[100] A final account, by a later fort commander and amateur historian, stated that the attack began when, on their way back from the fort to the crowd of Indians and Portuguese soldiers, the Guaikurú representatives gave a whistle, "with which they all understand one another as clearly as we do speaking." And "with this signal, every heathen with his club began killing the one before him, and some of the Portuguese even died in the laps of the Indian women."[101] The Guaikurús suffered no casualties and galloped off with all the goods they could carry.

Even with these discrepancies, colonial authors agreed on one point: that the 1778 massacre was the result of a "diabolical plan," which the Guaikurús "carried out like actors who had rehearsed a play for the stage."[102] And a few years later, several Guaikurú chiefs would proudly recount to a Spanish official that they had killed even higher numbers of Portuguese at the fort, after "faking peace and deceiving them."[103] Perhaps the massacre *was* premeditated, and in that case, the two brief encounters that preceded the massacre (in 1776 and 1777) would have been scouting expeditions, aimed at taking measure of Portuguese vulnerabilities and plotting the attack. But we also might consider the possibility that the Guaikurús arrived with intentions to trade but then read a series of ominous signs from the Portuguese. For example, if we trust the eyewitness report by the commander of Coimbra, perhaps the Guaikurús perceived the ringing of the chapel bells as a call for the troops to fire on their representatives, who had entered a dangerous space—the fort itself. Given their memory of past Portuguese (and Spanish) treacheries, it is possible that the Guaikurús suspected the soldiers' weapons, which had been put aside, would be used against them in a surprise attack. Colonial authors were so certain of Indian deceitfulness that they very rarely acknowledged the possibility that Native actions were provoked, or based on rational assessments of risk.

Other evidence from this period suggests that for Native peoples, the presence of firearms signaled that the Portuguese negotiated in bad faith. About a decade and a half after they had gotten "right in the muzzles" of Portuguese guns, a Juruna delegation arrived peacefully in the colonial village of Souzel, on the Xingú River. The village director described how the visitors gave the most convincing demonstrations of sincerity, communicating that they wanted to come live in the village so as to escape the depredations of their enemies, the Mundurukú. A short time later, the director dispatched an expedition to fetch them, and he made sure that it went heavily armed and "with much caution, so as to avoid any treachery." Once the expedition reached the Jurunas, these "received our people with little pleasure, saying that perhaps some other year they would come downriver [to settle in the village], and that it had not been necessary for so many armed people to come." According to the director, it was suddenly clear that the Jurunas had planned some treachery, "which they could not achieve due to fear of our guns." He assumed, in other words, that the Jurunas were planning to attack the expedition and desisted only because the men were armed. But it seems likely that the presence of the guns was what derailed the negotiations in the first place. The Jurunas responded accordingly, distancing themselves from men who had confirmed their untrustworthiness.[104]

In these charged situations, people with strategic knowledge of the enemy were extremely useful. This helps explain why many independent Indians incorporated people from colonial society, either as captives or voluntary recruits. By the second half of the eighteenth century, we know that the Mura and Guaikurú had accumulated—through force, attraction, or a mixture of the two—runaway Indians, fugitive Blacks, and remnants of other Native groups. They also counted upon scores of female and child captives taken from missions, colonial villages and cities, and passing expeditions.

The Mura, in particular, seem to have functioned as a kind of "alternative ethnic space" for people seeking to flee the colonial system.[105] Portuguese officials grasped this only slowly and with a growing uneasiness, as they came to interact with the Mura during the transition from warfare to peacemaking in the late eighteenth century (see chapters 2 and 3). When a group of Muras attacked the little frontier outpost of Maripí in 1782, officials noted that the village director was "most tormented" by the fact that a "a mulatto and a black" had accompanied the Mura warriors; he speculated that these two "had conceived the diabolical idea of burning the settlement, something the Mura had never done before."[106] Indeed, evidence from other regions of Brazil suggests that when they incorporated Black fugitives, autonomous Native groups might have become radicalized or more tenacious in their opposition to colonialism.[107]

"The Empire of these wretches is large, composed of many people of different languages," wrote another Portuguese officer in 1785, after the peace process had begun. There were "many people taking refuge among them, and also people kidnapped from the villages, all passing under the name of Mura. These refugees are the most difficult to dominate, and they were the ones who dissuaded some of the Muras from submitting to peace, because they go at their leisure among them, free from rowing canoes and the other jobs to which they are obligated in the [colonial] villages, and on which they die in such numbers."[108] Such individuals were known to have passed along intelligence to the Mura about which colonial outposts were most vulnerable to attack.[109] A few years later, a visiting naturalist noted that "not all of them are Mura by birth; rather, with this name and customs, some go disguised among them (and are perhaps the worst). They are the ones who, having been born and baptized in our settlements, were captured as children by the true Mura, who educated them in their ways."[110]

Soon the Portuguese were trying to distinguish between "legitimate" Muras and those who had been incorporated, a task that often proved difficult—if not impossible. One administrator in charge of overseeing a new, peaceful Mura settlement was asked to provide a detailed report on its residents. He dutifully counted 113 men and 98 women. But the administrator knew that his report was incomplete: "It is impossible to separate out those of the Xumana nation," he admitted, "because they cannot be distinguished from those of another nation who are some of the prisoners. *The Muras do not want to say where they are from, and they say only that they are all Muras.* Of these, only four people could be recognized by virtue of having their mouths [tattooed in] black, but due to the lack of an interpreter, their true nation could not be ascertained."[111] Among this group of Muras, then, there were Native prisoners as well as allied subordinates (in this case, Xumanas). The Mura evidently found it useful to assert, at least before the Portuguese, a united Mura identity for all.

Many newly incorporated peoples do seem to have undergone the cultural transformation that some colonial authors called "Murification." (One also encounters references to "Araucanization," "Comanchenization," and "Apacheanization" in the ethnohistorical literature from different parts of the Americas.[112]) The extent and nature of this process came into view of colonial authors only during the era of peacemaking, as they encountered such individuals face-to-face for the first time. These included parties of Murified captives who became central in the peace negotiations, described in the following chapter. Some spoke only the Mura language, having been captured as young children or born of captive mothers. A few had physical appearances that caught the attention of Portuguese officials, such as the eighty-year-old man, captured (probably as a child) from the old Jesuit mission of Abacaxis, "with a matted beard and completely white hair, and a Murified manner, but still very spry."[113] Even a half a century or more later, travelers would pointedly describe the Mura as having kinky hair and beards.[114]

A similar process played out among the Guaikurú, but it occurred within the structures of a more elaborate social hierarchy and long-standing (even precolonial) practices of captive-taking and alliance-making. As the Iberian chroniclers understood this hierarchy, the Guaikurú privileged lineage from the "nobles"—the captains, their wives, and their children. At the next social level were "soldiers," or warriors, who were free commoners. At the bottom was a large, ethnically diverse majority of Native tributaries and prisoners of war, along with their descendants. Many of these were called "captives" or "slaves," though it became clear to the Portuguese that the Guaikurú model of slavery differed dramatically from their own.[115] A Portuguese naturalist—the same one who had, just a few years before, written about captives of the Mura—took note of the many captives possessed by the Guaikurús whom he met at Coimbra Fort. "These are humanely treated by their masters," he acknowledged. "We call them barbarous"—referring to the Guaikurú—"but they, in these parts, do not disgrace humanity like the more refined nations of Europe, who . . . upon establishing themselves in America, seem to purposely devise ways of making the yoke of Black slavery heavier."[116]

The Portuguese marveled at how the Guaikurú managed to form a cohesive group out of so many captives and subordinates. In the eighteenth century, members of Guaikurú society included many groups of Guaná, neighbors who by the eighteenth century had submitted to Guaikurú authority and went on supplying the Guaikurú with tribute of food and female servants in a kind of unequal partnership or serfdom. The relationship with the Guaná tributaries was not maintained by Guaikurú military dominance alone; it also depended on marriages between Guaikurú captains and high-status Guaná women, so that the two groups were knit together as kin.[117] Other incorporated peoples were prisoners of war, who generally held a lower status than the Native tributaries; these included the Chamacocos, Bororos, Caiapós, Guatós, Chiquitos, and various other Native peoples, as well as smaller numbers of Blacks, people of mixed race, and whites captured from raids on colonial communities or attacks on expeditions. Captive children were often adopted and fully assimilated as Guaikurú, while attractive women might be incorporated as concubines; most war captives, though, tended to retain their servile status (as did their children), and normally they could be traded, rented out, and inherited.[118] At the beginning of the nineteenth century, one Portuguese fort commander estimated that among the two thousand Guaikurús who then kept up friendly relations with the Portuguese at Coimbra, most were actually Guanás, Chamacocos, or members of various other Indigenous groups or ethnicities. He estimated that only two hundred of the total number, or 10 percent, could be considered "true Guaikurús." Even the poorest of these was said to possess at least three or four captives. The same commander noted that, given practices of abortion and infanticide among Guaikurú women, the adoption of captive children and the incorporation of prisoners and tributaries like the Guaná made it possible for the tribe to replenish its numbers and continue to pose a threat.[119]

Those who voluntarily joined Native groups, or who preferred not to leave them after having been taken captive, played an important role in what might be considered psychological warfare against the colonial world. It is a sign of their moral outrage that both Spanish and Portuguese authorities used the term *apóstatas* (apostates)—meaning Christians who had renounced the faith—to refer to those who "went Native" or who passed in and then out of colonial society. Some Iberian authors considered Native "apostates" to be the most vicious of all: "The Indians who have abandoned our Holy Faith are more inclined to invade, steal, and murder than those who have never been converted," lamented a governor in northern New Spain.[120] A Portuguese officer defined apostates among the Mura in very similar terms: "Indians baptized in our settlements and civilized, who, absenting them, joined the Muras in the forests, and incited them and taught them, being even worse than the Muras themselves in the killings, thefts, and damage that they have done to the villagers and travelers, [both] whites and Indians, of the villages in the sertão."[121] With their insider knowledge of colonial society and their many grievances against the colonial system, the apostates were seen as particularly dangerous by the Portuguese—and as potentially useful by independent Indians. Their exhortations and threats had special currency: recall the renegade Indian villager who once led the Juruna, urging them not to fear Portuguese guns as they embedded their arrows in men from the Indian's former village. As the terrified survivors recounted, the Indian leader had "sent a message that he would soon come to this village for the head of the director, and of the priest."[122]

Christian Indians who did not want to stay with the Portuguese, and captives who did not want to be rescued—these interlinked phenomena undermined two deeply held articles of faith for colonists in Brazil, as in other parts of the Americas. The first was that "the Indians would want to be converted once they were exposed to the superior quality" of life in the colonial sphere. The second article of faith was "that no civilized person in possession of his faculties or free from undue restraint would choose to become an Indian." (Revealingly, the quotations are from a study of Anglo-America; the patterns of colonial presumption—and disillusionment—can be traced broadly across the hemisphere.)[123] Here is where the psychological warfare came in, as independent Indians knocked down, over and over again, these pillars of colonial ideology.

Take, for example, the joint Guaikurú-Payaguá attack on a Portuguese expedition along the Paraguay River in 1730. After killing some four hundred people (both whites and Black slaves), including the royal magistrate who accompanied the expedition, the Indians went on a kind of victory lap along the river in view of the Portuguese survivors, who had retreated behind some trees on the shore. One of the Native chiefs—probably a Payaguá—took that opportunity to deliver two symbolic blows. The first was a message communicated by a white boy who had been taken captive at age eight, just three years earlier, when his father (a prior expedition leader) had been killed. "If there are any men here who want to fight," the boy shouted on behalf of the chief, "come out of that thicket!" Getting no response, the boy then said that if the Portuguese didn't leave, the Indians would come to look for them. The Portuguese responded that they should go right ahead and then fired their guns—though the bullets could not reach the Indians. Then came the second insult: another captive, this time a man of mixed race (identified as a "bastard, or *carijo*"), mocked the Portuguese from across the water: "Oh, you scoundrels, vile and low, don't you know that the *caribas* (which is what they call the whites) have nothing on the Payaguás and Guaikurús?" Both captives evidently spoke the language of their captors and served as interpreters for the chief, though we cannot know how they felt about their roles. Finally, the Indians made sure that the Portuguese could see a young white woman, whose husband they had just killed. She now sat in a canoe at the feet of the chief, who sported the murdered magistrate's Order of Christ insignia around his neck as well as his fancy clothes.[124]

The demoralization of the Portuguese even extended into the era of peacemaking, as Christian Indians and Black captives of the Guaikurú refused to return to colonial society. Of all the captives who came with the Guaikurú to visit Coimbra Fort, only two old Chiquito women agreed to "pass out of the power" of the Indians and return to the Christian fold. Two elderly Black captives still knew some of the old prayers, but "no persuasion [was] strong enough to call them back to the bosom of the Church and tear them away from the customs and power of their masters." At a loss, the Portuguese finally told the Black captives that they could observe the Commandments and pray while continuing to live among the Guaikurú, and whenever they visited the fort, they could confess and attend Mass. In this way, the Portuguese reminded them, they could avoid going to hell. But the two old captives responded to everything "with the same interrogation: How do you know? And who has seen this?"—apparently referring to the phenomenon of lapsed Christians going to hell.[125]

Martha, the daughter of the captive Black interpreter Vitória (see chapter 3), similarly rebuffed offers to marry one of the Portuguese soldiers at Coimbra and to take a place of "esteem" among the very same people who originally had held her mother as a slave in the city of Cuiabá: "To all of these entreaties, she responds that she would rather enjoy her youth"—among the Guaikurú, that is—"and that when she is old, she will make a decision."[126] Like the Guaikurú with whom she lived, Martha would make the most of her present autonomy, while leaving open the possibility of some future movement.

Through many conduits of information and a wide range of encounters—some violent, some peaceful, and others in the gray area in between—autonomous Indigenous groups across Brazil came to know about, and make sense of, the colonial world. Many perceived, for example, that colonial peoples were diverse and divided among themselves and that their rivalries could be exploited and their particular vulnerabilities poked. Mistakes were made, sometimes at great cost, so grandparents and parents passed down stories of whites who had been dishonest and perfidious, in the hope that the younger generation would be more careful. Native peoples also came to know about colonialism—its mechanisms of control and its material manifestations in fortifications and churches, merchandise and guns. This process of intelligence-gathering played out unevenly across time and space and could be pushed forward or halted by Native groups themselves.

In the late eighteenth century, some of the most formidable autonomous groups in Brazil made more lasting peace agreements with the Portuguese. But peace was not a spontaneous or impulsive decision for the Indians—or for the colonists, for that matter. Instead, it came out of years of mutual surveillance, violent conflicts, and halting negotiations.[127] When, in 1791, some of the Guaikurús made peace with the Portuguese at the fort of Coimbra, they had been crossing paths with Iberians in the Chaco and Paraguay River Basin for more than two centuries without ceding their autonomy. "The more they come to know the Portuguese system of government," a fort commander wrote of the Guaikurú about a decade later, "the more they find it strange, and distance themselves from it, seeing obedience as coercive and public jails and punishments as an affront to the liberty of man." It was futile, the commander thought, to push for the full incorporation of the Guaikurú into the colonial world, because they already knew too much. "Their final conclusion," he wrote resignedly, "is that punishment and prison are born of our wickedness, and that all this is unnecessary among them, because their customs are more innocent, more in harmony with nature, more full of humanity . . . and because the natural tendency of their ways is tranquility, as proven by the independence in which they live."[128] The challenge—for the Guaikurú and so many other Native groups through history—was how to retain this autonomy and humanity, while drawing what they wanted from the world of the whites.[129] It would require all of their ingenuity in the years to come.

2 Why Embrace the Whites?

THE INDIANS CAME CLOSER. Stepping onto the sandy expanse of the river beach, they laid down their bows and arrows. The Portuguese mirrored the gesture and put aside their guns. A pair of interpreters, both captive women, stepped forward to communicate the friendly intentions of each side. Men made themselves slightly vulnerable in ways that could provoke smiles or awkward laughter: the Portuguese might remove their jackets and shirts, standing bare-chested to watch as Indians donned their clothes. Native women emerged cautiously from the tree cover or crossed over from the far side of the river to see the newcomers with their heaps of gifts. Beads, knives, mirrors, fishhooks, and bundles of cloth passed from hand to hand for inspection. Finally, the two groups shared food and drink, music and dancing. It was so good—following days of high-alert trekking and reconnaissance—that some even forgot to eat or sleep.[1]

Rituals of approximation and peace were well-established among Indigenous and colonial groups, going back to the era of first contacts on the coast of Brazil. What stunned many Portuguese observers was their sustained use, in the last quarter of the eighteenth century, among the "indomitable nations." These Indigenous groups had violently resisted colonization for a half century or more. Why, then, did major factions of the Karajá and Javaé (1775), Caiapó do Sul (1780), Mura (1784–1786), Xavante (1788), Guaikurú (1791), and Munduruku (1795) make peace with the Portuguese? Half of the explanation is already well known to us. It involves shifting colonial policies toward Indigenous peoples and the intensifying rivalry between Portugal and Spain, which drove a search for new allies. The other half of the explanation is just as important, though admittedly more difficult to trace through the written sources. It has to do with what Indigenous peoples saw as being intriguing, obtainable, empowering, or simply the lesser of two evils, as they looked toward the people and resources concentrated within the expanding network of colonial forts and frontier towns.

Peacemaking is considered here not as "pacification"—a state-led program, for state aims—but as a process that hinged on the motivations, interests, and customs of non-state peoples. Autonomous Native groups had their own ideas of why and how peace should be made. These ideas, furthermore, compelled even the most cynical colonial officials on the ground to make concessions and compromises. The extent to which Indigenous peoples could direct or influence this process has been obscured from our view, and not just because of the one-sidedness of the documentary record. Its obscurity is also the result of the overall trend toward increasing state power over Indigenous peoples and their territories. We know how things turned out; we read the past retrospectively. In doing so, we miss some of the complexity and contingency that must have made this earlier era seem full of possibility.

Perspectives on Motive

Let us begin, briefly, with the more accessible explanation for this turn of events in the late eighteenth century. First, it is no coincidence that parallel peace agreements with Indians played out in neighboring Spanish colonies during the same period. The demarcation of a new border between Spanish and Portuguese territories in South America after the 1750 Treaty of Madrid and the 1777 Treaty of San Ildefonso intensified the rivalry for Native allies. Both Crowns sought to claim territory on the basis of occupation by Native peoples, who could be called "subjects" and "vassals." In this period, colonial records make clear "that not only territory but also people were up for grabs and that both could be possessed and become the property of one power or the other."[2] The submission of Indigenous peoples was thus linked with territorial preservation for the Crowns.

For centuries, colonial agents had asserted that "heathens are the bulwarks of the *sertões*," or remote interior lands. Like the imposing stone walls of a frontier fort, autonomous Indigenous polities were thought to prevent other Europeans from entering regions of strategic importance.[3] Iberian policymakers came to believe that Indians would do this job better as willing allies than as hostile enemies, *and* do it in ways that might stand up to the legal scrutiny of a border demarcation commission. With the Enlightenment-era conviction that Native groups might be persuaded to make rational choices that were in their own self-interest, reformist Crown officials proposed engaging in "friendly" contacts with those who had resisted conquest and previous attempts at incorporation.[4] It is important to note that this shift toward policies of "attraction" in Spanish America and Brazil occurred even as the use of punitive expeditions and armed violence against Indigenous groups continued. Higher authorities might denounce the "barbarity and tyranny of the old *sertanistas*" (backwoodsmen) in their treatment of Indigenous peoples, but the state's control over local actors in remote regions was limited in this period. And sometimes it was simply convenient for royal officials to blame ongoing frontier violence on rogue colonists or trigger-happy soldiers.[5]

However tenuous, peace with independent Indigenous polities brought a measure of frontier security. The territories long controlled by autonomous Indians, after all, were refuges not only for Indigenous groups but also for other kinds of people—convicts, deserters, fugitive Black slaves, and runaways from the missions—who evaded control and threatened colonial populations, sometimes in direct cooperation with independent Indians.[6] With the opening of safer passages, through which colonial people and products could move, the Iberian Crowns hoped that extractive or agricultural industries, as well as permanent settlements, might take root in new territories. Flotillas and caravans full of miners, ranchers, merchants, soldiers, and missionaries plied the strategic river and overland routes of the interior, looking for opportunities to get rich, earn recognition, or save souls. By the end of the eighteenth century, these travelers did not have to worry quite so much whenever they passed a towering *sumaumeira* (kapok) tree, portaged over rapids, or navigated through a treacherously narrow spot along the river—places where before they might have expected a deadly shower of arrows.[7]

Though it did not carry the same risks and costs of a military operation, peace was not free. Colonial fort commanders and governors were expected to host, entertain, and bestow gifts upon visiting Indians, giving rise (in Spanish America) to the much-lamented budget category of *gastos de indios*, or "Indian expenses."[8] But Iberian officials could recoup some of their expenditures by trading for livestock, hides, or raw forest products with the visitors. Native peoples often obtained some of those trade goods through raiding in other colonial areas—and this did not seem problematic to colonial officials, as long as it terrorized their rivals. Regarding his orders to buy horses that the Guaikurú had likely stolen from Spanish ranches, the Portuguese governor of Mato Grosso went so far as to suggest that the trade would be to the benefit of his side and to the detriment of the Spanish: "In seeing their livestock disappear, the Spaniards might abandon those establishments, or guard them, offending the Guaikurú with their hostility; these, once aggravated, they will have as irreconcilable enemies for many years, to the total ruin of these new ranches of theirs."[9] (Spanish officials were justifiably skeptical when their Portuguese counterparts denied supporting and encouraging Guaikurú raids.[10]) Autonomous Indians might even have special skills that could be exploited for economic gain: "They navigate with indescribable velocity," one Portuguese official said of the canoe-borne Mura, "and although they are presently worthless for constructing houses, gardens, or any other basic establishments, they will be of great use for discovering the treasures [of the forest], which their ferocity has until now hidden from us."[11]

Finally, Iberians continued the time-honed practice of using Indigenous polities as strategic allies against other Native groups, a practice that went back to the earliest years of conquest and colonization.[12] The cast of characters and regional settings changed over time, but the method remained one based on manipulation and disdain for Native lives, as two examples from Brazil in the 1780s reveal. When the Portuguese governor of Goiás recruited a group of Akroás to counterbalance a large contingent of Caiapó warriors who had recently migrated to a state-run village, he claimed the Akroás would be useful to have in the village "because of the opposition this nation has against the Caiapó, and because as Indians they could more easily detect some treachery in the Caiapó."[13] Hundreds of miles to the north, a Portuguese official noted that although the Mura had been "pacified," the Mundurukú were now pushing into the same territory with greater ease. "Freed from one [pest], navigation is always infested by another," in a kind of historical cycle that the Portuguese, in the official's view, had to tolerate as their colonial lot. "But at least there will be fewer enemies to combat, and when it is time to castigate them"—referring to the Mundurukú—"the Mura will be of great help and advantage."[14] Alliances could be used to inflame rivalries between Indigenous polities or among factions of groups, all for colonial gain. As emissaries or military auxiliaries of Iberian Crowns, Native allies could also convince—or compel—other independent Indian nations to come to the colonial negotiating table. Alliance with one Native group sometimes directly facilitated colonial relations with another (related or subservient) group, as the Portuguese clearly perceived in their dealings with the Guaikurú and the Guaná, or with the Mura and the Xumana.[15]

If the benefits that accrued to peacemaking Iberians seem clear, Indigenous motives for establishing peaceful relations remain more shadowy. To explain why some Native polities aligned themselves with Iberian powers, scholars have rightly emphasized the many hardships facing Indigenous populations during the late colonial period: reduced territorial control, epidemics of measles and smallpox, ecological crises like droughts, and threats from both European and Indigenous enemies.[16] These pressures and challenges were very real, and the sources make clear that they intensified during the latter half of the eighteenth century as Iberians sought to expand mining, ranching, and farming enterprises into new regions and to secure the navigational routes and territorial borders of their colonies. But is this a complete picture of Indigenous motivations to make peace?

This chapter aims to go beyond external pressures or "push factors" in explaining why some Native groups moved closer to the whites in this period. In representing themselves to their Portuguese interlocutors in Brazil, Native groups tended not to paint themselves as being stuck between a rock and a hard place—in other words, as being forced by dire circumstances to find new allies. Instead, they often framed theirs as a proactive *choice* to ally with the Portuguese against a common enemy (often, the Spanish).[17] This new proximity was envisioned on their own terms: "When they decided to abandon their forests, *it was to live with the whites*," they explained, and they did not want to be resettled at the distant, unhealthy, or barren sites occasionally proposed by colonial officials.[18]

Such realignments opened up a whole range of new social, political, and economic possibilities. These included access to livestock, participation in wider trade networks, recovery of captives, domination of rivals, and social interaction with Indigenous groups already living in colonial villages and cities. Such advantages, Indians found, could be gained without relinquishing traditional patterns of seasonal mobility. Allied groups came and went from the colonial settlements as they pleased—after reprovisioning themselves with metal tools and food supplies, of course.[19] Temporary stays in the colonial sphere even offered opportunities to learn the enemy's language, technologies, and tactical weaknesses. These lessons might prove useful if open hostilities began anew.[20]

Sources and Distortions

Peace agreements between Europeans and Native peoples took many forms, and just one of these was the formal, written treaty.[21] This helps explain why the documentary remains of the peacemaking process are diverse and scattered, more likely to be discovered in regional archives than in national or overseas collections. In Brazil, we find traces of the process in the letters of administrators and military men who found themselves stationed at remote forts or at the head of backlands expeditions. Both types of Portuguese officials described how they hosted contingents of visiting Indians; supervised the distribution of gifts; negotiated conditions of friendship; broached the possibilities of resettlement, evangelization, and military cooperation; and arranged for Indians to visit the outpost in the future, or even to visit the governor in the capital. The records of these colonial field agents reveal a great deal about the participation of Indians in peacemaking. They even can be read, cautiously, for Native perspectives on the process.[22]

On-the-ground sources often described Native actions and behavior in detail: how Indians approached or received colonial officials, what gifts exchanged hands, and how they comported themselves in the garrison, expedition camp, or frontier settlement. Occasionally, colonial authors reported what Indigenous people said, either purporting to quote them directly, or providing a summary. They named or described the Native men whom officials perceived—or wished to perceive—as leaders of extended kin groups (*malocas, tolderias,* parcialidades) or as representatives of Indigenous polities or "nations" (*nações*). Sometimes they paid attention to the women who accompanied these leaders as family members and interpreters—and, more broadly, as symbols of peaceful intentions.[23] Much ink was spilled, too, on personal interactions that were seen as important milestones in the peace process. The sources might tell us that high-ranking Indians sat down to share a meal with the Portuguese commander; that the two groups staged "friendly" demonstrations of their respective weapons (firearms, bows and arrows); that Native women were permitted to join the peacemaking festivities; or that the Portuguese were invited to enter the Indigenous village. In some cases, the documents described how Native leaders responded to proposals that they settle in *aldeamentos*, nuclear settlements overseen by missionaries or secular administrators, or that they serve as military auxiliaries against other Indigenous groups. Occasionally, Indians' conditions or demands were listed: protection against enemies, a steady supply of metal tools or food supplies, or assurances of their safety in the process. These negotiations might end in a pact (written or unwritten) or, more ambiguously, a promise to meet again in several "moons" or at some unspecified time in the future.

As valuable as they are, these written records distort our understanding of the peacemaking process in several ways. The first has to do with ego and pretension. Colonial officials were loathe to admit how difficult it could be to dominate Native peoples, tending to portray peace as unilaterally imposed rather than the result of compromise between the two parties. Seeking recognition and rewards, colonial officials often glorified their own roles in the negotiations and claimed greater authority over Indians than they really had.[24] Subordinates might flatter their superiors in written accounts of peace agreements: "Our most Excellent Governor has had the satisfaction of liberating the populace of this Captaincy from those beasts that had once devoured its entrails," referring to the Xavante, who had recently made peace. The governor, in this telling, had achieved "the incomparable glory of having gained for the church an equal number of children, plus as many vassals for the Portuguese Empire." These policies were rife with contradictions—so starkly apparent in the depiction of the Xavante as bloodthirsty beasts *and* children and vassals—but colonial authors did not bother to analyze them.[25] Instead, they congratulated each other in ornate language: "The brilliant talents of Your Excellency and their assiduous application to the benefit of the Crown," wrote one governor to another, "have brought about, like a miracle, the pacification of the terrible Caiapó Indians."[26] With these pretensions, authors often downplayed the extent to which Indians imposed conditions for peace and extracted concessions from them—concessions that provided Indigenous groups with many of the same benefits previously obtained through raids.[27] There is also plenty of evidence to suggest that Native peoples did not see themselves as "pacified" or "domesticated." The same year that the governors crowed to each other about the achievement of Caiapó pacification, the Caiapó were living in or near the capital city, waiting for their new village to be prepared for them (in a location of their choosing) and bartering goods with their former enemies. One eyewitness account described how a group of Caiapó men had come upon a group of slaves struggling to drag a massive wooden beam along the ground, while their merchant owner supervised. Laughing at the merchant's efforts to shoo them away, the Caiapó hoisted the beam onto their shoulders "as if it was a stick"—a move that recalled their traditional log races—and carried it to the merchant's house. As one historian notes of this episode, these "were not dispirited and defeated men forced to acquiesce to a humiliating subjugation; rather, they were warriors proud of their speed and strength."[28]

Second, colonial authors almost always described the peacemaking process through a lens of deep suspicion. Native peoples were seen as inherently untrustworthy and mercurial in their loyalties, as captured in the label "*inconstante*," or inconstant, applied to Indians in the writings of military men, administrators, and missionaries throughout the Iberian colonial world.[29] Strongly associated with nomadism—which contemporaries described as "living like beasts . . . wandering about without ever truly settling"[30]—the notion of Indian inconstancy profoundly shaped colonial understandings of Native actions and words. Iberian authors occasionally did recount the explanations given by Indians for switching sides or turning against their former allies, but they usually framed these as deceptive. We would do well to give such explanations more credit than contemporaries did and to read them for evidence of Native political strategies, attitudes, and choices. Indeed, the perception of fickle and mercurial behavior could be reciprocal: Indians, too, made accusations of broken promises and complained of insults received from their Spanish and Portuguese allies.[31]

Colonial officials may have misread as fickleness what was really just the result of many different Indigenous groups each pursuing different local interests and strategies or disagreeing among themselves as to which path to follow.[32] This leads us to the third major problem with the colonial sources, which is their tendency to identify Indians as members of generic "nations" rather than factions or internally divided groups. Applied to delegations of Indians, such an identification might represent a kind of wishful thinking on the part of colonial authors: not just a small group, but rather a whole polity could be considered "pacified" or on its way to pacification. For borderlands administrators and military men, there were real incentives for making such claims, as the Royal Treasury typically sent supplies and funds in accordance with the presumed importance and size of the target group.[33] The colonial categorization of Indian "nations" thus presents a picture of unity that is unhelpful for reconstructing the ebb and flow of Indigenous alliances. A number of documents cited in this book, however, show that the colonial record *does* contain evidence of Native factionalism. It simply can be harder to find amid all of the triumphalist accounts.

A final, related problem has to do with inclusion. The peacemaking activities of some Indigenous groups in colonial Brazil were much better documented than others, corresponding to their relative power (whether actual or perceived) and the frequency and intensity of their contacts with colonial populations. So many Indigenous groups left only fleeting traces in the documentary record of peacemaking. What do such traces look like? We have, for example, an intriguing document from the Portuguese Amazon in 1766 that describes how the "Aritú nation" hosted a group of colonial emissaries for three days in their village, situated on a small waterway off a tributary of the Amazon River. The Aritú were said to be able to converse and share news with the emissaries—who were Native people themselves—in the Jesuit-devised língua geral. This linguistic detail, as well as the Aritús' alleged statement that "their ancestors had always said that there would be good people of God who would come look for them," suggests an earlier connection to the missions of Amazonia; these may have been descendants of former mission residents, or perhaps mission runaways had been incorporated with them at some point in the past. From the same document, we know that three Aritú chiefs sent their sons to visit the colonial settlement of Vila Franca, at the junction of the Amazon and Tapajós Rivers. The visitors' response was ambivalent: they thought the houses in the village already too full of people. More houses, they said, would have to be built before they could bring the rest of their kin to settle there. And that is where the story of this particular peacemaking venture ends—or at least the single account of it that made it into in the archives.[34]

Taming the Whites

The Guaikurú were keenly alert to the new commercial and political possibilities of peace. As detailed in the previous chapter, various Guaikurú groups had made intermittent peace agreements with Spaniards in Paraguay since the sixteenth century and often visited Asunción to trade. Some had even experimented with Jesuit mission life at the short-lived mission at Belén (1760–1767). When they attacked the Portuguese, witnesses reported that the Guaikurús often uttered Spanish words or phrases, and the bodies of any Guaikurús killed during the skirmishes might be found with firearms, wool cloth, glass beads, or silver ornaments.[35] But by the 1770s, the Guaikurú had begun raiding the newly established Spanish ranches north of Asunción for livestock, and some groups looked for new trading partners on the other side of the border.[36] They, like other Chaco peoples, also looked for new ways to survive in a changing ecosystem, as game animals grew more scarce due to overhunting (stimulated by the colonial trade in hides) and supplies of wild plant food diminished or became less accessible (as cattle ranches advanced into Native territories).[37]

It took time for trading with the Portuguese to become normalized, given the traumas of recent history. Guaikurú groups must have debated fiercely among themselves about the differences between Spanish and Portuguese: was one nation less traitorous than the other? At the forefront of everyone's minds was the 1778 massacre of more than fifty unarmed Portuguese soldiers at Coimbra Fort by a Guaikurú party (see chapter 1). Would the Portuguese exact revenge? Would the Guaikurú inflict such devastating losses again? Nerves were frayed, too, after so many years of long-distance sightings and mutual surveillance. The Indians had watched the passage of colonial cargo canoes along the Paraguay River and the circulation of daily patrols from the fort and garrison town. The Portuguese, for their part, had often found "fresh signs of heathens" (cut wood, the ashes of fires, and hoof prints from large herds of livestock) in the vicinity of their outposts along the Paraguay River.[38] Later, a commander would describe Coimbra before the peace as "a true exile, with its garrison confined to the area of the stockade, at the edge of a barren hill, full of rocks, where no one fished or hunted except under armed guard. Even so, the Guaikurús, lurking and waiting in ambush, killed some people as soon as they sensed any opening or carelessness; and on dark nights, they sometimes attacked the sentinels in their watchtowers."[39] A much later generation of Brazilians—early twentieth-century employees of the Indian Protection Service, or SPI—would describe what this surveillance felt like: it was an "unbearable nervous affliction caused by the state of feeling incessantly surrounded, watched, and studied in one's smallest acts, by people one cannot see, and whose numbers cannot even be known."[40]

Peaceful contacts began, haltingly, around 1790. Instead of silently approaching Coimbra Fort under cover of darkness and stormy weather—as they had been known to do in the years following the massacre—a large party of some forty Guaikurús appeared in front of the fort one afternoon and gave a few loud shouts. And instead of packing their guns with powder and firing at them, a group of soldiers went to see what the Indians wanted. Although there was no interpreter to translate for them and the two groups communicated at a great distance, the Portuguese were able to gather that the Guaikurú planned to return on friendly terms. So they did, a few months later. On higher orders to attempt a peaceful interaction through gifting, the fort commander gave them some presents, which "left them very satisfied and quite happy, and they went off with the promise to bring their products to trade." A few months after that, the same commander reported that the Guaikurú came constantly to the fort, bringing livestock to trade. Among them was the chief Caimá—whom a visiting naturalist described as "one of the tallest Indians that I have ever seen."[41]

Distrust still ran high on both sides. For example, when a new fort commander, Joaquim José Ferreira, arrived at Coimbra near the end of 1790, the Guaikurú stayed away from the fort and would only send their captives to visit and trade. The chief who had visited before, Caimá, finally accepted Ferreira's invitation to return to Coimbra in early 1791, but he was said to have spent the three-day voyage to the fort repeatedly asking his Portuguese escort whether he was going to be tied up and have his throat cut in retribution for past insults. Commander Ferreira described how, upon his receiving Caimá hospitably, the chief "got up, embraced me, and said in a loud voice that he wanted to be my friend." When Ferreira replied that he still expected the chief to break whatever promises were made—in keeping with the stereotype of the inconstant Indian—"he said to me, very annoyed, that he was Caimá, and that Caimá would not break [a promise]."[42] Yet the chief remained on high alert during these initial visits and generally did not permit his people to bring their families to Coimbra, "saying that this was a land that did not have women, so their women should not come, either."[43]

It was thus significant that Caimá brought his own wife to the fort, and it helps explain why a remarkable pair of portraits was made of the couple when they overlapped there in 1791 with the royally appointed naturalist, Alexandre Rodrigues Ferreira, and the artists of his expedition (figure 2.1). The portraits are rich in detail: Caimá

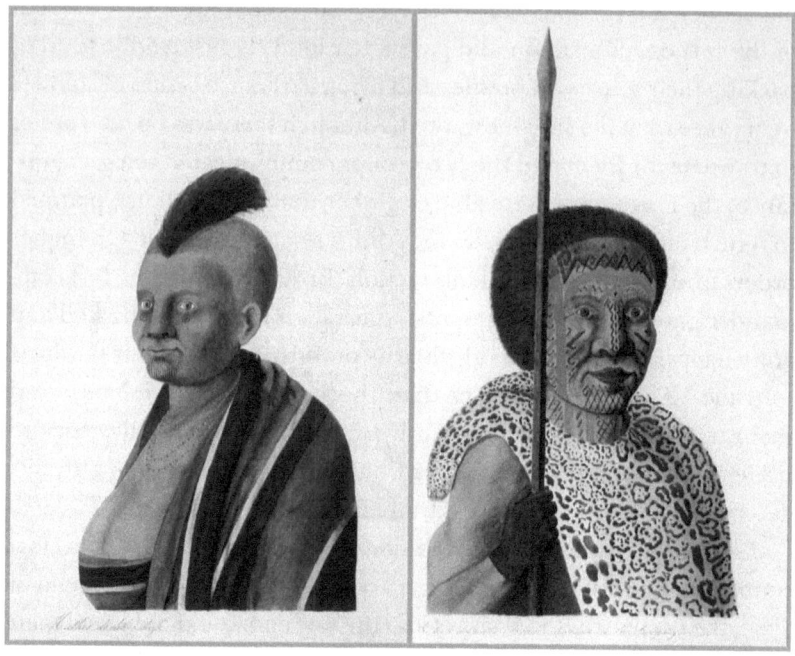

FIGURE 2.1 Portrait of the Guaikurú chief Caimá and his wife in 1791.

Source: Joaquim José Codina, from the Alexandre Rodrigues Ferreira collection at the Museu Nacional de História Natural e da Ciência da Universidade de Lisboa, Portugal.

wears a jaguar cloak, his face and body are decorated in red urucum and black *genipapo* paint, and his muscular arm holds a metal-tipped lance. His wife, described as a "beautiful Indian woman" who would later be given the Portuguese name of Joaquina, is dressed in a typical striped cotton mantle and sports a hairstyle for married women that, according to the naturalist, evoked the crest of a curassow bird (*mutum*). The couple also appear with plucked eyelashes and eyebrows, a sign of proper grooming and beauty.[44] Caimá's subgroup was known as the Eyibegodegis (or Ejueos), meaning the "hidden ones," whose lands lay on the eastern side of the Paraguay River near the Bodoquena Mountains, more than thirty leagues southeast of Coimbra. He would play a starring role in the peacemaking of the next several years, until his death by Spanish guns in 1796.[45]

Some Guaikurú groups had, in effect, "followed the market" at a time when Spain's ability to import trade items was hampered by the

British blockade of the 1790s.[46] The new economic and political relationship with the Portuguese was first affirmed by two large groups of Guaikurú—one led by Caimá, the other by a chief called Emavidi Xané—at Coimbra Fort in 1791. It was formalized later that year with a written peace agreement, upon the visit of the two chiefs to the capital of Mato Grosso, Vila Bela. According to that agreement, the chiefs said that "in their names and in those of all the other chiefs of their nation, their compatriots, and their descendants, they declared and promised from this day forward . . . to maintain the most intimate peace and friendship with the Portuguese," serving the king "loyally and obediently, in the same way that all of his vassals do."[47]

These promises on behalf of all Guaikurú were, of course, aspirational for both peacemaking parties; Caimá and Emavidi Xané did not actually speak for all of the chiefs. Theirs was a dispersed system of political organization, based on shifting alliances and networks of kinship. (Caimá's wife Joaquina, for example, was identified as the daughter of Emavidi Xané, a marriage that must have cemented the connection between the two peacemaking chiefs and their respective groups; a few years later, she would separate from Caimá and marry the leader of another Guaikurú group farther to the south, which thereafter entered peaceful relations with the Portuguese.[48]) At that time, the Guaikurú were divided into at least six parcialidades, or regional groups, each of which was divided into further subgroups with subordinate leaders (see chapter 1). Some of these parcialidades, especially those toward the south and on the eastern side of the Paraguay River, allied with Spain and remained openly hostile to Portuguese.[49]

But as relationships with Spaniards deteriorated in the context of intensified raiding and reprisals, many Guaikurú groups did transfer to the Portuguese side, with their vast herds of horses in tow. In 1797, the Portuguese reported that some southern groups of Guaikurú had stolen more than nine thousand animals from Spanish ranches over the course of the past half year; they then sought refuge across the border.[50] Reports make clear that this migration ebbed and flowed over time, according to the seasons and the political climate. "Lately we have begun to see columns of smoke on the western side [of the

Paraguay River], certainly at a diminishing distance," wrote the commander of Coimbra in 1796, "which shows that as the plains are drying out, they are coming closer."[51] In 1802, "the flow of Indians was greater than ever before," with members of an important Guaikurú subgroup, the Kadiwéu, arriving every day to take refuge at Coimbra. Another group of some four hundred Kadiwéus waited farther downriver for the floodwaters to recede, so that they could transport their livestock safely to Coimbra, while Spanish emissaries allegedly came to harass them and "tell them a thousand bad things about the Portuguese."[52] Frequent reverse migrations occurred, too, as some Guaikurú leaders and groups responded to new Spanish overtures or simply kept crossing back and forth over the border for their own purposes.[53] The important thing, from the perspective of Native peoples in the borderlands, was to maintain ties to a range of different colonial outposts, so as to better control conduits of goods and information between the two empires. The Fecho dos Morros, an area where the Paraguay River narrowed around an island, seems to have been seen as a kind of geographical division during the peacemaking era, with the Guaikurú groups south of that point remaining mostly connected to Spanish outposts, and those to the north gravitating more toward Portuguese ones (see map 1).[54]

By the beginning of the new century, many Guaikurú groups (including the Kadiwéu) were living seasonally in the vicinity of the Portuguese military outposts of Coimbra, Albuquerque, and Miranda, which served as "entrepôts of attraction for native populations [and] outposts for establishing political relations with *caciques*," or chiefs.[55] In exchange for gifts and protection, the Guaikurú supplied the Portuguese soldiers and Mato Grosso's royal ranches with horses, including animals stolen from Spanish pastures. If the Guaikurú were anything like the Comanche of North America, they would have aimed to sell these stolen "colonial" horses rather than their own domestically raised animals, which had been trained and bred to suit their preferences. We do know that they sometimes tried to sell old, sick, or lame horses.[56] The Guaikurú also passed along intelligence about Spanish forces and made assurances of military assistance in the case of a Spanish invasion.[57]

This profitable peace with the Portuguese strengthened some Guaikurú factions and leaders over others. The first chiefs to formalize peace, Caimá and Emavidi Xané, consolidated their power as they accumulated goods and prestige, and as other Guaikurú and Guaná groups decided to incorporate with them over the course of the 1790s.[58] Caimá was said to have claimed the title of "general governor of all the Guaikurú"; his stated goal in early 1791 was to go to Vila Bela to receive the ceremonial "staff of office, as chief of his people."[59] The "apparition" of superior chiefs satisfied colonial desires to identify a single leader with whom to negotiate peace, but it surely also had to do with Indigenous decisions to organize more broadly against Iberian threats to their territory and autonomy.[60] Guaikurú leaders knew that they were riven by internal disagreements and that their own authority was limited; they also knew that their people straddled a colonial border with dangers and opportunities on both sides. In some moments, cohesion made sense and was possible. At other times, they preferred—or could not avoid—fragmentation.

With their new base of operations in what is now the Brazilian state of Mato Grosso do Sul, Guaikurú raiding parties continued to cross the border to sack Spanish ranches and yerba mate plantations. They went on taking captives among less powerful Indigenous groups like the Chamacoco and Guató, even as Portuguese officials sought to discourage or obstruct such ventures (see chapter 3). Many Guaikurú chiefs also worked to maintain their long-standing symbiotic relationship with the Guaná, when they perceived that the Portuguese were working to undermine that relationship.[61] For many years, colonial authorities tried negotiating directly with the Guaná chiefs, sending them to Vila Bela to be wined and dined by the governor, and proposing resettlement sites intended exclusively for them. In their writings, officials highlighted the diligence and cooperation of the Guaná, in contrast with the "haughty" Guaikurú. In response, the allied Guaikurú reportedly changed tactics: one fort commander described how they began "calling the Guanás their friends and relatives, inviting them to their parties and even to my table. They feared this change, because with it they would lose women, part of their subsistence, and their forces, for they invite them always on their bellicose expeditions."[62] The Guaikurú chief Emavidi Xané, for example, promoted his image as a kind of benefactor to the Guaná: he hosted them in his residence, visited their camps, and treated their leaders as worthy dining companions at Coimbra Fort—rather than scorning, as most Guaikurú captains did, the idea of sitting down to eat with those they called captives.⁶³

The Portuguese officials who interacted with Guaikurús found that they disconcertingly mirrored colonial attitudes and aims. Ricardo Franco de Almeida Serra, the longtime commander at Coimbra, fulminated that the Guaikurú considered themselves "the first and dominant nation of Indians, counting all others as their captives, not judging themselves inferior even to the Spanish and Portuguese." He provided a few examples of this, recounting how "my box of tobacco was on a bench, and next to it sat a Guaikurú. I asked him for it, and he responded, very insolently, 'Call the Black slave.' They responded the same way when some Portuguese asked to have a light for his cigarette."⁶⁴ Even more provocatively, the Guaikurú went around "boasting daily that even though we are very fierce, they know how to tame us."⁶⁵

Commander Serra asserted that such "taming" had a sexual component. This seems purely salacious, until we consider that both Guaikurú and Guaná women could, by this time, be found in the bunks of Portuguese soldiers at Coimbra, Albuquerque, and Miranda, and that Serra himself took a Guaná wife, with whom he had two children.⁶⁶ The commander claimed that "the Guanás value and advertise the companionship of their women," openly requiring payments for sexual favors. In contrast, the Guaikurús denied that prostitution was taking place, "saying that the friendship of their women is chaste and without malice; and that whatever they give is out of gratitude, *for the Portuguese being tamed.*"⁶⁷ In Serra's opinion, the Guaikurú still had their eyes on the money that could be exchanged for sex; their claims to the contrary only solidified his views on Guaikurú arrogance and dissimulation. But despite these conveniently reinforced conclusions, it is hard to imagine that Serra completely fabricated the Indians' statements. If the Guaikurú (or their interpreters) actually used the words *amansado* (tamed) or *manso* (tame), perhaps it was because the Portuguese commonly applied that adjective to horses as well as to Indians who were the targets of their pacification efforts. A late-eighteenth-century dictionary, after all, defined *manso* as "broken, i.e., a tame horse" or like "tame Indians who live in settled villages, and engage in trade, and show subjection to Portuguese ministers."[68] For an equestrian, conquering people like the Guaikurú, the connection between taming horses and men would have been clear. Perhaps Portuguese men could be kept, figuratively, under saddle and reins. The Guaikurú, it seems, had turned the colonial narrative of pacification on its head: they were the ones pacifying, or taming, the whites. It would not be the first time or place where such a reversal left its traces in the historical or ethnographic record.[69]

And so the peacemaking process continued, in all of its ambiguity. Using the discourse of friendship and alliance, the Guaikurú visited the Portuguese forts and even the capital city to obtain tobacco and *aguardente* (cane liquor) as well as information. Commander Serra claimed that the visiting Guaikurú spoke fluent Portuguese only when they were intoxicated; at all other times, they pretended not to speak or understand even a word of it, so as to better eavesdrop upon their "friends." He also suggested that they had a kind of secret pidgin language, one that could not be understood even by non-Guaikurú who had lived in their company for many years and who were otherwise employed as interpreters; he thought they used this language whenever they were discussing particularly sensitive matters.[70] According to Serra, news could be transmitted among the Guaikurú over long distances by the sounds of whistles, pipes (*gaitas*), and even the movements of their oars on the water. (Interestingly, the Mura were likewise thought to have a secret, guttural language that they used in plotting rebellion, thefts, or murders. Although the Mura language is extinct, modern linguists studying the related dialect of Pirahã have confirmed that the language features five different channels or modes of speech, including "humming" speech, which can be used for secretive communications, and whistling speech, used by men to communicate while hunting or by boys in belligerent play.[71]) The Guaikurús at Coimbra, for example, were said to have known that the chief Caimá had died as soon as a canoe appeared in the distance. For the Portuguese, these sophisticated Native methods of gathering and transmitting information were both blessing and curse: they were advantageous in the competition with Spain but also fed fears of the "inconstant Indian," who could never be trusted.[72]

More than twenty years after the initial peace agreement with the Guaikurú, another Coimbra commander was convinced that one of the main protagonists of the 1791 treaty—the chief Emavidi Xané, whose Portuguese title was Capitão Paulo Joaquim José Ferreira—was still living as a spy among the Portuguese. Too old to go raiding in Spanish territories with the rest of his group, he was said to remain at the Portuguese fort, eager "to spread to the entire nation all [the intelligence] that he can gather around here."[73] The irony was, of course, that the Portuguese wanted to keep the Guaikurú under surveillance at the fort but found this difficult, given the Indians' frequent absences. Though tinged with colonial paranoia, these descriptions nonetheless suggest that the Guaikurú saw peace as more than simply as a survival strategy. It was an initiative by which they could more efficiently obtain Portuguese goods, power, and knowledge.

Intensifying and Expanding Social Relations
The Mura, long known as the "river corsairs" of Brazil, made peace with the Portuguese in the Amazonian borderlands between 1784 and 1786. Reconstructing why this unfolded when it did—just after Mura attacks had achieved maximum terror among colonial travelers and villagers across a vast area of the Upper and Middle Amazon—tells us more about shifting Native priorities than it does about Portuguese policies. In fact, as one scholar has described it, Mura overtures of friendship were "so unexpected by the Portuguese that they were incredulous at first, and then unanimous in attributing it to divine intervention." A military engineer, Henrique João Wilkens, even wrote an epic poem on how the Mura went from making war to offering peace. It featured a heavenly angel who convinced the Mura to join the fold.[74] For Wilkens, who was part of the joint Portuguese and Spanish boundary demarcation commission, the Mura peace was truly a gift from above: the place where the Mura first came to "adhere" to the Portuguese side was situated on one of the very rivers contested by the two Iberian Crowns along the western frontier of the Portuguese Amazon.

For many Muras, the shift toward peacemaking in 1784 was driven by social connections, old and new, to the world of the colonial Indian villages. Dotted all along the main tributaries of the Portuguese

Amazon, most of these villages were former missions, secularized in 1757 under the power of the colonial state. They had individual Portuguese or Brazilian "directors" (according to the administrative regime known as the Indian Directorate) but maintained some Native leadership structures and traditions of local autonomy until the end of the eighteenth century. And although the Directorate imposed the menacing demands of draft labor, the villages offered the relative security of residence in a state-sponsored, corporate community.[75] The Mura were familiar with many of these settlements because they had a long history of raiding them for people and goods. Many Muras were, in fact, people who had been born and raised in these communities before their capture or voluntary incorporation. They had been, as colonial authors described it, *murificado*, or "Murified" (see chapter 1).

One such group of Murified men initiated the peace process. Five of them appeared in July of 1784 at the little frontier village of Santo Antônio de Maripí on the Japurá River (see map 2). There, they found only a petrified vicar and one soldier, quaking in his boots. The vicar had enough presence of mind to send some Indian boys to find the village director, Mathias Fernandes, who was in the forest working on the fabrication of a new canoe. Fernandes must have thrown down his tools and hurried back to the village, because he quickly appeared. After a brief conference between the director and the vicar, a fateful decision was made: they would let the visitors come in peace, for they themselves were very few in number, and the Mura (they suspected, correctly) were many.

This meeting at Maripí with Director Fernandes was not an arbitrary choice on the part of the Mura, and in fact there was a deeper history on both sides. Fernandes himself had participated in bloody expeditions against the Mura in the past, and groups of Muras (though probably not the same ones) had attacked Maripí various times.[76] As recently as 1781, Mura raiders had allegedly carried off manioc roots and fruit from the ripening gardens of the residents. In 1782—a year that one higher official identified as the peak of "daily insults" by the Mura[77]—a large Mura raiding party had surrounded the village for three days and threatened "in loud voices" to burn it down until gunfire deterred them. Portuguese higher officials, for their part, saw

Maripí as a key outpost, necessary to preserve in the face of Spanish territorial pretensions and the ongoing negotiations with Spain over the demarcation of the imperial border along the Japurá River. They even stationed a small military detachment there.[78] Maripí, then, carried a kind of symbolic importance for both Portuguese and Indians in the same way that Coimbra Fort did: it was a site of bloodshed, of past confrontations between enemies, but it also held strategic value in the broader contest for territory and control.

The five peacemaking Indians who came to Maripí all communicated in the língua geral that they had spoken as children in the colonial villages of the region, before they were captured by the Mura. Some had been taken from Castro de Avelãs, far up the Solimões River, and others from Airão, on the Rio Negro; the immense distance between these two villages of origin corresponds with what we know of the territorial reach of Mura raiding and captive-taking. They told Fernandes that there were many more of their kind among the large group of Muras hiding in the vicinity—and indeed, the village priest spotted some forty Muras, in ten watercraft, waiting nearby. Despite their superior numbers, the Muras promised that they would not kill any more villagers in Maripí. This intention was emphasized by what the visitors said next: they noted that they had seen all of the village canoes leave, and they wanted to warn the Portuguese that "behind those canoes went a larger number of more barbarous Muras, who do not accept among themselves any *gente ladina* (acculturated people) from the colonial villages, who spare no one and kill everyone in their path." Having provided this warning, which would have terrified the Portuguese and Native villagers alike, the visitors received twenty-five knives, one axe, one harpoon, and a bushel of manioc meal from Director Fernandes, who played along with this exchange of goodwill despite his deep distrust of the Mura. Once they had gone turtle hunting and had finished destroying some enemies farther along the Japurá River, the visitors promised to return.[79]

A different group of Mura interpreters showed up at Maripí about six months later, bringing five turtles and a few roots of sarsaparilla as presents, and an unnamed Mura chief felt safe enough to visit in person the following day. The military commander at Maripí first tried to ascertain how this new group was connected to the first one that had visited, and it emerged that they knew of the broader plan to make peace. He then made his pitch: would the chief be interested in visiting the Portuguese lieutenant downriver? This would entail several days' travel down to the Solimões River, to the border demarcation headquarters at the town of Ega (modern-day Tefé). Assured that he would receive many gifts there, the chief agreed to go. But then the commander told him that he would have to be escorted by soldiers, who would go in a separate canoe. At this, the chief balked: "He said that he had an upset stomach and that he could not bear to travel with whites."[80] Despite this initial reluctance, the chief did end up traveling to Ega several days later—though most of his party refused to go anywhere close to the town. It would be the first of many such visits by Mura groups.

In the peace negotiations that followed over the course of the next several years, the main protagonist was also a Murified Indian, whom the Portuguese called Ambrósio. They identified him as the leader of the group that had sent the first Mura translators to Maripí, and which had its main base on the Amaná Lake, just off the Japurá River. This lake was connected via a labyrinthine network of waterways to both the Solimões River and the Rio Negro; for that reason, it would become a region of great strategic interest to colonial officials.[81]

The Portuguese wrote about Ambrósio with a level of biographical detail that is extremely rare in the colonial sources. There are a few possible reasons for this. First, they found him physically imposing: "He has a heavyset, almost gigantic figure," one official wrote with a mixture of fascination and fear, "being taller, more robust, and more muscular than me." Second, Ambrósio's family history and his own life story made him stand out as a kind of archetype, familiar to any colonial official of that place and time. Like so many "colonial Indians," his family had deserted the village of Nogueira when it was still a mission, probably back in the late 1740s. While living in a fugitive community, they had been attacked by the Mura, who killed the men in Ambrósio's family (including his father) but adopted the women and children, among them the young Ambrósio, at least one sister, and his mother, Joana. Rising to prominence as a warrior among his new people, Ambrósio was "Murified, even down to the two bones shaped like large teeth that he wears in his lower and upper lips," and went on to lead a group that staged raids along the lower Japurá River, the northern bank of the Amazon-Solimões River, and as far as the Rio Negro.[82] Now, relying on Joana as translator (since he spoke the língua geral poorly), he embraced the role of "chief reconciler of the Mura."[83] This, of course, was the third reason why the Portuguese wrote so much about him: accurately or not, they saw him as the one upon whom the whole peace project depended.

In mid-1785, Ambrósio and his group showed up in Nogueira, his family's former village on the Solimões River, where one of their relatives served as a Native officer. They came during the annual festival in June, when the whole village erupted in dancing and celebration—another sign of divine providence in the eyes of at least one Portuguese observer. After several days of joyful partying on the village beach, the Mura offered twenty of their children for baptism. As godfather, they chose Lieutenant Colonel João Batista Mardel.[84] Another group of Muras headed to the village of Moura, on the Rio Negro, because one of them (who served as an interpreter) had been captured from there as a child and had evidently convinced them that this was the best place to visit and perhaps settle.[85] The freedom to visit old friends and kin in the colonial villages was clearly important to the peacemaking Mura, and especially to the women, some of whom gravitated toward the rituals and festivities of the village churches.[86] Joana, who spent time in Nogueira recuperating from an illness, apparently "never missed going to Church to [fulfill] all the obligations and devotions of the rest of the populace."[87]

In 1786, peacemaking Indians also arrived in waves to Borba, a garrison town on the Madeira River. Higher authorities identified them as "Muras," but correspondence from the commander at Borba makes clear that the picture was more ethnically complex, including groups that might have been considered subordinate allies of the Mura. The visiting parties grew larger over the course of several months and demonstrated the Indians' increasing trust: they spent the night dancing and partying in the village, returned two captives who had been taken long ago from Borba, and even invited the commander to visit their home village (which he did). Finally, a large group of 143 men and women showed up in the town. Described as Mura, Torá, Irurí, and Jarauary Indians "all mixed together," some of the visitors had kin connections with Indians in Borba. In fact, as soon as the Torás set foot in the town, they went into the house of their female kin—presumably a large, multifamily house—and shared their pet monkeys.[88] If among contemporary Native Amazonians the exchange of tame animals like monkeys is a way of affirming kin relationships, in this case it may have helped bring together members of an Indigenous group that had been split between the colonial and extracolonial spheres and integrated with other groups. Again, women played key roles in building (or rebuilding) these social connections.[89]

The visitors lingered in Borba for several days because they wanted to see the villagers raise the flagpoles of the Divine Holy Spirit and Saint Anthony—referring to the ceremonial flagpoles made out of large pieces of wood and decorated with flowers and ribbons, commonly used in saint's day celebrations in rural Brazil to this day. The visitors were quite insistent on this point, the garrison commander noted: "They said that they wanted to come [again] to see the festival, and that I should send someone to tell them, or they would come to find out, when it was happening."[90]

But curiosity about Christian festivities did not imply a renunciation of Native practices, as a visiting archbishop discovered in the same town a few years later. By then, about a thousand Muras had come to live at Borba, at least seasonally, and many of their children had been baptized. The archbishop, however, described them as completely unassimilated in language and culture and said that "they conserve the same brutish customs with which they were raised in the forest, and the chiefs have seven, eight, or nine wives." The Mura men put on a show for their aghast visitor, painting themselves for the occasion and dancing in a line, some playing long wooden flutes and others displaying their bows and arrows. Adding to the archbishop's disappointment was the local priest's admission that the Mura mothers feared the baptism of their children—especially when it came time to put the blessed salt in their mouths, at which point the mothers snatched the children away and removed the salt as quickly as possible. Such was the ambiguity of baptism among Native groups: it was often sought out as a possible cure for sickness, but it could also be associated with death or harm. It is also worth noting that the groups of Muras who came to Borba in the late 1780s were among those most directly threatened by the incursions of the Mundurukú. For them—more than for the Mura groups along on the north bank of the Amazon-Solimões River and the northern tributaries—the militarized town may have provided protection from those attacks, but at a cost. Tellingly, the women all stayed away from the town during the archbishop's visit.[91]

What about the Mura groups that were more distant from the Mundurukú but closer to the imperial border zone upriver? One scholar has argued that in the context of a brutal, decades-long war with the Portuguese, and especially at a moment when Iberian representatives were gathering in intimidatingly large numbers at the border demarcation headquarters of Ega and heading out in large expeditions to survey the surrounding rivers, some factions of Mura may have been on the lookout for alternatives to armed conflict. Women and elders—especially those with prior connections to the colonial villages—may have convinced the young Mura warriors to consider the social benefits of peace.[92] Ambrósio apparently suggested as much. Asked by one colonial official whether he had decided to settle in a permanent place, "he said yes, for he was tired of wandering in this life, and his mother, who was already old, did not want to wander in this life either."[93] It is an evocative image that surely reassured the Portuguese: the fearsome warrior and his elderly mother had grown weary of their peregrinations and were ready to settle. Perhaps it reflected real sentiments on the part of Joana and others. An elderly Caiapó man named Romexi said much the same thing during peace talks with the Portuguese in 1780, according to the colonial governor who spoke with him. When urged to leave the colonial village (where he had been visiting) and go back to his homelands as an emissary of the new peace agreement, the old man said "that he was already tired of wandering through the forest; that he wanted to live and end his days among us, the whites."[94]

Ambrósio himself, however, showed no signs of slowing down or staying put. In fact, he appears in the sources as constantly, enthusiastically on the move during those years. Peace afforded opportunities to continue what the Mura already did very well, which was incorporating other peoples into their network of clans and mobile settlements.

Ambrósio, his brother-in-law, and several other leaders were active in persuading (or coercing) other groups of Mura as well as Xumana, Torá, and Irurí to join them in making peace and forming large settlements in locations closer to the Portuguese. In March of 1785, Ambrósio was planning to engage in peace talks with Mura groups along the Juruá River, "pacifying them and settling them."[95] A few months later, he claimed to have established peace with the Muras along the northern bank and tributaries of the Amazon River. "Showing great satisfaction," he also reported having sent his brother-in-law to spread the peace proposal among the Muras of the Rio Negro.[96]

One of the artists on the Alexandre Rodrigues Ferreira expedition—the same one who painted the portraits of the Guaikurú chief and his wife in figure 2.1—drew the likeness of a Mura who showed up in the Rio Negro village of Airão (figure 2.2). This unnamed man had arrived in late 1786 and stayed for several months, along with an interpreter who was originally from that village; in all, his group of Muras consisted of twenty-one men, twenty-two women, nine boys, and seven girls. The portrait was clearly intended to be representative: he wore the typical woven leaf headdress, lip ornaments, and an apron of twisted palm fibers with a long pipe (for inhaling the narcotic snuff called *paricá*) stuck into the belt; he also carried bamboo-tipped arrows and a long bow braced against his foot for shooting. (Several of these items are numbered in the drawing since the naturalist was sending examples of them back to Portugal.)[97]

The Portuguese called such Muras "*novos*," or newly contacted ones, and described them as "extremely fierce in appearance and gesture," supposedly never seen before by whites. But when these newcomers came to colonial settlements with Muras who had already made peace, they quickly joined the celebratory singing and dancing. In at least one instance, a mixed group of Muras even offered (like the Caiapó warriors mentioned earlier) to help the settlers carry some logs out of the forest, in what must have been a display of strength and agility.[98] In the case of the Muras visiting Airão, they were "almost everyday here in the village," as one priest noted, "the men as well as the women, and the latter sometimes come alone, without any fear or terror whatsoever, as if they were already domesticated"—a term commonly applied to

FIGURE 2.2 Portrait of a Mura, 1787.

Source: Joaquim José Codina, from the Alexandre Rodrigues Ferreira collection at the Museu Nacional de História Natural e da Ciência da Universidade de Lisboa, Portugal.

colonial Indians.⁹⁹ "They presented themselves to the Director of the Indians in this village," one author wrote of the Mura visitors in Airão, "to whom, in the name of all, one of the two interpreters in their party said they wanted to settle and establish themselves together with the other domestic Indians, as a result of the new Agreement of Peace and Friendship, which they have all just contracted with the Whites and with the Indians settled along the banks of the Japurá, Solimões, Amazon, and Madeira Rivers."¹⁰⁰

Ambrósio's recruiting activities mirror those of other Native leaders who allied with the Portuguese, seeking to gain power and prestige among their own people and over rival groups. The Portuguese were often blind to the political and interethnic complexities of such a project, but these do emerge in the documents, from time to time, in the form of expressed confusion or bewilderment. Officials puzzled over their meetings with Mura factions that claimed never to have met Ambrósio, despite his claims to have brought them into the colonial fold.¹⁰¹ Gradually, they began to perceive a divergence of aims between Mura groups who lived to the north and to the south of the basic dividing line that was the Amazon-Solimões River. The southern groups (including those in the Autazes and along the lower to middle Madeira River) were apparently less convinced of the benefits of peace, at least initially, and seemed less influenced by Murified captives; they were also said to live in larger and more powerful kin groups, or malocas. Informants told the Portuguese that Ambrósio had threatened the southern groups to the effect that "if they wanted to deceive the whites, and not form a settlement, he intended to make war against them with his [people] and all the others who are his allies."¹⁰² The southern groups seem to have changed tactics only when the Mundurukú began advancing into their territory, beginning in 1786.

The Portuguese also fretted over attacks on a handful of colonial settlements and canoe expeditions by factions of Muras that remained hostile. Some of these were thought to be led by particularly vicious ex-villagers who had joined the Mura voluntarily—the "bad" Murified ones, in counterpoint to Ambrósio and his collaborators.¹⁰³ After being accused by his superior of writing reports about the Mura that were full of discrepancies, one officer (the poetically inclined Henrique João Wilkens) tried to explain the complexity of the situation. The Mura, he said, were a nation made up of "many republics," which inhabited different watery corners of the Basin and were each governed by different chiefs and customs. "They customarily attack one another when they meet as strangers or even when they find unconvincing the arguments proposed to them. They side with whoever wins." This was perceptive, in that it recognized internal diversity and factionalism; somewhat less insightful was Wilkens's conclusion that a life of river piracy and long-distance wandering had produced an innate "inconstancy" in the Mura.[104]

Another way to understand what the Mura were doing in this period is to look at how contemporary Native peoples in lowland South America remember their decisions to move toward white society in the twentieth century. The way some groups frame it may seem paradoxical. The Wari' of the southwest Amazon, for example, describe their approximation of whites as a movement toward *Indigenous* society and social life, which had been so disrupted by the arrival of white settlers. The anthropologist Aparecida Vilaça observes that moving into greater contact with others was an opportunity for the Wari' to regain "a social life in all its complexity," with the sharing of song, dance, food, and homes, as well as competition and conflict. One of her informants, who had spent years living in the forest with a small kin group, described how he felt when he came to live with other Wari' in proximity to the whites: "I was so happy. At last there were people for me! The ache in my heart went away. I stayed there."[105]

For Ambrósio, at least, we have a glimpse of how this process played out over time—though filtered through the understanding of the colonial officer, Wilkens, who was one of his main contacts in the late 1780s. The Portuguese were, at this point, trying to understand why conflicts with some groups of Muras continued several years after the initial peacemaking. Perhaps for this reason, Wilkens seemed at pains to report Ambrósio's responses as precisely as possible, with little of the flair that usually characterized his writings. It is thus a revealing record of the Mura leader's thinking. Asked about a recent Mura attack on a military canoe on the Içá (Putumayo) River, Ambrósio explained that it must have been carried out by a group that had not yet been in contact with him. It was not for lack of trying: he had sent a canoe to make contact with them and had not yet received a response. But he said that since he saw Wilkens was very worried about the situation, "he himself would go to speak with them." These Muras on the Içá River were, he said, quite different from those downriver; they did not even have hammocks to lie in, and instead just "sleep on the ground like pigs." (Using the same swine epithet that colonial authors had applied to the Mura, Ambrósio likely knew the negative connotations of such sleeping arrangements for the Portuguese, but ethnographic evidence suggests that this was also a common distinction made by Indians when referring to other Indigenous groups.[106]) "But he would go there," Ambrósio told Wilkens, "and he would try to bring their chief and other leaders—not by force, nor by killing, but by persuasion. *Because what he wanted was for the Muras not to do harm to the whites, nor to the Indians of the villages; but also for the whites not to do harm to the Indians.*"[107]

From the Japurá River downward, Ambrósio promised that day, "everything was in peace and friendship; and so it would remain as long as he lived, for he would not allow anything else. He assured me," Wilkens wrote, "that soon the same would happen in the upriver parts, as far as there are Muras."[108] Such a campaign would, of course, involve more than "persuasion." The evidence shows that it brought Mura factions into conflict with one another, and it extended beyond the Mura to ensnare other Indigenous groups who were their junior allies, captives, or simply weaker neighbors. But it also gave warriors and their families the chance to gather on a beach, unarmed, during the village festival season that they had heard so much about from those among them who remembered it from childhood. They could crowd inside the small whitewashed church to hear a new kind of music and singing, and perhaps they would consent to the priest pouring holy water over their children's heads. The leaders and interpreters among them could travel to Ega or Barcelos to meet, and even share a meal, with the Portuguese officers in their fancy tricorn hats and powdered wigs. The Mura could, in short, experience a new social universe, one that had not been open to them before the peace.

▼▲▼▲▼▲

Not surprisingly, colonial authors often credited external forces with pushing Native peoples to make peace in the Brazilian borderlands. The refrain was a kind of reassurance: "necessity obliges them to seek our friendship."[109] According to a Portuguese governor, the Mura were driven to negotiate because of the threat they faced from their expansionist enemies, the Mundurukú—despite the fact that the Mundurukú offensive began in 1786, in a region hundreds of miles downriver from the place where the Mura first offered peace in 1784. The Mundurukú themselves, many of whom made peace with the Portuguese in 1795, were said to be motivated by a punitive expedition that the Portuguese had sent against them in the previous year. The appeal of such analyses lay in their assurance that Indigenous groups negotiated from a position of vulnerability or weakness and in their suggestion that, in the not-too-distant future, such people could be turned into useful vassals.[110]

Other colonial authors were more pessimistic. At a time when hundreds of Mundurukús were showing up to declare peace at the garrison town of Santarém, in the Lower Amazon, one official warned the governor that "Your Excellency ought to know that they do not intend to establish themselves in our lands. Their only aim, which they declare through gestures, is to have a free trade, by which they can better obtain the tools that are needed for their farming. This is well proven by some of the small malocas that have descended to these villages, only to then withdraw with some tools that they take, steal, and never return" (levão, robão, e mais não voltão).[111] This more cynical analysis reduced Native motivations to a kind of crude materialism.

The evidence examined in this chapter works against these colonial assumptions and highlights the importance of understanding the peacemaking process from a Native perspective and through a careful reading of ground-level sources. Although threats from Indigenous and European enemies, epidemics, resource shortages, territorial losses, and other external forces are important factors, they do not fully explain why groups of significant military prowess moved to establish peaceful relations with Iberian powers. Dominance over others (Native and non-Native), the expansion of social relations, and the chance to gather intelligence about Europeans—without ceding autonomy—also led Indigenous groups to extend, accept, or disseminate offers of peace.

3   Practices of Peace

THE VISITORS SEEMED INSATIABLE. They ate all the manioc meal, smoked all the tobacco, and drank all the cane liquor, and when they were done, they demanded more. Native leaders took stock of one another and then bent the ear of the nearest colonial official: Why did *that* chief have a silver-tipped staff of office? Why was his *own* coat not cut from the same thick red cloth? Why did *that* group receive gifts without giving anything valuable in return? Perhaps better treatment might be sought elsewhere, they suggested. But for now, they would make themselves comfortable in the courtyard of the fort or garrison. When the bells rang at sunset, signaling that the Indians must depart to their camp, they would drag their feet. They preferred to sleep within the walls of the fort, they said, for safety's sake and out of affection for their friends, the Portuguese soldiers and officers. Would they be made to leave, or could they stay for the night, as they had come to expect?[1]

For autonomous Native peoples across the Americas, peace was not a fixed state of being; instead, it was tested, renegotiated, and sometimes nearly broken. Celebratory narratives of pacification, often found in high-level official correspondence or chronicles, veil this long-term process of maintaining a fragile and flawed peace.[2] To see it more clearly, we again turn to reports from the front lines of colonial contact with independent Native polities. It is in these sources—with their expressions of frustration and then accommodation in the face of Native customs and demands—that we can find evidence of Europeans having to play by Indigenous rules of peacemaking. Concessions and compromise are most obvious in two main arenas of long-term interaction: peace talks and gift exchanges. This chapter will consider each in turn.

Often tacking back and forth between Portuguese- and Spanish-claimed territories, autonomous Indian groups carried their own expectations of gifts, titles, and accommodations that in turn determined what the two imperial rivals were willing to concede to them. Colonial authorities often followed the peacemaking script and played their customary parts. What emerged from these transborder negotiations were common conventions of treatment and patterns of interaction between Iberian officials and the Indians they could not conquer but hoped to win to their side. For these reasons, the much larger scholarly literature on Spanish American peacemaking is relevant to the Luso-Brazilian cases examined here, and even to those that involved Indigenous groups not in direct or regular communication with Spaniards.[3] Also relevant, as in the previous chapters, are studies of contemporary Indigenous groups in situations of contact. Taking this broader view will help us perceive the cultural logics and political strategies behind what colonial authors all over the Americas described as Indian "insatiability."

Peace Talks

Peace negotiations between Native peoples and Europeans were hybrid affairs, with metaphors, modes of speech, symbols, and rituals drawn from the traditions of both parties. A remarkably well-documented case in Central Brazil shows that although there were divergences in meaning, the negotiations could still proceed as if all were understood.[4] For this episode—which comes from peace talks held in 1775 on Bananal Island in the Araguaia River—we have formal statements recorded for each side: the Portuguese and the Karajá.

The peace proposal from the governor of Goiás, read by a colonial interpreter, assured the Karajá of "the purity and tenderness of heart" with which the governor desired their friendship. It also offered them the protection of the Portuguese king, "master of the lands that you inhabit," who existed "on the other side of the great Ocean Lake" and sent valuable gifts to his "sons" in Brazil. (The Karajá, the governor added, could see what material benefits might accrue to them from the "small display" of gifts that had been sent to them on this occasion.) If the Karajá showed "fidelity in the vassalage owed to our common Father, the undefeated King of Portugal," they could receive assistance in the form of gunpowder, shot, and men who know how to use such things, with the caveat that weapons "cannot be employed without royal permission," and be free of the depredations of their Xavante enemies.[5]

The Karajá chief, Abuênonâ, composed a reply to this proposal, with the assistance of a colonial scribe and a Karajá woman captured by the Portuguese some two decades earlier, who served as interpreter under the colonial officer leading the negotiations. The chief's words, however imperfectly translated and recorded at the time, are worth quoting in full:

> In my land your people arrived, Sir, giving us many things that we esteem, may God reward you; and a paper [i.e., the proposal], which is speaking good things to us. And your son [the Portuguese officer] tells us that you have a good heart and that the Great Father of the whites, who lives on the other side of the great Lake, wants to take care of the people of our skin; and thus it is appearing [credible] to us, seeing that your people do not do us harm. I want you to speak to them, so that it always remains thus; and for you to free us of the Xavante, so that we remain in comradeship for all time. When your son goes to your land, I will send my son to visit your house. I hope that you, Sir, send him back again, so my heart does not remain aching.[6]

Both the governor's proposal and the chief's reply invoked father-son relationships. Portuguese (as well as Spanish and French) negotiators had long ago selected this as the best functional equivalent for communicating to Indians the idea of a monarch-subject relationship: the king ruled over his vassals like a father over his sons. But functional as it was, the principle did not have the same meaning for the Indians and was not used in the same way.[7]

In his proposal, the governor asserted that the King was "our common Father," whose vast dominion already included the territories inhabited by the Karajá. This father figure offered the Indians material succor and protection against enemies in exchange for their loyalty and vassalage, which for the Portuguese implied absolute obedience and submission to his authority. The Karajá chief, however, used the term in a central but more limited way. In his framing, the king was "the Great Father of the whites" but not of the Karajá, though he did offer them desirable things and protection against both Indigenous enemies *and* the Portuguese—who, for a change, had not done harm to the Karajá during this encounter, and, the chief hoped, could be persuaded not to do any harm in the future. The chief said nothing about ceding sovereignty over land or submitting to Portuguese rule, only affirming a desire for comradeship. He also drew a parallel between the Portuguese officer with whom he negotiated (the governor's "son") and his own son; each could serve as a negotiator in this peace, on equal footing, as they paid reciprocal visits to the centers of Karajá and Portuguese power.

This case hints at the difference between "capitulation" accords (signed with relatively weak Native polities) and treaties that recognized Indigenous sovereignty (signed with more formidable Native groups). The former required Indians to make sweeping concessions: they might have to return captives, agree to live in restricted areas (often close to military installations), travel only with official license, pay colonial tribute or tithes, serve as military auxiliaries, supply the labor draft, or produce their own food through farming and raising livestock. In the latter scenario, Indians might formally agree to be vassals of the Portuguese king, but they could still retain a kind of "de facto independence" while receiving long-term supplies of rations and other gifts.[8] This was the kind of treaty signed on Bananal Island in 1775. Revealingly, the chief also set a number of conditions on the way the peace talks were conducted: the Portuguese peacemaking expedition could not cross the Araguaia River into the heart of Karajá territories without permission, and the men had to stay out of the Karajá villages and gardens; the Karajá, however, could visit the Portuguese in their camp.[9]

Similar peacemaking language appears in the formal treaty drawn up by the Portuguese and signed by two bands of Guaikurú in 1791.

That document stated that the Guaikurú promised to uphold "the most intimate peace and friendship" with the Portuguese and to give their "loyalty and obedience" to the king. In exchange, the governor promised to always protect the Guaikurú and do all that was needed for their spiritual and material satisfaction.[10] There were no territorial concessions or resettlement promises made, though these were certainly long-term aspirations for the Portuguese in their dealings with the Guaikurú. From the perspective of the Guaikurú groups, the treaty was likely a sign of respect for (and even tribute to) their power and status. Indeed, as a seemingly endless supply of gifts flowed from colonial warehouses into Guaikurú hands, Portuguese officials began to wonder if they were in fact paying tribute to a Native polity.[11]

The Guaikurú certainly did nothing to discourage this impression of reverse tribute. When Serra convened the allied Guaikurú chiefs together to read the king's and governor's orders on settlement and intermarriage and also warned that supply shortages at Coimbra meant that they needed to plant corn, beans, and raise pigs for their own sustenance—and for which they would have been given tools, cloth, sugar, and aguardente—the Guaikurú did not accept the terms unconditionally.

> They had a large meeting among themselves, at the end of which Capitão Paulo [Emavidi Xané], in the name of all, responded that all of this was very good and what they wanted. But [they wanted to know] how many slaves would be sent by His Excellency to make those plantations, for they themselves were not slaves. They said the same with respect to the houses; the wood was for them very hard, and it hurt their shoulders; they all wanted [the houses], but the Portuguese would have to make them for them.

This response echoes other Guaikurú expressions of disdain for manual or agricultural labor—work that they considered only fit for their own Native captives or the Black slaves of the Portuguese. The chiefs' view of the orders on intermarriage was even more pointed: "With regard to the marriages, they all said that they wanted Portuguese wives. But they thought it unacceptable, as well as unnecessary, to impose the condition that they could not part until death or [require] that they should be baptized before contracting such marriages."[12] Serra recounted this anecdote years later to paint a picture of Guaikurú arrogance, and it is likely exaggerated. He also did not disclose whether he agreed to any of these conditions. But it does correspond with what we know of the Guaikurú tendency to use the language of hierarchy and privilege in their peace negotiations. Perhaps this irritated the Portuguese precisely because it was so familiar to their own culture.

Martial symbols and rituals, commonly used in the peace talks, also found resonance in the warrior cultures of both Indians and Europeans. Military titles were bestowed on Native leaders; promises were made to fight common enemies; and "rituals of respect functioned as the redemptive erasures of past slurs on the battlefield."[13] Thus, in 1791, the two Guaikurú chiefs who traveled to the Portuguese capital of Vila Bela to formalize their peace agreement received military uniforms and decorations fit for high officers. They took up ceremonial staffs of office and accepted military commissions (*patentes*). The military title of Capitão and an honorific Portuguese name completed the transformation: the cacique Caimá became Capitão João Queima de Albuquerque, after the governor of Mato Grosso; the other cacique, Emavidi Xané, gained the title of Capitão Paulo Joaquim José Ferreira, after the commander of Coimbra.[14]

The titles, patentes, and decorative items all fit well into Indigenous hierarchies of leadership. The Indians distinguished "small" and "great" captains among themselves, and they also applied these gradations to the Portuguese officials with whom they interacted.[15] Commander Serra described how a Guaná chief, Capitão Aires Pinto, carried his patente slung over his shoulder, even while helping to transport loads of mud for a construction project at the fort. From time to time, he would pause in his labors and "take the patente out of its tinplate box to show to the first person he encountered, even if it was a Black man, saying that he was a Capitão Grande." (Serra added that the chief was later told not to do the construction labor himself, but rather to supervise the rest of the Guaná workers, which he did enthusiastically.)[16] Serra's comments were derisive, but even so, they afford us a glimpse of how these patentes may have been displayed by allied Indians as markers of status and loyalty.

When the Guaikurú believed that the Portuguese had breached their peace agreement, they turned their indignation upon these symbols first. The year 1798 was particularly tense, as rumors spread among the Indians that the Portuguese had imprisoned members of another Native group in Western Brazil, the Bororo, and that they would soon do the same to their allies. Two officers from Coimbra, one of whom knew the Guaikurú language, along with a Black interpreter named Vitória, were dispatched to the Guaikurú and Guaná encampments to investigate, bearing gifts of tobacco and aguardente. There they encountered Capitão Luiz Pinto, who had just received his patente two years earlier. Now he was in a state of agitation, preparing to desert Portuguese territories, "with his uniform and his patente ready to send back to [Commander Serra] or to be the first things to feel his wrath, if the Portuguese came after him." Other worrisome encounters followed, as the official party traveled to the encampment of Capitão Paulo (Emavidi Xané), one of the original chiefs to make peace and who always had been distinguished among the Guaikurú "for having deserved the honor of possessing a patente" signed by the governor. Paulo immediately asked the officers if it was true that the governor had ordered the Bororo to be imprisoned. They reassured him that the imprisonment was not meant to do that group any harm; it was simply a way to "bring the Bororo closer to us," since they had received so many presents and then shown themselves to be ingrates. Paulo was reportedly "calmed" by these words, though one wonders whether he believed such a dubious explanation. The same encampment was home to the Guaná Capitão Aires Pinto, who, just several months before, had been proudly showing off his patente to anyone he met. Now he saw the Portuguese party and jumped on his horse, joined by his women and children, having already prepared to flee with all their belongings. It took many reassurances—and generous amounts of aguardente and tobacco—to convince him to come back.[17]

As this example suggests, peace negotiations depended on individuals endowed with special skills for crossing cultural boundaries. They might be groomed for the task by a colonial officer or governor, but, crucially, they were often described as "beloved" and "chosen" by the

Indians. One such figure was the Portuguese soldier António Batista da Silva from Coimbra Fort. Having visited the Guaikurú encampments many times, escorting the Indians back and forth from the fort during the 1790s, he was the one "who was most in their good graces, for accommodating himself to their gestures and ways."[18] They referred to him as the "son" of Joaquim José Ferreira, the Portuguese commander who had first affirmed peace with the Guaikurú in 1791, and honored him with the title of Capitão Comandante Guaikurú. He was even invited to marry within the Guaikurú nation, which would have made him kin. Pointing to "his docile nature" and good treatment of the Indians, one colonial commander claimed that Batista da Silva was responsible for having "sweetened and moderated the barbarity of these Indians; he still today exercises authority over them, and everything he tells them is done."[19] Though such assessments were embellished and self-serving, they also hinted at the possibility of genuine affection and trust between Native groups and a select few interlocutors.

Peace talks were almost always conducted through interpreters—despite the fact that many participating Indians knew some Portuguese, Spanish, or the língua geral, either through long-term contacts with colonial populations or because they had been born into colonial society and then later incorporated into Indigenous society. Insisting on the use of interpreters in the peace talks, Native peoples avoided situations in which they would have to express themselves in a foreign tongue.[20] They also tended to select their own interpreters and maintain them over time as trusted intermediaries. In their meetings with the Portuguese, the Guaikurú insisted on the presence of the aforementioned Vitória, a Black woman whom they had captured some two decades earlier, at age twelve, as she fled from colonial slavery along the Paraguay River. She appears frequently in the documentation from the first peace talks in 1791 through at least 1801, which speaks to her centrality in the ongoing negotiations around peace, settlement, provisioning, defense, and border crossings. Portuguese commanders also came to depend on Vitória, who traveled with the Guaikurú back and forth to the fort: "I cannot go without her here, given the agitation in which the Indians find themselves," admitted Serra during a particularly tense time at the fort. Yet the Portuguese never seemed entirely certain of where Vitória's loyalties lay.[21]

Captivity, then, was one of the main cross-cultural institutions that made communication possible between peacemaking parties.²² The Mura, for their part, depended on a number of Murified individuals—people who had incorporated with the Mura either voluntarily or involuntarily—to serve as translators. Among them was Joana, the mother of the leader Ambrósio, who spoke the língua geral well, having been captured by the Mura as an adult. She accompanied her son on most of his trips to speak with different colonial officials. As a captive who had been incorporated with the Mura, she had two "Murified" daughters, in addition to Ambrósio, and had taught many of the "legitimate Muras" to speak the língua geral.²³

Colonial authors seemed to have found the Mura language impenetrable, and without skilled interpreters, verbal communication was impossible. One visiting archbishop lamented that he had no sense of their receptivity to Christianity, given the language barrier. It was only through pantomime that the Muras made their wishes known to him: "What they did was grab me by the tunic and open their mouths, indicating that they wanted clothes and manioc meal."²⁴ It is also rather striking that the Portuguese never recorded (as far as I know) even a single Native-language name for any of the Muras with whom they interacted in the late eighteenth century. Even important interlocutors, like chiefs, whose names we would expect to be rendered phonetically (if inaccurately), were simply identified along the lines of "the chief who came to see me at Ega," or "the one who came here last month," or "the chief in Ambrósio's company." Although the Mura language went extinct sometime around the middle of the twentieth century, a closely related dialect survives today among the remote subgroup known as the Pirahã. Interestingly, that dialect is tonal and has only three vowels and eight consonants, so many of the words are long and almost impossible for a foreigner to grasp. (In the first decade of the twenty-first century, only three non-Indigenous people spoke Pirahã fluently, all of them missionaries or former missionaries.) Studies of Mura-Pirahã suggest that it is a language isolate, unrelated to other Indigenous languages in the region. It is impossible to know whether this was the case in the eighteenth century, of course, since so many languages were extinguished over the years of conquest and colonization.²⁵

Because linguistic and cultural intermediaries were so essential in negotiations with the Mura, the Portuguese had to set aside their suspicions of them. They also had to accept that captives would remain in the possession of Indians; they could not be "rescued" and returned to colonial society without a cascade of negative consequences for the peace process. Such was the case with an unnamed Indian boy from the colonial village of Alvarães. We know only a few things about the boy: that he had been captured by the Mura and adopted by the leader Ambrósio and that his mother wanted him back with a kind of maternal fierceness that comes across even in the staid official report. Ambrósio had brought the boy with him once, when he came to speak with the Portuguese lieutenant João Batista Mardel. The Mura leader had then left the boy in the custody of his mother in Alvarães—but not without extracting a promise that he could have him back at any time. When that time came, the mother refused. Lieutenant Mardel was resolute in this "impious, but necessary" decision: the boy *would* be returned to Ambrósio to avoid undermining the trust-building process with the Mura. If the mother had kept her son, Mardel thought Ambrósio would have gone to retrieve him "through rivers of blood" and would then have spread this "bad faith" to all the other Mura groups, bringing a return to war. Ambrósio—"that monster," Mardel called him, betraying his own emotions around this episode—showed great satisfaction when the boy was given back to him.[26]

Another test of faith played out several years later, when a Xumana woman, identified in the documents as Ambrósio's concubine, returned to live with her relatives in the colonial village of Ega. After Ambrósio was rumored to have threatened the woman's family, a colonial officer persuaded the family to take her back to the house in Nogueira where Ambrósio had originally deposited her. The precariousness of the moment, from the Portuguese point of view, made such a resolution—in effect, facilitating concubinage—necessary. Spaniards were at that time suspected of making overtures to Native groups along the nearby frontier; epidemic fevers in the region were making the Mura skittish about contact and resettlement; Ambrósio had plans in the works to convince a recalcitrant group of Mura to make peace; and he himself had not yet committed to a permanent place of residence.[27]

It is worth underlining that this was in 1789—nearly five years since the peace process had begun.

In such contexts, Indians were able to extract concessions from their allies. They could also interpret the terms of the original peace agreements in ways that were highly selective in the eyes of their colonial partners. Like the Karajá and Guaikurú, the Mura clearly saw their (unwritten) truce with the Portuguese as an agreement, first and foremost, to end mutual hostilities—to make *"camaradagem,"* comradeship with former enemies. This sentiment was captured in the slogan, shouted between Mura canoes and colonial parties when they encountered each other along the river, as a means of signaling peaceful intent: "Camarada Mathias!" they called, referring to the old Indian fighter, Mathias Fernandes, who went from making war on the Mura to receiving their representatives hospitably (if suspiciously) when they first came in peace to Maripí (see chapter 2). The slogan traveled far and wide in less than a month—surprisingly fast, given the decentralized political structure of the Mura—along with news of the events at Maripí and the advantages to be gained from the new relationship with the whites. It was as if the news "flew on the wings of the wind."[28] But the slogan and the circumstances under which it was used—two canoes meeting on a river or lake, each often engaged in fishing, hunting turtles, or harpooning manatee—also staked a kind of claim. It soon became clear that the Mura intended not only to keep their access to traditional fishing and hunting grounds but to be welcomed in new areas opened up by the peace agreement. Many such areas were turtle-rich beaches and lakes teeming with fish, easily accessed because they were on or near the main river highways of the Amazon and Madeira. These became regular sites of social interaction between colonial expeditions and Mura groups, where impromptu trades of manioc meal for turtles might be made.[29]

They were also sites of potential conflict and competition. One problem was that the Portuguese believed in proprietorship of fishing grounds—and even in the notion that beaches, lakes, and all their aquatic creatures could be designated the property of a distant king. These, however, were exactly the places where the Mura wanted to establish themselves after the peace agreement, as they moved closer to the Portuguese. An administrator of a royal fishery on the Amazon River noted that the Mura had set up camps all around the royal lakes, and that he needed to find an interpreter who could more effectively communicate to them that they should not enter the large lake designated "as belonging to the king, for since they are very close to it, they easily do [enter]." They also had to be made to understand "that they can no longer fish on the lakes that are located in front of where they are situated, because they have driven off all [the fish]."[30] What might the Mura have made of this concept of proprietary fishing grounds? Like other native groups, the Mura probably recognized communal rights to particular lands and resources, with an understanding that access could be negotiated through alliances or kinship connections.[31] If the attitudes of contemporary Amazonian peasants are any indication, however, the idea of an individual laying claim to an entire lake and everything living in it would have seemed absurd. The anthropologist Mark Harris writes that, for Amazonian river dwellers today, "Water and its resources are for communal stewardship. . . . Water, and in particular fish, cannot be owned by anybody because, for example, fish cannot be controlled. As one person told me: 'Fish are looked after by nature and swim where they want.'"[32]

Tensions around turtles, a food staple for both colonists and Indians, flared in late 1787. First, colonial fishermen confronted a group of Muras led by Ambrósio about their unauthorized hunting of turtles at the royal beaches of Jauató, which were considered the property of the king. The Muras indignantly replied that "they had lots of arrows, and they had no fear, for the whites were few, and they were many."[33] Figure 3.1, a drawing based on the writings of a naturalist who traveled through the region in this same period, seems to depict such a scene. Although it is not a situation of outright conflict—as signaled by the Mura men continuing their work of loading turtles into a canoe and by the presence of Mura women and children in hammocks—there is a sense of competition between the Muras and the colonial canoes just offshore. The Mura man at the center of the picture carries a bow and arrows and seems to be looking directly at the canoe boss who, one assumes, is not welcome to order his men to land.

Only a few days after the incident at Jauató, the Portuguese learned that on some beaches just upriver from the demarcation headquarters of

FIGURE 3.1 Muras hunting turtles, c. 1800.

Source: Alexandre Rodrigues Ferreira collection at the Biblioteca Nacional, Brazil.

Ega, a violent encounter had occurred between a group of Muras and a party of Spanish soldiers and Indians (who were working on behalf of the Spanish representatives involved in the demarcation commission at Ega). The Muras were shooting at turtles with their bows and arrows, hunting them for meat, whereas the Spanish group intended to collect the turtle eggs to make a kind of "butter," commonly used as a cooking oil. When the Spaniards ordered the Muras to leave and to stop scaring off the egg-laying turtles, they refused. Some kind of altercation followed, and the Portuguese official in Ega was alarmed to discover that the Spanish group had requested supplies of gunpowder and shot from the garrison, making it known that they intended to attack the Muras.[34] A few weeks later, Ambrósio was prodded to explain the incident. He admitted that there had been some arguments with the Spaniards on the beaches but brushed off the incident as unimportant. The Spaniards "had a point," he said, "because they wanted [turtle egg] butter, and the Muras had a point, because they wanted to kill turtles to eat, not caring about butter." This effort to diffuse the situation was not enough, though, and conflicts over the Muras' insistence on open access to fishing and turtle hunting grounds continued well into the nineteenth century (see chapter 4).[35]

In the negotiations around resettlement, colonial officials generally accommodated Mura preferences, as long as they remained in Portuguese-claimed territory. General João Pereira Caldas, who was overseeing the Portuguese boundary demarcation process, proposed transferring one group of Muras from their scattered encampments on the lakes and rivers near the royal fishery of Puraquequara to a new settlement at a place called Manacapurú, farther upriver on the Solimões: "They should be persuaded that it will be better for them to go there all together and make a larger town, rather than splitting up into so many small groups," presumably because this made supervision easier and helped solidify Portuguese territorial claims on the basis of effective occupation. "But this must be communicated to them gently," he warned, "so that they do not become distrustful; and they must not be forced in any way if they do not want to go or move themselves." An interpreter was summoned but apparently had little success in persuading the Mura group to move to the new settlement at Manacapurú. The official in charge of the royal fishery wrote to

Caldas to break the bad news, though he tried to couch it in positive terms: "After the interpreter's speech, they are ready and very happy to settle anew on the river and make their village. But they say they do not want to move to Manacapurú. . . . They responded that at their present spot they could make a large settlement, too, and that there were also very many of them, and that they were awaiting their compatriots."[36] Like Ambrósio, this group of Muras evidently knew that the promise of bringing more people (their "compatriots") into the colonial fold gave them more bargaining power in negotiations.

Though the Mura did not seem to ever have entered into peace talks with Spaniards, they must have been aware that the possibility of a Spanish alliance gave them additional leverage with the Portuguese—who asked them repeatedly not to let Spaniards enter their camps and not to speak to them through their interpreters. Of particular concern to the Portuguese, the Mura learned, was a man named Fernando Rojas. Having first gone upriver as a fugitive Black slave, Rojas ended up serving as interpreter for the Spanish boundary commissioner, since he spoke many of the Indigenous languages from the region, as well as the língua geral (see figure 1.1). The Portuguese were convinced that Rojas had recruited the Xumana for the Spanish side, and the Xumana were known to have close relationships of kinship, alliance, and captivity with the Mura in this same period.[37]

Some Mura groups, such as Ambrósio's, also hailed from the Japurá River, one of the waterways at the center of Iberian disputes over territory during the 1780s. The Spaniards and Portuguese could not even agree on where the westernmost mouth of Japurá lay, which had been established by the 1777 treaty as a point along the imperial borderline. Between the two possible river mouths was an island-filled stretch of the Solimões River that saw a great deal of mutual surveillance from Spanish and Portuguese boundary commissioners.[38] All the while, the Mura plied those same contested waters, watching the demarcation teams go about their work. Around the end of the century, some Muras even allegedly removed the boundary marker that had been erected on the Auati-Paraná canal that linked the Solimões to the Japurá. The heavy stone marker was said to have disappeared completely, perhaps having been pushed into the depths of the water.[39]

During the resettlement talks, the Mura did not let their canoes dry out. (Literally: according to one author, the tree bark out of which they were made would crack if left to dry, so the canoes were usually submerged in the water for storage.[40]) To hear colonial officials tell it, Indians were like "bands of gypsies" who moved simply for the sake of moving—or for more sinister, inscrutable reasons.[41] But seasonal changes, in fact, governed many of their movements: the migration of turtles and fish, the ripening of palm fruits and nuts, the coming of dry weather for making their bark canoes. Just as longtime residents of the colonial missions and villages had learned to do, the Mura also moved to avoid epidemics.[42] The result was that the new, state-sponsored settlements were often empty or occupied only by children, the elderly, and the sick—as officials found to their exasperation when they went to carry out population counts. One Portuguese administrator described the Mura as "volante" (itinerant) and said that they regularly left the settlement to visit their original lands, giving him the excuse that they needed to go gather food.[43] Perhaps for this reason, higher authorities thought it would be ideal if Indians could be settled far from the siren song of these homelands, a thousand or more miles downriver. But as General Caldas admitted, back in the early months of the peace, "it probably will not be possible to persuade and convince them of this."[44] Lieutenant Mardel put it this way: peace with the "wandering" Mura could be kept only "by following, for now, the path of patiently suffering the lack of persistence that one always sees in them."[45]

Aided by their own reputation for inconstancy and also by shifting Crown policies, the Mura were often successful at evading the obligations of colonial Indian life. Even as they moved closer to colonial settlements and (occasionally) offered their children to be baptized en masse, the Mura continued to be seen as "heathens" who might leave or turn on their hosts at any time.[46] Officials received orders to treat the Mura "with affability and gentleness" and to ignore, "for now, whatever rudeness or missteps they commit."[47] They should not require of them "any work that is contrary to their customs, lest they return, annoyed and offended, to the licentious life that they just left."[48] In these instructions, one can see signs of the Crown reform movement that was gaining traction in this period and that brought about the abolition, in the late 1790s, of the Indian administrative system known as the Directorate. One governor wrote in 1795, during peace negotiations with the Mundurukú, "Experience has shown that to introduce parish priests and directors among these new and hardly secure friends is the same as making them return to the forest." Instead, Crown reformers proposed allowing private parties to contact, resettle, and employ Indigenous groups, while state officials and religious authorities would oversee the education and indoctrination of particularly promising Indian youths in the cities. The goal was to send them back to their communities as emissaries of "civilization."[49]

Among the Mura, however, this last scheme apparently met with angry resistance. An archbishop, who visited a new Mura settlement on the Solimões River in 1788, described how one woman, when asked to give up her little boy to him, grew "enraged, set her eyes on me, and began to mutter and make some kind of threatening signs with her hands. I understood that she was trying to say that I had many white relatives, and that I should content myself with them."[50] Persistence did not pay off. In 1804, a different bishop traveled to the Rio Negro and repeatedly tried to bring a few Mura boys back with him, but he could not obtain a single one; the parents were "excessively protective of their small children and would not consent to be separated from them."[51]

The Mura also shunned nearly all types of contract labor well into the nineteenth century. They were sometimes willing, on an informal and unsupervised basis, to collect forest products, fish, or turtles in exchange for trade goods, but there is no record of them ever participating in the regular labor draft rotation or serving on royal construction crews.[52] Selectively, they pursued agreements with individual settlers (see chapter 4). One of these settlers was an entrepreneurial cacao planter in the Lower Amazon who wrote to the governor to pitch an elaborate scheme involving the establishment of a town for the Mura and putting them to work collecting forest products. The settler's self-interest was clear, but so was the Muras'. Apparently, they had told him that if he did not go ahead with the plan for the town—which, of course, was to include houses and gardens built for them by local laborers and a supply of tools funded by the government—"they will go back to their original habitations and live like beasts . . . conspiring against us once more with eternal enmity, and also now knowing the weaknesses of some towns and ranches." The governor turned down the settler's proposal, noting that building a whole new town was unnecessary and encouraging the settler to instead settle the Mura on his plantation, harnessing them to regular work and helping them to construct their own houses and gardens. This was in keeping with Crown priorities to farm out some of the cost of "pacification" to private parties, but it likely did not have the same appeal for the Mura. Perhaps as a result, settlers in that region continued to complain about Mura raids on the homesteads of white settlers and Indian villagers alike, as well as a spate of killings of Black slaves.[53] After describing Mura depredations near Óbidos in the early 1790s, one local author linked their mobility with the long-standing competition over fishing and hunting grounds. "With the same ease by which they establish themselves," he wrote, "they withdraw after a few weeks have passed: their only profession is driving off the game animals, whether by sea or by land."[54]

The Guaikurú likewise were adamant about maintaining their mobile way of life and an independent foreign policy.[55] Reports from Coimbra Fort, situated right on the contested border, seethed with controversies around these issues. The Portuguese became determined to control Guaikurú raiding across the border, because it led to diplomatic tensions with Spain, or even prompted Spanish punitive expeditions into Portuguese-claimed territories. Portuguese officials also hoped to prevent the friendly visits that groups of Guaikurús sometimes made to Spanish outposts. But colonial efforts to stop or control Native border crossings and raids—mainly through licensing requirements, verbal exhortations, or (beginning in 1803) river patrols—failed miserably. If they even bothered with licensing, the Guaikurú might get permission to go on a sanctioned errand but then would visit, surreptitiously, the Spanish forts of Borbón and San Carlos to trade and carouse with their erstwhile enemies, or they would go on captive-taking expeditions in Chiquitos (map 1).[56] The Portuguese sometimes gave their stamp of approval to Guaikurú plans to raid for captives among a "hostile" Native group, only to find out later that they had attacked a group that was friendly with the Portuguese, throwing that fragile relationship into chaos.[57] (Portuguese officials could only protest to the Guaikurú, with a growing sense of futility, that "His

Majesty and the Portuguese love all of the peoples of this district and detest offensive war, which no nation has the right to conduct."[58]) Guaikurú bands that had successfully pillaged goods on the Spanish side mocked the Portuguese upon their return, saying "with irony, that they had only gotten rich because they had gone over to Spain."[59] And when officials did manage to dissuade the Guaikurú from going on a planned raid, large quantities of desirable goods had to be distributed, so that they could not allege necessity for the raid.[60] Shaped by Portuguese as well as Native practices of peace in the borderlands, negotiations might suffer setbacks from a colonial perspective, while opening up new possibilities from an Indigenous point of view.[61]

Well into the nineteenth century, the Guaikurú disdained sedentary life, preferring to organize themselves into what one fort commander called "aldeias volantes," or itinerant villages that were adapted to seasonal flooding and the availability of pasturage for their herds. Kin groups traveled far and wide in search of good grazing grass as well as palm fruit and game like deer, alligators, and capivaras.[62] A dozen years after the peace agreement, a fort commander made the case in a major report to the governor that many advantages had "resulted from the peace and friendship with the Guaikurús, *even without their settlement and perfect reduction.*" In essence, he advocated for keeping them as a kind of autonomous ally.[63]

One revealing episode occurred in 1796, when colonials officials pressured the Guaikurú to transfer all of their encampments to the eastern side of the Paraguay River. The reason was that those lands were "positively" Portuguese, whereas the western side remained in dispute with Spain. However, the Portuguese had founded Coimbra Fort—the site of all this peacemaking with the Guaikurú—on the western bank. Thus the Guaikurú responded (rather provocatively) "that when the Portuguese move [to the eastern bank], they will do so as well."[64] The keen sense of colonial hypocrisy, the awareness of geopolitical pressures, and the willingness to drive a hard bargain: these were all characteristics of Indigenous dealmaking in this period. Native peoples sought to decide for themselves where to live or travel, how to gain their subsistence, and what rules of conduct they would observe in their relations with the Portuguese. They also determined how much their friendship would cost.

Gifting

"They are quite skilled in the art of demanding," Commander Serra complained of the visiting Guaikurús and Kadiwéus at Coimbra Fort. But he would continue to gratify them, in light of recent desertions to Spanish territories on the far side of the Paraguay River.[65] "These vacillating men yield to one side today, and tomorrow they lean toward the other," he wrote in 1802, more than a decade after the original peace agreement. "Very crafty, they know how to take advantage of friendship with us and with the Spaniards, selling it to both Nations, often lying, and at other times telling the truth, everything an abyss of confusion." The fort commander then signed off with what had become a refrain at the end of his letters: "For now, this is all I have to report hastily to Your Excellency; I say hastily because from barely sunrise until sunset, the Kadiwéus do not give me a moment's rest, asking for things with the greatest nuisance and impertinence."[66] It even served as an excuse for sending a late report to the governor: "These Captains, and their old and miserable wives, bother me in my quarters day and night, impeding everything I do, even the prompt dispatch of this mail."[67]

The Portuguese commander felt righteous in his complaints; after all, he was joining a chorus of colonial authors throughout the hemisphere who likewise described Indians as "a very craving people." This raises two important possibilities: first, that ritual weeping, demanding, and posing as pitiable or starving were cultural performances common to many Indigenous groups when dealing with nonkin, especially with threatening outsiders; and second, that Europeans anticipated such performances when they interacted with Indians. Some of the examples that follow suggest that Native peoples may even have played the part of craving in "an ironic imitation of white expectations."[68]

Complaining loudly, at least among themselves, eighteenth-century Iberian officials spent enormous sums of money on Indians whose cooperation was needed to meet important Crown objectives, and especially when other European powers vied for Native loyalties.[69] Indigenous peoples were well aware of these bargaining chips. The Guaikurú, probably more than any other Native group in Brazil, used their long history of trading and gifting with the Spanish in their forging of advantageous exchange relations with the Portuguese, constantly reminding the Portuguese of the silver, cattle, and beads that they had received from the Spanish and threatening to return to their former territories on the Spanish-claimed side of the border.[70] "The greatest difficulty that I find," wrote a Portuguese governor, "has to do with the locale in which they live—between Portuguese and Spanish, who ceaselessly seek to attract them into friendship. They manipulate these contrary aims with great shrewdness, and in this way they obtain what they want from both, without either work or subjection."[71] Clearly, the Guaikurú did not want their political loyalty to be taken for granted. It was something that had to be nurtured over the years.

What this meant is that the supply of "gifts" and rations extended far beyond the period of initial peacemaking in 1791. By the end of the century, there were some eight hundred Guaikurú living near Coimbra and visiting the fort regularly, along with about six hundred Guaná Indians (some of whom were considered "captives" of the Guaikurú). This total number of Indian visitors nearly doubled several years later, as the Guaikurú amassed hundreds of Chamacoco captives and as additional bands of Guaikurú (from the Kadiweú subgroup) crossed into Portuguese territories. Other Guaikurú and Guaná groups visited the nearby garrison of Albuquerque and the Miranda fort. At that point, in 1803, the Portuguese estimated that the Guaikurú had received some 16,000–20,000 cruzados-worth of goods over their twelve years of living in the most "intimate friendship" with the Portuguese.[72] What could such a quantity of money buy in late eighteenth-century Brazil? For comparison, a wealthy planter could obtain about 14 sugar mills with the same sum, or approximately 145 skilled slaves, or as many as 540 horses of the highest quality, fit for the viceregal guard.[73] In a good harvest year, in the opulent sugar zone of coastal Bahia, two large plantations might receive around that much money for all of their sugar combined.[74]

Native demands also ensured the supply of certain quantities and types of goods. The fort commanders found themselves under heavy pressure, for example, to give the Guaikurú guns instead of knives. Though the governor reminded them that guns should not be traded with such a "brave warrior nation," as it was against the law and also foolish, there is evidence that the Guaikurú did receive firearms and perhaps even military training from their allies.[75] Commanders also passed along Guaikurú preferences for specific products to Vila Bela: the Indians wanted blue or red woolen cloth (the color of "ox blood") instead of the more readily available yellow, new (not used or repaired) axes and knives, salt and lard with which to flavor their food (to which they had become accustomed since living near the Portuguese), and always more alcohol and tobacco.[76] In first-contact situations, when there was no way to communicate by speech, Native wishes could be made clear in other ways: a friendly group of Caripuna who encountered a passing colonial expedition along the Madeira River made the chopping sounds that axes make on wood to express their interest in receiving those tools, while isolated Native groups targeted for contact by state agents in the twentieth century left models of machetes or scissors carved from wood to indicate what they hoped to find when they next visited gift exchange sites in the forest.[77]

We can imagine colonial officials learning to apply Native criteria, as a young Claude Lévi-Strauss did at the wholesale trimmings markets of Paris in the 1930s, when he bought supplies of gifts for his return trip to Brazil: "I set about choosing the smallest of the embroidery beads.... I tried to bite through them to test their toughness; I sucked them in order to make sure that they were made of tinted glass and that the color would not run at the first contact with river water; I varied the amounts purchased in accordance with the basic Indian colour scheme: first, black and white in equal quantities; next red; then a much smaller quantity of yellow." The anthropologist had already learned, in his first expedition among the Kadiwéu and Bororo, about the "fastidious tastes of the Indians" (figure 3.2).[78]

One list of Indian expenses from Coimbra, which covered expenditures for gifts and rations at the fort for nearly three years, included a whopping ~2,200 gallons of manioc meal, ~750 gallons of beans, ~400 pounds of lard, and many other foodstuffs. There were also ~300 shipments of alcohol; almost 1,000 units of tobacco; different kinds of textiles, beads, and decorative objects; and a large variety of tools and hardware. In all, the list contained fifty-one different categories

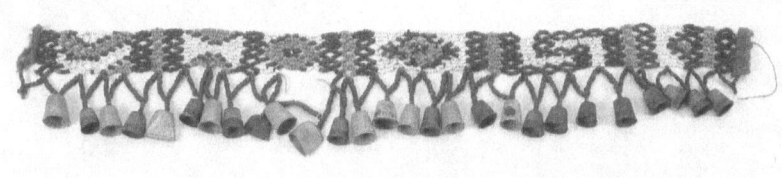

FIGURE 3.2 Kadiwéu necklace, early twentieth century. The Guaikurú and Kadiwéu wanted only blue and white beads, according to the commander at Coimbra (Serra, "Continuação do parecer," 395). In this necklace, created about a century later, the Kadiwéu combined white and two shades of blue glass beads with accents of red wool and a row of metal thimbles likely acquired from the Indian Protection Service (SPI).
SOURCE: Collection of Sasha Siemel, courtesy of the National Museum of the American Indian, Smithsonian Institution (catalogue no. 19/6909). Photograph by NMAI Photo Services.

of goods given to the Guaikurú, Kadiwéu, and allied Guaná at the fort between 1800 and late 1802 (figure 3.3).[79] "They well know the value of all the things they receive," noted Commander Serra, but it was never enough. When given alcohol, "they say that it is simply peed out; the food is similarly excreted; the woolen fabric, white cloth, handkerchiefs, and calico they say has been torn; the iron [tools] are worn out, and likewise the rest."[80]

In their correspondence, officials lamented shortages in these products, which caused such a stir among the Guaikurú. Commander Serra described how, if anything was denied (especially the alcohol and tobacco), the Guaikurú "grow melancholy, and then they shout that it must be given to them, because Your Excellency only sends it for them." The only way to quell these protests, he said, was to show them the empty warehouses.[81] "As soon as [our supplies] run out," fretted another commander, "I am quite convinced that they will abandon our alliance."[82] What followed was a plea for more (and better) supplies to be shipped to the frontier.

Frontier authorities also continued sending elite Indians to be feted and entertained in large towns and capital cities, even after authorities ordered that these expensive visits be discouraged.[83] Why did the visits continue? Because the Guaikurú and the Mura insisted. The first thing

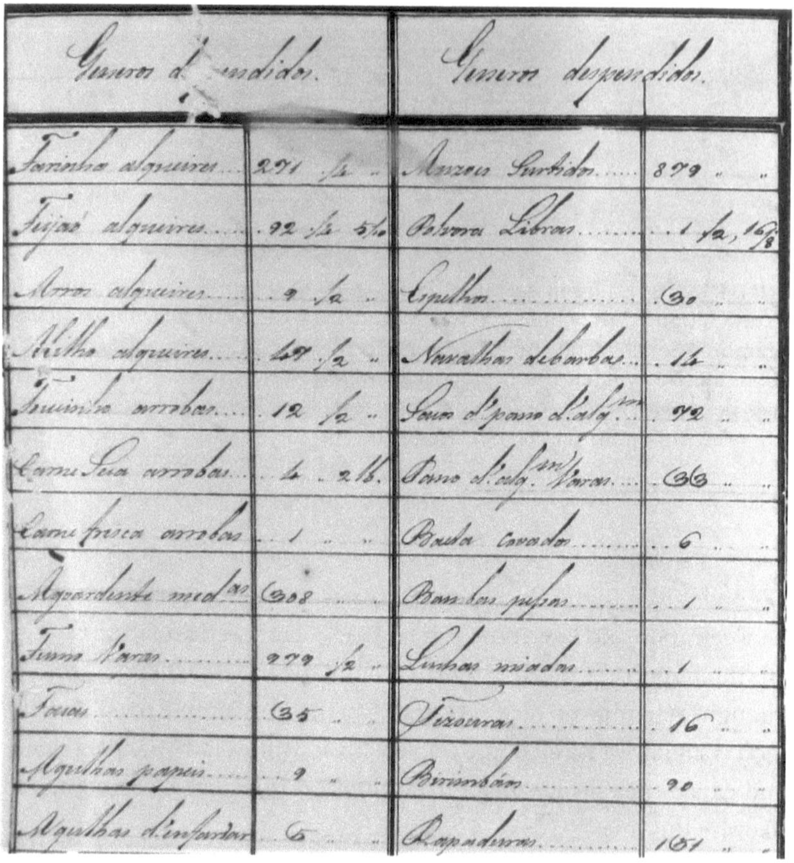

FIGURE 3.3 Indian expenses at Coimbra, early 1800s. This extract of goods dispensed at Coimbra Fort covered the period from January 1, 1800, to October 31, 1802.

Source: APMT, PRFIO.MP, Cx. 8, Doc. 426. Photograph by the author.

that a Mura chief said to authorities after arriving in a village on the Rio Negro was that "he wanted to go meet Your Excellency, and at the same time see the land of the Whites." This chief also had spoken with another group of Muras, passing through the village on their way back from visiting Barcelos, whose leader had boasted of the gifts and good treatment they had received there; this only served to increase the chief's "fervor" to make the trip, too. So as not to upset him (or his group of about a hundred people), village authorities permitted him to go, despite the official policy of deterrence.[84] Similarly, a military commander on the Madeira River reported that the Muras were constantly "pestering me with their desire to go" to visit the governor in Barcelos. They ended up going in a large group of over twenty people, and General Caldas was clearly displeased by their arrival, given the shortage of manioc meal rations, though he still handed out gifts to all the members of the party.[85] The Guaikurú were even more forceful about going to the city. They had a "willful spirit about going to Cuiabá," a commander noted of one group. Having come to the fort without their wives, the Guaikurús "said that they wanted to go, profit, and return." (To this, the commander responded that they could go only if they brought their women—a sign of good faith—and that the visits would have to be lengthy.)[86] One Guaikurú captain even threatened that "either he would go on this occasion to embrace the knees of His Excellency"—in the capital of Vila Bela—"or he would never see the Portuguese again."[87]

Anthropologists studying patterns of exchange among hunter-gatherer-horticulturalists have identified a similar set of practices called "demand sharing." They have described it as a way of testing a relationship or asserting a claim in an uncertain or shifting social context.[88] Elizabeth Ewart, who has worked among the Panará—descendants of the Caiapó do Sul—in Central Brazil reflected in 2013 that "Like many anthropologists, I experienced an often unrelenting and sometimes materially as well as emotionally draining stream of demands from Panará people. It seemed that no matter what I brought and how hard I tried to ensure that all who asked received something, there would always be somebody who would point out that she had no beads left, or that her flip-flops were worn out, or that the cooking pot was old and broken, and why had I not brought more beads, some new flip-flops, a new cooking pot?"[89] Even across a distance of some two hundred years, there are echoes with the way that the Guaikurú framed their demands of Iberian officials. As Ewart and other anthropologists make clear, it is not just that Indigenous groups *need* these items, nor is it about holding outsiders to some ideal of Native generosity. Rather, it is about establishing difference: the Panará, Ewart notes, almost never demand things directly like this from one another. It is also about maintaining autonomy: if outsiders are "good only as long as they are materially useful" (as another anthropologist put it), then their power over Indigenous peoples is, in a sense, limited.[90]

What did testing a relationship look like, as gifts changed hands in the late eighteenth century? Commander Serra recounted that one day's worth of presents to a visiting Guaikurú chief and his wife included knives, soap, bolts of cloth, and a mirror, as well as a couple dozen blocks of raw sugar, but that the couple began "haranguing" him as soon as they received these items. (Irritable colonial authors everywhere asserted that Indians were prone to haranguing.) The Guaikurú, Serra realized, were insisting that he "give them something that is mine, because they know that however much they have just received . . . none of it was mine, but rather all was ordered to be given by Your Excellency [the governor]." Clearly, the Guaikurú leadership wanted Serra to sacrifice on their behalf, to have a personal stake in the relationship they were building at the fort. They wanted gifts, not transactions ordered by a distant governor. (They would attempt to forge personal connections with the governor, too, through visits and gifts that they sent to him in the capital.)[91] What they wanted, perhaps, was an attitude like that of one lieutenant in the Lower Amazon, who, when hosting hundreds of peacemaking Mundurukús in 1795, claimed to have gone to extremes: "I no longer have any clothing," he wrote to the governor, "because I have given it all away." (He reassured the governor that he was, of course, having a new outfit made for himself.) The benefactor role seemed to suit him, and possibly it suited the visiting Mundurukús, too: "All of my effort is spent on pleasing them," the lieutenant claimed; "I am their Saint Anthony"—referring to the patron saint of the poor.[92]

The Guaikurú also insisted upon the context in which these personal exchanges would occur: within the fort walls, in close proximity with the Portuguese, their former enemies. Controversies inevitably ensued, with officers complaining to commanders that it was dangerous to let the Guaikurú chiefs sleep in their quarters, and governors grumbling that Indians should not be allowed to enter the fort with weapons and in such large numbers. One commander felt the need to defend his policies on hosting the Indians, telling the governor, "In my time, the Guaikurú Indians have never slept within this Royal

Fort, except for Captains Paulo and Queima" (Caimá) and their families; "not a single one entered after the Ave Maria," referring to the ringing of the chapel bells in the evening, "and the gate is locked from this time onward so as to impede them" from entering during the night. The arms that the Guaikurús brought with them when they entered the fort, he explained, were simply the arrows, lances, clubs, and knives that they needed for their daily hunting and for defending themselves against jaguars or hostile Indians. Seeking to placate the governor further, the commander added the Guaikurús "are so gentled, that they say goodbye to this garrison with tears" and always return when sick, "willingly subjecting themselves to the harshest remedies."[93] Some two decades of documentation from Coimbra show that the Guaikurú were quite successful in their efforts to retain access to the fort and its inner chambers, not to mention its precious supplies of food and medicine.

Native peoples also dodged Portuguese attempts to use gifts and hospitality as a means of cultural assimilation or as a reward for it. One of the most vivid descriptions from Coimbra centers on a Guaná man named Joaquim. Having been baptized on his travels with a merchant to Cuiabá, São Paulo, and Rio de Janeiro, he returned to the fort wearing shoes and fine clothing. The fort commander hosted Joaquim for dinner—which, one suspects, increased his indignation at what ensued: "Two hours later, he came to see me, very pleased, naked but for the cloth in which he was wrapped, plucked of eyelashes and eyebrows, greased with urucum and painted with genipapo, with a woman he found here, whom he had just in that moment married." The same thing was said to have happened with another Guaná visitor at the fort: "esteemed by the scribe of the royal treasury" and baptized "with all pomp in Cuiabá," he showed up at Coimbra dressed and groomed in colonial style, only to eagerly transform back to his original appearance that same day.[94]

Another learning curve for officials involved dispensing gifts and hospitality in accordance with the hierarchical sensibilities of their allies. The Guaikurú chiefs, or "captains," along with their wives and extended family members, expected to be hosted by the commander in his quarters and to eat at his dinner table each day—as, indeed, they were, during their stopovers at the fort over the course of more than a decade. These visiting dignitaries may have, in fact, outnumbered the sixty to seventy Portuguese soldiers stationed at the fort during much of this period.[95] At these dinners, colonial officials learned to privilege the Guaikurú over their other, less demanding Native allies like the Guaná. One commander noted that the Guaikurú captains and their families would eat whatever he ate at his own table, while the visiting Guanás had to sit on the floor with humble plates of beans. This distinction could even be quantified. The same commander noted that he always adhered to a proportional distribution of alcohol, giving ten times more to the Guaikurú than to the Guaná. He could give Guaná captains extra food or rations only "on the sly."[96] The governor noted after entertaining two Guaná elites in the capital that adherence to such a division of goods was necessary so as not to "scandalize" the Guaikurú, who considered the Guaná to be their captives or servants.[97] It is revealing that such attempts to abide by Native expectations of gifting were made over the course of decades, not just in initial peace talks.

As these examples suggest, the Portuguese had to learn not just *what* to give, but *how* to exchange gifts. Colonial officials sometimes kept lists of things given to the Indians and what they received in return—a selection of metal tools for turtles, in the case of the Mura, or for horses in the case of the Guaikurú—as if they were trading commodities and the goal was to profit or at least achieve a balance of trade.[98] It was a futile exercise, as some Portuguese on the front lines realized. When Ambrósio and his band of Muras showed up in the town of Ega to meet with the Portuguese boundary commissioner there, the latter was wise enough not to object when the turtles given to him as "presents" were promptly eaten by the Muras themselves. It is unclear whether the commissioner was expected to join in this feast, but he did adhere to his expected role in distributing cloth and other gifts to the visitors.[99] The epithet "Indian giver," widespread in North America at this time, would have resonated with the Portuguese officer: it evoked the image of a calculating, deceptive Indian who gave a gift, only to take it back or expect something much greater in return.[100]

What the "Indian giver" epithet obscures is that Indigenous peoples had their own reasons for exchanging goods with outsiders in this way, seeing continual generosity on the part of the Portuguese—or

Native indebtedness, in another frame—as key to the relationships with nonkin that were constituted through trade. Settling a debt or refusing to keep up one's side in the ongoing exchange effectively ended the relationship.[101] Perhaps this explains why peacemaking Indians sometimes gave children (often girls or captive boys) to the Portuguese: these individuals embodied the ideal of an enduring exchange, based on personal relationships that would grow over time. The Portuguese would benefit from the labor of the children while feeding, clothing, and "civilizing" them; the Indians, in turn, might expect to see the fruits of that fictive-kin relationship when they returned to visit (and receive gifts) at the colonial outpost or garrison. (As described earlier in the chapter, however, the Mura adamantly refused to give up their children when asked to do so by the Portuguese; it had to be on their own initiative during peace negotiations.)[102]

These exchanges of children, however, did not always work out as planned. Engaged in peace talks with the Tatuoca on the Japurá River in the early 1780s, the officer Wilkens had given presents to the chief on two occasions. But when the chief offered to give him some captive girls and boys on their third meeting, Wilkens rejected the offering. He attempted to turn it into a teaching moment: "I responded affably that I did not want anything, and that my only interest was that they come out of the forests to become children of the Church, to save their souls, and to become vassals of the Queen." Wilkens said that "this response astonished" the chief and speculated that he had been expecting an answer more like that of the rapacious river traders, who were always trying to swindle the Indians out of their captives. But it seems much more likely that the Tatuoca chief was offended by Wilkens's refusal to take the children. It may have been seen as terminating a relationship that had only just begun.[103]

Over their many years of gifting, the Portuguese at the front lines must have had some inkling that their manufactured goods were not simply functional items to Native peoples—that they had symbolic and social value, too.[104] These meanings, however, remained opaque to colonial authors. Lieutenant Mardel seemed baffled, for example, when a visiting Mura chief went into Mardel's own residence and, finding some employees eating at the dining table, "threw himself at it without a word, and snatched a knife, spoon, and fork," after which he "went off without saying or explaining a thing."[105] The Muras had taken the cutlery as they were about to depart from the garrison, heading upriver to meet with other Mura groups; once there, the knife, fork, and spoon must have entered Indigenous networks of exchange. One anthropologist, writing about the Waiwai of the northern Amazon in the twentieth century, puts it this way: "Western goods symbolized commodities and much more: they represented the whites and all of the painful contradictions resulting from contact, at the same time as they served as a vehicle for the Waiwai to be able to control the conditions that gave rise to such contradictions."[106] Thus, cutlery—a marker, for Europeans, of civilization—was taken out of its original context and took on new significance, perhaps as a kind of "avatar" of the whites.[107] Left empty-handed in front of his plate of food, the colonial diner may have seen nothing more in this episode than proof of Native caprice. But he relinquished his knife, spoon, and fork and did not insist upon an explanation.

▼▲▼▲▼▲

Both Spain and Portugal devised cynical policies and practices toward independent Native polities in the second half of the eighteenth century, leading one Spanish viceroy to describe the overall strategy as "peace by deceit." Some of these practices were of Iberian design. Others were clearly inspired by English and French methods for increasing Native dependency on European trade items (especially "vices" like alcohol and tobacco) and thus weakening Native cultural defenses. The principal aim of peace agreements, after all, was to neutralize the threat presented by autonomous Indians.[108]

This comes across clearly in official correspondence from Brazil, which condescendingly referred to Indians as people who could be duped—through promises and gifts—into accepting peace. One governor gave these instructions to an officer in charge of negotiating with a group of autonomous Bororo in Mato Grosso:

> By every possible means you will try to find out the number of individuals that compose [their group], inquiring as to whether they are just one nation under a single cacique, or whether they have dif-

ferent chiefs. . . . Take care that they do not distrust the reason for this examination, and tell them that the motive for wanting to know how many they are is that we want to know how many houses to make for them, and how many tools to have prepared for them.[109]

Throughout the late colonial period, Crown authorities advocated dissimilation and manipulation as the best strategies for making peace with autonomous Native polities and for turning them into obedient and useful subjects. Some officials, at their most disturbingly candid, proposed that if peace did not work out, perhaps Indians simply could be tricked into killing each other. According to one Portuguese officer (Lieutenant Mardel) involved in peace negotiations, the Mura leader Ambrósio might be used to either "facilitate the surrender of the other [Mura factions], or to seed such confusion among them that they end up killing off one another, making it easier for us to extinguish them completely. I have taken care in this regard, fomenting among them competition and jealousy from the very beginning, at the same time as I offer them all the greatest friendship."[110] The provocation of interethnic strife, a technique honed by the Portuguese over the course of earlier Indian wars in Brazil, had never been completely disavowed; it had always existed alongside (and sometimes in concert with) colonial practices of peacemaking.

But there were very real limits on these colonial schemes. Independent Native peoples, after all, had co-created the conditions under which peacemaking in the borderlands took place. They could threaten a return to war, withhold their assistance in bringing other Native groups into the peace, or accept the invitations of another imperial power. In this context, Indians' political strategies had to be reckoned with and their practices of peace observed and learned by colonial officials on the ground. These were always considered temporary accommodations, of course; Iberians never intended to continue making concessions to Indians. But they lasted longer than expected, in large part because autonomous Native peoples demanded them so effectively.

4   A Return to War Is Always Possible

IN LOW VOICES, the women talked among themselves. Their husbands, they agreed, were fooling no one with their acts of bravado. Everyone knew what had happened to the village downriver—its houses burnt, its gardens pillaged, its people hiding in the woods. They had heard the stories of babies being snatched from their mother's arms. They knew that their own young men, who had left in search of firearms and other trade goods, might never return. What would become of their families if the worst should come to pass?

The men debated, too. Some voices were defiant: we must paint our bodies black for war and go to arrow these enemies. Other voices urged caution: we must go deeper into the forests, they said, and cover our tracks. As in any group in the throes of change, there were those who perceived opportunities for personal gain and those who felt a strong sense of duty to protect the group. The younger disagreed with the older, the children with their parents. Lacking consensus and without a clear path forward, some took radical initiatives—often with weapons in hand.[1]

Tumult and uncertainty had reached deep into Brazil's interior and reverberated along its borders. The first decades of the century saw the unprecedented transfer of a royal court to its colony, fleeing Napoleon's armies, and the opening of Brazilian ports to foreigners (1808). From his new perch in Brazil, the Portuguese prince regent authorized brutal wars against various Native polities (1808–1811). As Brazil's neighbors cast off Spanish rule, another Portuguese prince oversaw Brazil's independence (1822), establishing a Brazilian monarchy that attempted to maintain key continuities with the old regime. But demands for social, political, and economic transformation grew louder and more insistent over time, especially in areas distant from the center of power in Rio de Janeiro. From 1831 to 1840, Brazil had no effective leader, just regents governing in place of a child emperor, and the country teetered on the edge of civil war and territorial fragmentation. Massive rebellions convulsed the northern, northeastern, and southern provinces. It was only around the middle of the century that governing elites consolidated their power on a platform of order and slave-owning prosperity. They saw little or no role for Indigenous peoples in the Brazilian Empire—though attempts to "civilize" the Indians continued, and Native labor still powered some parts of the country.[2]

This chapter takes up the challenge of understanding these social, political, and economic changes from the perspectives of Native peoples who lived mostly beyond the effective control of the state but entered into frequent contact with settlers and government officials. How did different groups position themselves during these decades of instability and escalating violence? As the balance of power tipped further toward the Brazilian state and local oligarchs, autonomous Indians fought to preserve what they had gained from past alliances with whites. These struggles took many forms. Some groups made war against their former allies; others joined the regional rebellions; and still more experimented with new, often risky forms of contact.

Narrowing Paths
When a high-ranking official from São Paulo anchored in the port of Albuquerque in 1801, a party of about a hundred Guaikurús gathered to welcome him. The Indians would have noticed that although he distributed gifts, he did so grudgingly, only because (as he himself admitted) he was under orders to appease them. A few days later, another group of several dozen Guaikurús arrived and stayed about

a week at the garrison, including a young Guaikurú noblewoman whom the official described in condescending terms ("one of the grand personages of their Court"). He did not bother to hide his disdain for the Guaikurú: "Their indomitable arrogance gives us no hope that they will subject themselves as vassals to the laws of God and Kingdom"; instead, they "keep their independence as allies, with the same extreme superstitions and depraved customs." He also lamented their possession of firearms, "in whose use they are extremely skilled."[3] Within a few months, the official had come to find the whole scene at Albuquerque intolerable, like a tableau from the "Kingdom of Satan," as he put it. There were "more than 200 Guaycurú Indians, both men and women, encircling the military camp with a continuous clamor day and night . . . deafening the ears of the spectators with the hammering of the rocks they use to break open the coconuts called *bocaiúvas*, whose nuts they eat." Meanwhile, their many horses surrounded the houses of Albuquerque, leaving piles of manure in their wake. All of this convinced the visiting official of the "disorder and disruption" of the Indians' presence and reminded him of "the vigilance needed among infidels."[4]

This scornful vision contrasted with what some colonial officials on the ground were still arguing at the dawn of the nineteenth century: that friendship with the groups like the Guaikurú was strategically useful, even if the Indians continued to live autonomously and cost a great deal to maintain as allies.[5] That argument, which had informed both Spanish and Portuguese policies for several decades in the previous century, was increasingly rejected by those in positions of power at every level of government. Years and sometimes decades after the initial peace agreements, the extent of Native autonomy came to be seen as more galling and the "pacification" as woefully incomplete. Both Brazilian and Spanish American authors drew portraits of "irredeemable savages"—though Brazilians were certain that "their" Indians were worse.[6] They complained that most allied Native peoples refused to settle permanently or do any kind of regular labor for whites—though some authors acknowledged that Indians did engage in seasonal work, and that many traded their wares and foodstuffs in colonial towns. Few were baptized or had ever accepted a missionary in their midst—and in most cases, missionaries did not even attempt to make overtures. What existed between Indians and whites was only an "apparent friendship," as one late-colonial governor in the Amazon wrote.[7] Native groups like the Mura were characterized as "stupid" and "less disposed to receive any benefit that one wishes to give to them," which made it easier to justify slashing the expenses of gifting and diplomacy.[8] Of course, distrust and contempt had always been palpable in Iberian writings about Indians; we might recall, from the previous chapter, that Lieutenant Mardel referred to the Mura leader, Ambrósio, as a "monster." But Mardel had continued to negotiate with Ambrósio, in the pursuit of what he saw as a higher purpose.[9]

A new, harder line toward Indigenous allies runs through the official correspondence of the new century, which describes even submissive, vulnerable groups in barbed terms. When a group of some four hundred skinny, terrorized Guanás traveled about eighty leagues on foot from their villages in Spanish territory to reach the Portuguese garrison at Miranda, seeking refuge after an devastating massacre of their people, the Portuguese commander expressed nothing but cynicism. One would need a mountain of tools, cloth, and other gifts, he claimed, to "appease these barbarous people (though they claim that the majority of them are baptized)," and besides, "experience has shown that all one gives them is for naught." The Guanás, he said, tried to cajole him with "the affectionate expressions . . . with which these Indians know how to delude us, saying that they came to seek the patronage of the Portuguese, because they have heard that we are very good, and other flattering words." But the frontier commander would not be budged—and in any case, he claimed that he had nothing to offer them. "These Indians even dare to say that they are very inclined toward agriculture, but since they go around mixed up with the damned Guaikurús, soon they drink the same poison, and end up as professional thieves, assassins, traitors, and idlers."[10] One can imagine the disappointment of the Guaná survivors as they realized that safe haven among the Portuguese was a mirage, or perhaps something available only to previous generations of border-crossing Guanás.

Royal policies likewise reflected the shift toward contempt and repression of independent Indians. In 1798, a royal decree specified that the Mura, Mundurukú, and Karajá—among other unspecified Native groups at peace—could be compelled to serve the settlers, as long as their contracts were registered with government officials and the Indians were baptized and educated during their term of service. The stated principle was that all Indians were "free" as long as they were not at war with the Portuguese, but it was now legal to transport them out of their homelands, bind them to labor contracts, and treat them as wards of the state. Language about Native consent was entirely absent.[11] Most scholars have seen the royal instructions of 1798 as giving new, official sanction to raids and enslavement of Indigenous communities—which had lacked this stamp of approval for about half a century.[12]

Native peoples with a reputation for intractability found themselves targeted even more aggressively in this period. Soon after the royal court arrived in Rio de Janeiro, in 1808, a "war of extermination" began in the forests of Minas Gerais and Bahia, in eastern Brazil. First, the prince regent authorized an offensive war against the "cannibalistic" Botocudo—a catch-all name for various Native groups in the region, who were accused of eating human flesh by those seeking to justify armed expeditions.[13] This war, the prince told the governor of Minas Gerais, "will not end until you have the satisfaction of taking possession of their habitations and of making them recognize the superiority of my royal arms"—and indeed, the war authorization was not revoked until 1831. All Botocudos—again, a generic category—found bearing weapons should be taken as prisoners of war, to serve the colonists. They even could be kept in chains if they "did not show proof of having abandoned their ferocity and cannibalism." As if this were not clear enough, the prince regent ordered the governor to suspend, until further notice, all humane treatment of the Botocudo.[14] One historian has argued that in this language lay the origins of the Indians' "state of exception": they were considered to be outside of the law but were still subject to its most extreme penalties.[15]

The 1808 authorization of war cast a wide net across Brazil, ensnaring Indians far beyond the Botocudos (or supposed "Botocudos") along the eastern seaboard. Officials in other captaincies (or provinces, after independence) argued for the necessity of offensive warfare, asking for the "grace" of the war authorization to be extended to their districts.[16] This is exactly what happened between 1808 and 1811, when the Kaingang, Karajá, Apinajé, Xavante, Xerente, and Canoeiro were officially targeted in southeastern and Central Brazil. In an 1811 decree, the prince regent acknowledged that the hostility of these groups could be attributed to past depredations on the part of those in charge of colonial Indian settlements; after all, several of these groups had made peace agreements and had settled, at least for a time, in the colonial sphere. But he affirmed his conviction "that there is presently no other path to follow except to intimidate and even destroy them if necessary."[17] Some officials did not even ask for authorization to make war; they simply assumed that in the case of "obstinately fierce" tribes—such as the Gamela in Maranhão—it would be "indispensably necessary to treat them in conformity" with the 1808 orders on the Botocudo.[18] Other independent Native groups, such as the Caiapó do Sul along the Paraná River, were not slated for elimination, and they continued negotiating and trading with white settlers and missionaries in the early decades of the nineteenth century. But captives were increasingly obtained even in the context of ostensibly peaceful trades: parents felt pressured to give up their children in exchange for salt, tools, and trinkets, and the young Caiapós were then distributed to settlers in the city to work as servants. When it came time to determine the fates of these captive Caiapós, regional authorities relied on a very broad interpretation of the royal authorizations on taking prisoners of war, which included a sentence of fifteen years of unpaid labor.[19] These interpretations were most enthusiastically championed by those who hoped to take advantage of Native labor—including the authorities themselves.

The state, after all, was not absent from the frontier regions where slave raiding and child trafficking ran rampant; rather, many state authorities were deeply invested, alongside settlers, in the revival of Indigenous slavery.[20] Provincial officials liked to refer to the trade in Indigenous captives, particularly children, as the "innocent trade." It should be promoted and expanded, they said, as a means of bringing more Indians out of their "primitive state" and perhaps even supplanting African slave labor—if that other, more notorious trade were to end.[21]

When foreign travelers began exploring Brazil in the 1810s and 1820s, they got an earful on the topic. Government officials and plantation owners enjoyed regaling their foreign guests with tales of exploits in the Indigenous captive trade, describing these as efforts to bring whole tribes out of the forests to work on their downriver plantations.[22] In the Rio Negro captaincy, settlers told of undertaking *amarrações*—from the word *amarrar*, to tie up or to bind together—in what was clearly a reference to the way Indians were captured.[23] Military commanders on the expanding agricultural frontiers of the country claimed to have "pacified" formidable groups through sheer terror. In Mato Grosso, a district commander (who was also a wealthy ranch owner) received royal authorization for an expedition against the Bororo. The Indians had allegedly killed about a dozen of his Black slaves; later, the commander told a group of foreign travelers how he taken his revenge many times over, killing 450 Bororos and imprisoning 50 more, including the chief. He was proud of his stratagem, by which the chief, in exchange for his freedom, agreed to bring the rest of his people into peaceful relations and to work as herdsmen on the commander's ranch.[24] In 1827, these surviving Bororos visited the French artist Aimé-Adrien Taunay and the German botanist Ludwig Riedel in the house where they were staying in Mato Grosso. Taunay captured the scene in watercolor, with Riedel sitting in a hammock, seeming to engage a Bororo man in conversation, and Taunay himself drawing at a desk, while another man and child look on with curiosity (figure 4.1).[25] Perhaps the strange, book-laden men had seemed like appealingly different interlocutors, of another breed than the district commander and his ilk.

If so, it was a misplaced hope. Many foreign travelers made the leap to complacency—and complicity—rather quickly during this era of opened ports and new scientific expeditions into the Brazilian interior. In 1819, the Bavarian naturalists Carl von Martius and Johann Baptist von Spix visited the sprawling Amazonian plantations of one Francisco Ricardo Zany, an Italian-born colonel who became one of their main collaborators. The naturalists described how Zany's twenty thousand coffee trees, among other crops, were worked by a large labor force of Passés, Yurís, and Macunás whom he had "ordered to come out of the forests of the Japurá River." (About a decade later, Zany was said to have

FIGURE 4.1 Party of visiting Bororos, 1827.
Source: French artist Aimé-Adrien Taunay during his travels in Mato Grosso with the Langsdorff Expedition. Now in the collections of the Russian Academy of Sciences in Saint Petersburg.

three hundred Indians working on his estate on the Solimões River.) But their friend's Indigenous captives seemed happy and docile, Spix and Martius asserted.[26] The travelers apparently accepted the idea that private parties should play a role in "civilizing" Indians and incorporating them into the labor system—a notion that gained traction all over Brazil in this period.[27] (A rare Brazilian critic noted that all one needed was a "roll of coarse cloth, a case of axes and knives, and a flask of gunpowder to go the Japurá" to obtain Indians for one's own use.[28])

Colonel Zany himself would propose exactly such a plan for harnessing independent Indians to a labor regime—the only Indian policy proposal considered by the Portuguese parliament in 1822, on the eve of Brazilian independence. But in 1820, Zany was still out in the field, actively carrying out his vision of how one ought to "bring Indians, now wandering as vagabonds through the forest, into our civil society."[29] He guided Martius on an expedition up the Rio Japurá, where the party engaged a Miranha chief to obtain some captives for them:

adult Indians for Zany and some children for Martius. Known as João Manoel, the chief was described as clever but villainous, his authority based on his control of the expanding slave trade with whites. Through his commercial contacts, he was said to have "acquired some European habits; he took pride in always wearing pants and a shirt, eating from a china plate, and daily shaving the little beard he had." When the chief returned with a load of war captives from a rival subgroup of Miranhas, he sold five children to Martius: two girls and three boys.[30]

Years later, when Martius wrote about his travels for a wider audience, he took care to depict the children as an unwanted gift—which he only accepted as an act of charity. The five child captives, he wrote, would have met an unfortunate end in the possession of the "barbarous" Chief João Manoel. This was likely an effort to justify an episode that we know, from his later diaries, came to weigh heavily on Martius's conscience. One of the captive girls was called Isabella, or simply Miranha. She made it all the way to Munich with the Bavarian travelers, where she died as a young teenager. For about a year after crossing the ocean, she had company, a Yurí boy named Johannes whom Martius had purchased from Zany's estate, though they did not speak the same language. Perhaps the two children had learned to communicate with one another, reviving some of the memories of the people and places they had left behind, before their premature deaths in 1821 and 1822.[31]

The participation of the Miranha chief in the captive trade is an important part of this nineteenth-century story. João Manoel's role can be understood in the context of intensifying exchange relations between independent Indians and white settlers, as well as shrinking options for maintaining autonomy in this period. Martius, for all of his deprecatory comments about the chief and his people, described this group of Miranhas as a people who had not submitted. He credited the leadership of João Manoel for their living in a "state of primitive liberty," as the traveler put it, "distant from the whites, able to avoid the forced labor that is such a horror to all the other Indians, and constituting a powerful tribe, independent from the rest." They seemed healthy and "robust," and their numbers were said to be strong, with some six thousand individuals. João Manoel told the travelers that his people occupied the forests from the Japurá River into the deep interior, and that it took some fifteen days to travel to the outer edge of their territory.[32]

The description of a second chief, who came to meet with Martius's party along a lower stretch of the Japurá, reveals another facet of these contact strategies. Pachico, chief of the Kueretú of the Apaporis River, appears in the travelogue as a kind of caricature—"the perfect likeness of an African chief who makes slave trafficking his business"—but the recorded details about him suggest a more sophisticated approach. Pachico presented himself to the travelers in a fancy blue coat and carried a silver-tipped staff of office, which had been given to him by the Portuguese boundary commissioners back in the 1780s in recognition of the Kueretús' hospitality and cooperation. "He was by far the most astute and bold Indian I had yet encountered," Martius wrote. "He finds it convenient to present himself as a loyal vassal of the King of Portugal," and he spoke Portuguese well. (In fact, he may have visited the Portuguese governor in Barcelos, some thirty years earlier: an unnamed son of a Kueretú chief had gone there on a diplomatic mission in 1787, during which the governor urged him to relocate his people from the upper Apaporis River to a spot closer to the Portuguese. The chief's son said he would attempt to persuade his father but promised nothing. Perhaps a blue frock coat was among the gifts he received on this occasion.) But despite Pachico's self-presentation and rhetoric, Martius described the chief as "no less opposed to the whites than the others I met." While making war upon his Indigenous neighbors to supply traders with captives, he "sought to keep his tribe in the forest, far away from the whites."[33]

Many Native groups sought to avoid the slave raiders by withdrawing from the banks of the main river highways and heading for the more distant tributaries. A British naval officer who traveled along the Amazon in the late 1820s lamented that with the abundance of fish and turtles and the chances for employment along the main river, this was where Indians should "naturally be the most numerous and the least barbarous," yet there were relatively few.[34] Those who had moved upriver competed with one another for resources and struggled to fend off raiding parties, while chiefs like João Manoel and

Pachico came to dominate exchange relations with whites. Yet many saw this as preferable to staying close to the main rivers and fronts of settler expansion.

Native groups that remained in zones of intensive, unrelenting contact paid a high price for their proximity during this period, and foreign travelers noticed (and even capitalized on) the signs of social disintegration and loss. A French botanist, Auguste Saint-Hilaire, who traveled in the early 1820s along the Jequitinhonha River in Minas Gerais, noticed that "there were already no children among the tribes that have the most communication with the Portuguese, and to sell more of them still, these tribes waged wars with other, more distant ones." But despite condemning the practice of enslaving and trading Native children, the Frenchman went on to acquire a boy, referring to him as "my Botocudo."[35] The German naturalist Georg Wilhelm Freyreiss likewise criticized the crude violence of the settlers who carved out ranches among the "hordes" of Purís on the banks of the Paraíba River, but he himself cajoled with alcohol and then pressured a group of hungry, desperate Purís to sell one of their male children to him. The Purí women protested bitterly but were overruled by the head of the family, who carefully considered the shirt, knives, and trinkets he would receive. At first, he attempted to sell Freyreiss an unhealthy child, but the boy's poor stature and distended belly did not pass muster; the traveler insisted that he offer a different one. Freyreiss went on to receive one of the early land grants to European immigrants, part of the Crown's effort to incentivize the settlement of those eastern forests still inhabited by independent Indians.[36]

The dynamics of the interimperial borderlands changed, too, in the early decades of the century. As Brazil's neighbors fought for independence from Spain (and fought each other for political dominance), the long-standing border contest between Spain and Portugal became less relevant. Rival European Crowns no longer vied for Native loyalty, and funds were scarce for peacemaking, in any case. As a result, diplomatic channels narrowed on both sides of the border.[37] Chiefs like Pachico continued to travel to the capital cities to seek audiences with governors, and some Native leaders even went all the way to Rio de Janeiro to visit the royal court in the years after 1808. But the gifts they received on these visits were less generous, and Indians might resort to trading with those they encountered along the way, so as not to return empty-handed—they might exchange a child captive, say, for a couple of axes. (Indeed, this is what Martius paid for the "pretty boy Yurí," Johannes.[38])

Indigenous peoples who had long crossed back and forth over colonial borders noticed worrisome changes, too. In the 1810s and 1820s, Native spies near the Paraguay-Brazil border puzzled over the signs of "agitation, the movement of forces to the south, the fleeing of some people, the imprisonment of others."[39] During the upheavals of war and the militarization of the border zone, safe refuge became harder to find—even as it became more necessary.[40] The Guaná survivors of a Spanish massacre could not count on Portuguese protection at the garrison town near the border, as discussed earlier, while the Guaikurú and Kadiwéu encountered more overt disdain and intolerance from authorities at the frontier outposts they visited in Brazil and Paraguay. In 1812, a group of Kadiwéu—angry about their increasingly hostile treatment at the Paraguayan fort of Borbón (Olimpo), where they had been, "by long-standing custom, treated with kindness by all the commanders"—decided to steal the fort's herds of cattle and besiege it until its small number of soldiers abandoned the place, at which point the Indians ransacked it for weapons and other loot.[41] A few years later, the dictator of the newly independent Republic of Paraguay declared a war of extermination against the Guaikurú and Kadiwéu, much like the one declared by Brazil's prince regent on the Botocudo, leaving them with fewer options for trade and transborder mobility than before.[42]

Other groups felt themselves under more heavy-handed surveillance as they followed their customary routes. During turtle egg-laying season, government sentinels patrolled Amazonian beaches, warning the Mura not to harvest eggs prematurely and imposing strict quotas on how many turtles could be killed for meat. To get the sentinels off their trail as they moved toward turtle-nesting areas, the Muras had to hide their canoes underwater.[43] Perhaps these new restrictions help explain why the same groups of Muras began working as fishermen for Colonel Zany and other settlers along the Solimões River. But although the Mura remained mobile and relatively autonomous, the new work surely came with some negative consequences. We know, for example, that Zany was a vocal proponent of using the Mundurukú, longtime enemies of the Mura, to intimidate Native groups into submission or at least cooperation. When he traveled around the region, visiting Native communities and encampments, he liked to bring a Mundurukú man along with him for this very purpose.[44]

The more centralized policies of the Portuguese Crown, with their recent emphasis on strategic alliances with Indians and protectionist legislation, were giving way to a tangle of local initiatives in Brazil. These were dominated by landowners, military men, provincial officials, missionaries, and other would-be supervisors of Indian labor, who sometimes collaborated but often competed against one another.[45] Ideas for Indigenous policies ran the gamut, from philanthropic proposals to more aggressive ones, with Colonel Zany's scheme (mentioned earlier) falling in the latter category. Very little consensus existed on the national level. Although Brazil's new constitution (1824) defined citizenship broadly and inclusively based on birthplace, Native peoples went unmentioned. Representatives of the Constituent Assembly had argued, in fact, that autonomous Indians should be excluded because they were not part of "civilized" society, whereas incorporated Indians might qualify as citizens, but none of that language made it into the Constitution itself.[46] One historian has described the Indian legislation for the first half of the century as "greatly impoverished, and mostly of an ad hoc character."[47] The same was generally true of the Spanish American republics, where individual provinces and even cities developed their own idiosyncratic policies and approaches toward independent Indians, many of them motivated only by short-term goals.[48]

Chaotic processes of "internal colonization" accelerated all across Brazil, as Portuguese colonial rule ended and regional oligarchs rushed to pursue their own agendas.[49] Pressure on Native lands and resources grew, fueled by settler population growth and the expansion of extractive and agricultural enterprises. Indigenous peoples watched as fruiting palms and other useful trees along the banks of the Amazon and its main tributaries were felled with startling speed to make room for row after row of planted cacao trees. A few decades later, around the middle of the century, wild latex extraction became profitable, beginning the rubber boom that would reshape the landscape and demography of Indigenous homelands in Amazonia. In Western Brazil and the Pantanal, cattle multiplied rapidly across the grasslands, and ranchers took up residence in new clearings with access to prime riverfront. The thirst for Indian labor—for people to clear the forests, work the cacao groves, tap the rubber trees, and herd the cattle on the ranches—was greater than ever, wherever Indigenous populations were still numerous and African slaves remained more expensive.

Indian labor was therefore at the center of independence-era power struggles in many parts of the country, especially in Northern, Central, and Western Brazil. In the Amazon, escalating violence against Indigenous groups coexisted with new, liberal ideas about Indians' rights over their own labor. Independent Native groups got wind of these ideas (and the bitter debates they provoked) through missionaries, incorporated Indians, slaves, and settlers. We know, for example, that a priest, known for his radical views on Native freedom from forced labor, worked with Mundurukú and Mawé groups. At the other end of the spectrum were landowners who used the political opening around independence to press for unrestricted access to Indian labor—especially the labor of those who still lived autonomously in the forests and upriver areas.[50] The Mundurukú, for example, were pressed into service for the first time in the 1810s, having long held an exemption from any kind of draft labor in return for their provisioning of manioc meal for the capital city. Indignant, the Mundurukú withdrew farther into the interior forests between the Tapajós and Madeira Rivers—until around 1820, when they successfully negotiated a return to the old agreement.[51] A few years later, in 1824, armed groups of Indigenous and mixed-race villagers, along with some Black slaves, staged attacks along the Lower Amazon, targeting influential landowners and allegedly claiming to be "lords of themselves."[52]

With all these interests and agendas at play, autonomous Native peoples found it even more difficult to read the intentions of those with whom they interacted. Some crisscrossed provincial lines in an attempt to find new, better interlocutors.[53] Others preferred to negotiate only with Native emissaries like the famous Damiana da Cunha, who led five official expeditions into the interior (1808–1830), shedding her clothes and painting her body in genipapo and urucum, so as to better recruit her brethren among the autonomous Caiapó do Sul to settle in her state-sponsored village in Goiás.[54] Many other Native peoples assumed the worst of all those outside their own group. When a Portuguese military officer in Central Brazil took stock of the attitudes of Indigenous groups in 1824, in the wake of Brazilian independence, he described them as filled with "the most profound hatred for civilized people"—a hatred fueled by the forced labor to which they were subjected and by the dispossession of their territories.[55] In the central Amazon, according to one observer in 1826, the Mura were convinced that the "magistrates" were out to enslave them, and they remained "distrustful and disloyal."[56] The following year, in 1827, the Guaikurú were reputed to be "fearsome for the disloyalty with which they act, suddenly severing friendly relations, in the midst of peace and during the exchange of sentiments that seem cordial."[57] While these assessments drew on common stereotypes about Native peoples as recalcitrant, they contained a kernel of truth, too. At their core was Indians' rejection of the false choice held out to them by government officials and local oligarchs, between "civilization" and extermination.

Defiance, Audacity, and Revolt
The acts of violence committed by "friendly Indians" in this period seem, at first glance, to be almost random. The Indians, the story goes, simply erupted "in the midst of peace," turning on their former allies without warning or provocation. But it is worth remembering an argument developed in the first chapter of this book: that Native actions in war often came out of direct provocations and grievances and that Indians, too, made rational assessments of risk. A closer look at the evidence shows that strategies of alliance and warfare were intertwined in Indigenous peoples' efforts to counter new threats to their survival, to maintain autonomy, and to reassert authority over people and territory.[58]

The Guaikurú peace agreement with the Portuguese, formalized by two subgroups in 1791 and then affirmed by others in the years that followed, had long provided a measure of security. Guaikurú bands could always head north and east to the forts and garrisons of Coimbra, Albuquerque, or Miranda if conditions worsened on the other side of the border or if they needed to escape retribution for a raid on Paraguayan soil. At the Portuguese forts, they accepted hospitality (however cynically offered) and trade goods in exchange for ceasing hostilities and helping with frontier surveillance and intelligence gathering. But the balance of power had gradually shifted over the three decades of peace with the whites and with the end of Portuguese colonial rule.

One shift was that the Guaná, who had long supplied the Guaikurú with food and women, began linking their fortunes to settler communities like Albuquerque and cementing their ties to Luso-Brazilian fort commanders and prominent landowners rather than to the Guaikurú chiefs. By the early 1820s, the old interethnic alliance between the Guaikurú and Guaná had deteriorated, even as local power brokers in Brazil offered less and less in exchange for Native loyalty.[59]

Another shift was underway in the relations between Paraguay and Brazil. By the 1820s, the dictator of Paraguay seemed bent on the destruction of the Guaikurú, going so far as to send four hundred soldiers to burn down the vast bocaiúva palm groves upon which the Indians depended for their subsistence.[60] This was the context in which officials in Paraguay insisted that their Brazilian counterparts stop buying stolen goods from the Guaikurú and Kadiwéu, as well as decline to sell them guns and fix their old firearms. The Brazilian authorities agreed (at least in theory) to abide by these demands, so as to "conserve with the Republic of Paraguay the most perfect harmony and good intelligence."[61] However short-lived, the two nations' efforts at cooperation put the Guaikurú in a decidedly less advantageous position in the border zone.

The long-standing debate among Native peoples about the characters and intentions of "Spaniards" versus "Portuguese" grew heated again in 1826. (Well into the nineteenth century, Indigenous groups in Brazil continued to use these old designations: "Every white, brown, or black man is 'Portuguese'; the Indians never refer to them as Brazilians, and the Paraguayans are still, to them, 'Spaniards.'"[62]) The details of what happened in 1826 are vague, but we know that a Kadiwéu chief named Calabá stood at the center of the controversy. Calabá had come to the Paraguayan fort of Borbón to visit a popular Brazilian merchant, who was passing through the area. Upon Calabá's arrival at the fort, the merchant (acting on the Paraguayan fort commander's instructions) invited him to enter the fort in his company. As soon as the chief stepped through the gates, however, soldiers arrested Calabá and put him in chains. He was sent to Asunción, where people said he was put to death on the dictator's orders.[63]

In this episode, the Guaikurú saw proof of the collusion of Spaniards and Portuguese (or rather, Paraguayans and Brazilians) against one of their chiefs. The Brazilian merchant claimed to have been acting in good faith, ignorant of the Paraguayan fort commander's plot against Calabá, but it was too late. A coalition of five Guaikurú groups, including the Kadiwéu, broke their long-established peace agreement with Brazil.[64] For the first time in several decades, Guaikurús raided the forts of Coimbra and Miranda, the symbols of Brazilian military authority on the frontier. They also ambushed traveling military convoys and attacked Brazilian ranches, stealing hundreds of cattle and horses and killing a handful of white settlers and their Native servants. Provocatively, two Guaikurú chiefs went about wearing accessories from the military uniform of a Brazilian officer they had killed.[65]

As Guaikurú attacks on Brazilian property and lives continued through 1826 and into 1827, the government chose to negotiate. The stated rationale was that the province of Mato Grosso "lacked all the necessary means to succeed in such a war" against the Guaikurú, who were said to have more than two thousand warriors.[66] The province was short on able-bodied men as well as funds, which meant that any armed expedition would be likely to fail—especially during the long flood season, when the waters of the Pantanal formed a labyrinth of rivers, channels, lakes, and swamps known only to the Indians.[67] Even if troops managed to pursue the Guaikurú through this watery maze, the Indians could cross into Paraguay in an effort to escape retribution.[68] (Cooperation with Paraguay, after all, only went so far: the Paraguayans were said to be gloating over the Brazilians' new Indian problems, and they would have been unlikely to allow Brazilian troops to pursue the Indians across the border.[69]) For these reasons, provincial authorities in Mato Grosso decided to take a mostly "soft" approach that harkened back to the old peace negotiations. But it was an approach that attempted to exploit Guaikurú weaknesses in a systematic way and to take advantage of the changed circumstances of the borderlands.

The first weakness was internal factionalism. A Brazilian military engineer, who offered an influential proposal for how to respond to the threat of Native rebellion along the frontier with Paraguay, framed the solution in these terms: "We should find a way to bring to the attention of the Guaikurú captains that the provincial government's resentment is only against their principal leader, who, deluding the rest, was the cause of breaking the peace and good harmony with us, which they themselves sought, and so many years ago swore solemnly to uphold." The Guaikurú, he suggested, should be told that the government would be "inclined toward a lasting reconciliation, for reciprocal peace, if they returned to their duties." The ends always justified the means: "In this way, sowing division among those chiefs, we will obtain the most secure path to achieving the goals that best fit our circumstances, and as soon as one of them peels away, the others will not take long to imitate him."[70]

A military commander with long experience on the Paraguay River was dispatched at the head of a large expedition, with instructions to negotiate an end to the rebellion. To that end, Commander Jerônimo Joaquim Nunes heaped the blame on a single Guaikurú chief, Beque de Ayona (who, ironically, was also known by the Portuguese name Joaquim Nunes, after the very same commander now charged with restoring peace to the frontier). The "youngsters" among the Guaikurú were said to have been spurred on by this charismatic leader, who encouraged them to reject their elders' focus on maintaining the peace. Even the son of the chief Emavidi Xané—who, back in 1791, had gained the title Capitão Paulo Joaquim José Ferreira upon formalizing the peace agreement with the Portuguese—had gone over to the side of the rebels. By late 1827, though, the "youngsters" were said to be returning to the fold—to the "elders" and to their encampments close to Brazilian establishments—and Commander Nunes had managed to convince other chiefs to become well-paid spies and collaborators. Even Beque de Ayona agreed to make peace, only to be killed, shortly thereafter, by a rival Guaikurú faction. His death was celebrated by the Brazilian authorities as an act of divine providence, freeing the province from the influence of a "bad Indian." But the Guaikurú were nonetheless reprimanded for their audacity in killing a chief "within view of a Brazilian garrison," and the perpetrators of the murder were briefly detained until several prominent Guaikurú chiefs demanded their release).[71]

The second weakness of the Guaikurú was their deteriorating alliance with the Guaná. The Guaná, one Brazilian official proposed, "should be treated with all good faith and courtesy . . . giving gifts to their principal chiefs and praising their constancy and loyalty to friendship."[72] Commander Nunes made a special visit for this purpose to the Guaná at a mission near Albuquerque. There he met up with the Capitão Aires Pinto, one of the first Guaná chiefs to receive a government patente back in the 1790s (see chapter 2) and now a very old man. According to Pinto, the Guaikurús had told all the Guanás that the Brazilians would kill them for their association with the rebels, and the only way to escape this fate was to come away with them. The commander was alarmed at this possible defection, because the Guaná were seen as essential to provisioning Brazil's frontier outposts; they, and particularly the Kinikinau subgroup, were an agricultural people who, he noted approvingly, even had learned to use the plow in their fields. To dissuade Pinto and his people from joining the Guaikurú, the commander distributed that old trio of vices—tobacco, alcohol, and blocks of brown sugar—and reassured the chief that his military forces were simply for their protection. A few months later, Pinto would receive a new, better patente for his loyalty.[73] Other Native groups in the region, such as the Guató and the Guaxí, were likewise targeted for special treatment during the rebellion, with the goal of "stimulating the antipathy that they have toward the Guaikurú, and thus tightening the bonds of friendship [with us]."[74] Brazilian military patrols counted on various Native informants and guides as they tried to track down Guaikurú parties with stolen livestock.[75]

For the Guaikurú, the rebellion of 1826–1827 had been an effort to reassert their place in an unpredictable borderlands and among new, post-independence actors. Given the precariousness of Brazilian defenses along the frontier, they saw an opportunity to avenge the wrongful death of a chief and to compel the Brazilians to return to the old terms of alliance—and avoid what would have been a "slow and ruinous war" for the newly independent, cash-strapped Brazilian Empire.[76] The outcomes of the rebellion, from a Guaikurú perspective, were likely ambivalent. They failed to convince the Guaná to abandon the Brazilians, and the rebellion seemed to have deepened political and generational cleavages among the Guaikurú themselves. But upon negotiating with the Brazilians to cease hostilities, leaders received new infusions of gifts and reaffirmations of goodwill from frontier authorities, while retaining their fearsome reputation in the region and much of their autonomy.[77] Indeed, just a few years later, in 1830, groups of Guaikurú and Kadiwéu agreed to be armed by frontier settlers and accompanied by troops from Mato Grosso for a joint cattle-raiding expedition in Paraguay.[78]

Living in a region that likewise saw rising tensions and bloodshed in the years after independence, the Mura charted their own difficult course. Two aspects of Mura existence stood out to travelers and priests who wrote about them in the 1820s: deep distrust of government officials and stubborn independence from the forced labor system that was so prevalent in Amazonia. "They do not want to join the villages and hamlets," one priest lamented, "because of the opinion among them that they will be enslaved like the other Indians."[79] The other reason was that "they know they are despised by those same Indians, because they are not, like the other heathens, workers of the soil"—though everyone agreed on their being "expert fishermen."[80] Spix and Martius noted of the Muras whom they met in the same period that their "hostility has been tempered, at least in part," but that they still "scorn serving the whites, more than any other tribe, and only the desire for alcohol can sometimes turn them into servants for short periods. Without this talisman, the appearance of a Mura among whites would be a strange occurrence." As a result of this self-enforced distance, few Muras spoke the língua geral in the 1820s, though by the 1840s many had begun to use it to communicate with white traders.[81]

Several decades after the message of peace with the Portuguese "flew on the wings of the wind" to reach Muras on distant tributaries, their malocas (or extended family groups) were still scattered over the central Amazon, many of them established on lakes that could be reached only via intricate networks of seasonal channels and creeks.[82] They still communicated with each other in sophisticated ways; as one chronicler noted in the 1840s, Muras far up the Madeira River would know of a boat, "with the most precise details, two or three days before its arrival, because from the mouth of the River, or even farther afield, the Muras report it, along with whatever else they can find out about it, a tactic that once served them well in their assaults." Although years of warfare with the Mundurukú had taken a toll on their population, the total number of Muras was still thought to be large. Just as had existed during the peacemaking era, there were geographical differences: the Muras of the Autazes core region and in the homelands of the Lower Madeira River were described as more populous and better established in the nineteenth century than the small, dispersed Mura groups that lived near the more heavily trafficked Amazon-Solimões River.[83]

These differences extended to the ways in which Mura individuals and groups engaged with the outside world. Some were known as river highwaymen and small-scale raiders, "roaming about in small bands," considered "more troublesome than dangerous, for their small thefts."[84] More threatening episodes flared up now and again. In 1832, some Muras from the region of Maués (between the Tapajós and Madeira Rivers) joined a group of soldiers who had risen up against their pro-Portuguese commander in Manaus. The rebelling soldiers allegedly recruited the Muras by saying that if the Portuguese returned to retake power in the country—as some nativist Brazilians feared—all Muras would be enslaved. Before the uprising was repressed by troops from the capital, the Muras attacked the town of Serpa and went on a killing spree in the town of Maués (at that time called Luzéia), targeting around thirty soldiers and whites assumed to be Portuguese or to have Portuguese loyalties. The next year, a group of Muras mounted attacks on the old colonial outpost of Borba, on the Madeira River, murdering local whites and kidnapping some of the women. Among their leaders was one of the rebellious soldiers from Manaus, which shows that the relationship between the Muras and the soldiers was ongoing; indeed, it was probably essential to the regional rebellion that followed.[85]

Other Muras, however, maintained a reputation for relatively peaceful engagement in this period. As mentioned earlier, some worked for Colonel Zany and for other white settlers as fishermen and forest collectors. A prominent Mura chief known as Severino was described in the early 1820s as "very fond of the whites, having been solemnly baptized as a child, along with many others, at the village of Borba"—likely referring to the mass baptisms of the late 1780s (see chapter 2).[86] Some Muras traded with settlers, exchanging turtle egg butter for alcohol or manufactured goods; young men participated in long-distance canoe trips with white settlers from time to time; and family groups caught and salted fish to supply ranches and farms. Spix and Martius remarked that "despite their great repugnance for serving the whites, and as stubborn as they have been in dodging any obligation to the government, one sees examples of whites who have remained unharmed among them for a long time, thanks to a wise approach."[87]

Perhaps this deeper history of resistance and selective alliances explains why, during the late 1830s, some Mura groups took part in the Cabanagem Rebellion (1835–1840)—the bloodiest, longest, and most geographically expansive rebellion in Brazil's history, with perhaps 20,000–30,000 fatalities across the northern region. Countless other Muras were simply swept up in this violence—and to this day, Mura oral histories of the Cabanagem tell of people having been abducted to fight on the rebel side.[88] The movement began with mostly white, elite leadership in the downriver port city of Belém but quickly spread upriver and into the interior, where it was taken up by new rebel leaders with more radical (if little known) agendas.[89]

The sources produced during the rebellion—nearly all documents of repression—tell us almost nothing about the motivations of the Muras who joined a mosaic of other social groups in taking up arms in this period. Some of these rebels were fighting against the structures of imperial rule; others against the impositions of local oligarchs; and still more against soldiers who came to destroy them for no apparent reason other than their identity as Indians.[90] Most documents referred only to generic "Indian" rebels, occasionally distinguishing between "heathens" (*gentio*) and those who came from the villages established for incorporated Native peoples in the colonial period (almost all of whom joined the rebellion).⁹¹ Rarely did they name specific ethnic groups, and sometimes the only clue to Mura participation is reference to a rebel stronghold located on a lake or river closely associated with them. A few authors later blamed outside agitators or "wicked people" for having "aroused the stupid and brutal animosity of the Muras against the whites." But this is best recognized as a refrain of Brazilian elites on the imperial side, as they attempted to explain why their fledgling empire faced massive rebellions across the country. It was easier to blame the outsize influence of just a few radicalized individuals than to acknowledge grievances among larger groups.⁹²

What we do know is that the Mura became formidable enemies once again. They used their knowledge of the labyrinthine river system to launch surprise attacks on imperial forces, to escape when pursued, and to communicate warnings to other Muras. The oral history evidence suggests that they established fortified points near the mouths of lakes or rivers and used rot-resistant trunks of trees to construct underwater barriers across waterways to impede their enemies. Ideally, these barriers would smash into the undersides of heavy watercraft, causing them to sink, while the Muras' bark canoes crossed easily. Well into the twentieth century, white settlers in the Autazes region worked on removing these stubborn wooden barriers; some may still be trying today.⁹³

Using such tactics, the Muras killed one of the most (in)famous military commanders on the imperial side, Bararoá (whose full name was Ambrósio Pedro Ayres). A prominent settler on the Rio Negro, Bararoá was known for his cruelty against Indians and for the large groups of soldiers he recruited; Muras alive today still recall Bararoá as "the chief of killing the Indians."⁹⁴ In 1838, he led some 130 soldiers to the Autazes, the Mura heartland, with the aim of "disinfesting" the region of rebels. Instead the troops found only Mura women and children camping beside a lake, who must have been terrorized by this encounter. The troops went on to Sampaio Lake, known to be a rebel hideout, where they located a defensible point that was quickly abandoned by the few men standing guard there. But as soon as Bararoá and a small detachment of soldiers split off from the main troops to head back down the Madeira River, they were ambushed by seven canoes of men ("the majority of them Muras"). Those Muras—likely affiliated with the rebels at Sampaio Lake—used the time-honed strategy of attacking as their target passed between two islands, where the river narrowed. Bararoá and others who tried to escape on foot were pursued and killed by the Muras. The commander himself was said to have been deposited in the river for the enjoyment of the piranhas.[95]

The Mura bore the brunt of the imperial response to the growing rebel threat along the Amazon-Solimões River and its tributaries, as the government sent expedition after expedition into Indigenous territories to destroy villages and encampments, burn crops, and torture and kill any suspected rebels—who were often identified on the basis of physical appearance as Indians. Many groups of Mundurukú aided in this destruction, having been recruited—or having offered—to punish the Mura, their historical enemies.[96] Epidemic fevers also took their toll during the later years of the war. Finally, in 1840, nearly a thousand rebels surrendered in response to an amnesty offered by the government. They came to the town of Maués to hand over their weapons, which included rifles as well as bows and arrows—suggesting that many had been Indigenous fighters.[97]

The repression of the Cabanagem Rebellion took countless Mura lives. Those who survived were among the main targets of the notoriously abusive workers' corps (1838–1855), established during the height of the repression, which aimed to corral Indians, people of mixed race, and Blacks into public and private service. In a militarized province that stigmatized Native mobility and autonomy, Mura were especially vulnerable to being rounded up for forced labor. To this day, Muras speak of the "Pega-Pega" (the Big Catch)—a time of fear, violence, kidnappings, and separations from kin—that is closely associated with the era of the workers' corps.[98] The many official reports of Mura murders, assaults, and other skirmishes with white settlers and local oligarchs in the decades after the end of the rebellion should be understood in this context.[99]

The rebellion also solidified the status of the Mura as the most reviled Indians of Amazonia. The Mura were "spoken of as the worst upon the river," according to an American traveler, William Edwards, in the mid-1840s. He regretted hiring a Mura canoe crew in the capital to accompany him upriver a few years after the end of the rebellion, as he became convinced that the men were either plotting to desert the expedition or to steal all its supplies.¹⁰⁰ The British naturalist Henry Walter Bates, who visited a Mura settlement on the Solimões in the late 1840s, reflected that "the Muras have a bad reputation all over this part of the Amazons, the semi-civilized Indians being quite as severe upon them as the white settlers. Everyone spoke of them as lazy, thievish, untrustworthy, and cruel. They have a greater repugnance than any other class of Indians to settled habits, regular labour, and the service of the whites; their distaste, in fact, to any approximation towards civilised life is invincible." Other travelers repeated this same assessment of the Mura character, year after year, sometimes admitting that it was based on hearsay.¹⁰¹ Only one of the post-rebellion travelers emphasized positive traits among the Mura: their fame as the best fishermen and hunters of turtles, their skill at canoe-building, and the bounty of food they gathered from their rivers and lakes.¹⁰²

If the trajectory of the Mura in this period reveals one way in which strategies of resistance and alliance might be intertwined, the case of the Mundurukú highlights another. The Cabanagem had given the Mundurukú a chance to establish themselves more firmly as collaborators of the state against the "hated Muras" and other rebels. In the mid to late 1830s, many of the Mundurukú chiefs presented themselves to legalist authorities to declare their allegiance to the "forces of order" during the rebellion—offering, at one point, some 3,000–4,000 warriors to do battle with the rebels.¹⁰³ When Bates visited a Mundurukú group on the Tapajós River in the late 1840s, he was particularly impressed with the bearing of a chief named Joaquim Fructuoso, who had received a commission in the Brazilian army for his assistance in putting down the rebellion. The chief spoke good Portuguese, having traveled multiple times to the large cities of the region; he wore a shirt and pants over his intricately tattooed body; and neither he nor his people insisted that Bates's party share their expedition supplies. Though considered one of the most warlike nations in the Amazon—engaged at the time of Bates's visit in destroying a neighboring Native group with the help of their firearms—the Mundurukú had been, ever since their peace agreement with the Portuguese in the 1790s, "firm friends of the whites."¹⁰⁴

The friendship offered by the Mundurukú was very deliberate, as Bates acknowledged: "It is remarkable how faithfully this friendly feeling has been handed down amongst the Mundurucús, and spread to the remotest of the scattered hordes. Wherever a white man meets a family, or even an individual of the tribe, he is almost sure to be reminded of this alliance."[105] As Chief Joaquim told another foreign traveler: "I love the whites and have never betrayed them. I left my friends, my cacao plantations, and my house on the banks of the Madeira to defend them."[106] The same savvy positioning extended to labor and trade relations. Having negotiated (and, over time, renegotiated) an exemption from draft labor in recognition of their role in supplying the province with huge quantities of manioc meal and other forest products, the Munduruku always required traders to pay them months in advance with cloth, iron tools, cutlery, and alcohol. Yet many Munduruku groups lived at a distance from Brazilian towns; as Bates put it, "They show no aptitude for the civilized life of towns."[107] In the middle years of the nineteenth century—as steamboats began to ply the rivers and settlers fanned out across the Amazon Basin to make their fortunes in rubber and Brazil nuts—such an autonomous existence was hard won.

Evading—and Playing—the New System

In the aftermath of the regional rebellions and just before midcentury, a new decree put an end to the long official silence on matters of Brazilian Indian policy. There would now be a General Director of Indians, nominated by the emperor for each province, and he would have a whole raft of supervisory duties over the Native peoples of his province. He would "inquire," "examine," "investigate," and "watch over" their resources, customs, and movements. He would "prevent" some activities but "approve," "promote" and "give license" to others. And he would, in theory, inform the imperial government of all the relevant details—making extensive lists of workers, expenses, and earnings—and propose various measures to increase the productivity of the lands inhabited by Native peoples.[108]

The Regulation Concerning the Missions of Indian Catechism and Civilization was the first general Indian legislation in decades and one that would shape land tenure and labor relations until the end of the empire. The Regulation of 1845 drew on old, time-worn models for converting and "civilizing" Indigenous peoples—the Jesuit missions and the Indian Directorate of the colonial period—but added a distinctly nineteenth-century zeal for assimilation and modernization.[109] The General Directors were prominent men, who often had military leadership experience and personal histories connected to Indian affairs.[110] Lower in the bureaucracy were the many civil "directors"—usually local landowners and entrepreneurs with direct interests in exploiting Native labor—who were supposed to oversee the settlement of local Native groups; and the missionaries, many of them Capuchins from Italy.[111] A centerpiece of the new legislation was the development of *aldeamentos*. These were state-administered settlements that would, if all went according to plan, turn "wild" Indians into "tame" villagers whose labor could be harnessed and whose lands could be occupied by the new waves of colonists in the interior. Much has been written about the 1845 legislation and its effects on Native peoples who lived in the aldeamentos—many of whom had been part of Brazilian society, or at least resident on its margins, for a long time, despite the rhetoric about "wild Indians." Historians have come to understand the Regulation of 1845 as a significant step toward the dispossession of incorporated Native communities, as it established a process by which Native villagers' lands (those deemed to be unused or "abandoned") could be leased to white settler families.[112] But we know less about Indigenous peoples who refused to settle in the aldeamentos or who made a mockery of their structures and expectations. What were such groups doing during this post-rebellion surge of "civilizing" campaigns? How did they dodge, as well as take advantage of, the new system? The reports of travelers and officials who interacted with Guaikurús and Kadiwéus during the first four years of the decree provide some clues.

The year was 1845. Encountering a group of Guaikurús (figure 4.2) at the frontier garrison of Albuquerque, the French naturalist Francis de Castelnau found out that they had arrived from the Chaco only a few days before: "They told us that they had massacred the population of a Spanish town [in Paraguay] and that, being pursued, they came to place themselves under the protection of the Brazilian garrison." Another group, whom Castelnau identified as a "much more savage" band of Kadiwéus, had just crossed into Brazil from Paraguay, to escape retribution from an Indigenous enemy.[113] It is clear from Castelnau's

FIGURE 4.2 Portrait of a Guaikurú, 1845. The Kadiwéu "paint the body with genipapo, covering it with precise figures made of concentric lines and beautiful arabesques.... They also frequently paint their hands black, giving the impression of wearing gloves" (Castelnau, *Expedição*, 366–67).

Source: Francis de Castelnau, *Expédition dans les parties centrales de l'Amérique du Sud, de Rio de Janeiro à Lima et de Lima au Para*, vol. 2: *Vues et Scènes* (Paris: P. Bertrand, 1852). Courtesy of the Oliveira Lima Library at the Catholic University of America.

account that transborder raiding remained common in the 1840s and that the areas between forts in Brazil and Paraguay still effectively belonged to mobile bands of Guaikurú and Kadiwéu in this period. After the Frenchman visited the Paraguayan fort at Olimpo, he was escorted back to Coimbra Fort on the Brazilian side by a group of soldiers who were terrified to venture into open spaces. On high alert for Guaikurú raiders, "every grass mound of the Chaco seemed to them a Guaicuru ready to attack." (The Guaná guides who accompanied the party, in contrast, seemed unconcerned and slept soundly through their overnight stop.) The Paraguayan soldiers' fears were later justified: upon Castelnau's return to Brazil, he was told that the Guaikurú had been tracking the party and would have attacked it, had it not been for the presence of the French travelers. He also discovered that the Guaikurú had already given the Brazilian commander at Coimbra a precise accounting of every minor detail of the trip to Olimpo, fulfilling their long-standing role as borderland spies and informants.[114]

In 1846, a Brazilian officer explored two small waterways off of the Paraguay River, one known as the Queima and the other as the Paulo. "It seems that these Indians have for a long time resided temporarily at this place," the officer wrote of the Guaikurú and Kadiwéu, "for the names Queima and Paulo are those of the two chiefs who, in 1791, went to Mato Grosso to request peace and friendship from the Captain-General Luís de Albuquerque." Commemoratively named to celebrate the alliance between the Guaikurú and the Portuguese and to strengthen Portuguese territorial claims over those of their Spanish rivals, the two waterways had come to mean something different over time: they were now testament to an Indigenous territoriality that could not be erased easily from the landscape. In describing the continuity of Guaikurú and Kadiwéu seasonal occupation of the Pantanal wetlands—they "*have for a long time resided temporarily*" at these sites—the Brazilian officer recognized what few of his contemporaries had been able to wrap their heads around when they looked at the Indian encampments with their transient shelters (figure 4.3).[115] "Still, since they are very traitorous," the same officer warned, "one should be cautious in navigating from Coimbra to Olimpo and make sure to guard well at night, especially when landing on the right [western] bank of the river."

FIGURE 4.3 "Encampment of Guaycuru Indians" near Albuquerque, 1845. This is likely the encampment that Castelnau described as inhabited by the Uatedeos subgroup of Guaikurús, with open-walled shelters arranged in a semicircle. Although the Uatedeos were described in this account and in official reports from the 1840s as "aldeado" (settled in an aldeamento), other evidence suggests that they remained mobile and autonomous.

Source: Francis de Castelnau, *Expédition dans les parties centrales de l'Amérique du Sud, de Rio de Janeiro à Lima et de Lima au Para*, vol. 2: *Vues et Scènes* (Paris: P. Bertrand, 1852). Courtesy of the Oliveira Lima Library at the Catholic University of America.

The Indians could approach by canoe or horseback, and in addition to cutlasses, lances, and clubs, they made good use of firearms.[116]

So it was in 1847. A party of twenty Kadiwéu men and women arrived at Albuquerque, riding bareback on fine horses, with an even larger group of horses following alongside. The adventurer João Henrique Elliott, who met them there, described the Kadiwéus with that familiar mix of admiration and scorn: "Their faces were painted with *urucum* and *genipapo* ink; their weapons were long lances and cutlasses slung over their shoulders. The men were for the most part tall and thin, and they had an arrogant and disdainful look, affecting a certain air of superiority." Their chief was "an old Indian, mounted on a lovely bay horse, which he handled with great skill and elegance." Approaching the district commander, who had recently come to the garrison, the elderly chief waited for an interpreter to be called and then announced in his own language:

> "I heard that the Senhor Comandante was here in Albuquerque, and since I am a comandante, too, I came to visit you."
> "Where are your people?" asked the commander.
> "Behind the Bodoquena Mountains," the Indian replied.
> "So you have come only to visit me?"
> "I also come to sell some horses and to buy aguardente. We are about to put on a big feast, as soon as I return from here."
> "I suppose that means you have just been fighting the Enimas," the commander countered.

The chief denied having gone against this Indigenous group from the Chaco, but the Brazilians were certain that this was why they had come with so many horses to sell.[117] Elliott did not say whether the Kadiwéu were successful in making a sale or not, but at this point, they had been peddling stolen horses to Luso-Brazilians for over half a century.

In 1848, the report of the recently created General Directorate of the Indians in Mato Grosso (which now oversaw the handful of aldeamentos in that province) claimed of the Kadiwéu that "no other nation has received so many gifts from us, but we have not been able to get them to abandon their errant life." They were, the administrator thought, in a completely different category than the "tame, peaceful, and hospitable" Guaná, who lived in two large aldeamentos and worked in a range of industries, from agriculture to river navigation to weaving. The report went on, deeply pessimistic about the Kadiwéu:

> Although they interact with us, frequent our towns, and even come to the capital, they seem determined to persist in their vagabond lifestyle. They have not taken advantage of the good treatment and gifts that we have given them. Just a few years ago, they expressed the desire to settle themselves at Albuquerque, which the government facilitated, ordering them to be given farming tools. But after just a brief time, a quarrel came up between some of them and other Indians, and they took off, having first sold their tools in exchange for aguardente.[118]

Recalling the old image of the "inconstant Indian," untrustworthy and always susceptible to the siren song of the wilderness, the administrator suggested that little rational thought or strategy informed the Kadiwéus' decisions to come and go. But in fact these comings and goings were part of a larger effort to manipulate the system of state-sponsored settlements for maximal gain with minimal commitment.

These four snapshots of the Guaikurú and Kadiwéu in the 1840s show that strategies of mobility and patterns of seasonal occupation were still important features of Indigenous lives in the border region, despite all the changes that had occurred. About a generation after the rebellion of 1826–1827, it is clear that they had rebuilt their alliance with the Brazilians while retaining their fearsome reputation as warriors; this was especially true of the Kadiwéu subgroup. Aldeamento had failed: Brazilian authorities acknowledged among themselves that Guaikurú villages were "far from resembling the aldeamentos laid out in the Regulation" of 1845, and by the late 1850s, the Guaikurú were no longer included in the aldeado category in official reports.[119] The sources from these years also reveal the ways in which Indians sought to preserve their access to merchandise and their efforts to tap into the new resources made available by the legislation of 1845.

An eclectic combination of old and new strategies seemed to have worked best. In capital cities across Brazil during the second half of the nineteenth century, for example, Indigenous chiefs made appearances at government palaces. This was a well-known negotiating tactic, going back to the colonial period, but now the visiting Indians paid homage to a portrait of Emperor Pedro II and adopted new rhetoric. Promises to the effect that Native groups would "entirely abandon their savage lifestyle" were made all too easily, to the frustration of authorities, who accused the Indians of "deceiving the government."[120] In these cases, Indians had to find other, more receptive authorities—which was certainly possible, if they were willing to travel—or wait until their past promises might be judged to have expired.

Some groups took a more aggressive approach to soliciting gifts. In the early 1880s, for example, the Xerente of northern Goiás traveled to the capital, led by one Capitão Raimundo de Souza. The provincial president described how they "demanded gifts from me, especially goods, livestock, and firearms. I ordered the naked ones to be dressed, provided the captain with a harnessed animal, and distributed to him tools, thereby spending 127$500. I refused to give them firearms, and they went so far as to demand them with threats. And they left disgruntled."[121] The request for guns was controversial, as authorities tended to think it "imprudent" to supply Native peoples with firepower. The Xerente knew it, and they pushed as hard as they could under the constraints of peace.[122]

Ethnic reinvention and the manipulation of cultural signs was another possible tactic. Because the aldeamento system aimed to attract "wild" Indians, providing more generous funds for such efforts, some Indigenous groups reinvented themselves as new arrivals. In São Paulo in the 1860s, for example, a party of Guarani-Kaiowá presented themselves to the office of the provincial president as newly contacted Indians. They even painted their bodies for this "lovely spectacle," when allegedly they been circulating in and out of the aldeamentos for some time.[123] Similarly, a group of baptized Maxacali migrated across provincial lines into Minas Gerais, where they claimed not to speak any Portuguese so as to "pass" as new arrivals from the forest and receive gifts from local authorities.[124]

Indigenous groups, then, did not simply avoid contact with aldeamentos and settlers. What often emerged instead was a complex mix of attraction and repulsion that has characterized the responses of Native peoples to missions for centuries. A provincial president's description of an aldeamento on the Rio Branco, in the northwest Amazon, is typical, if oversimplified, in its reading of Native motivations: "The number of indigenes is constantly varying and uncertain, for many come to the mission only on visits, with a spirit of curiosity, attracted by the desire of receiving some present; as soon as they acquire it, they withdraw again to their home villages, leaving the missionary with only the people of his entourage."[125] Many Native peoples lived in dispersed villages and seasonal encampments in the vicinity of mission centers. They made an appearance only during festivals or when they needed something from the visiting or resident missionary—a dose of medication, a new supply of fishhooks, protection from an angry rancher.[126]

The Mura were one of many groups that made use of the revolving doors of the aldeamentos in the 1840s through the 1880s, blurring the lines between the categories of "tame" and "wild" Indians.[127] Muras often came and went from a village known as São José do Matari (or simply Matari), situated on a desirable tract of *terra firme* along the main channel of the Amazon River near its junction with the Madeira. The community was said to have begun as a maloca, or extended family group, led by a Murified captive—an origin story that was common among Mura groups.[128] Back in the 1820s, a missionary, known for his tireless work among the Mundurukú, had been sent to try his luck among the Mura families at this promising site, directing them to plant crops, construct a chapel, and build a block of houses. He also forbade the trade in aguardente with river traders—so ubiquitous along this great river highway—though the Muras found ways of getting around the missionary's prohibition by meeting travelers just out of sight and a little farther along the river.[129] The fledging mission was destroyed during the Cabanagem; by which side, it is hard to say, though at least one author blamed the rebels.[130]

When the travelers Bates and Edwards each passed through Matari in the mid to late 1840s, they described a mostly ruined place, though Edwards remarked on its still-picturesque location on an elevated bank over the river and on the fact that its small chapel was still standing. The government had, per the Regulation of 1845, recently installed a director to oversee the small numbers of Muras who still lived in the vicinity, "with the intention of bringing the hitherto intractable savages under authority." This imposition, Bates thought, had caused many families to withdraw to "their old solitary haunts on the banks of the interior waters." The few Muras at Matari at the time of Bates's visit were wary of the strangers; Bates said they offered no hospitality and "did not even pass the ordinary salutes, which all the semi-civilized and many savage Indians proffer on a first meeting." They focused only on obtaining alcohol, "which they seemed to consider the only good thing the white man brings with him"; indeed, this was likely one of the only reasons to come to a place like Matari, on such a heavily trafficked river and under the oversight of a new director. When Bates's canoe boss refused to give them alcohol for the turtles they promised to get, the Muras became angry, and the travelers weighed anchor in a hurry.[131] In his grim portrayal of Matari and its inhabitants, Bates was surely influenced by rumors of the Muras' disagreeable character and by assumptions of the ill-fated nature of Amazonian settlement schemes.[132] To contextualize what the naturalist described, we can turn to a wide range of other sources that document systemic problems and resentments in this period: corrupt directors, a scarcity of willing and able missionaries, dwindling financial support, epidemics (some of which may have been intentionally introduced among Native peoples), alcohol abuse, and rapacious traders.[133]

In the same vein as their open relationships with the aldeamentos, many Muras chose to work on a seasonal or short-term basis for plantation owners, canoe bosses, and provincial elites. They consistently chose river-based labor.[134] Even the elderly leader, or *tuxáua*, of the Muras at Matari worked on Edwards's canoe crew, along with his five sons and their family members. Hired in the capital city of Belém, where they were likely visiting to trade, this Mura family earned wages and goods for a month-and-a-half stint of service on the expedition's canoe. Along the way, they attended a saint's day festival in a riverside town, visited another encampment of Muras, hunted and fished, and traded for alcohol in settler towns. When they reached Matari, however, the Muras disembarked and refused to go any farther—even though that meant forgoing the bonus they would have received at the destination city. (It is worth pointing out that this was probably a year or two *before* a civil director had been appointed to oversee Matari, which might have changed the Muras' calculus.)[135] Several decades later, the Mura were still known for abandoning canoe bosses, leaving them stranded by jumping in the water or disappearing at stopping places en route. One chronicler took a longer view, writing that "in this way the Mura takes revenge, to this day, for colonial persecution."[136]

Short-term labor arrangements may have represented alternatives not only to the structures and requirements of aldeamento life but to the post-rebellion workers' corps that aimed to press independent, mobile Native peoples into service. When an American naval officer visited Barra (now Manaus), the provincial capital of Amazonas, in the early 1850s, he noted the presence of Muras in the vicinity. His hosts said that the Muras led "an idle, vagabond life," organized around hunting and fishing, though some occasionally worked for white residents of the town. Interestingly, most of these Muras brought their children to be baptized in Barra. The American traveler assumed (perhaps incorrectly) that they had little interest in the ceremony itself; rather, they aimed to "persuade some good-natured white man to stand as godfather, which secures the payment of the church fee (a *cruzado*), a bottle of spirits to the father, and a yard or two of cotton cloth to the mother." One of the most prominent local traders, an Italian immigrant, boasted that he was godfather to "half the tribe," who remained (as the American wrote) "thorough savages" after their baptism.[137] The Amazon was not the only region where such arrangements were common during the nineteenth century. In other parts of Brazil, too, Indigenous groups forged alliances with frontier settlers, often symbolized by the offering of children for baptism and reaffirmed by their parents' willingness to do periods of work on the settlers' estates or canoes.[138]

It mattered that Native peoples had control over the choice of patrons, and this may have been especially true of contexts in which autonomy had to be more fiercely defended. One group of Mundurukús, who lived near a rapidly expanding settler town in the 1840s, disappointed a visiting bishop by refusing to accept white godparents for their children's baptisms. They also insisted that the baptisms occur not in the town's church, but in their own village. (The bishop had little choice but to give his grudging consent.)[139] That same year, a war-ravaged group of Botocudos in Minas Gerais went to the opposite extreme, offering several of their children as gifts to a visiting dignitary in the region. Their purpose, they told the powerful white visitor, was to keep him "tame."[140]

In 1828, a Munduruku man permitted the French artist Hercule Florence to draw his portrait (figure 4.4). Perched on the edge of the canoe that belonged to the Russian Imperial Scientific Expedition, dipping his toes in the waters of the Tapajós, he seems content with the knife he had just acquired in trade.[141] Behind him are two

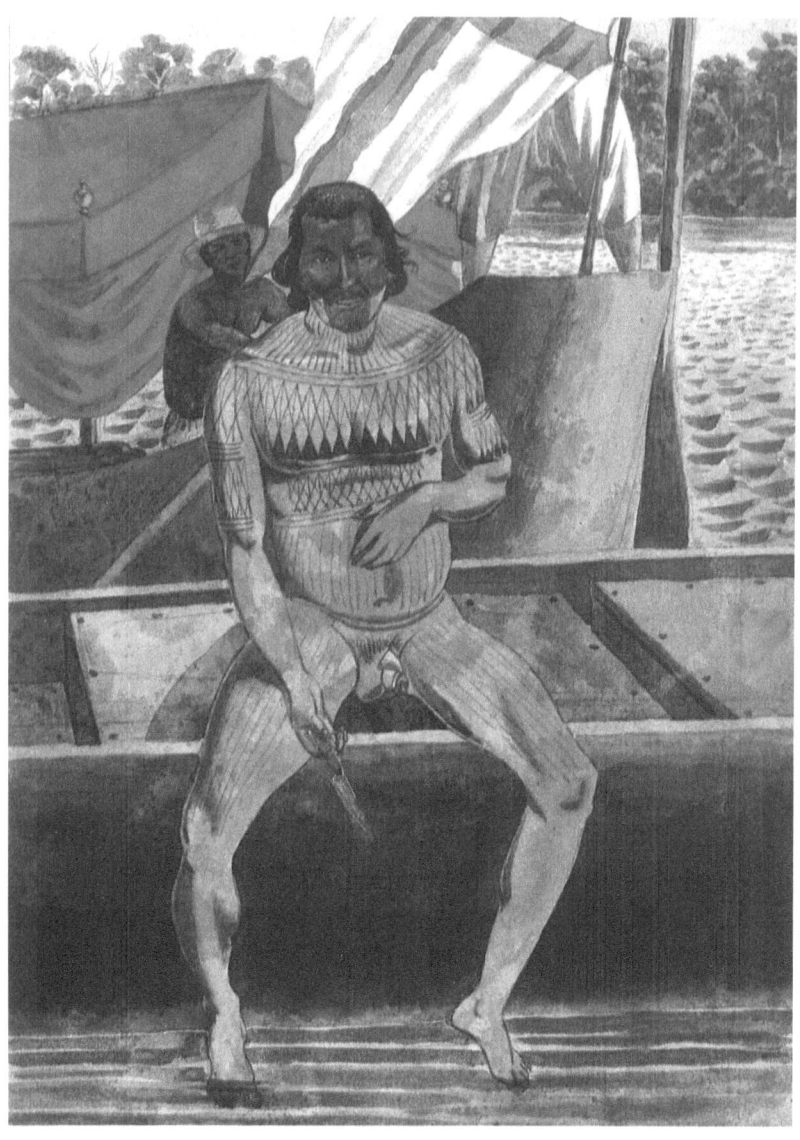

FIGURE 4.4 Portrait of a Mundurukú on the Tapajós River, 1828. The flag in the background is that of the Russian Navy.

Source: Hercule Florence, from the collections of the Russian Academy of Sciences in Saint Petersburg.

men from the expedition crew, one dark-skinned and the other white (judging from his lower legs, the only body part in view). The image suggests an easy coexistence between the various racial and ethnic groups of post-independence Brazil.

But looks could be deceiving, and Florence may have found the scene intriguing for that very reason. The Frenchman had just spent several years listening to white settlers describing their successful frontier conquests, and he also knew—from his tense passage through Guaikurú territories along the Brazil-Paraguay frontier in 1826–1827—that a return to Native warfare was always possible. As they pushed farther into the forests and rivers of the interior during the middle decades of that increasingly prosperous century, Brazilians may have ignored or forgotten this lesson, but they did so at their own peril. Famous Native warriors continued to live in their midst: they passed through towns and trading posts, temporarily resided in missions, rowed settlers' canoes, showed up uninvited at ranches and homesteads, and used the same fishing and hunting grounds.[142]

From time to time, there were ominous tidings. In 1854, a trader who claimed to oversee a Mura settlement on the Purús River wrote to the provincial president to warn of a regional plot reminiscent of the Cabanagem. Some Muras from Manacapurú, a large maloca-turned-aldeamento on the Solimões River, had recently come to the Purús on a secret mission. Among them was one José Capuham, charged by his chief, Vitoriano, to "invite all the Muras of this river to assassinate the whites living here." He was said to have gone around "telling his relatives that the whites pursue them for service"—forced labor, in other words—"so as to do away with them, and that it was necessary to close in on the whites."[143] The specificity of this information—the kin networks linking Mura groups from two major rivers and the named protagonists in the alleged plot—must have given it some weight among authorities, who were used to hearing nonspecific rumors of Native conspiracies. The notice, though unverified, likely led to increased official surveillance along the Purús and perhaps some preemptive attacks on Indigenous groups in the region. Perhaps the Muras desisted, or could not recruit enough participants from distant rivers; it is also quite possible that the plot never existed in the first place.[144] Either way, private efforts to develop trade and labor relations with so-called savage nations continued all along Brazil's extractive frontiers. They were too profitable to give up.[145]

Other reminders of a possible return to violence came when the Brazilians found themselves once again in desperate need of allies. The Guaikurú fought on the Brazilian side in the Paraguayan War (1864–1870), inflicting heavy losses on their longtime enemies in Paraguay but also making their allies chronically uneasy. Brazilian officers, like their Portuguese predecessors, fretted about relying on Guaikurú spies, scouts, and soldiers in the war.[146] As one provincial president complained, they "carry out only surprise attacks and do not enter into regular combat until after the conflict is already won, and then it is difficult to curb their excesses in killing and pillaging the losers." From the perspective of the Guaikurú, they were fighting a war within the broader war against the Paraguayans: their goal was to regain control over territory that had been lost to both countries over the decades.[147] About a thousand miles to the north during this same period, the Mura wanted nothing to do with the Paraguayan War, a bloody conflict far from their homelands. When authorities came to the Madeira River to draft Muras for military service in the war, beginning in 1867, Mura groups fled into the interior. Much later, Mura oral histories would connect these times of forced conscription to their longer experience of what they called the Big Catch.[148]

In 1883, an ancient Mura man and a group of Mundurukús hitched their canoes to a steamboat full of engineers charged with planning the Madeira-Mamoré railroad. The Indians were heading to work in the rubber groves near Humaitá on the Madeira River, and catching a lift from the steamboat shortened the trip considerably. Each man brought a bow and arrows and a hunting dog, animals "which they greatly esteem." The Mundurukús were of a "good appearance," still reputed to be "close friends of the whites to the point of fighting on their behalf," and the railroad commission secretary lauded their "dedication." The Mura man stood out as "more than a hundred years old, but still hardworking, and extremely dark and ugly in appearance." The big toe of his right foot was deformed, jutting away from the rest of his toes, from years of bracing his long bow when shooting arrows.[149]

Though the account almost surely exaggerated the Mura's age, one cannot help but wonder if the old man had been born around the time of the peace negotiations of 1784–1786. Even if he had come into the world a decade or two afterward, his parents and extended family members would have remembered the preceding half century of war against the whites and would have told vivid stories of the warriors' bravery and tenacity. Given his advanced years when the railroad engineers encountered him on the steamboat, we can assume that he had lived through the revival of Indigenous slavery in the early decades of the nineteenth century and the instability and militarization of a newly independent Brazil. Surely, he remembered the carnage of the Cabanagem Rebellion, much of it inflicted on his people by the Mundurukú, whose descendants were now his traveling companions and perhaps his bosses.[150] In his middle age, he would have experienced the menace of the workers' corps and the founding (and abandonment) of aldeamentos in Mura territories, as well as the ever-growing encroachment of cacao planters, river traders, nut collectors, and rubber tappers as the Amazon became the destination and final resting place of an enormous labor diaspora.[151]

Now, as he approached the twilight of his life, he had traveled far from his kin to do work that linked him to the voracious global demand for rubber. Perhaps he would die alone in the groves of Humaitá. But he was hardly "the last of his tribe," as some romantic writers of that century would have liked to believe.[152] Many Muras had gone before him, and many more would follow, hooking their canoes to steamboats, saving their strength for what lay ahead.

5   Against Extinction

WHEN THE MEN HEADED BACK from the rubber groves, the river turtles were just hauling themselves onto the beaches to deposit caches of eggs. The Indians did not stop, tempting as it was. They rowed steadily toward home—first down the big, turbulent river, then along the quiet streams that wound through the forest—and slowed only when their canoes pulled along familiar lakeshores. Parents, siblings, wives, and children were waiting to receive them. There were trade goods to share—aluminum pots, matches, axe heads, salt—and a flood of questions to answer about what they had seen and experienced during their time away. Distant kin came to visit, and all celebrated the return of the men and the abundance of the season.

The days that followed were spent fishing or hunting with the young people, who asked to hear the old stories as they passed through the landscape. That opening in the forest? It is the path to the place where the ancestors lived, and where the best urucum trees still grow, heavy with fruit. There you can see a deep, dark hole in the river, where the giant snake lies in wait; all canoes must avoid passing over it. And yes, this is the place where our warriors proved their bravery and drove away our enemies. They told the stories, the young people listened, and everyone knew: it had been a time of rubber and much more besides.[1]

When the white traveler arrived, he asked questions of a different sort. Notebook in hand, he addressed them one by one: How many had died in the last sickness, and how many were left in the maloca? Did any among them still speak the old language? He went inside their homes to inspect things. Why did they not make ornaments with feathers anymore, or canoes from bark? What did they buy at the trading post, and how much did they owe the trader there? He took pictures with his camera, bartered for a few old arrows, scribbled in his notebook, and then was already on his way. The Indians tried to stop him—to make him understand that even with all of their losses, they were not lost. But the man would not listen; his mind was made up. Perhaps he could hear only the settlers from the town downriver, who liked to say that there were no longer any real Indians in those parts.[2]

The narrative that Native peoples were disappearing into oblivion— that they were people without a history and without a future—was constructed in the nineteenth century and reaffirmed in the early decades of the twentieth century.[3] All across the Americas, writers described vanishing Indians or remnants of Indigenous polities. The genre has come to be known as "salvage ethnography." Whether the ethnographers worked in Brazil or the United States, whether they were amateurs or professionals, the images were similar: Indians succumbing to poverty, addiction, and demographic collapse, or else disappearing through mixture with other groups.[4]

The extinction narrative was taken up by policymakers and settlers, too. It fit like a puzzle piece into neocolonial visions of a hierarchy of races, in which civilization inevitably triumphed over barbarism. It also conveniently reinforced the land claims of whites, justifying Native dispossession and removal—or sweeping that whole violent, painful process under the rug.[5] As one French geographer wrote in the 1890s, having been commissioned by a Brazilian governor to explore the Tapajós River, "it will not be long before nothing remains of these errant gangs. But their lands, now widowed, will be there, still beautiful, rich, and awaiting the goodwill of men."[6] An American explorer, writing about the war-ravaged Botocudo, agreed: "There was this compensation for the loss of the tribe—that it would open up a richly endowed region to the benefits of civilization and Christianity."[7]

The argument rang loudly through the halls of power in Brazil, as in other parts of the Americas: if no "true Indians" remained, then their land was free for the taking.[8]

The aim of this chapter is to move beyond simple (and sometimes self-serving) narratives of Native decline and disappearance. If we place the "salvage ethnographies" in a broader frame of reference and alongside other historical sources about Brazil's Native peoples, new meanings and purposes come into view. What appeared to those writers—and to some present-day scholars—as signs of decadence were not always what they seemed. Sometimes they were processes of engagement, innovation, and adaptation that had been unfolding for a very long time.[9]

Rereading the Salvage Ethnography

In 1902, a search party found Guido Boggiani's camera, tripod, and glass plate negatives smashed and buried near his bones. These remains, scattered across a remote area of the Brazil-Paraguay borderlands, confirmed the murder of the Italian traveler a year earlier and led investigators to a little-known Chamacoco subgroup called the Tumrahá, who (it was said) had associated Boggiani's photography with witchcraft.[10] The Kadiwéu, in contrast, had permitted Boggiani to take dozens of portraits during his extended stay among them in 1897. The women were especially eager to pose for his camera, for which they received hair pomade, glass beads, cloth, and sugarcane alcohol.[11] The surviving negatives—those not destroyed at the time of his death—were later developed and published as an album of postcards, exotically appealing in their depiction of "Indigenous types," many of them in elaborate body paint (figure 5.1).

In his travel diaries, Boggiani expressed a sense of urgency in recording Kadiwéu artistry and other practices. He did so not because he foresaw his own untimely death, but because he viewed the Kadiwéu as the last vestiges of an Indigenous culture that soon would live only in memory, annihilated by imported diseases and vices like the very alcohol that he distributed.[12] He wrote in 1897,

> If all the photographs I have taken come out well, this single collection will be of considerable value. It will not only preserve the

FIGURE 5.1 "Caduveo (Mbayá) Indian Woman, Nabileque River," c. 1897. Photograph by Guido Boggiani.

Source: Robert Lehmann-Nitsche, *Colección Boggiani de tipos indígenas de la América Central* (Buenos Aires: Casa Rosauer, 1904).

character of a tribe that is historically and ethnographically among the most interesting and that is on the verge of total extinction; it will also preserve the memory of its extraordinary aptitude for ornamental art, which gives it special distinction among all the indigenous tribes of South America.[13]

While Boggiani was producing voluminous records of Native life on the margins of Brazil, other kinds of sources were going silent. As "civilizing" aims became increasingly marginal to state concerns, Indians faded from official view.[14] Ministerial reports, which once had whole sections devoted to Native settlement and catechism, began in the 1870s to neglect these topics altogether or addressed them only superficially. Flowery Latin phrases, quotations from European thinkers, and Positivist slogans increasingly took the place of empirical documentation. Even the old General Directorate of the Indians, which had produced detailed annual reports for provincial presidents since the late 1840s, could not be counted upon as a source of official information about incorporated and unincorporated Indigenous groups. The director responsible for the 1872 report from Mato Grosso, for example, simply reproduced, nearly verbatim, a report from two and a half decades earlier—perhaps confident that his superiors would not notice or care.[15] Meanwhile, local authorities charged with supervising activities in the Native aldeamentos often claimed that their Indian residents had disappeared. They peppered their reports with words like "few," "dispersed," "remnant," "mixed," and "civilized" to promote the idea that most Indians had either died or been successfully acculturated into the Brazilian masses—and that their communal lands were now open for private investment.[16]

Even as they reproduced similar ideas about decline and acculturation, Boggiani's diaries and photographs from 1892 and 1897 represent a treasure trove of information about the Kadiwéu, as well as their Chamacoco "servants" and kin. In the Italian's footsteps came a second traveler, a French surveyor named Émile Rivasseau, who spent two weeks in Kadiwéu villages around the very end of the century, participated in the demarcation of their territory, and lived in the region for about two decades.[17] Though neither was a professionally trained ethnographer, both men aimed to observe and record Kadiwéu cultural practices, and they sought to do so through participation in the daily activities of the group. Boggiani even acquired a basic facility in the Kadiwéu language, and he collected vocabulary words and a large variety of place names in the little-known interior of Kadiwéu territory.[18] His descriptions of the waterways, grasslands, seasonal rhythms, and plant and animal life are striking for their understanding of the complex ecology of the Pantanal wetlands.

For the Mura, we have an important pair of early ethnographies, too: the French missionary and linguist Constantin Tastevin and—right on his heels, with a sense of having been beaten to the chase—the German-born ethnologist Curt Nimuendajú. Tastevin lived for about twenty years in Tefé, the town on the Solimões River that had once been called Ega; readers will remember that groups of peacemaking Muras had been hosted there back in the 1780s, when it was the largest colonial town for miles around. Tastevin's contacts with the Mura dated to 1922, when he visited their villages in the Autazes; the region's "greatest wealth," he asserted, was "its indigenous population, the Mura Indians." Though he relied on an interpreter, the missionary collected Mura vocabularies and myths, and his text on the Mura became a standard reference point for ethnologists.[19] Most directly, it informed the work of Nimuendajú, who went searching for the "bastion of the ancient customs of the Mura" several years later, in 1926.[20] But as he traveled through the Autazes region, Nimuendajú's disappointment grew. "I fear now, based on the collected information, that Father Tastevin already saw everything that was worth observing," he lamented.[21] The Muras he encountered would have been the subjects of "a wonderful study—if I had come at least thirty years earlier! Today these remains of the Mura are ethnographically almost worthless. . . . Their traditions are forgotten and the language almost extinct." His dependence on the sale of Native artifacts to museums might explain some of this bitterness.[22] Nimuendajú's disillusionment, however, should not lead us to discount what he *did* produce on the basis of his fieldwork among the Mura. This included a series of letters to a museum director friend about his travels, several academic essays, a synthesis of Mura history and culture for the *Handbook of South American Indians*, and a handful of surviving photographs.[23]

One of these is a sepia-toned portrait of a woman in a cotton shift, with a woven palm wall in the background (figure 5.2). No one would ever print it as a postcard, and there is nothing to identify the woman as Mura other than the ethnologist's handwritten label on the reverse.[24] Taken to document a process of decline and itself poorly preserved in a distant archive, the photograph carries the assumptions of salvage ethnography. At the same time, the woman's gaze is arresting, as if challenging the viewer to see that Mura history would not be so easily erased.

The ethnographers' sense that time was running out for them to document Native groups was not entirely ideological (or commercial). It did have a basis in the demographic realities of the day, as epidemics of smallpox, measles, yellow fever, and tuberculosis laid waste to Native communities during the second half of the nineteenth century and first decades of the twentieth century.[25] Efforts to more precisely measure Native populations, however, were deeply flawed. Counting people as "Indians" or as members of a particular ethnic group meant putting them in fixed and bounded categories, and it meant *not* counting people if they showed signs of mixing with other groups. It also required being in enough contact with people to count them in the first place. This might entail visiting villages dispersed through the forest or located on remote waterways, a difficult and potentially dangerous endeavor. For each community, one would have to account for demographic shifts that occurred seasonally, as people left to go trekking or paddling in search of sustenance, or to engage in trade or short-term labor contracts.[26] The act of counting was itself controversial within many Native communities. Nimuendajú, presenting his own demographic figures for the upper Rio Negro region, acknowledged that Indigenous groups tended to distrust those who arrived to count them—and with good reason, as censuses had been used for centuries as an instrument of state control.[27]

Numbers of Native peoples were also politicized, especially after the creation of a new federal agency, the Indian Protection Service (SPI), in 1910. The SPI built on earlier regimes of state tutelage and "pacification," with the goal of turning Indians into a stable rural labor force for an expanding extractive economy.[28] To this end, SPI officials

FIGURE 5.2 "Mura Indian woman from the village of Jauary-Autaz," c. 1926. Photograph by Curt Nimuendajú.

Courtesy of the Acervo Museu do Estado de Pernambuco/FUNDARPE.

visited Native communities and attempted to get more accurate head counts. They were often disappointed by what they found, and some turned to denouncing the circumstances that had led to the decline. According to one official who toured the Autazes villages in 1911, the Mura were "the bravest nation of yore, today transformed into groups of poor, addicted Indians, degraded and humiliated by the civilization to which they were welcomed." Many Indigenous people were ensnared in exploitive labor contracts—including with the very state appointees charged with their "protection." Some said there were three thousand Mura left in the Autazes region and others said five thousand; no one knew for sure.[29] It was around a decade later that Nimuendajú decided to take his own population counts among the Mura, since he had learned not to trust the assessments of local settlers or officials. He visited twenty of the twenty-five Mura villages he knew to exist to the south of the Amazon River, which included the Autazes region, and calculated a total Mura population of 1,150, with an additional 125 across the five villages that he did not visit.[30] But just a few years after his trip, in 1931, a state investigation determined that no Indians at all existed in the four municipalities that encompassed the lower Madeira River and Autazes—the Mura heartland. Backed by settler interests in the region, the investigation aimed to undercut the SPI's efforts to demarcate Mura territories.[31]

Putting such unreliable numbers aside, another approach is to look at the ethnonyms as they changed over time in the sources. At the beginning of the nineteenth century, the Kadiwéu had been described as one of six subgroups within the larger Guaikurú polity.[32] Six subgroups were still described in the 1840s, but this number dropped to just three in the 1860s, and only the Kadiwéu appeared in the sources from the 1890s onward.[33] As this trajectory suggests, the nineteenth century was a fatal century for the Guaikurú, as it was for so many other Indigenous groups throughout the Americas.[34]

But this was no simple history of extinction. The emblematic case that comes to mind is that of the Caiapó do Sul, who made appearances in earlier chapters of this book. After two centuries of intensive contacts with colonists in Central Brazil, the Caiapó do Sul were assumed to have disappeared around the early twentieth century, another casualty of the conflicts around land and labor that intensified as settlers expanded into Native territories. A generation of scholars wrote about them in the past tense.[35] But in the late 1970s, new linguistic evidence suggested that the Caiapó do Sul had never really gone "extinct." A Native group that lived on a remote tributary in northern Mato Grosso—many hundreds of miles away to the northwest—spoke the same language, and they called themselves Panará, which old vocabulary lists collected among the Caiapó do Sul translate as "the people." Sometime in the nineteenth century, it seems they had divided in two, following radically different trajectories. Panará oral histories even tell how they originally came from the east, where the whites were exceptionally wild and fierce, and had killed many of their ancestors.[36]

"Extinction"—like "isolation" or "integration"—is a bureaucratic category long used by the Brazilian state. It tells us very little about these wrenching histories of political division, or about divergent experiences of contact and withdrawal.[37] But perhaps the assumption of Caiapó extinction helped the survivors evade their enemies. At last, no one was looking for them; they did not have to cover their tracks.

Strategic Friendships and Useful Outsiders
The Kadiwéu leader known as Capitãozinho, or "Little Captain," dressed up for his formal portrait with Boggiani. His jacket, cut from dark wool, is ornamented with golden braid decorations, shiny buttons, and shoulder knots (figure 5.3). Likely earned by an ancestor in the Paraguayan War several decades earlier, the uniform confirmed that its wearer had powerful friends; in its finery, it affirmed Capitãozinho's status as a leader among the Kadiwéu. For similar reasons, Kadiwéu men in this period carried flintlock rifles that had been imported from Europe during the war, while their leaders proudly sported Remington rifles. Antiquated as they were, these uniforms and firearms featured prominently among Indigenous peoples in Brazil's western borderlands, well into the twentieth century.[38]

Many writers took a condescending view of such displays: Indians, they implied, had delusions of grandeur about their historical roles as allies. The French aristocrat Francis de Castelnau, who encountered one formally dressed Capitão at Albuquerque back in the 1840s,

FIGURE 5.3 "Caduveo (Mbayá) Indian, 'Capitancinho', Nabileque River," c. 1897. Photograph by Guido Boggiani.

Source: Robert Lehmann-Nitsche, *Colección Boggiani de tipos indígenas de la América Central* (Buenos Aires: Casa Rosauer, 1904).

ridiculed his use of an old tricorn hat and musty suit, which he claimed had been worn backwards. The outfit had been inherited from the leader's grandfather—perhaps one of the captains involved in the late-colonial peace negotiations—and Castelnau thought it looked a bit worse for its generations of wear.[39]

If some described them as shabby remnants of the past, what did these symbols mean to the Guaikurú and to their descendants, the Kadiwéu? The military uniforms, weapons, and titles harkened back to the initial peace agreement with the Portuguese in 1791 and to the moments when the alliance had been renewed over the course of the past century. After the Guaikurú and Kadiwéu fought in the Paraguayan War (1864–1870) on the Brazilian side, these items represented Native sacrifices on behalf of the nation. They could be used to remind imperial leaders of the most important form of compensation—land—that was owed to allies.

To this day, the Kadiwéu say that the Brazilian emperor, Dom Pedro II, promised the territorial reserve to the Kadiwéu after the war. As historians have pointed out, no document has ever been found to definitively trace the donation back to the emperor. But in telling this story down to the present day, the Kadiwéu (like other Native groups in Brazil) invoke the legendary figure of the emperor to legitimize their claim to territory.[40] Rivasseau added another essential detail from his informants: the reserve had been cemented by a political alliance the Kadiwéu made in 1898 with a regional strongman who, in recompense for the Indians' service as mercenaries during a time of political unrest, advocated their cause in the halls of the newly constituted government.[41] Against significant odds, a reserve of 373,024 hectares was successfully demarcated in 1899–1900 and formally recognized by the state of Mato Grosso in 1903. The alliances and martial sacrifices made by generations of Kadiwéus were frequently invoked by their descendants when describing the historical origins of the reserve. "These lands cost the blood of our grandfathers," one Kadiwéu man told an anthropologist in the 1980s.[42]

To outside observers, strategic friendships could look a lot like subordination or debasement. The late-nineteenth-century ethnographers noted, for example, that the Kadiwéu made alliances with individual ranchers—and even with those who actively encroached on Kadiwéu territory. The Indians provided temporary labor on the ranches or transport canoes in exchange for benefits like protection from enemies or desirable trade goods.[43] This would seem to be a traditional patron-client relationship, with the Kadiwéu in a position of dependency, but there is evidence (explored later in this chapter) that ranchers needed to behave like allies if they were to remain in Kadiwéu territories.

Native groups were as vulnerable to factionalism as ever—divisiveness was embedded in their social organization and intensified with contact—and so it should come as no surprise that some Kadiwéus rejected the alliances altogether, or aligned themselves with opposing factions of ranchers. Boggiani described one aging Kadiwéu leader, Nauvilla, as "more or less the vassal" of Colonel Antônio Joaquim Malheiros, a Portuguese immigrant and former Indian administrator who claimed a vast tract of land traditionally used by the Kadiwéu. Other (younger) Kadiwéu leaders like Capitãozinho, however, despised Malheiros as an interloper and tyrant. In the late 1890s, Nauvilla allegedly aided a punitive expedition sponsored by Malheiros, guiding it to the Kadiwéu village of Nalique, which was then sacked and destroyed. In retribution, the Nalique villagers forced Nauvilla and his band to flee their homes and live like fugitives.[44] Boggiani found himself at the center of these disputes when he urged the Kadiwéu to make peace with their long-time adversary. Other ranchers, aligned against Malheiros, then plotted to have the Italian traveler killed, as such a peace agreement would have deprived them of valuable Kadiwéu assistance in cattle rustling. They supposedly convinced a Kadiwéu man to carry out the assassination, and he, in turn, fabricated a story about how Boggiani had been paid by Malheiros to betray the Indians. Luckily for Boggiani—who later found out that he was "within a hair's breadth of being assassinated"—Kadiwéu leaders at Nalique came to his defense. (He had reminded his hosts that if he were planning such a betrayal, he would not have given them gunpowder and bullets for their weapons!)[45]

Many Kadiwéus likely counted Boggiani as a key ally, because he was one of the first whites to live among them like a Kadiwéu, eating as they ate, dressing as they dressed, and participating in their games and dances.[46] Boggiani even took a Native "wife" for a very brief time: a Chamacoco slave whom he bought for "ten meters of cotton cloth, some brightly colored scarves, and a few small things of little importance." He was surprisingly candid in his diaries about this "nuptial" contract, which came to an end when the woman returned to her original master, taking some of the Italian's belongings with her.[47] Boggiani may have been unique in the extent of his immersion among the Kadiwéu, but his experience reflected deeper patterns. Short-term, selective alliances with useful outsiders—some of whom were incorporated as Indians, drawn into their economic networks, and embroiled in their disputes—go back to the colonial period.

When Nimuendajú visited the Mura in the Autazes region, he, too, found himself quickly drawn into Mura struggles against rapacious settlers and traders. "Instead of an ethnographic collection," he admitted to his friend, "I brought back a bundle of complaints about land invasions and other poor treatment at the hands of the *civilizados*."[48] Some Muras had tried to "compel me to stay among them, to help them in the defense of their rights against the intruders. They even offered me the few products they had, wanting to give me Brazil nuts (*castanhas*), etc. They later went to Manaus to demand at the Inspectorate of Indians that I be returned to them!"[49] The Muras' engagement with Nimuendajú was part of their broader effort to respond to an interrelated set of impositions. These included the coming of the SPI as a new institution attempting to exert state control; the intensification of extractive activities in the region after the end of the rubber boom, as settlers focused their attention on other valuable export products, such as Brazil nuts; and the escalation of land-grabbing schemes involving settlers, local officials, and SPI administrators. In the 1910s, Mura chiefs had gone to Manaus to protest predatory labor recruitment; they also tried to denounce abusive practices when newly installed SPI officials came through Mura communities on inspection tours.[50] By the 1920s, the Mura would have been on the lookout for new intermediaries and allies, as the competition over the resource-rich rivers and lakes of the interior grew more fierce. They would have taken note of Nimuendajú's habit of traveling to villages alone in a small boat, and his focus on gaining their trust and acceptance while he stayed with them.[51]

The Mura had a long reputation for harboring outsiders, especially those who rejected (or were rejected by) mainstream society. Back in

1785, one colonial official had written that there were "many people taking refuge among them, and also people kidnapped from the villages, all passing under the name of Muras."[52] Almost a century later, in 1875, they were described by a visiting official as "very swarthy," with kinky hair and beards, which "shows us that this tribe from time immemorial has served as a refuge for deserters and fugitive Blacks."[53] Father Tastevin framed it as an inverse historical choice, and one with an unexpectedly positive dimension: "The Mura never had a good reputation. As a nation in love with liberty and vagabondage, incapable of understanding the advantages that Portuguese domination brought to them, they refused until the end of the eighteenth century to make friends with the whites. Conversely, as a nation generous and hospitable to the weak, they served as a refuge for all the martyred slaves and for all the Indians reduced to servitude. From there came the mixture of blood visible in their descendants." During his visits to Mura communities in the Autazes in the early 1920s, Tastevin found ample evidence of Afro-Brazilian cultural influences on Mura songs and dances, as well as terms borrowed from other Indigenous languages, the língua geral, and Portuguese.[54]

The salvage ethnography also shows that the Mura of the Autazes sustained far-flung networks with Native groups on the Purús, Juruá, Madeira, Solimões, and Japurá Rivers.[55] Some Muras even became leaders among other, less powerful ethnic groups. In the 1870s, for example, an American missionary on the Purús River told the story of a Mura river trader who was "endowed with more than ordinary intelligence." He "left his tribal horde and mingled with" the Paumari people, "who speedily recognized unusual abilities in the stranger, and elected him tuchana [*tuxáua*, or chief]" despite his outsider status. A likely factor in this choice was the Mura trader's commercial savviness. Indeed, the missionary had heard of his scheme to float a raft full of turtles some five hundred miles down the Purús, "so as to barter them for dry goods and hardware in the wet season when fish and game is scarce." The missionary emphasized that that the Mura trader was still gullible—apparently, he had been tricked by a Brazilian merchant en route into accepting a relatively small cash note—but the more notable aspect of the story is the Mura's rise to prominence among the Paumari, thanks to his entrepreneurial approach to interethnic trade.[56]

Yet the standard image of the Mura in this period was one of degeneration through mixing. Inspired by ideologies of scientific racism, one SPI official wrote in 1912 that "what exists in the region of Autaz under the denomination of Mura Indians is a crossed population, mixed with diverse ethnic elements. . . . The pure indigenous racial type, that of the Autaz, has disappeared completely, along with the traditions and customs of the heathens." The contemporary Mura, in the official's view, were only "so-called Indians."[57] Tastevin, to his credit, turned this image on its head. It was the "bohemian" lifestyle—with its mixed marriages, cultural borrowing, and long-distance trading and socializing by canoe—that was the very definition of Mura-ness.[58]

Modes of Consumption and Exchange

Indigenous groups not only forged relationships with a range of non-Indigenous people; they also appropriated outsiders' goods and practices. The early ethnographers tended to see this process as degrading to Indians, and it should come as no surprise that alcohol (*aguardente, pinga,* or *cachaça*) featured prominently in these nineteenth-century discussions about Native dependence on products of Western origin. Alcohol abuse is still invoked in the narratives of decline that thread through Indigenous history—in Brazil as in other parts of the Americas and Oceania.[59] But we would be missing a great deal if we looked only at the destructive aspects of alcohol consumption and exchange in that history.

Castelnau, who visited the Kadiwéu back in the 1840s, said that the "passion for aguardente" had already taken hold of a group camped out near the Brazilian garrison of Albuquerque, and that they even sold their horses and firearms "to satisfy their fatal inclination" to drink.[60] This would not seem to bode well for cultural integrity. Neither do the early passages of Boggiani's diary, from 1892. When he arrived in Nalique, the main Kadiwéu village at the time, Boggiani found himself bombarded with requests for alcohol and entreaties of "*o meu amiiiiiigo!*" The Indians would ask for large or small bottles of pinga, or even just a cup, on credit. Boggiani claimed it was impossible to avoid getting entangled in trades involving his supplies of alcohol, and soon he was conducting an irresistibly good business in hides, meat, and artifacts.

The hidden cost for him was that he could not sleep well at night after making a trade, because the whole village erupted in singing and dancing until all the pinga had been consumed.[61]

A deeper reading of Boggiani's diaries reveals, however, that Kadiwéu consumption of alcohol was at this time sporadic, occasioned by the appearance of outsiders. The villagers would obtain a bottle or two, drink them immediately with total immoderation and collective festivity, and then go for several weeks without any. They may well have been addicted to the "delicious liquid," but they were not making the changes in their way of life that would have ensured a regular supply.[62] Rivasseau put it (rather idealistically) this way: "The Guaycurus consider it a weakness, an extreme lowness, to submit oneself to the demands of civilized life for Indians. They know it very well, and they prefer to renounce this life completely.... To guard [their liberty], they would rather die than consent... to becoming slaves of another's will." But they could still go to local trading posts to obtain a small supply of alcohol, maté tea, or tobacco; or they could work for a few weeks as cowhands, in order to gain temporary access to these products.[63] Indigenous leaders could expect to have their authority affirmed by outsiders who occasionally visited them, via gifts of alcohol that were then shared with the rest of the village. Boggiani, for example, had to be careful to favor Capitãozinho, the leader of Nalique, in his distribution of pinga.[64]

Similar modes of exchange and consumption can be seen in the colonial-era sources about the Guaikurú. In military commanders' reports from the late eighteenth and early nineteenth centuries, one finds evidence of the same low-stakes, short-term trading for alcohol and the desire to stay at some remove from the world of the whites while taking advantage of periodic contacts. Despite the intensity of this acquisitive process—which played out during the dry season, when the floodplains of the Paraguay River could be traversed with vast herds of horses—the Guaikurú were known for maintaining their social distance and habits of mobility.[65]

The ethnographies from the end of the nineteenth century show that the Kadiwéu still had many horses and firearms, half a century after Castelnau predicted they would sell them all for aguardente. This balancing act was difficult; by the mid-twentieth century, there is evidence that Kadiwéu herds had dwindled and that alcohol dominated the trade within and across the boundaries of the reserve.⁶⁶ But for a longer period than scholars have generally acknowledged, Indigenous peoples managed to appropriate, or "capture," the knowledge and goods of the whites without having to join white society or live according to its norms. And even when significant damage had been done, there was always the possibility of rejection and reversal.⁶⁷

For Indigenous peoples, this mode of temporary approximation has been historically important.⁶⁸ From a Catholic mission in Paraná, in southeastern Brazil, we have a fascinating expression of these purposes from a Kaingang chief named Manoel Aropquimbe. Writing in the late nineteenth century, a missionary lamented of Aropquimbe that "I was unable to make him realize the error of his ways, nor could I convince him that polygamy was a sin." When confronted,

> the old polygamist, instead of showing a desire to be educated, replied to me that he could not give up having his four women, because he was "*tremani*" (which means valiant). In living with us, he went on, he was not trying to find happiness—for he was much happier in the virgin forests, where game, fish, and fruit were more abundant, and where he never lacked provisions for his own sustenance or that of his large family. The true motive that justified his stay among us was that he could no longer go without our tools. [He said that] it was too late to accept a new religion, since he was already old; he could never even learn to make the sign of the cross.⁶⁹

It was a startlingly clear rebuke, one that few missionaries wanted to hear or record for posterity: the Kaingang leader had nothing but disdain for the evangelist message, and instead his primary motive was access to Western goods and technology—"the possession of which would guarantee him prestige, honor, and lots of women."⁷⁰ What might appear as abject dependence, in other words, could actually serve a broader goal: that of making whites and their products useful in the reproduction of Native power and prestige.

The crucial struggle, for Indigenous peoples, was against the "conquest of the palate," as one historian has described a centuries-old effort on the part of missionaries, state officials, and settlers. These would-be users of Native labor hoped that a taste for alcohol, salt, sugar, and tobacco would compel Indians to stay fixed in place and would harness them to work regimes. Exchanges of these products had long been essential to cross-cultural trade, going back to early contacts between whites and Native groups. By the nineteenth century, they bound clients to patrons, in exploitive relationships that became widespread across rural Brazil in that period and continue up to the present day.[71] Tastevin denounced the role of SPI officials in cynically promoting vice products among the Mura in the Autazes region, revealing one aspect of the rivalry between missionaries and secular officials. "Entering the village of Murutinga," he noted after his trip there in the early 1920s, "two things immediately catch one's eyes: a cantina where only alcohol and supposed perfumes are sold, the first to stupefy men and the second to seduce the women; and a stocks for breaking rebels. . . . For a liter of rum, for a few grams of hashish, for a bit of tobacco, the Mura is ready to give everything he has."[72] Similarly, Nimuendajú described how he made the long, difficult journey to the Mura village of Juma—rumored to be one of the last cradles of traditional Mura customs—only to find it deserted, its houses in a ruined state. Later, he came across thirty people from the abandoned village, a small fraction of those encountered by Tastevin a few years earlier. They were working on a settler's ranch in exchange for hashish, perpetually in a state of drunkenness.[73]

But alcohol use among Native groups in Brazil has a deeper and more complex history than these bleak descriptions would suggest. Unlike their Native counterparts in North America or Australia, Brazilian Indians had long concocted drinks from fermented manioc, corn, fruit, and plant sap; intoxication was central to their ritual life. The Mura, for example, made their own fermented drinks and also used paricá, a hallucinogen made from the roasted seeds of an Amazonian tree, long before they began consuming trade liquor. The settlers' distilled alcohol was, of course, stronger; back in the seventeenth century, when they first encountered French "fire wine," Native Brazilians remarked on how it left a pleasurable sensation of warmth in the belly and "clouded the heads" of those who drank large amounts. But whether a Native- or Western-style brew, alcohol could be used by Indians in ways disadvantageous to missionary or state control, and this may be why the aguardente trade was officially (if ineffectively) prohibited in colonial Indian villages in the mid-eighteenth century.[74] Indigenous groups often used alcohol or narcotics in defiance of such state (or Church) edicts, rejecting the standards of behavior that those attempted to enforce.

Intoxication was a means of alleviating, too, the tensions that arose from contact itself, with the penetration of alien beliefs and practices and the corrosion of Native lifeways.[75] As one group of Mura told Tastevin in the village of Capivara, laughing as they passed a joint around a circle, "It makes everything forgotten."[76] But this does not mean that all community norms were discarded. As Boggiani noted during his time with the Kadiwéu, community members who did not comport themselves "decently and tranquilly" when drunk were expelled from the community. Just one word from Capitãozinho was enough.[77]

Defense of Territory
When a group of Kadiwéu men returned to their village after a hunt, the women greeted them with songs and happy shouts, "as in the old days, when upon the return of combat expeditions, the women would come to receive their brave husbands." Walking ahead of the men and horses and carrying their weapons and some of the game, the women made "a triumphal entrance into the village"; Rivasseau thought they must have recalled the era when their men returned with plunder and a haul of new captives.[78] By the end of the nineteenth century, however, the Kadiwéu no longer conducted raids across the border, which was heavily patrolled by the Paraguayans. Rivasseau maintained that the last Kadiwéu raids in their old Chaco stomping grounds had occurred seven to eight years before his visit in the late 1890s. By that time, the Kadiwéu were obtaining their slaves mostly through barter instead of war. The French traveler described them as essentially defensive in their posture and said that they tried to hide from, rather than engage, the armed expeditions that were sent against them by land-hungry ranchers. In general, the late-nineteenth-century sources described the Guaikurú or Kadiwéu as warriors whose glory lived on only in stories and bravado, mock fights staged for visitors, or ritual combat during festivals.[79]

There is evidence in these same accounts, however, that Kadiwéu armed resistance was hardly a vestige of the past. In the 1890s, Brazilian settlers and traders still feared them and were reluctant to accompany the rather intrepid Boggiani into their territory. Upon arriving at the first Kadiwéu tolderia (encampment) along the Nabileque River, one of Boggiani's traveling companions fell into a dark mood, "his head filled with all kinds of stories and fears of nocturnal assaults, thieves, serpents, ferocious beasts, and all the great dangers to which we were exposed." To venture farther into Kadiwéu territory, Boggiani had to send the rest of his fearful party back to the main Brazilian trading post. He was then accompanied to the Kadiwéu village of Nalique only by his Chamacoco servant, who presumably had little choice in the matter.[80] Boggiani also noted that even peaceful Kadiwéu trading parties were viewed with suspicion by Indigenous groups in the Chaco. On a trip to Paraguay several years earlier, he had seen how the local Indians reacted to the arrival of several Kadiwéu itinerant traders, who were assumed to be spies: the Indians hastily packed up their tolderias to evade what they feared was an approaching war party of Kadiwéus.[81]

Again, these fears were not completely unfounded. Kadiwéu violence still shaped power relations and the control of territory around the end of the nineteenth century, as the Indians raided homesteads of settlers who had swindled them and issued orders of expulsion to those they did not consider friends. Boggiani described how one settler ignored such an order and then had his property invaded by Kadiwéus, who sought "to carry off as many objects as they could get their hands on, and to rip out the manioc roots" from the garden. Only Boggiani's intercession on the settler's behalf saved the place from being completely looted and secured him permission to remain for several more months in Kadiwéu territory.[82]

The Kadiwéu described themselves as surrounded by enemies, who were determined to seize their land on the pretext that the Kadiwéu had stolen horses and cattle. These allegations, the Kadiwéu told Rivasseau, "were all lies." They went on to say that many years before the Portuguese settler Antônio Joaquim Malheiros "had come to take possession of the land, where he had established various ranches, the Guaycurús were already fixed, established, rooted, and occupied in the raising of cattle and horses. Their 'NATION'—for that is how they designate their tribe—had been the first to occupy and settle all of the fields of this region and to possess cattle and horses, and they had always been livestock farmers and ranchers."[83] As this statement makes clear, the Kadiwéu had learned to adopt the discourses of rootedness, land usage, and territorial sovereignty that non-Indians often used to press their claims to land.

The necessity of such rhetorical moves is made clear in a description of a different Indigenous group, the Kaingang, by a provincial president in the 1880s. Alfredo d'Escragnolle Taunay described how "a semi-naked gang of these people wandered the streets of Curitiba, demanding tools, clothing, money, etc., and whining about having been mistreated by Brazilians and dispossessed of the lands that belonged to them." Not inclined to believe the Kaingang, he went on: "I proceeded to question them, and I saw that their complaints were vague, obscure, and without a precise objective. After all, what they framed as their possessions occupied enormous areas that could only satisfy their habits of nomadism and mere vagabondage."[84] In the last chapter, we saw how nineteenth-century legislation treated the territories of independent Native groups as "vacant" or "unused" and thus part of the public domain, with only small portions being reserved for use by Native peoples. Local authorities, furthermore, decided who was a "true Indian" (with potential right to land) and who was not.[85]

Territory thus became increasingly connected to Native identity over time, as Indigenous peoples became more wedded to legal definitions of "Indianness," established by the state, that bound them to specific territories. As they worked to have their lands demarcated and their boundaries protected from the encroachments of loggers, poachers, miners, and ranchers, new concepts of territory as something bounded and exclusive came into use—even among historically mobile peoples. Documentation of historical occupation and mapping of territory also became important tools in their political struggles, further shaping the process of territorialization.[86]

It makes sense that the Kadiwéu focused their armed efforts on a more geographically circumscribed space by the end of the century, once the reserve became politically possible. They selected this space, they recounted later, "not only because it was rich in game but because it was easy to defend against Indian hunters and Brazilian cattlemen."[87] By the time Rivasseau visited the Kadiwéu, the process of demarcating the reserve had begun, and Rivasseau himself was involved in the surveying of boundaries. It was also during this period that the Indians entered a period of full-blown "war" with Malheiros, with whom any kind of alliance had become impossible. Even a century later, in the 1990s, the Kadiwéu invoked the violent conflicts with Malheiros to commemorate the successful defense of their territory.[88]

Even as they affirmed their commitment to protecting the reserve—with arms, if necessary—the Kadiwéu continued traveling and working far beyond its limits. They followed old trails and made new ones. With the arrival of a railroad that linked São Paulo to western Mato Grosso and the Paraguay River, the Kadiwéu crossed the Bodoquena Mountains to make regular trips to a nearby train station—inaugurated in 1912 and named, appropriately enough, "Guaicurus"—where they sold animal hides for aguardente.[89] As one of Capitãozinho's sons, João Matexua, told an anthropologist decades later, the Kadiwéu had never been destined to be rich; instead, their fate was to always travel the Pantanal, as their ancestors had done. At the same time, Capitãozinho's legacy of defending territory lived on. "My father died, but I am still happy to fight for this land," Matexua asserted. "The Kadiwéu will never let this land be lost, because it is theirs."[90]

The picture that comes down to us of Mura territories in the late nineteenth century is grimmer. A French traveler described how "a strange sadness seems to imbue the very air you breathe" on the blackwater canals and lakes of the lower Japurá River: "At every step we are reminded of decayed missions and villages, of dispersed or extinct nations, on whose territory there now wander, rather than dwell, tribes who have themselves been ousted from their native soil. These large black sheets of water, when we first saw them, appeared as if they were in mourning for those who once peopled their shores." The Mura, the traveler noted correctly, had expanded into this territory in the eighteenth century, when much of the region had been depopulated by colonial slaving and epidemics (see chapter 1). But he went on to claim that "a dull apathy and savage melancholy have replaced in these

Indians their ancient warlike, ferocious humor."[91] The implication was clear: even the fearsome Mura warriors were fated to follow this same path of exile and extinction. They had already been reduced to small, "errant" bands.

The gloom lifts a bit if we remember that movement and dispersal are central to Mura history and identity. One anthropologist has described Mura territoriality as formed by a "process of departure from places, arrivals, returns—in short, displacements of their own accord"; "fragmentation and collapse are not the only motors."[92] Along the winding creeks, lakes, and channels that branched off of the main river tributaries, the Mura had developed a fishing and foraging life that, for them, represented a positive choice—rather than something forced upon them by desperate circumstances.[93] In the nineteenth and early twentieth centuries, the fame of Mura fishermen was still widespread among Indians and non-Indians alike. Tastevin wrote that he would "never forget the almost religious admiration with which an old Catauixi man told me of their feats"—and the Catauixi were renowned fishermen themselves.[94]

This helps explain why most Mura struggles in this period revolved around efforts to continue traveling, migrating, and collecting aquatic and forest resources as they pleased. During the rubber era—remembered by Native peoples of the region as the "time of the bosses" (*tempo dos patrões*)—migrants from Northeastern Brazil poured into the Amazon to work in the extraction of latex, occupying Indigenous territories and igniting new social conflicts. At the same time, prominent settler families, merchants, and commercial firms moved aggressively to turn those territories into private properties. They often found willing collaborators in local and state officials.[95] Mura oral histories describe how traditional Mura territories came to be sliced up and sold and how their ancestors were coerced into serving as peons for the new owners of the land. To this day, their descendants might still pay "rent" (in goods or labor) to the heirs of the original usurpers, in order to remain in their homelands.[96]

Beginning in the 1910s, SPI agents began demarcating scattered lots of land for the Mura—though not without angry opposition from settlers, who questioned whether the Mura were even Indians. The lots tended to be small and vulnerable to legal challenges. The SPI demarcation program was based on the notion that Indians, as legal minors, needed state protection from rapacious settlers and traders. At the same time, it aimed to restrict the Muras' mobility by confining them to ever smaller areas.[97] These, of course, were not new ideas or aims. They built on colonial sedentarization projects (missions, secular villages) and campaigns against Indigenous mobility and absenteeism that dated back to the seventeenth and eighteenth centuries. The SPI also created "inspection posts" in Mura territories and villages. At these posts, agency officials monitored trade between Indians and river merchants; they tried to incentivize smaller population groups to move into closer proximity; and they directed the development of small-scale agricultural plots.[98] According to Tastevin, state officials in Manaus and local Indian administrators ordered that Mura chiefs not permit their men to go on long trips or lengthy absences, though such orders likely went unheeded.[99]

Alongside land usurpation, the demarcation of small lots, and efforts to restrict Indigenous mobility, this period saw constant efforts to lay claim to the rubber trees and Brazil nut groves in Mura territories. The most productive areas were effectively cordoned off for settlers' exclusive use. Some commercial houses in the Amazon even set up their bases of operation at the mouths of rivers, in an attempt to block any navigation to resources upriver.[100] The closing of waterways and nut groves struck at the heart of Mura lifeways and subsistence practices. Some Muras moved to more isolated and inaccessible places; others stayed put under new patronage relationships; and still more relocated to cities like Borba or Manaus, where they formed their own Mura enclaves.[101]

Other Mura groups responded to these provocations with violence. Nimuendajú, for example, reported that the Muras of Sapucaia-Oroca and Vista Alegre had killed an engineer who had gone to demarcate a plot of land within their territory on behalf of a settler. Already indicted and condemned for the murder, they were now reduced to "miserable, dispersed remnants." Locals told him that these Muras had lost all cultural distinctiveness, but Nimuendajú knew better than to take this assessment at face value. "One cannot trust the information given here in Borba," he noted, as it was a place where he had "noticed a great hostility against these poor people and against the Inspectorate of the Indians [or SPI], which sometimes takes their side."[102]

Occasionally, outside observers listened to the Mura themselves. A surprisingly sympathetic military engineer named João Augusto Zany—likely a descendant of the Colonel Francisco Ricardo Zany, who appeared in chapter 4 as both employer and tormentor of the Mura—visited the Autazes as part of an official expedition in 1911. The Mura, he wrote, might be dispersed and itinerant, but they "consider themselves to be the legitimate owners of the land that they occupy, and they always hope that the government will legalize their lands so that they can feel secure, without fear of losing the fruits of their labor."[103]

One apocryphal story, which circulated in the decades following bust in Brazil's rubber fortunes, is that the Mura had helped the British interloper Henry Wickham gather the rubber seeds that he smuggled from Santarém down the Amazon River and back to Britain in 1876. Called "the most fateful cargo ever to descend that river," thousands of the seeds were successfully transplanted in Southeast Asia, and those new plantations soon broke Brazil's global monopoly on rubber. Wickham's name would be forever reviled in Brazil, and the Mura would go down in history as his willing assistants in biopiracy—despite any clear evidence that they served in such a role.[104] The tale of Wickham's Native assistants, however, is revealing of more than long-standing settler antipathy against the Mura as the original "river corsairs" or paranoia about foreigners seeking to extract profit from the Amazon. Given the death and dispossession that always attended the extraction of latex in Native territories, there is some poetic justice in it, too.

The shores of Sampaio Lake, just off the Madeira River, were layered with history. Elaborate funeral urns—with human shapes and facial features molded out of clay—emerged from patches of dark, fertile soil that always hinted at sites of ancient habitation.[105] Generations of Mura families had lived beside its waters and nourished their children with its abundant fish. During the Cabanagem Rebellion, Mura warriors had set up a fortified spot on the lake, and from there they had gone to ambush and kill the notorious settler known as Bararoá. As the rubber crisis plunged the region into new levels of violence, the place had served as a refuge from forced labor recruitment.[106] When Nimuendajú visited Sampaio Lake, he found a group of about one hundred Muras still living there. "By their appearance and culture, I never would have recognized them as Indians," he admitted. "Nevertheless, they affirmed that they were Mura, even though none of them knew even one word of the primitive language."[107]

This exchange, recorded in the 1920s, echoes an episode from a century and a half earlier, recounted in a previous chapter of this book. A colonial administrator, having counted some two hundred Indians at one of the settlements established just after the peace agreement of the mid-1780s, reported that he could not discern which were Muras and which belonged to other ethnic groups. The Muras, he complained, refused to say where the other Indians were from, "and they say only that they are all Muras."[108] Over the centuries, as these examples suggest, outsiders have been far more preoccupied with cultural purity than Native peoples have ever been.[109]

Fewer than two hundred Kadiwéus remained in the 1890s, according to Boggiani.[110] When the young French anthropologist Claude Lévi-Strauss came to the reserve in 1935, he, too, asserted that there were only about two hundred Kadiwéus left in three main villages. He saw wretchedness and decline everywhere he looked. But between his visit and the writing of *Tristes Tropiques*, he read some of the earlier ethnographies, especially Boggiani's diaries. Lévi-Strauss admitted in his book that what he initially viewed as unstable or decadent had been recorded by other visitors in almost exactly the same form. For example, he feared that it had been his last opportunity to collect Kadiwéu face-painting designs but was then gratified to see that the anthropologist Darcy Ribeiro managed to gather nearly identical designs more than a decade later, at the end of the 1940s. Both of these collections, furthermore, closely resembled the designs compiled by Boggiani, some forty years earlier.[111] Ribeiro, as it turned out, also perceived these continuities when he brought Boggiani's book—brimming with portraits and body art motifs from the 1890s—with him into the field. As the Kadiwéu leafed through the book, they warmly remembered the Italian traveler from almost a half century earlier; and when Ribeiro shared the news of Boggiani's death at the hands of the Tumrahá, the Kadiwéu began celebrating him as one of their own fallen warriors, since he had been killed by their historical enemies. The book's bearer, Ribeiro, came to be identified as the "son" or "nephew" of Boggiani, and the book itself circulated throughout the village. At the end of the twentieth century, the elders still remembered both men as honorary Kadiwéus, their allies in the world of the whites.[112]

It should come as no surprise that, like their predecessors in the field, the twentieth-century anthropologists had to pay dearly for the portraits they took of the painted Kadiwéu women. Lévi-Strauss described how the women compelled him to pay to photograph them, *and* to photograph them so he would have to pay. "Hardly a day went by," he wrote, "but a woman came to me in some extraordinary get-up and obliged me, whether I wanted to or not, to pay her photographic homage, accompanied by a few milreis. Being anxious not to waste my film, I often just went through the motions and handed over the money."[113] Here, again, one sees the opportunistic way of dealing with foreigners and the appropriation of the photographic project. Rather than "proof of decadence," this was an example of the Kadiwéu adapting some of the modes of interaction with outsiders that had worked for them in the past. This only becomes clear when we (or Lévi-Strauss) consider a longer-term record with new eyes.[114]

The Indigenous peoples of Brazil, John Monteiro once wrote, "were not simply consumed by the steamroll of an advancing civilization, as supposed by the nineteenth-century thinkers (and a few from this century) under the assumptions of evolutionism, nor were they all decimated."[115] Like many other Native groups, the Kadiwéu and Mura survived and reinvented themselves in ancestral territories, officially demarcated reserves, and the expanding cities of Brazil's interior.

Conclusion

FOR A LONG TIME, contact has been framed as something exclusively done *to* Native peoples. There is good reason for this. Over the centuries, contact was imposed by the slave trader, on his armed expeditions to the interior, and by the missionary, as he looked for souls to save. The *sertanista* (backwoodsman) was officially contracted to achieve it, as he strung a line between trees in the forest and decorated it with sharp machetes and flashing mirrors. For decades now, the process of contact has been pushed heedlessly along by bulldozers, excavators, and chainsaws, as they clear trees, cut roads, and dig mines in or near Native territories. The loss of life that has accompanied the introduction of new pathogens and new forms of violence and exploitation is of such a magnitude and has occurred over such a long temporal scale that we can hardly comprehend it, much less put a precise number to it.

Many of those who survived initial contact were then subjected to a long-lasting assimilationist project. Its basic premise was that "pacified" Native peoples would perceive the advantages of civilization, shed their Native ways, and, finally, cease to be Indians.[1] Since at least the middle of the eighteenth century, the Luso-Brazilian state has claimed responsibility for paving the road to integration. Although the methods and outcomes varied widely over time, these efforts were almost always linked to control of territory—because the lands of Native "subjects" could be claimed by the Crown or because the alleged disappearance of Indians meant that their land could be more easily claimed by settlers. FUNAI (Brazil's National Indian Foundation, which succeeded the old SPI in 1967) was for several decades more protectionist than integrationist, but this is changing; the latter agenda is now promoted at the highest levels of government, especially among those who look nostalgically upon the days of military rule in Brazil. The current president often speaks of bringing isolated Native peoples into national society—"just like the Army, which did a wonderful job of it, incorporating Indians into the Armed Forces"—and opening up their lands to development.[2] As this example suggests, contact can be a euphemism for forced assimilation and erasure.

But contact has very often been initiated and controlled *by* Native peoples, to quite different ends. In the preceding chapters, we have seen how Indians developed a whole repertoire of creative strategies for maintaining their autonomy while engaging the colonial world in all its dangerous complexity. They decided to host—or kill—interlopers, to make alliances with the Portuguese (or the Spanish on the other side of the border), to take captives and negotiate the release of others, and to offer their services as guides or interpreters or mercenaries. They learned a new language, experimented with Christian rituals, adopted the horse and the gun, and acquired new tastes as well as vices. Many groups moved closer to whites temporarily—even seasonally—and then withdrew again into the forests and rivers of the interior to evade diseases and other threats to their survival. Others kept up intensive contacts over long periods of time without ever agreeing to settle, convert, or provide regular labor to the state or to settlers. Their Portuguese and Brazilian interlocutors were pleased, baffled, frustrated, or threatened by such choices, which is often why we know about them.

These contact strategies should not be seen as timeless continuities. Instead, they have been rooted in local experiences and shaped by the changing dynamics of colonialism as they played out from the early modern era to the present. What they have in common is the aim of self-determination. If Indigenous peoples wanted to be like whites, adopting their goods and practices, "they wanted to become so in their own way—and had no wish to remain so forever." This statement, from an anthropologist working among the Wari' peoples of the southwest Amazon, has broad historical relevance.[3] It affirms the basic principle that cultures are dynamic and grounded in lived experiences, rather than in fixed past traditions, and it emphasizes Native peoples' capacity for cultural persistence through transformation.

This emphasis is all the more important, I believe, in the current climate of rabid hostility toward Indigenous lives and rights in Brazil. Many non-Indigenous people who follow these developments—whether as scholars or allies—suspect that the gains of recent decades have been lost; they fear that the struggle is now futile, given the magnitude of the political, environmental, and public health problems that have arisen in the past few years. But not only is this defeatist, it is shortsighted. Indigenous communities in Brazil have lived through many eras of change and loss, yet they affirm their collective identities and bonds to one another and to the land. They still speak of hope. There is joy, pride, and sustenance to be found—even in homelands that have been burned or contaminated, even in communities that have been razed repeatedly to the ground. There are plans and aspirations, discussions of how things are and how they ought to be.[4]

In Brazil as in other parts of the world, opposition to Native self-determination runs deep. In recent years, the powerful agribusiness lobby has peddled the image of "fake" or "invented" Indians, so as to turn public opinion against processes of Indigenous land demarcation. Even billboards on rural highways proclaim the existence of such false Indians. They are rumored to be landless peasants, incited by anthropologists to identify themselves as Indigenous or encouraged by a "politicized" FUNAI to make such claims. Some are even accused of being migrants from neighboring countries like Paraguay, masquerading as Native Brazilians so as to claim territory and other resources. If real Indians *do* still exist in Brazil—so the story goes—they are only isolated "nomads" who wander aimlessly over the land, thus forfeiting any legitimate right to it, or they are violent "invaders," bent on the destruction of Brazilian farms and ranches.[5]

Against accusations of inauthenticity, contemporary Native groups across Brazil have powerfully affirmed their spiritual, historical, and ecological roots in particular places. They also have reminded their detractors that doing things associated with non-Indigenous people—like adopting new technology, spending time in cities or abroad, participating in the market, or pursuing higher levels of education—does not negate their Native identity. As this book has shown, such forms of engagement have been central to their collective survival for a very long time.

Confronting the old stereotype that they are nomadic and have no place in the modern Brazilian nation, Joênia Wapichana—the first Indigenous woman to be elected to Brazil's Chamber of Deputies—argues that "we have to fight this narrative that the indigenous peoples are an obstacle to development." Native peoples, she notes, contribute to the production of domestic food staples, to the tourism industry, and to the knowledge and protection of the country's biodiversity.[6] As hundreds of Indigenous activists asserted in an open letter before the 2012 meeting of the UN Conference on Sustainable Development, "[Our] traditional knowledge can bring about a better world." These convictions were reflected in the 2019 UN Global Assessment Report on Biodiversity and Ecosystem Services, which calls for "recognition of the knowledge, innovations and practices, institutions and values of Indigenous Peoples" and argues that "their inclusion and participation in environmental governance" is crucial to reversing the trend toward destruction of nature.[7] A glance at a satellite map makes this clear. In Brazilian states like Pará, Mato Grosso, and Rondônia, many Indigenous territories form forest islands—patches of vividly green landscape surrounded by a monotonous sea of soybean farms and cattle ranches.

With their lands legally demarcated—a process initially aided by Brazil's 1988 Constitution, which guaranteed Native peoples the right to live according to their own customs in their own traditional territories—some of the larger Indigenous groups have been able to prioritize economic self-sufficiency and local autonomy in the provisioning of goods and services. The Kayapó, for example, have their own truck drivers, pilots, policemen, medics, teachers, accountants, lawyers, and mechanics; the Xavante have established their own NGOs, which promote collective, sustainable enterprises like beekeeping and the production of handicrafts.[8] In general, seasonally mobile groups have found it much more difficult to get their lands demarcated—despite the fact that they, too, maintain strong attachments to the territory where they fish, hunt, and gather. They know its boundaries, navigational routes, and flora and fauna better than anyone, and they work to defend their lands against loggers, prospectors, poachers, and farmers of soy and sugarcane. Within the Americas, Brazil still has the largest number of groups recorded as "isolated"—with over a hundred such groups recognized by the state[9]—but far more Native peoples in Brazil would describe themselves as connected. Many have chosen to participate in networks of national and international solidarity and activism, framing their struggle as part of global Indigenous initiatives to secure political rights and territorial sovereignty.[10]

To counter the portrayal of Native peoples as instinctively violent, carrying out acts of senseless destruction against private enterprise, Indigenous leaders have emphasized what is purposeful and carefully planned in their actions, particularly when it comes to land reclamations. They have told of systematically reoccupying the land where their ancestors are buried—removing barbed wire or electric fences, dismantling bridges, replanting and restoring the landscape, and returning to do so after multiple evictions. They have denounced the violence directed against their communities, from anonymous death threats to harassment by police to drive-by shootings. On camera, they have shown their scars.[11] On the anniversary of the reclamation of their land in Western Brazil some two decades earlier, one Guarani-Kaiowá woman framed the struggle this way: "After many years, we came back here to die, in our own Jaguapiré! We're still here today. It's here that we're going to live and here that we're going to die."[12]

As I write this in 2020, the coronavirus is spreading rapidly throughout Brazil and Amazonia. Indigenous peoples have tended to understand the nature of this threat more quickly than others, since previous epidemics and strategies for controlling contact are preserved in their collective memories. Many groups have decided to isolate themselves, closing their villages to outsiders and blocking points of entry into their territories. Then, they have organized. They are working to ensure their food supply by saving seeds and organizing community fishing and collecting expeditions, circulating information about medicinal plants and other traditional remedies, setting up new or faster internet connections to obtain medical information without having to travel, translating public health guidance into indigenous languages, seeking international donations of hygiene products and protective gear, and putting in place special protections for elders.[13] Isolation is, of course, very difficult to maintain. In many villages, people live in large, communal houses, with several generations under one roof, sharing the same hammocks and food. Individuals are vulnerable to hunger and unrelated health issues, which may force them to travel to the city in search of social services and emergency funds. Meanwhile, outsiders pose a constant threat, as illegal gold miners and loggers are using this time of chaos and distraction to invade Indigenous territories. The federal government, for its part, actively promotes the disorder.[14]

Yet Indigenous peoples are still here. They mourn their elders who have died, but they refuse to be seen as collectively doomed in this crisis, rejecting the old idea that Native populations will inevitably disappear. They are recording their own accounts of this pandemic, reflecting on the experiences of their ancestors in times of sickness and isolation. The Tariano graduate student Jonilda Gouveia recently wrote about the memories shared by her grandmother, an 86-year-old Baniwa woman: "When she heard of the arrival of coronavirus in the city of Manaus, she felt desperate and afraid, remembering her childhood. My grandmother said that when her parents heard stories of horrible diseases, they went to isolate themselves in the midst of rocky formations (which she called the 'house of stone') located in the vicinity of their garden-homesteads and close to the streams. Remembering this, she wanted to go away to these places, to protect herself from the current situation."[15] As people all around the world confront the existential distress of ecological collapse and pandemic disease—which are, of course, intertwined processes—it is worth remembering that Indigenous societies have been dealing with these forms of disruption for a very long time.[16]

▼▲▼▲▼▲

How have the Kadiwéu (descendants of the Guaikurú) and the Mura carried on the struggle for autonomy in recent years? Autonomy is, as always, a relative term; neither group lives beyond the reach of the state or the global economy. Instead, they live at the edges. Like many other Indigenous communities, they receive intermittent state services, interact with agents of the state, and depend financially on arrangements with private parties, but they also seek to create or maintain their own forms of ethnic identity, community-building, and self-governance.[17]

About fifteen hundred Kadiwéus currently live on their reserve in Mato Grosso do Sul, which encompasses over two thousand square miles on the edge of the Pantanal wetlands. Their politics is often confrontational, molded by the past and present attempts to encroach upon their land. Since the 1970s, the Kadiwéu have kidnapped government representatives and contractors to protest policies favoring ranchers, expelled anthropologists and other researchers from their villages, and occupied ranches established within the limits of their territory. They remain internally divided over the leasing of ranchlands to private parties, a controversial practice that began under the SPI in the 1950s and continues under Kadiwéu oversight in the present. As in the past, fragile peace agreements with the ranchers alternate with occupations, which have escalated in recent years.[18]

In these ranch occupations, the Kadiwéu have emphasized that their territorial rights derive from the alliance they made with Brazil during the Paraguayan War, back in the nineteenth century. "We fought with the Brazilian Army to defend the fatherland," a Kadiwéu captain explained in 2012—a year during which the Kadiwéu occupied some two dozen ranches within the reserve. "That's why today there are Brazilians here in Mato Grosso do Sul. If it were not for our fighting, that of our ancestors, this territory would belong to Paraguay.... But if back then we fought side by side, now we are fighting against. We didn't want it to get to this point, but now our fight is against the officials, soldiers, and the government."[19] As in previous relations with the state, a return to open conflict is always possible.

In the 1990s, the filmmaker Lúcia Murat hired Kadiwéu actors for *Brava Gente Brasileira*, a fictionalized depiction of the eighteenth-century interactions between the Kadiwéu and the Portuguese at Coimbra Fort.[20] She recently returned to the reserve to make a documentary. It shows that electricity, television, and evangelical churches have arrived in Kadiwéu villages, and most young men now range across the reserve on motorbikes instead of horses. They also go to regional cities like Bodoquena, Miranda, Aquidauana, or even the state capital of Campo Grande, where they sometimes experience poverty or social alienation. (The young man who starred in the original film is now a gas station attendant in the city.)[21] But even amid these changes, the Kadiwéu continue to make a forceful case for their territorial rights, cultural integrity, and historical alliance with Brazil. The Indigenous Community Association of the Kadiwéu Reserve (ACIRK), for example, has worked over the past decade and half to replace dozens of old (and often suspiciously missing) border markers along the edges of the reserve with larger, much heavier concrete monuments that will endure (figure C.1).[22] Today the Kadiwéu may

FIGURE C.1 Kadiwéu Reserve boundary marker 19.
Source: Photograph by Fernanda Prado Santana, courtesy of the Projeto Noleedi.

live and intermarry with the Terena and Kinikinau—whose histories, as descendants of the Guaná, have been long intertwined with theirs—and also with select whites, but leadership qualifications and social prestige are still attached to Kadiwéu ancestry.[23]

In 2019—Brazil's infamous "year of fire"—the Kadiwéu Reserve saw the largest number of fires of any Indigenous territory in the country, with over twelve hundred hotspots that season. Some were set on purpose by local ranchers and farmers; others were fueled by the dry grass and brush that remained after the illegal logging of forested areas; and all have been intensified by climate change. In response, more than two dozen Kadiwéus organized into firefighting brigades. They used their knowledge of fire's behavior in the landscape to more effectively battle the blazes, while employing traditional controlled burns to protect villages.[24] They also began collaborating with a team of scientists who are studying the effects of fire—both good and bad—on the complex ecosystems of savannas, forests, and wetlands that make up their territory. It is appropriately called the Noleedi Project, using the Kadiwéu word for fire.[25] This year, however, as the drought-stricken Pantanal region burns with even greater ferocity, Kadiwéu firefighters have had to make a difficult but necessary choice: to limit their work to the reserve to avoid exposing themselves to the coronavirus and bringing it back to their villages. Like other Indigenous communities across Brazil, the Kadiwéu are waiting to turn their collective energy toward "taming the fire" once again.[26]

There are now more than eighteen thousand Muras, spread across more than forty reserves (at various stages of legal demarcation) as well as in neighborhoods in Amazonian cities like Manaus, Borba, Autazes, and Manicoré. To this day, Mura communities often incorporate other ethnic groups through marriage and formal "pacts of collaboration," building on their earlier histories of Murification. Appropriating the regional term *caboclo*—which normally refers to a person of mixed race and is often used as a deprecatory term for an acculturated Indian—many Muras identify themselves as the "legitimate caboclos" of the rivers and lakes of Amazonia. They are a people that has been transformed through their long history of contact with other kinds of people, and they insist upon this identity in the face of allegations that they are too mixed or acculturated to be real Indians.[27]

A growing cohort of Mura teachers have advocated for a reframing of their people's history. They want to deemphasize histories of attacks, exploitation, and devastation, because they see these as reinforcing the belief that the Mura were eliminated in the past. Instead, their hope is to recover useful histories of resistance, going back to the time of warfare against the Portuguese in the eighteenth century and to the Cabanagem Rebellion in the nineteenth century.[28] In 2017—a year of particularly ruthless attacks by local landowners, in coordination with municipal police and politicians—Mura communities and individuals did not back down. They denounced illegal logging on the reserves, demanded the right to be consulted about potassium mining, dismantled private fishing nets on rivers, corralled water buffalo that had been turned loose on their land, and confronted those opposed to the legal demarcation of Indigenous territories. They also protested in newly visible ways (figure C.2).[29]

Many Muras have come to take pride in self-identifying as *ciganos* (gypsies) or *andejos* (wanderers)—words that have been leveled against them

FIGURE C.2 First march of the Mura Indigenous people, 2019. A large Mura group from Autazes marches in opposition to potassium mining in their territories. A sign lifted above the others reads "Eu Sou Mura" (I am Mura); the woman on the right of the banner wears a T-shirt featuring a Mura portrait from the colonial period.

Courtesy of José Rosha/Conselho Indigenista Missionário (CIMI).

since the colonial period. One anthropologist noted that the phrase she heard most often during her fieldwork was "O Mura não para": the Mura doesn't stop moving, doesn't stay still.[30] Their leaders and shamans play a central role in keeping kin groups together as they move through the landscape of Amazonian rivers, lakes, and streams.[31] They frequently cross the imposed (and often arbitrary) boundaries of the reserves to go hunting and fishing, to visit relatives and friends in other Mura territories and to attend festivals or political meetings. They go frequently to the cities to spend time in Mura enclaves there. Many Muras speak of the satisfaction of going in their canoes—now equipped with outboard motors—from place to place. In these movements, they affirm a migratory way of life with deep roots, and they reintegrate territories that were fragmented by the state a century ago. Instead of many small, scattered reserves, they envision a larger whole, in which "each place, each native village, is seen as a legitimate destination for constant Mura migrations."[32]

In these pandemic times, the strategies have necessarily shifted. Mura leaders from the villages of the Autazes region, for example, have worked in recent months to restrict movement in and out of their communities. They have refused entry to people arriving via the highway between Autazes and Manaus, and they have set up river patrols to prevent unregulated access to the villages by water, especially at night. One Mura resident of Autazes, anthropology graduate student Ana Mary Azevedo, described how Indigenous leaders decided to take the lead in fortifying the barriers to their communities, after seeing that the edicts of municipal authorities did nothing to stop the flow of outsiders.[33] We might recall the barriers built in the time of the Cabanagem, when Mura groups installed heavy logs across waterways to halt the invasion of their enemies. These protective barriers—old and new—will remain in the collective memory of communities throughout the Autazes, ready to reconstruct whenever needed.[34]

Indigenous groups across the Americas are often described as resilient, able to cope and adapt in the face of adversity. But resilience is a slippery concept. For all its positive connotations, resilience can be a burden borne by individuals and communities, who must face danger and instability on their own—a state of precarity that is then normalized.[35] What many Native peoples are seeking, in Brazil and elsewhere, is not a deeper well of collective resilience. Instead, their goal is a sea change in the attitudes and institutions of non-Indigenous society. They demand respect for Indigenous lives and cultures, recognition of their forms of autonomy, and legal confirmation of their territorial rights. ("Demarcation now!" has been the main rallying cry of recent mobilizations in Brazil's capital.) The territories of isolated peoples and those in recent contact deserve special protection, they remind the state, and their right to decide to live in isolation ought to be respected. On the other side of the coin, Indigenous leaders call for the redefinition of development as a process in which Native peoples can choose to participate, shaping its aims and outcomes while limiting its capacity to ravage people and nature.[36]

To bring about such transformations, Brazil's Indigenous peoples have long histories of collaboration and confrontation upon which to draw. Among themselves, they know how to build consensus while navigating the inevitable disagreements over which path to follow. They know when to invite non-Indigenous people to find common ground with them: shared goals, responsibilities, and attachments to local places. Against their opponents, they know how to wage battles that take many forms and last for many years, while remaining open to the potential for negotiation. Perhaps most importantly, they know how to cross boundaries—of geography, culture, technology, and language—in the ongoing quest for knowledge and understanding. Holding these histories close, they look to the future.

APPENDIX

Indigenous Groups Discussed in the Text

Alternate ethnonyms, spelling variations, and autodenominations (the latter italicized) are indicated in brackets.

These groups can also be found in the index.

Sources: Instituto Socioambiental, Povos Indígenas no Brasil, http://pib.socioambiental.org/en; Curt Nimuendajú, *Mapa etno-histórico do Brasil e regiões adjacentes* (Rio de Janeiro: IBGE, 1981 [1944]).

Akroá [Acorua]: A people in the Jê language family who were closely related to the Xavante and Xerente. Their historical territories encompassed northern Goiás (now the state of Tocantins) and Piauí.

Apinajé [Apinayé, Timbira Ocidentais]: Part of the Jê language family, they live in a region bordered by the Araguaia and Tocantins Rivers in what is now the state of Tocantins. Their population is about 2,280.

Bororo [*Boe*]: They currently live in discontinuous territories in Mato Grosso, and many still speak the Bororo language, which is considered part of the Macro-Jê linguistic branch. Their population is about 1,820.

Botocudo: An umbrella term used by Luso-Brazilians to refer to various different Indigenous groups located in the Atlantic rainforest region and the Southeast.

Caiapó do Sul [Cayapó / Kayapó do Sul / *Panará*]: Inhabitants of a vast expanse of Central Brazil and speakers of a Jê language, they disappeared from the historical sources in the early twentieth century. Linguistic and ethnographic evidence suggests, however, that they divided in the nineteenth century, with one group migrating northward into the forests of northern Mato Grosso and southern Pará. These descendants are known as **Panará**.

Chamacoco [Xamacoco / *Ishir*]: Part of the Samuko language family, small numbers of the Chamacoco live in Mato Grosso do Sul; a larger population lives in neighboring Paraguay.

Guaikurú [Mbayá / Guaykuru / Guaycuru / *Eyiguayegui*]: Speakers of a language in the Guaikurú family (shared by many peoples of the Chaco) and historically dubbed *índios cavaleiros*, or horsemen Indians, they occupied a vast territory in the Paraguay River Basin and Northern Chaco, extending from around the Taquari River in the modern Brazilian state of Mato Grosso do Sul to the Rio Jejuí in Paraguay. In the late eighteenth century, many subgroups of Guaikurú moved north and east into lands claimed by Brazil on the eastern side of the Paraguay River. Their descendants are known as **Kadiwéu**.

Guaná: An Aruak-speaking people living primarily in what is now the state of Mato Grosso do Sul, though some inhabited Mato Grosso and São Paulo. The Terena and Kinikinau are descendant subgroups of the Guaná, and their combined population is about 26,700.

Guarani-Kaiowá: Tupi-Guarani speakers, about 31,000 now live in in the southern region of Mato Grosso do Sul, while others live across the border in Paraguay.

Guató: Inhabitants of the Pantanal region with lands in the states of Mato Grosso and Mato Grosso do Sul, their language was little studied but thought to be within the Macro-Jê branch. Only a few speakers of Guató remain, and their population is about 420.

Juruna [Yudjá, Yuruna]: Inhabitants of Xingú River Basin in Pará and Mato Grosso, they speak a Tupian language. Their numbers are estimated at around 880.

Kadiwéu [Caduveo / Cadiueo / Cadigegodi]: Descendants of the Guaikurú (and speakers of a language in that family), their territory is in Mato Grosso do Sul to the east of the Paraguay River; it includes part of the Pantanal region. Their population is about 1,500. See also **Guaikurú**.

Kaingang [Kanhgág]: They live in the Southeastern states of São Paulo, Paraná, Santa Catarina, and Rio Grande do Sul. Their language is part of the Jê linguistic family. Their population is about 45,620.

Karajá [Carajá / Canajá / *Iny*]: Part of the Macro-Jê linguistic branch, they live in the Araguaia River valley, including the fluvial island known as the Ilha do Bananal. Their population is around 3,370.

Kayapó [*Mebêngôkre*]**:** Speakers of a Jê language, they occupy a huge area of the Central Brazilian plateau in the states of Pará and Mato Grosso. Their population is 11,680.

Kueretú [Cueretu]: Speakers of a language in the Tukano family with historical territories in the Japurá River region, they now live in Colombia, mostly in the vicinity of the Apaporis River.

Mbayá-Guaikurú: See **Guaikurú**.

Miranha [Miranya]: Living along the middle Solimões and Japurá Rivers in Amazonas state, with a smaller population across the border in Colombia, they speak a variant of the Bora language. About 1,460 live in Brazil.

Munduruku [Mandurucu / Mondurucu / *Wuyjuyu*]: Inhabiting territories throughout the Tapajós River valley, mostly in the states of

Pará and Amazonas, they speak a language in the Tupi branch. Their population is 13,750.

Mura: Originally speakers of a language isolate, they adopted Nheengatu (a lingua franca) and later Portuguese. With a historical territory that encompassed vast areas of the central Amazon (including the Solimões-Amazonas, Purús, Madeira, Japurá, and Negro River basins), most Muras now live in the region between the Madeira and Purús Rivers. Some also live in Mura enclaves in the cities of Amazonas state. Their population is 18,230. See also **Pirahã**.

Panará: Descendants of the Caiapó do Sul, they live in northern Mato Grosso and southern Pará near the Iriri River and Peixoto de Azevedo watershed. Their language is in the Jê family, and their numbers are estimated at about 540. See also **Caiapó do Sul.**

Payaguá [Paiaguá / *Evueví*]: Known as *índios canoeiros*, or canoemen Indians, of the Paraguay River Basin and Northern Chaco region, they belonged to the Guiakurú language family. The last Payaguás were documented as living near Asunción, Paraguay, in the mid-twentieth century.

Pirahã (*Hiaitsiihi*): A descendant subgroup of Mura who still speak a related dialect, they live in small groups along the Rio Maici, a tributary of the Marmelos River in Amazonas state. Their population is about 590. See also **Mura.**

Purí: Inhabitants of the Vale do Paraíba in what are now the states of Minas Gerais and Rio de Janeiro, they spoke a language in the Macro-Jê linguistic branch. Their population is 675.

Sateré-Mawé [Mawé / Maué / Mague]: Part of the Tupi language family, they live near the Amazon River at the border of Amazonas and Pará states. Their population is thought to be around 13,350.

Ticuna [Tikuna / *Magüta*]: Speakers of a language isolate, they occupy territories along the Upper Solimões River in Amazonas. In Brazil, their population is about 53,540; smaller numbers of Ticuna live in Colombia and Peru.

Torá [Turá]: Historically, a people of the Madeira River; they now live near the mouth of the Marmelos River in Amazonas state. Their language was little studied, and these days, they speak Portuguese. Their population is 330.

Xavante [Chavante / *A'uwe*]: Part of the Jê linguistic family and closely related to the Xerente, they lived in Central Brazil and gradually moved west to be wholly in Mato Grosso state. Their population is now around 22,260.

Xerente [Cherente / *Akwe*]: Speakers of a Jê language similar to that of the Xavante, they now live in Tocantins state. Their population is 3,510.

Xumana [Chumana / Jumana / Yumana]: An Aruak-speaking group that lived in the vicinity of the Japurá River.

Yurí [Jurí]: Part of the Ticuna linguistic family, they historically occupied territories between the Caquetá and Içá (Putumayo) Rivers; small numbers now live in Colombia near the Brazilian border.

Notes

Introduction

1. These details come from the documentary film *Estratégia Xavante*, dir. Belisário Franca (Giros and IDET, 2007).

2. Interview with Cidancri, *Estratégia Xavante*. On the challenges facing the Xavante during the 1950s–1970s, see Seth Garfield, *Indigenous Struggle at the Heart of Brazil: State Policy, Frontier Expansion, and the Xavante Indians, 1937–1988* (Durham, NC: Duke University Press, 2001), chs. 5–7.

3. Aracy Lopes da Silva, "Dois séculos e meio de história Xavante," in *História dos índios no Brasil*, ed. Manuela Carneiro da Cunha (São Paulo: Companhia das Letras, 1992), 357–78; Mary C. Karasch, *Before Brasília: Frontier Life in Central Brazil* (Albuquerque: University of New Mexico Press, 2016), 49–52, 107–11.

4. Paulo Cipassé Xavante, "Histórias de um líder Xavante," interview by Tereza Ruiz, Museu da Pessoa, November 25, 2014, http://www.museudapessoa.net/pt/destaque/historias-de-um-lider-xavante.

5. Laura R. Graham, "Fluid Subjectivity: Reflections on Self and Alternative Futures in the Autobiographical Narrative of Hiparidi Top'tiro, a Xavante Transcultural Leader," in *Fluent Selves: Autobiography, Person, and History in Lowland South America*, ed. Suzanne Oakdale and Magnus Course (Lincoln: University of Nebraska Press, 2014), 235–70.

6. Jurandir Siridiwê, who stayed in São Paulo, was a co-producer of *Estratégia Xavante*.

7. Amy Turner Bushnell, "Indigenous America and the Limits of the Atlantic World, 1493–1825," in *Atlantic History: A Critical Appraisal*, ed. Jack P. Greene and Philip Morgan (Oxford: Oxford University Press, 2009), 191; see

also David J. Weber, *Bárbaros: Spaniards and Their Savages in the Age of Enlightenment* (New Haven, CT: Yale University Press, 2005), 12.

8. Juliana Barr, "Geographies of Power: Mapping Indian Borders in the 'Borderlands' of the Early Southwest," *William and Mary Quarterly* 68, no. 1 (2011): 5–46; Daniel K. Richter, *Facing East from Indian Country: A Native History of Early America* (Cambridge, MA: Harvard University Press, 2001); Kate Fullagar and Michael A. McDonnell, eds., *Facing Empire: Indigenous Experiences in a Revolutionary Age* (Baltimore, MD: Johns Hopkins University Press, 2018).

9. Heather F. Roller, *Amazonian Routes: Indigenous Mobility and Colonial Communities in Northern Brazil* (Stanford, CA: Stanford University Press, 2014).

10. I follow David Weber in noting that independence is a relative term and is not meant to discount the kinds of independence that incorporated Indians managed to find within the colonial system. Weber, *Bárbaros*, 281n45.

11. On this aspiration among contemporary indigenous groups, see Cristiane Lasmar, *De volta ao lago de leite: Gênero e transformação no Alto Rio Negro* (São Paulo: Edusp/ISA, 2005), 257; I originally came across this reference in Janet M. Chernela, "Directions of Existence: Indigenous Women Domestics in the Paris of the Tropics," *Journal of Latin American and Caribbean Anthropology* 20 (2015): 204.

12. Patrícia Melo Sampaio, "Política indigenista no Brasil imperial," in *O Brasil Imperial*, ed. Keila Grinberg and Ricardo Salles (Rio de Janeiro: Civilização Brasileira, 2009), 1:197, quoting a report from the Ministry of Agriculture in 1877.

13. For a critique of the convention by which *colonial* serves only as a chronological marker, see Jean-Frédéric Schaub, "Is the 'Colonial Studies' Category Indispensable?," *Annales. Histoire, Sciences Sociales* 63, no. 3 (2008): 625–46.

14. The Mura were in a linguistic family of their own, whereas the Mbayá-Guaikurú were part of the larger Guaikurú language family (which encompassed the Abipón, Mocovi, Toba, Pilagá, Payaguá, and Mbayá peoples). The Mbayá occupied the northernmost territories, and in the eighteenth century, many of them migrated from Spanish-claimed territories on the western side of the Paraguay River to Portuguese-claimed territories on the eastern side. While Mbayá has remained the preferred Spanish ethnonym for this group, the Portuguese simply referred to them as Guaikurú or as *índios cavaleiros*, "horsemen Indians." In the eighteenth century, they called themselves Eyiguayegui, or "people of the eyiguá palm," referring to an important source of food. José Sánchez Labrador, *El Paraguay católico* (Buenos Aires: Imprenta de Coni Hermanos, 1910), 1:5.

15. On paying attention to different kinds of cultural landscapes, see Cynthia Radding, *Landscapes of Power and Identity: Comparative Histories in the Sonoran Desert and the Forests of Amazonia from Colony to Republic* (Durham, NC: Duke University Press, 2005).

16. This was the case, for example, with the military engineers and fort commanders Joaquim José Ferreira and Ricardo Franco de Almeida Serra, as well as the royally appointed naturalist Alexandre Rodrigues Ferreira, who each encountered the Mura and the Guaikurú in the late eighteenth century.

17. Bushnell, "Indigenous America," 208.

18. Perhaps the only others are the Mundurukú, Caiapó do Sul (Panará), Tupinambá, Xavante, and Bororo.

19. The most useful study of the Guaikurú across the Spanish-Portuguese divide is Francismar Alex Lopes de Carvalho, *Lealdades negociadas: Povos indígenas e a expansão dos impérios ibéricos nas regiões centrais da América do Sul (segunda metade do século XVIII)* (São Paulo: Alameda, 2014).

20. Stephen Warren makes this argument against the exceptionalism of the Shawnee in *The Worlds the Shawnees Made: Migration and Violence in Early America* (Chapel Hill: University of North Carolina Press, 2014), 18–19. About the Comanche, Pekka Hämäläinen writes that they "may have been exceptional in degree—no other Native American society seems to have managed to exert such concentrated and long-lasting dominance at colonial frontiers—but not in kind." Pekka Hämäläinen, "The Politics of Grass: European Expansion, Ecological Change, and Indigenous Power in the Southwest Borderlands," *William and Mary Quarterly* 67, no. 2 (2010): 206–7.

21. Pierre Lamaison and Pierre Bourdieu, "From Rules to Strategies: An Interview with Pierre Bourdieu," *Cultural Anthropology* 1, no. 1 (1986), 112–13.

22. Paul Cohen, "Was There an Amerindian Atlantic? Reflections on the Limits of a Historiographical Concept," *History of European Ideas* 34, no. 4 (2008), 388–410; Bushnell, "Indigenous America."

23. António Vilela do Amaral to Alexandre Rodrigues Ferreira, "Tratado da agricultura particular do Rio Negro," Barcelos, April 20, 1787, BNRJ, 21, 2, 020. Logs painted with urucum were taken as signs of Native defiance by members of colonial expeditions, according to Manoel da Costa Pereira, "Registo de hum Diário feito por Manoel da Costa Pereira da segunda entrada que fez com a Bandeira para a reducção dos Gentios Bororos e Araviras," October 1796, APMT, Cod. 25, fls. 122v–23v.

24. On the absence of a "bright frontier line," see Sean F. McEnroe, "Sites of Diplomacy, Violence, and Refuge: Topography and Negotiation in the Mountains of New Spain," *The Americas* 69, no. 2 (2012): 182. On European sovereignty as partial and limited to corridors and enclaves, see Lauren Benton, *In Search of Sovereignty: Law and Geography in European Empires, 1400–1900* (Cambridge: Cambridge University Press, 2010); Jeffers Lennox, *Homelands and Empires: Indigenous Spaces, Imperial Fictions, and Competition for Territory in Northeastern North America, 1690–1763* (Toronto: University of Toronto Press, 2017).

25. On the importance of local awareness of territorial extent, see Tamar Herzog, *Frontiers of Possession: Spain and Portugal in Europe and the Americas* (Cambridge, MA: Harvard University Press, 2015), 8–9.

26. The crab comparison is from the Franciscan friar Vicente do Salvador, *História do Brasil* (Curitiba: Juruá, 2007 [1627]), 39.

27. R. Brian Ferguson and Neil L. Whitehead, "The Violent Edge of Empire," in *War in the Tribal Zone: Expanding States and Indigenous Warfare*, ed. R. Brian Ferguson and Neil L. Whitehead (Santa Fe, NM: School of American Research Press, 1992), especially 3, 12–15.

28. This is the useful framing of Michael Witgen, *An Infinity of Nations: How the Native New World Shaped Early North America* (Philadelphia: University of Pennsylvania Press, 2011), focusing on the Anishinaabe and Dakota peoples of the interior of North America.

29. Jeremy Adelman and Stephen Aron, "From Borderlands to Borders: Empires, Nation-States, and the Peoples in between in North American History," *American Historical Review* 104, no. 3 (June 1999): 814–41.

30. Pekka Hämäläinen and Samuel Truett, "On Borderlands," *Journal of American History* 98, no. 2 (2011): 352. Important examples of this approach to South American borderlands include Guillaume Boccara, *Los vencedores: Los Mapuche en la época colonial* (San Pedro de Atacama/Santiago, Chile: Línea Editorial IIAM, 2007); Elisa Frühauf Garcia, *As diversas formas de ser índio: Políticas indígenas e políticas indigenistas no extremo sul da América portuguesa* (Rio de Janeiro: Arquivo Nacional, 2009); Silvia Espelt-Bombin, "Makers and Keepers of Networks: Amerindian Spaces, Migrations, and Exchanges in the Brazilian Amazon and French Guiana, 1600–1730," *Ethnohistory* 65, no. 4 (2018): 597–620; Mark Harris, "The Making of Regional Systems: The Tapajós/Madeira and Trombetas/Nhamundá Regions in the Lower Brazilian Amazon, Seventeenth and Eighteenth Centuries," *Ethnohistory* 65, no. 4 (2018): 621–45; Jeffrey Alan Erbig Jr., *Where Caciques and Mapmakers Met: Border Making in Eighteenth-Century South America* (Chapel Hill: University of North Carolina Press, 2020). For North and Central America, see Kathleen DuVal, *The Native Ground: Indians and Colonists in the Heart of the Continent* (Philadelphia: University of Pennsylvania Press, 2006); Juliana Barr, *Peace Came in the Form of a Woman: Indians and Spaniards in the Texas Borderlands* (Chapel Hill: University of North Carolina Press, 2007); Claudia García, *Etnogénesis, hibridación y consolidación de la identidad del pueblo Miskitu* (Madrid: Consejo Superior de Investigaciones Científicas, 2007); Pekka Hämäläinen, *Comanche Empire* (New Haven, CT: Yale University Press, 2008); Caroline A. Williams, "Living Between Empires: Diplomacy and Politics in the Late Eighteenth-Century Mosquitia," *The Americas* 70, no. 2 (2013): 237–68. A recent collection that reflects these new approaches while transcending traditional geographic divisions is Danna A. Levin Rojo and Cynthia Radding, eds., *The Oxford Handbook of Borderlands of the Iberian World* (Oxford: Oxford University Press, 2019).

31. "Imformação do Rio da Madeira, e dos mais rios que dezagoão nelle, de seos certoens, gentios delles, e de seos costumes, ritos, e ceremonias," n.d., Biblioteca Pública da Évora, Cod. CXV 2-15, no. 5, fls. 44v–45. I have

dated this document to 1714, because it refers to an episode in "the past year 1713" (fl. 43). It was likely written by João de Sampaio, a Jesuit at the mission of Canomã. I am grateful to Mark Harris for sharing a copy of this relatively unknown document with me, and to Marta Rosa Amoroso for helping me to decipher and interpret the passages about the Mura, especially the one that likely describes feasts and ritual combat. Curt Nimuendajú and others have described a different document, also by a Jesuit in 1714, as the first historical mention of the Mura, but that letter simply lists the Mura as one of many Native groups inhabiting the Madeira River: Bartolomeu Rodrigues to Jacinto de Carvalho, Guaicurupá dos Tupinambarana, May 2, 1714, in *Corografia histórica, cronográfica, genealógica, nobiliária e política do Império do Brasil*, ed. Alexandre J. de Mello Moraes (Rio de Janeiro: Tipografia Brasileira, 1872), 4:363; see also Curt Nimuendajú, "The Mura and Pirahã," in *Handbook of South American Indians*, ed. Julian H. Steward (Washington, DC: Smithsonian Institution, 1948), 3:255.

32. Alcida Rita Ramos, *Indigenism: Ethnic Politics in Brazil* (Madison: University of Wisconsin Press, 1998), 48–49.

33. John M. Monteiro, "The Heathen Castes of Sixteenth-Century Portuguese America: Unity, Diversity, and the Invention of the Brazilian Indians," *Hispanic American Historical Review* 80, no. 4 (2000): 703–5; Ângela Domingues, *Quando os índios eram vassalos: Colonização e relações de poder no Norte do Brasil na segunda metade do século XVIII* (Lisbon: Comissão Nacional para as Comemorações dos Descobrimentos Portugueses, 2000), 329.

34. "Imformação do Rio da Madeira," 45.

35. Ramos, *Indigenism*, 36 ("archetype of ferocious nomads"); David Louis Mead, "Caiapó do Sul, an Ethnohistory (1610–1920)," (PhD diss., University of Florida, 2010), 96 ("an 'errant' and 'pillaging' people"). Iberian debates about the validity of the territorial claims of mobile Native groups are summarized in Erbig, *Where Caciques and Mapmakers Met*, 58–60.

36. Hal Langfur, *The Forbidden Lands: Colonial Identity, Frontier Violence, and the Persistence of Brazil's Eastern Indians, 1750–1830* (Stanford, CA: Stanford University Press, 2006), 243–45. The most famous of the early accounts was Jean de Léry's description of Tupinambá cannibalism: *History of a Voyage to the Land of Brazil, Otherwise Called America*, trans. Janet Whatley (Berkeley: University of California Press, 1990 [1556]).

37. The key study of how Indian wars could be overtly manipulated in this way comes from northern New Spain. Sara Ortelli describes a situation in which local officials and settlers invoked the threat of war with "the Apache"—like "the Mura," a catchall term—so as to protect their own interests in the context of a royal reform effort at extending control over this frontier region. Sara Ortelli, *Trama de una guerra conveniente: Nueva Vizcaya y la sombra de los apaches (1748–1790)* (Mexico City: El Colegio de México, Centro de Estudios Históricos, 2007). On such "convenient wars" in the

Brazilian borderlands, see Carvalho, *Lealdades negociadas*, 151–57. On the Crown's assessment that Native groups might advantageously block the access of unwanted migrants and rivals, see Langfur, *The Forbidden Lands*; Nádia Farage, *As muralhas dos sertões: Os povos indígenas no Rio Branco e a colonização* (Rio de Janeiro: ANPOCS, 1991).

38. However, descriptions of Native peoples by state officials were often contradictory, ranging from images of their (potential) utility and loyalty to denunciations of their (presumed) insolence and hostility. On these images in the late colonial period, see Domingues, *Quando os índios eram vassalos*, 323, 336–42.

39. The best study of Native enslavement in Brazil, focusing on colonial São Paulo, is John M. Monteiro, *Blacks of the Land: Indian Slavery, Settler Society, and the Portuguese Colonial Enterprise in South America*, ed. and trans. James Woodard and Barbara Weinstein (Cambridge: Cambridge University Press, 2018).

40. For challenges to stereotypes around the "nomadism" of Native Brazilians, see Ramos, *Indigenism*, 33–40. The classic study of the mobility and other evasive tactics of those who were "barbaric by design" is James C. Scott, *The Art of Not Being Governed: An Anarchist History of Upland Southeast Asia* (New Haven, CT: Yale University Press, 2009).

41. James Axtell, "Prologue: The Ethnohistory of Native America," in *Natives and Newcomers: The Cultural Origins of North America* (Oxford: Oxford University Press, 2001), 1–12.

42. Yanna Yannakakis, "Bárbaros in the Archive" (panel, annual meeting of the American Historical Association and the Conference on Latin American History, Atlanta, January 8, 2016).

43. The quotation is from Guido Boggiani, *Os Caduveos* (Belo Horizonte: Editora Itatiaia, 1975), 140–41. Other nineteenth-century descriptions of the Kadiwéu using urucum can be found in Francis de Castelnau, *Expedição às regiões centrais da América do Sul* (Rio de Janeiro: Itatiaia, 2000), 366–67; Alfredo d'Escragnolle Taunay, *Scenas de viagem: Exploração entre os rios Taquary e Aquidauana no districto de Miranda* (Rio de Janeiro: Typographia Americana, 1868), 114–15.

44. Ailton Krenak, "O eterno retorno do encontro," Instituto Socioambiental, Povos Indígenas no Brasil, last modified April 27, 2018, https://pib.socioambiental.org/pt/O_eterno_retorno_do_encontro. See also Antonio Porro, "Os povos indígenas da Amazônia à chegada dos europeus," in *História da Igreja na Amazônia*, ed. Eduardo Hoornaert (Petrópolis: Vozes, 1992), 11.

45. Such a complex history of contact is traced for the Yanomami people of the Northwest Amazon in Bruce Albert, "A fumaça do metal: História e representações do contato entre os Yanomami," *Anuário Antropológico* 89 (1992): 151–89.

46. Carlos Fausto and Michael Heckenberger, "Introduction: Indigenous History and the History of the 'Indians,'" in *Time and Memory in Indigenous*

Amazonia: Anthropological Perspectives, ed. Carlos Fausto and Michael Heckenberger (Gainesville: University Press of Florida, 2007), 17.

47. Glenn H. Shepard Jr., "Ceci N'est Pas un Contacte: The Fetishization of Isolated Indigenous People along the Peru-Brazil Border," *Tipití: Journal of the Society for the Anthropology of Lowland South America* 14, no. 1 (2016): 135, 137. See also Neil Whitehead, "Native Peoples Confront Colonial Regimes in Northeastern South America (c. 1500–1900)," in *South America*, vol. 3, pt. 2 of *The Cambridge History of the Native Peoples of the Americas*, ed. Frank Salomon and Stuart B. Schwartz (Cambridge: Cambridge University Press, 1999), 386, 431.

48. Luísa Tombini Wittmann, *O Vapor e o Botoque: Imigrantes alemães e índios Xokleng no Vale do Itajaí/SC (1850–1926)* (Florianópolis: Letras Contemporâneas, 2007), 203, citing the report of SPI administrator Eduardo Hoerhann from 1921.

49. On the ways in which a colonial system based on slavery and coerced labor likely exacerbated the epidemics of centuries past, see Rafael Chambouleyron, Benedito Costa Barbosa, Fernanda Aires Bombardi, and Claudia Rocha de Sousa, "'Formidable Contagion': Epidemics, Work and Recruitment in Colonial Amazonia (1660–1750)," *História, Ciências, Saúde—Manguinhos* 18, no. 4 (2011): 987–1004.

50. Carlos Fausto, "'Vamos fazer lockdown na aldeia': governança indígena e desgoverno," *Nexo*, June 11, 2020, https://www.nexojornal.com.br/ensaio/debate/2020/'Vamos-fazer-lockdown-na-aldeia'-governança-indígena-e-desgoverno; Bruna Rocha and Rosamaria Loures, "In Amazonia, Libraries Are Being Set Alight," *OpenDemocracy*, July 21, 2020, https://www.opendemocracy.net/en/amazonia-libraries-are-being-set-alight/.

51. Alcida Ramos, "Indian Voices: Contact Experienced and Expressed," in *Rethinking History and Myth: Indigenous South American Perspectives on the Past*, ed. Jonathan D. Hill (Chicago: University of Illinois Press, 1988), 230; Albert, "A fumaça do metal," 181. For a call to consider the very different ways in which Indigenous peoples might conceptualize the arrival of Europeans—in some cases giving it a different emphasis or little importance at all—see Olivia Harris, "'The Coming of the White People': Reflections on the Mythologisation of History in Latin America," *Bulletin of Latin American Research* 14, no. 1 (1995): 9–24.

52. Marta Rosa Amoroso, "The Once and Future Amazon: New Horizons in Amazonian Studies" (workshop, Brown University, Providence, February 23, 2019).

53. Interview with Barreto Mura (Antônio da Silva Barreto), in Márcia Nunes Maciel (Márcia Mura), "Tecendo tradições indígenas" (PhD diss., Universidade de São Paulo, 2016), 1: 581–82. The poem is Henrique João Wilkens's *Muhuraida, ou O Triumfo da Fe, 1785* (Manaus: Universidade Federal do Amazonas, 1993).

54. John M. Monteiro, "Rethinking Amerindian Resistance and Persistence in Colonial Portuguese America," in *New Approaches to Resistance in Brazil and Mexico*, ed. John Gledhill and Patience A. Schell (Durham, NC: Duke University Press, 2012), 26–30.

55. Ricardo Franco de Almeida Serra, "Parecer sobre o aldeamento dos índios Uaicurus e Guanás com a descripção dos seus usos, religião, estabilidade e costumes (1803)," *Revista do Instituto Histórico e Geográfico Brasileiro* 7 (1845): 204–5.

56. Eduardo Viveiros de Castro, *From the Enemy's Point of View: Humanity and Divinity in an Amazonian Society* (Chicago: University of Chicago Press, 1992); Bruce Albert and Alcida Ramos, eds., *Pacificando o branco: Cosmologias do contato no Norte-Amazônico* (São Paulo: UNESP, 2002); Carlos Fausto and Michael Heckenberger, eds., *Time and Memory in Indigenous Amazonia: Anthropological Perspectives* (Gainesville: University Press of Florida, 2007); Aparecida Vilaça, *Strange Enemies: Indigenous Agency and Scenes of Encounters in Amazonia* (Durham, NC: Duke University Press, 2010); Carlos Fausto, *Warfare and Shamanism in Amazonia* (Cambridge: Cambridge University Press, 2012). A recent synthesis can be found in Michael L. Cepek, "Indigenous Difference: Rethinking Particularity in the Anthropology of Amazonia," *Journal of Latin American and Caribbean Anthropology* 18 (2013): 359–70.

57. Bruce Albert, "Introdução: Cosmologias do contato no Norte-Amazônico," in *Pacificando o branco: Cosmologias do contato no Norte-Amazônico*, ed. Bruce Albert and Alcida Ramos (São Paulo: UNESP, 2002), 15.

58. Fausto and Heckenberger, "Introduction," 16 (quotation). On the narrative of "pacification" in Brazilian history, see Hal Langfur, "Myths of Pacification: Brazilian Frontier Settlement and the Subjugation of the Bororo Indians," *Journal of Social History* 32, no. 4 (1999): 879–905; João Pacheco de Oliveira, "Pacificação e tutela militar na gestão de populações e territórios," *Mana* 20, no. 1 (2014): 125–61. Compelling challenges to such conventions in Spanish American historiography include Matthew Restall, *Seven Myths of the Spanish Conquest* (Oxford: Oxford University Press, 2003); Laura E. Matthew and Michel R. Oudijk, eds., *Indian Conquistadors: Indigenous Allies in the Conquest of Mesoamerica* (Norman: University of Oklahoma Press, 2007).

59. On this tension in the literature and the need for epistemological caution, see Frank Salomon, "Testimonies: The Making and Reading of Native South American Historical Sources," in *South America*, vol. 3, pt. 1 of Salomon and Schwartz, *The Cambridge History of the Native Peoples of the Americas*, 51. I thank Mark Harris for urging me, some years ago, to take a more critical approach to historical agency. See also Maria Cristina dos Santos and Guilherme Galhegos Felippe, "Apropriações possíveis de um protagonismo outro," *Revista Brasileira de História*, 37, no. 76 (2017): 115–36. On the denial of history and agency as part of a larger assault on Native autonomy, see Gerald Sider, *Living*

Indian Histories: Lumbee and Tuscarora People in North Carolina, 2nd ed. (Chapel Hill: University of North Carolina Press, 2003), 281–82.

60. Vânia Maria Losada Moreira, "Terras Indígenas do Espírito Santo sob o regime territorial de 1850," *Revista Brasileira de História* 22, no. 43 (2002): 166–67.

61. Davi Kopenawa and Bruce Albert, *The Falling Sky: Words of a Yanomami Shaman*, trans. Nicholas Elliott and Alison Dundy (Cambridge: Harvard University Press, 2013), 255.

62. Maria Regina Celestino de Almeida, "Os índios na história do Brasil no século XIX: Da invisibilidade ao protagonismo," *Revista História Hoje* 1, no. 2 (2012): 21–39. For in-depth portraits of these struggles for territory, see the recent documentaries *Martírio*, dir. Vincent Carelli, Tatiana Almeida, and Ernesto de Carvalho (Pragda, 2016), on the Guarani-Kaiowá of Mato Grosso do Sul; and *Tupinambá: O Retorno da Terra*, dir. Daniela Fernandes Alarcón (Repórter do Brasil, 2015), on the land reclamations of the Tupinambá of southern Bahia.

63. In referring to contemporary Indigenous groups in Brazil, I have followed the spelling conventions of the Instituto Socioambiental, Povos Indígenas no Brasil, https://pib.socioambiental.org. For useful reflections on problems of taxonomy for the Native Americas, see Frank Salomon and Stuart B. Schwartz, "Introduction," in *South America*, vol. 3, pt. 1 of Salomon and Schwartz, *The Cambridge History of the Native Peoples of the Americas*, 11–17.

64. John M. Monteiro, "Tupis, tapuias e historiadores: Estudos de história indígena a do indigenismo" (Tese de Livre Docência, Universidade Estadual de Campinas, 2001), ch. 3; see also Christophe Giudicelli, ed., *Luchas de clasificación: Las sociedades indígenas entre taxonomía, memoria y reapropiación* (Rosario, Argentina: Prohistoia, 2018).

65. See, for example, António José Pinto de Figueiredo to governor, Cuiabá, June 31, 1791, APMT, QM.TM.CA, Cx. 24, Doc. 1583.

66. Interview with Ondino Casimiro in the documentary film *Caminho de Mutum*, dir. Edson Tosta Matarezio Filho and Marília Senlle (Laboratório de Imagem e Som em Antropologia—Universidade de São Paulo, 2018). According to oral tradition among the Magüta, Yo´i fished their first people from a creek that remains a sacred site to this day: Marília Facó Soares, "Ticuna," Instituto Socioambiental, Povos Indígenas no Brasil, last modified August 20, 2018, https://pib.socioambiental.org/pt/Povo:Ticuna.

67. Jeffrey A. Erbig and Sergio Latini, "Across Archival Limits: Colonial Records, Changing Ethnonyms, and Geographies of Knowledge," *Ethnohistory* 66, no. 2 (2019): 249–73; and Beatriz Perrone-Moisés and Renato Sztutman, "Notícias de uma certa confederação Tamoio," *Mana* 16, no. 2 (2010): 401–33.

68. On ethnonyms among the Guaikurú, see Ana Lucia Herberts, "Panorama histórico dos Mbayá-Guaikuru entre os séculos XVI e XIX," in *Kadiwéu: Senhoras da arte, senhores da guerra*, ed. Giovani José da Silva (Curitiba:

Editora CRV, 2011), 17–19; Francismar Alex Lopes de Carvalho, "Etnogênese Mbayá-Guaykuru: Notas sobre emergência identitária, expansão territorial e resistência de um grupo étnico no vale do Rio Paraguai (c. 1650–1800)," *Revista de História e Estudos Culturais* 3, no. 4 (2006): 1–20.

69. Monteiro, "The Heathen Castes," 708; Christophe Giudicelli, "'Identidades' rebeldes. Soberanía colonial y poder de clasificación: sobre la categoría calchaquí (Tucumán, Santa Fe, siglos XVI–XVII)," in *América colonial: Denominaciones, clasificaciones e identidades*, ed. Alejandra Araya Espinoza and Jaime Valenzuela Márquez (Santiago de Chile: RIL Editores, 2010), 137–172; Garcia, *As diversas formas de ser índio*, 21; Cecilia Sheridan, "Social Control and Native Territoriality in Northeastern New Spain," in *Choice, Persuasion, and Coercion: Social Control on Spain's North American Frontiers*, ed. Jesús F. de la Teja and Ross Frank (Albuquerque: University of New Mexico Press, 2005), 125, 143; Marta Rosa Amoroso, "Documentos de Henrique João Wilckens: Introdução," in *Relatos da fronteira Amazônica no século XVIII: Alexandre Rodrigues Ferreira e Henrique João Wilckens*, ed. Marta Rosa Amoroso and Nádia Farage (São Paulo: Universidade de São Paulo / Núcleo de História Indígena e do Indigenismo, 1994), 11–13.

70. For synthetic treatments of ethnogenesis, see Stuart B. Schwartz and Frank Salomon, "New Peoples and New Kinds of People: Adaptation, Readjustment, and Ethnogenesis in South American Indigenous Societies (Colonial Era)," in *South America*, vol. 3, pt. 2 of Salomon and Schwartz, *The Cambridge History of the Native Peoples of the Americas*, 449–52; Jonathan Hill, ed., *History, Power, and Identity: Ethnogenesis in the Americas, 1492–1992* (Iowa City: University of Iowa Press, 1996). For a corrective to romantic visions of ethnogenesis, see James H. Sweet, "The Quiet Violence of Ethnogenesis," *William and Mary Quarterly* 68, no. 2 (2011): 209–14, which notes that "cultural mixture and ethnogenesis were rarely neutral exchanges among peoples of equal power, and it was through these hierarchies of power that collective identities emerged and evolved" (212). Influential case studies from Spanish America include Guillaume Boccara, "Etnogénesis mapuche: Resistencia y reestructuración entre los indígenas del centro-sur de Chile (siglos XVI–XVIII)," *Hispanic American Historical Review* 79, no. 3 (1999): 425–61; Garcia, *Etnogénesis, hibridación y consolidación de la identidad del pueblo Miskitu*.

71. Territorialization was originally discussed with reference to incorporated Native groups living in state-sponsored villages: João Pacheco de Oliveira, "Uma etnologia dos 'índios misturados'? Situação colonial, territorialização e fluxos culturais," *Mana* 4, no. 1 (1998): 47–77. Later, the concept was extended to the case of autonomous Native groups like the Mapuche: Guillaume Boccara, "Poder colonial e etnicidade no Chile: Territorialização e reestruturação entre os Mapuche da época colonial," *Tempo* 12, no. 23 (2007): 56–72.

72. Marta Rosa Amoroso, *Terra de índio: Imagens em aldeamentos do Império* (São Paulo: Editora Terceiro Nome, 2014), 79–80.

73. The best studies of this process focus on the Northeast of Brazil: José Maurício Andion Arruti, "A emergência dos 'remanescentes': Notas para o diálogo entre indígenas e quilombolas," *Mana* 3, no. 2 (1997): 7–38; João Pacheco de Oliveira, ed., *A viagem da volta: Ethnicidade, política e reelaboração cultural no Nordeste indígena* (Rio de Janeiro: Contracapa, 1999); Jan Hoffman French, *Legalizing Identities: Becoming Black or Indian in Brazil's Northeast* (Chapel Hill: University of North Carolina Press, 2009); Daniela Fernandes Alarcón, "O retorno da terra: As retomadas na aldeia Tupinambá da Serra do Padeiro, sul da Bahia" (MA thesis, Universidade de Brasília, 2013).

74. Maciel, "Tecendo tradições indígenas," 1: 409–10; Larry Rohter, "Language Born of Colonialism Thrives Again in Amazon," *New York Times*, August 28, 2005.

75. Erbig and Latini, "Across Archival Limits," 265–66.

76. Director Domingos de Macedo Ferreira to Henrique João Wilkens [?], Alvelos, December 31, 1788, AHU, Rio Negro Avulsos, Cx. 15, Doc. 558 (attachment).

77. Emilio Rivasseau, *A vida dos indios Guaycurús: Quinze dias nas suas aldeias (sul de Matto-Grosso)* (São Paulo: Companhia Editora Nacional, 1936), 64–65, see also 54–55.

78. The "most enduring divide" is from Hämäläinen and Truett, "On Borderlands," 355; on "bordered lands," see Adelman and Aron, "From Borderlands to Borders," 816.

Chapter 1

1. This reconstruction of what Native spies might have seen is based on a summary of forest collecting procedures for colonial expeditions written by Commerce Secretary Mathias José Ribeiro: "Formalidade, que se costuma observar no negócio feito nos Sertões," Belém, 27 November 1783, AHU, Pará Avulsos, Cx. 90, Doc. 7366; and on a mid-eighteenth-century description of the collecting expeditions written by the Jesuit missionary João Daniel, *Tesouro descoberto no máximo rio Amazonas* (Rio de Janeiro: Contraponto, 2004), 2:79–88.

2. This phrase comes from Kate Fullagar and Michael A. McDonnell, eds., *Facing Empire: Indigenous Experiences in a Revolutionary Age* (Baltimore: Johns Hopkins University Press, 2018).

3. For an innovative study of communication networks among Indians, Europeans, and Africans in the early American South, see Alejandra Dubcovsky, *Informed Power: Communication in the Early American South* (Cambridge, MA: Harvard University Press, 2016). On interethnic communication in Brazil, see Stuart B. Schwartz and Hal Langfur, "*Tapanhuns, Negros da Terra*, and *Curibocas*: Common Cause and Confrontation between Blacks and Natives in Colonial Brazil," in *Beyond Black and Red: African-Native Relations in Colonial Latin America*, ed. Matthew Restall (Albuquerque: University of New Mexico Press, 2005), 81–114.

4. José Simões de Carvalho to Manoel da Gama Lobo de Almada, 27 April 1787, APEP, Cod. 448, Doc. 9.

5. For a call to study how Native peoples constructed categories to make sense of the world, and how those categories were similar to, and different from, those of Europeans at the time, see Nancy Shoemaker, "Categories," in *Clearing a Path: Theorizing the Past in Native American Cultures*, ed. Nancy Shoemaker (New York: Routledge, 2002), 51–74.

6. Liminal figures are discussed in Shoemaker, "Categories," 60.

7. On the *cunhamenas* and their role in the slave trade and in negotiating resettlements of Native groups in colonial towns, see Barbara A. Sommer, "Colony of the Sertão: Amazonian Expeditions and the Indian Slave Trade," *The Americas* 61, no. 3 (2005): 401–28; and "Cracking Down on the Cunhamenas: Renegade Amazonian Traders under Pombaline Reform," *Journal of Latin American Studies* 38, no. 4 (2006): 767–91.

8. Heather F. Roller, "River Guides, Geographical Informants, and Colonial Field Agents in the Portuguese Amazon," *Colonial Latin American Review* 21, no. 1 (2012): 101–26; Ângela Domingues, *Quando os índios eram vassalos: Colonização e relações de poder no Norte do Brasil na segunda metade do século XVIII* (Lisbon: Comissão Nacional para as Comemorações dos Descobrimentos Portugueses, 2000), 238–45.

9. Colonial Indian legislation in Brazil often has been portrayed as contradictory and inconsistent, but some scholars argue that this was the result of laws and policies that purposefully distinguished between different categories of Indians, treating, for example, "friendly Indians" very differently from "hostile Indians." Beatriz Perrone-Moisés, "Índios livres e índios escravos: Os princípios da legislação indigenista do período colonial (séculos XVI a XVIII)," in *História dos índios no Brasil*, ed. Manuela Carneiro da Cunha (São Paulo: Schwarcz, 1992), 117; Pedro Puntoni, *A guerra dos bárbaros: Povos indígenas e a colonização do sertão nordeste do Brasil, 1650–1720* (São Paulo: Hucitec/Edusp/Fapesp, 2002), 60.

10. José Sánchez Labrador, *El Paraguay católico* (Buenos Aires: Imprenta de Coni Hermanos, 1910), 2:132. The Jesuit wrote this account after his expulsion, during his exile in Italy, probably in the early 1770s.

11. The Guaikurú exacted revenge nonetheless: they subsequently captured the governor's sister and two nieces and staged attacks on numerous properties near Asunción. Barbara Ganson, "The Evueví of Paraguay: Adaptive Strategies and Responses to Colonialism, 1528–1811," *The Americas* 45, no. 4 (1989): 474–75. Ganson adds that "memories of this tragic event lingered in the minds of the Chaco Indian tribes and were passed on through oral tradition to later generations who continued to resist the colonists" (475).

12. Sánchez Labrador, *El Paraguay católico*, 2:79–81(quotation on 81). The massacre occurred in 1678. See also the summary in James Schofield Saeger, *The Chaco Mission Frontier: The Guaycuruan Experience* (Tucson: University of Arizona Press, 2000), 12.

13. Sánchez Labrador, *El Paraguay católico*, 2:141–47. See also Francismar Alex Lopes de Carvalho, *Lealdades negociadas: Povos indígenas e a expansão dos impérios ibéricos nas regiões centrais da América do Sul (segunda metade do século XVIII)* (São Paulo: Alameda, 2014), 185–86, on this same episode.

14. Elizabeth A. Fenn, "Biological Warfare in Eighteenth-Century North America: Beyond Jeffery Amherst," *Journal of American History* 86, no. 4 (2000): 1552–80. The infected blankets were given to a group of Delaware dignitaries who were coming to parley with the British and urge them to abandon Fort Pitt; the smallpox spread among other groups surrounding the fort, such as the Shawnee and Mingo. Fenn asserts that "Fort Pitt account books make it clear that the British military both sanctioned and paid for the deed" (1554).

15. Sánchez Labrador, *El Paraguay católico*, 2:84. The Apacachodegodegis and Lichagotegodis of the eastern side of the Paraguay River were the Guaikurú subgroups among whom Sánchez Labrador worked most closely in setting up the mission at Belén, on the Ipané River. He also made friendly contacts with the Eyibegodegis (or Ejueos) and Cadiguegodis (Kadiwéu). On Belén and the attempts to establish missions among the Guaikurú, see Saeger, *The Chaco Mission Frontier*, ch. 2.

16. Sánchez Labrador, *El Paraguay católico*, 1:249.

17. Sánchez Labrador, *El Paraguay católico*, 2:159–60 (quotation on 160). A group of Payaguá who had settled near Belén under the Jesuit's supervision also protested his departure (Sánchez Labrador, 2:161).

18. João Antônio Cabral Camelo, *Notícias práticas das minas do Cuiabá* (Cuiabá: IHGMT, 2002), 16; "Anno de 1731," in *Annaes do Sennado da Câmara de Cuyabá, 1719–1830*, transcription by Yumiko Takamoto Suzuki (Cuiabá: Entrelinhas / APMT, 2007), 65.

19. "Anno de 1740," in *Annaes do Sennado da Camara de Cuyabá*, 72–73.

20. On the history of these attacks and the alliance between the Guaikurú and Payaguá, often dated to 1719–1768, see Sílvia Schmuziger Carvalho, "Chaco: Encruzilhada dos povos e 'melting pot' cultural, suas relações com a bacia do Paraná e o Sul mato-grossense," in *História dos índios do Brasil*, ed. Manuela Carneiro da Cunha (São Paulo: Companhia das Letras, 1992), 464–66; Branislava Susnik, *El indio colonial del Paraguay: El Chaqueño*, vol. 3, part 1 (Asunción, Paraguay: Museo Etnográfico Andrés Barbero, 1971), 64.

21. Daniel, *Tesouro descoberto*, 1:360.

22. This is from a more typical description of the Mura, "Imformação do Rio da Madeira, e dos mais rios que dezagoão nelle, de seos certoens, gentios delles, e de seos costumes, ritos, e ceremonias," likely written by a missionary at Canomã, c. 1714, Biblioteca Pública da Évora, Cod. CXV 2–15, no. 5, fls. 44v–45. For similar descriptions of the Mura by another Jesuit, see "Informação da Aldeia dos Abacaxis, que manda o P. Missionario Theotonio Barbosa ao P. Provincial, anno de 1749," Biblioteca Pública da Évora, Cod. CXV 2–15, no. 4, fl. 40v. For settlers' framing of Mura hostility

as "without cause," see the formulaic testimonies collected (or fabricated) during an investigation carried out in 1738: "Documento 3: Inquérito das 33 testemunhas juradas," in Universidade do Amazonas, *Autos da devassa contra os índios Mura do Rio Madeira e nações do Rio Tocantins, 1738–1739* (Manaus: CEDEAM, 1986), 17–89.

23. Daniel, *Tesouro descoberto*, 1:361; see also David G. Sweet, "Native Resistance in Eighteenth-Century Amazonia: The 'Abominable Muras' in War and Peace," *Radical History Review* 53, no. 1 (1992): 55 for an analysis of this account. The missionary who had begun working among the Mura before their deception was probably the Jesuit João Sampaio, who had founded the mission furthest upriver on the Madeira, called Santo Antônio da Cachoeira, in the 1720s: see Antonio Porro, "Uma crônica ignorada: Anselm Eckart e a Amazônia setecentista," *Boletim do Museu Paraense Emílio Goeldi—Ciências Humanas* 6, no. 3 (2011): 581.

24. Missions fortified against Mura attacks are described in Daniel, *Tesouro descoberto*, 1:360; competition with the Mura over turtles is mentioned in the missionary report from c. 1714, "Imformação do Rio da Madeira," fl. 44v. The quote is from Marta Rosa Amoroso, "Guerra Mura no século XVIII: Versos e versões, representações dos Mura no imaginário colonial" (MA thesis, Universidade Estadual de Campinas, São Paulo, 1991), 38.

25. On how to categorize the different types of armed expeditions into indigenous territories, see Mary C. Karasch, *Before Brasília: Frontier Life in Central Brazil* (Albuquerque: University of New Mexico Press, 2016), 63–67.

26. On war parties against the Mura, see the testimony of Diogo Pinto da Gaya in *Autos da devassa*, 89; "Observacções addicionaes a Illustração sobre o Gentio Mura, escripta por hum anônimo no anno de 1826," in Carlos de Araújo Moreira Neto, *Índios da Amazônia, de maioria a minoria* (Petrópolis: Vozes, 1988), 250–51. The indispensable source for the history of slaving in Portuguese Amazonia remains David G. Sweet, "A Rich Realm of Nature Destroyed: The Middle Amazon Valley, 1640–1750" (PhD diss., University of Wisconsin, 1974).

27. Primary sources on the measles epidemic of 1749–1750 include "Informação da Aldeia dos Abacaxis"; Daniel, *Tesouro descoberto*, 1:385–86; Teodósio Constantino de Chermont, "Memória dos mais temíveis contágios de bexigas e sarampo d'este Estado desde o ano de 1720 por diante," *Revista Trimensal do Instituto Histórico e Geográfico do Brasil* 48 (1885): 28–30.

28. José Gonçalves da Fonseca, "Primeira exploração do rios Madeira e Guaporé feita por José Gonçalves da Fonseca em 1749," in *Memorias para a historia do extincto estado do Maranhão, cujo territorio comprehende hoje as províncias do Maranhão, Piauhy, Grão-Pará e Amazonas*, ed. Cândido Mendes (Rio de Janeiro: Typographia de J. Paulo Hildebrandt, 1874), 2:296–314.

29. Fonseca, "Primeira exploração do rios Madeira e Guaporé," 311. I have never seen other references to these structures; it is difficult to know what they really were used for or who built them.

30. Sánchez Labrador, *El Paraguay católico*, 1:250. Similar descriptions of Guaikurú inquisitiveness and cleverness can be found in Francisco Rodrigues do Prado, *História dos índios cavaleiros ou da Nação Guaycurú (1795)* (Campo Grande: Instituto Histórico e Geográfico do Mato Grosso do Sul, 2006), 31; and Ricardo Franco de Almeida Serra, "Continuação do parecer sobre os índios Uaicurús e Guanás," *Revista do Instituto Histórico e Geográfico Brasileiro* 13 (1850): 362.

31. Sánchez Labrador, *El Paraguay católico*, 1:258–59; on how this subgroup, the Eyibegodegis (or Ejueos), remained mostly hostile to the Spanish and had only occasional friendly contacts with the Jesuits, see Sánchez Labrador, 1:266. They would later make peace with the Portuguese (in 1791) under the leadership of the chief Caimá. On Indigenous appropriation of liturgical items and vestments, which were associated with the special powers of the missionaries, see Carlos Fausto, "If God Were a Jaguar: Cannibalism and Christianity among the Guaraní (16th-20th Centuries)," in *Time and Memory in Indigenous Amazonia: Anthropological Perspectives*, ed. Carlos Fausto and Michael Heckenberger (Gainesville: University Press of Florida, 2007), 83.

32. Sánchez Labrador, *El Paraguay católico*, 1:314.

33. Stephen Hugh-Jones, "Yesterday's Luxuries, Tomorrow's Necessities: Business and Barter in Northwest Amazonia," in *Barter, Exchange, and Value: An Anthropological Approach*, ed. Caroline Humphrey and Stephen Hugh-Jones (Cambridge: Cambridge University Press, 1992), 59; see also Cesar Gordon, "The Objects of the Whites: Commodities and Consumerism among the Xikrin-Kayapó (Mebengokre) of Amazonia," *Tipití* 8, no. 2 (2010): 1–20.

34. A good discussion of the term *sertão* can be found in Hal Langfur, *The Forbidden Lands: Colonial Identity, Frontier Violence, and the Persistence of Brazil's Eastern Indians, 1750–1830* (Stanford, CA: Stanford University Press, 2006), 292–94. For further analysis of the map, see Juciene Ricarte Apolinário, "Os Akroá e outros povos indígenas nas fronteiras do sertão: As práticas das políticas indígena e indigenista no norte da Capitania de Goiás—século XVIII" (PhD diss., Universidade Federal de Pernambuco, 2005), 214–18.

35. On imperial control as limited to corridors and enclaves, see Lauren Benton, *A Search for Sovereignty: Law and Geography in European Empires, 1400–1900* (Cambridge: Cambridge University Press, 2010). Recognition of Native territorialities on European maps from the mid to late eighteenth century is explored in Jeffrey Alan Erbig Jr., *Where Caciques and Mapmakers Met: Border Making in Eighteenth-Century South America* (Chapel Hill: University of North Carolina Press, 2020), especially 82–83.

36. Regional studies of how autonomous peoples of the Americas achieved this repositioning between imperial powers include Claudia Garcia, *Etnogénesis, hibridación y consolidación de la identidad del pueblo Miskitu* (Madrid: Consejo Superior de Investigaciones Científicas, 2007); Pekka Hämäläinen, *Comanche Empire* (New Haven, CT: Yale University Press, 2008); Ryan Hall, *Beneath the*

Backbone of the World: Blackfoot People and the North American Borderlands, 1720–1877 (Chapel Hill: University of North Carolina Press, 2020); Erbig, *Where Caciques and Mapmakers Met*.

37. Pekka Hämäläinen, "The Shapes of Power: Indians, Europeans, and North American Worlds from the Seventeenth to the Nineteenth Century," in *Contested Spaces of Early America*, ed. Juliana Barr and Edward Countryman (Philadelphia: University of Pennsylvania Press, 2104), 49 ("kinetic regimes"), and 43 ("geographically privileged"). See also Stephen Warren, *The Worlds the Shawnees Made: Migration and Violence in Early America* (Chapel Hill: University of North Carolina Press, 2014), 14–15, and 81, on the Shawnee strategy of moving toward violent borderlands as places of opportunity.

38. "Imformação do Rio da Madeira," 44v, 43. The evidence in this document linking the Mura to the area near the Marmelos River is fascinating, because it suggests that the Pirahã, a Mura subgroup who today live on a tributary of the Marmelos (the Maici River) might have historical connections to this territory or at least to the broader region. The anthropological literature on the Pirahã, in contrast, suggests that they split off from the Mura and migrated to the Maici much later, perhaps in the mid-nineteenth century.

39. "Supplement" to the letter of Lieutenant Colonel João Batista Mardel to João Pereira Caldas, Nogueira, June 1, 1785, AHI, Cod. 340-4-6. On the archaeological evidence for the Autazes being inhabited by materially advanced groups before the Mura came to live there, see Curt Nimuendajú, "The Mura and Pirahã," in *Handbook of South American Indians*, ed. Julian H. Steward (Washington, DC: Smithsonian Institution, 1948), 3:256. The plots of terra preta in the region are described in Curt Nimuendajú, *Cartas do sertão, de Curt Nimuendajú para Carlos Estevão de Oliveira*, ed. Thekla Hartmann (Lisbon: Museu Nacional de Etnologia / Assírio & Alvim, 2000). On terra preta, see Johannes Lehmann, Dirse C. Kern, Bruno Glaser, and William I. Woods, eds., *Amazonian Dark Earths: Origins, Properties, Management* (Boston: Kluwer Academic, 2003).

40. Eliane da Silva Souza Pequeno, "Mura, guardiães do caminho fluvial," *Revista de Estudos e Pesquisas (FUNAI)* 3, no. ½ (2006), 142–43; Sweet, "Native Resistance," 54–59. The hypothesis that the Mura practiced swidden agriculture on the forested banks of the Madeira rests on the assertion by the chronicler of the 1749 expedition that the Mura were seen burning plots of land, with fires that burned night and day. Fonseca, "Primeira exploração do rios Madeira e Guaporé," 306.

41. Sweet ("Native Resistance," 59) argues that the secularization of the missions and the departure of the Jesuit missionaries left a "vacuum of authority in the wake of depopulation," to which he links the Muras' decision to move to the Autazes in the mid-1750s. But the transition to secular clerics and civil administrators (or "directors") under the Indian Directorate occurred relatively smoothly, as Crown reformers purposefully left much of the

structure and organization of the former missions intact, and their Native inhabitants were able to maintain long-standing patterns of mobility and subsistence. Heather F. Roller, *Amazonian Routes: Indigenous Mobility and Colonial Communities in Northern Brazil* (Stanford, CA: Stanford University Press, 2014), ch. 1. Nimuendajú ("The Mura and Pirahã," 3:256) characterized the Muras' migration as a "warlike expansion" toward colonial settlements that were unable to resist their advances.

42. Fleets traveling the Madeira route to Mato Grosso had to be escorted by armed guards, due to frequent Mura attacks. Amoroso, "Guerra Mura," 96. A description of Mura surveillance and attack on a commercial fleet traveling along the Madeira River can be found in Antônio Pires da Silva Pontes, "Diário histórico e físico da viagem dos oficiais da demarcação que partiram do quartel geral de Barcelos para a capital de Vila Bela da Capitania de Mato Grosso, em 1 de Setembro de 1781," *Revista do Instituto Histórico e Geográfico Brasileiro* 262 (1964): 357; this source also describes how Muras spied on the Portuguese boundary demarcation expedition as it traveled upriver through Mura territories (353–54).

43. Amoroso, "Guerra Mura," 111–12, 114–16. See, for example, the notice that the Mura had reached the banks of the Amazon River in the Captaincy of Pará, near the town of Óbidos. Manoel António da Costa Souto Maior to governor, Óbidos, January 1, 1774, APEP, Cod. 73, Doc. 66. On *Mura* as the standard term of comparison when describing hostile or recalcitrant Native groups, see João Pedro Marçal da Silva to governor, Baião, March 7, 1777, APEP, Cod. 271, Doc. 11; and José Gonçalves Marqués to governor, Porto de Moz, December 2, 1764, APEP, Cod. 140, Doc. 44.

44. This very rough estimation of travel time is based on a fold-out table in "Mappa geral classificado da população da Província do Gram-Pará," in Ignacio Accioli de Cerqueira e Silva, *Corografia Paraense, ou, descripção física, histórica, e política da província do Gram-Pará* (Bahia: Typologia do Diário, 1833).

45. Francisco Xavier Ribeiro de Sampaio, *Diário da viagem que em visita, e correição das povoações da Capitania de S. Jozé do Rio Negro fez o Ouvidor, e Intendente Geral da mesma . . . no anno de 1774 e 1775* (Lisbon: Typografia da Academia, 1825), 22–23.

46. Director Mathias Fernandes to governor, Japurá, April 12, 1778, APEP, Cod. 340, Doc. 9.

47. On the "convenience" of Indian wars for colonial officials in frontier regions, see Sara Ortelli, *Trama de una guerra conveniente: Nueva Vizcaya y la sombra de los apaches (1748–1790)* (Mexico City: El Colegio de México, Centro de Estudios Históricos, 2007).

48. Sergeant Major Henrique João Wilkens, quoted in Domingues, *Quando os índios eram vassalos*, 328. Absenteeism from the villages of the Indian Directorate was chronic—and difficult for officials to quantify or trace; the Mura must have been an easy scapegoat for thefts by this transient population.

49. Director Mathias Fernandes to governor, Japurá, April 12, 1778, APEP, Cod. 340, Doc. 9.

50. Governor Joaquim de Melo e Póvoas to Francisco Xavier de Mendonça Furtado, Barcelos, January 15, 1760, AHU, Rio Negro Avulsos, Cod. 1, Doc. 59.

51. On their use of channels between the Solimões and Madeira Rivers, see Ribeiro de Sampaio, *Diário da viagem*, 13; they also traveled via small waterways between the Japurá and Negro Rivers.

52. Francisco Mendes, "Carta . . . sobre las costumbres, religion, terreno y tradiciones de los Yndios Mbayás, Guanás y demas naciones que ocupan la region boreal del Rio Paraguay (1772)," June 20, 1772, in Do Tratado de Madri à conquista do Sete Povos, ed. Jaime Cortesão (Rio de Janeiro: Biblioteca Nacional, 1969), 54. Fray Mendes defined the northern boundary of Mbayánica as the Mboteteu River (later known as the Miranda River), but it is more commonly defined as running along the Taquari River. See Uacury Ribeiro de A. Bastos, *Expansão territorial do Brasil Colônia no Vale do Paraguai (1767–1801)* (São Paulo: Universidade de São Paulo, 1978), 126.

53. Maria de Fátima Costa, *História de um país inexistente: O Pantanal entre os séculos XVI e XVIII* (São Paulo: Estação Liberdade/Kosmos, 1999), 47; Sánchez Labrador, *El Paraguay católico*, 1:266.

54. On the Pantanal as a historical space, see Costa, *História de um país inexistente*. Costa defines it as the area between the mouth of the Jauru River to the mouth of the Apa River (21). For a similar case, in which "the horse was the catalyst" for Comanche expansion, see Pekka Hämäläinen, "The Politics of Grass: European Expansion, Ecological Change, and Indigenous Power in the Southwest Borderlands," *William and Mary Quarterly* 67, no. 2 (2010): 186.

55. Cândido Xavier de Almeida e Souza, "Descrição diária dos progressos da expedição destinada à capitania de São Paulo para fronteiras do Paraguai, em 9 de outubro de 1800," *Revista do Instituto Histórico e Geográfico Brasileiro* 202 (1949): 96.

56. Ricardo Franco de Almeida Serra, "Parecer sobre o aldeamento dos índios Uaicurus e Guanás com a descripção dos seus usos, religião, estabilidade e costumes (1803)," *Revista do Instituto Histórico e Geográfico Brasileiro* 7 (1845): 211–13.

57. Saeger, *The Chaco Mission Frontier*, 60.

58. Ana Lucia Herberts, "Panorama histórico dos mbayá-guaikuru entre os séculos XVI e XIX," in *Kadiwéu: Senhoras da arte, senhores da guerra*, ed. Giovani José da Silva (Curitiba: Editora CRV, 2011), 28–36.

59. Prado, *História dos índios cavaleiros*, 43–48. Missionary sources identify the Uatedeos (Guetiadegodis in Sánchez Labrador's account) as the Guaikurú subgroup that made the most use of canoes and had the fewest horses (Mendes, "Carta . . . sobre las costumbres," 56).

60. Commander Francisco Rodrigues do Prado to governor, Coimbra, January 2(?), 1794, APMT, Cod. 35, fl. 126v.

61. On the western side of the Paraguay River, from north to south, were the Guetiadegodis (Uatedeos) and Cadiguegodis (Kadiwéus); on the eastern side were the Eyibegodegis (Ejueos), Gotocogegodegis (Cotogeus), Lichagotegodis, and Apacachodegodegis, according to Sánchez Labrador, *El Paraguay católico*, 1:255–59; these appear with different spellings in Mendes, "Carta... sobre las costumbres," 55–56; and again several decades later in Serra, "Parecer," 207. The many spelling variations are clarified in Alfred Métraux, "Ethnography of the Chaco," in *Handbook of South American Indians*, ed. Julian H. Steward, vol. 1, part 2 (Washington DC: Smithsonian Institution, 1946), 217–18; Susnik, *El indio colonial del Paraguay*, vol. 3, part 1, 57–61. On the colonial category of parcialidad(e), see Guillaume Boccara, "Poder colonial e etnicidade no Chile: Territorialização e reestruturação entre os Mapuche da época colonial," *Tempo* 12, no. 23 (2007): 62n8.

62. Sánchez Labrador, *El Paraguay católico*, 1:260; Mendes, "Carta... sobre las costumbres," 55–56 (who mentions that the Guetiadegodis came to the encampments of the Eyibegodegis to sell jewelry from a Portuguese women they had taken captive upriver); Commander Ricardo Franco de Almeida Serra to governor, Coimbra, September 25, 1798, APMT, FC.CA, Cx. 6, Doc. 345.

63. Susnik, *El indio colonial del Paraguay*, vol. 3, part 1, 38; see also R. Brian Ferguson and Neil L. Whitehead, eds., *War in the Tribal Zone: Expanding States and Indigenous Warfare* (Santa Fe, NM: School of American Research, 1992).

64. Carvalho, *Lealdades negociadas*, 237–38, 250.

65. R. Brian Ferguson, "Blood of the Leviathan: Western Contact and Warfare in Amazonia," *American Ethnologist* 17 (1990): 238.

66. John Hemming, for example, wrote of the Guaikurú that "there was no purpose or strategy behind their fighting." *Red Gold: The Conquest of the Brazilian Indians* (Cambridge, MA: Harvard University Press, 1978), 391. For more nuanced approaches to the study of indigenous resistance to conquest in the eighteenth and early nineteenth centuries, see Langfur, *The Forbidden Lands*, chs. 6–8, esp. 215–16; Karasch, *Before Brasília*, ch. 4; and with a broader perspective on the topic for Spanish America, David J. Weber, *Bárbaros: Spaniards and Their Savages in the Age of Enlightenment* (New Haven, CT: Yale University Press, 2005), ch. 2.

67. Félix Feliciano da Fonseca, *Relaçam do que aconteçeo aos demarcadores portuguezes e castelhanos no certam das terras da collonia; opoziçam que os indios lhe fizeraõ, rompimento de guerra que houve, e de como se alhanaraõ todas as deficuldades*, Lisbon, c. 1753, John Carter Brown Library, Portugal and Brazil Collection, Internet Archive, https://archive.org/details/relaamdoqueacooofons/page/n4. Though the specific Native group was not named in the document, it likely referred to Guaraníes at Santa Tecla; if so, however, this was land historically occupied by the Minuanes, making the territorial claims of the envoys all the more interesting (Jeffrey Erbig, personal communications, June 29 and July 1, 2020). On the Guaraní War (1753–1756) that followed these Native

challenges to the boundary demarcation teams, see Erbig, *Where Caciques and Mapmakers Met*, 83–87.

68. Termo de Junta, Goiás, May 17, 1757, AHEG, Cod. 12, fl. 7v. The mission was São Francisco Xavier do Duro in northeastern Goiás; the Akroás there were trained as military auxiliaries by Wenceslau Gomes da Silva, who served as an administrator of the mission after having led the armed expedition to bring the Akroás out of the forest several years earlier. Apolinário, "Os Akroá e outros povos indígenas nas fronteiras do sertão," ch. 2. For parallels among the Caiapó do Sul, Xavante, and Xerente, see Mary C. Karasch, "Interethnic Conflict and Survival Strategies on the Tocantins-Araguaia Frontier, 1750–1890," in *Contested Ground: Comparative Frontiers on the Northern and Southern Edges of the Spanish Empire*, ed. Donna J. Guy and Thomas E. Sheridan (Tucson: University of Arizona Press, 1998), 129–32. Colonial allegations of "treason" by Indians who took up guns against colonists can be found in the royal war authorization (*bando*) against the Caiapó do Sul: Vila Boa de Goiás, October 25, 1762, copied in APMT, CVC.RQ, Cx. 1, Doc. 48.

69. On the Akroás' adoption of horses, see Governor Marcos de Noronha to king, Vila Boa de Goiás, February 10, 1751, AHEG, Cod. 1, fls. 50–51v. For a very broad treatment of the equestrian societies that emerged across the hemisphere, see Peter Mitchell, *Horse Nations: The Worldwide Impact of the Horse on Indigenous Societies Post-1492* (Oxford: Oxford University Press, 2015).

70. Ganson, "The Evueví of Paraguay," 475; Prado, *História dos índios cavaleiros*, 40–41.

71. Puntoni, *A guerra dos bárbaros*, 269; Carvalho, *Lealdades negociadas*, 395–97. On the Karajá, who were gifted guns during a 1792 diplomatic visit to the governor in Belém and who were seen as potential allies against the Apinajé, see "Diário da navegação que fez Thomáz de Souza Villa Real," 1793, AIHGB, Lata 281, Pasta 4, Doc. 3.

72. Juiz Ordinário of Pinhel to governor, Pinhel, 1805, APEP, Cod. 610, Doc. 157, referring to settlers from the town of Óbidos who were allegedly trading with the Mawé. I am grateful to Mark Harris for sharing this document with me. For similar concerns, see also Pedro Miguel Ayres Pereira to governor, Santarém, August 26, 1793, APEP, Cod. 497, Doc. 18. I suspect this trading post among the Mawé was seen as especially controversial because of older prohibitions on trade (since 1769) with this particular Native group, due to their perceived resistance to colonial resettlement attempts. Governor Fernando da Costa de Ataíde Teive to Pedro Maciel Parente, Belém, October 3, 1769, AIHGB, Lata 283, Pasta 10. In 1790, restrictions on trade with independent Indians were lifted, but the official ban on trade in guns, powder, and shot remained.

73. Karasch, *Before Brasília*, 126, notes that Indians only occasionally obtained guns in the late colonial period and often preferred not to use them.

On the Payaguá, see Ganson, "The Evueví of Paraguay," 465; Costa, *História de um país inexistente*, 48–50.

74. Director Lucas José Espinosa de Brito Coelho Folqman to governor, Pombal, February 21, 1772, APEP, Cod. 241, Doc. 33. The renegade (named Simão) was said to lead the Juruna along with his wife, Joana. Both were runaways from the village of Pombal.

75. According to one author, colonial canoe crew members customarily chopped up the bodies of any Indians they killed after ambushes, "perhaps for revenge, or to terrorize them with this treatment." Silva Pontes, "Diário histórico e físico da viagem," 357.

76. António de Morais Silva and Rafael Bluteau, *Diccionário da língua portugueza* (Lisbon: Oficina de S. T. Ferreira, 1789), 2:534.

77. António Vieira, "Carta II a El Rey" (1660), in *Cartas do P. Antonio Vieyra da Companhia de Jesu* (Lisbon: Congregação do Oratorio, 1735), 24, John Carter Brown Library, Brazil and Portugal Collection, Internet Archive, https://archive.org/details/cartasdopantonio01viei/page/n6; see also the eighteenth-century description of these tactics of warfare in Daniel, *Tesouro descoberto*, 1:319–20. Langfur, *The Forbidden Lands*, 258–59, makes the point that guerrilla tactics were used by both Indians and settlers, one of several examples of reciprocal "cultural borrowing" even in the midst of a brutal frontier war in Minas Gerais.

78. The Mura were described as fighting "face-to-face" in the missionary chronicle of c. 1714, "Imformação do Rio da Madeira," fl. 44v.

79. Fonseca, "Primeira exploração do rios Madeira e Guaporé," especially 301, 308–9. A nineteenth-century account suggested that the Mura turned to guerrilla-style warfare after their encounter with gunfire on the 1749 expedition, but this does not seem accurate. "Illustração necessária e interessante, relativa ao gentio da nação Mura . . . feita por um anônimo em 1826," in Carlos de Araújo Moreira Neto, *Índios da Amazônia, de maioria a minoria* (Petrópolis: Vozes, 1988), 250.

80. These attacks are mentioned in village correspondence at APEP. For summary reports, see Governor Joaquim de Melo e Póvoas to Francisco Xavier de Mendonça Furtado, Barcelos, January 15, 1760, AHU, Rio Negro Avulsos, Cod. 1, Doc. 59; Ribeiro de Sampaio, *Diário da viagem*, especially 76.

81. Sweet, "Native Resistance," 61.

82. On the strong correlation between episodes of frontier violence and colonial punitive expeditions, see Langfur, *The Forbidden Lands*, 217–21.

83. Sergeant Major Henrique João Wilkens, Ega, July 5, 1782, AHU, Rio Negro Avulsos, Cx. 5, Doc. 245 (attachment).

84. General João Pereira Caldas to Martinho de Melo e Castro, Barcelos, November 13, 1782; Director Mathias Fernandes, July 25, 1782 (attachment); Lieutenant Colonel Theodósio Constantino de Chermont to João Pereira

Caldas, Santo Antônio de Maripí, August 16, 1782 (attachment), all in AHU, Rio Negro Avulsos, Cx. 5, Doc. 250.

85. Carvalho, *Lealdades negociadas*, 399, quoting Francisco Rodrigues do Prado, who commanded the troops and Guaikurú auxiliaries.

86. Serra, "Continuação do parecer," 370.

87. Langfur, *The Forbidden Lands*, 247, 250.

88. Serra, "Continuação do parecer," 369.

89. John Hemming, *Amazon Frontier: The Defeat of the Brazilian Indians* (Cambridge, MA: Harvard University Press, 1987), 188, quoting the traveler Johann Emanuel Pohl, who described such an episode near a garrison on the Tocantins River in 1812. See also Karasch, *Before Brasília*, 98.

90. David Murray, *Indian Giving: Economies of Power in Indian-White Exchanges* (Amherst: University of Massachusetts Press, 2000), 7.

91. Anne-Christine Taylor, "Sick of History: Contrasting Regimes of Historicity in the Upper Amazon," in *Time and Memory in Indigenous Amazonia: Anthropological Perspectives*, ed. Carlos Fausto and Michael Heckenberger (Gainesville: University Press of Florida, 2007), 138. For vivid depictions of this dynamic in the eighteenth-century documentation, see, for example, João Pedro Marçal da Silva to governor, Baião, March 7, 1777, APEP, Cod. 271, Doc. 11; *Cabo* (Canoe Boss) Bernardo Fernandes Brazão to Director António Gonçalves de Sousa, Vila Franca, 1777, APEP, Cod. 317, unnumbered doc., fl. 114.

92. Captain Miguel José Rodrigues to Luís de Albuquerque de Melo Pereira e Cáceres, Coimbra, October 14, 1776, in Cáceres, "Exploração do Rio Paraguay e primeiras práticas com os índios Guaikurús," *Revista Trimensal do Instituto Histórico Geográfico e Ethnographico do Brasil* 28 (1865): 71–84; and Commander Marcellino Rodrigues Campones to Luís de Albuquerque de Melo Pereira e Cáceres, Coimbra, October 17, 1776, in Cáceres, "Exploração do Rio Paraguay," 87; "Anno de 1776," in *Annaes do Sennado da Camara de Cuyabá*, 107–9. On the Guaikurú leader Lorenzo (Lourenço), see Sánchez Labrador, *El Paraguay católico*, especially 2:82–83.

93. Prado, *História dos índios cavaleiros*, 53.

94. Captain José was mentioned by name in the eyewitness report of this event. A much later document named Captain Felipe as one of the representatives who had entered the fort on the day of the 1778 massacre. Francisco Rodrigues do Prado to governor, Coimbra, January 8, 1795, APMT, FC.CA., Cx. 4, Doc. 197. This document does not indicate what subgroup Felipe was from, but it says that his son married Joaquina, the daughter of Captain Emavidi Xané (Paulo), who belonged to the Uatedeos (or Guetiadegodis) subgroup; she was also the former wife of Captain Caimá (Queima) of the Eyibegodegis (or Ejueos) subgroup. This corresponds to what we know of the kin relationships that linked Guaikurú subgroups. Because of the Lourenço/Lorenzo connection and the location near the Fecho dos Morros where they were first encountered, my best guess is that the Guaikurús involved in the contacts of

1776–1778 were Apacachodegodegis who spoke Spanish as a result of their contacts with Sánchez Labrador and the missionaries and secular priests who followed in his footsteps. In the 1776 encounter, the Guaikurú even mention one of these priests. See Captain Miguel José Rodrigues to Luís de Albuquerque de Melo Pereira e Cáceres, Coimbra, October 14, 1776, in "Exploração do Rio Paraguay," 82; Prado, *História dos índios cavaleiros*, 63.

95. Sánchez Labrador, *El Paraguay católico*, 1:261 described the Guaikurú using smoke signals to communicate with other parcialidades or subordinate leaders.

96. Marcelino Rodrigues Camponês to governor, Coimbra, January 22, 1778, APMT, FC.CA, Cx. 1, Doc. 25.

97. Prado, *História dos índios cavaleiros*, 54.

98. Marcelino Rodrigues Camponês to governor, Coimbra, January 22, 1778, APMT, FC.CA, Cx. 1, Doc. 25.

99. Marcelino Rodrigues Camponês to governor, Coimbra, January 22, 1778, APMT, FC.CA, Cx. 1, Doc. 25.

100. "Anno de 1778," in *Annaes do Sennado da Camara de Cuyabá*, 111.

101. Prado, *História dos índios cavaleiros*, 54.

102. Raul Silveira de Mello, *História do Forte de Coimbra* (Rio de Janeiro: Imprensa do Exército, 1959), 2:112.

103. Félix de Azara, "Al Virey, sobre demarcación" (Abril 12, 1784), "Correspondencia oficial e inédita sobre la demarcación de límites entre el Paraguay y el Brasil," in *Colección de obras y documentos relativos a la historia antigua y moderna de las provincias del Río*, ed. Pedro de Angelis (Buenos Aires: Imprenta del Estado, 1836), 4:6. I assume this is in reference to the 1778 massacre at Coimbra, though the timeline described by Azara does not quite match. Three Mbayá (Guaikurú) caciques told him they had killed 164 Portuguese at the fort, but he added that a priest at the mission of Belén revised this number—most likely lowering it—after some Guaikurús (sporting Portuguese rifles) showed him some kind of knotted device upon which they had recorded the deaths. I first saw reference to this intriguing instance of Native record keeping in Jeffrey A. Erbig, "Forging Frontiers: Félix de Azara and the Making of the Virreinato del Río de La Plata" (MA thesis, University of North Carolina, Chapel Hill, 2010), 28n35.

104. Director Luís da Rocha Lima to governor, Souzel, September 8, 1788, APEP, Cod. 449, Doc. 34.

105. Amoroso, "Guerra Mura," 147; see also Sweet, "Native Resistance," 63–64.

106. Lieutenant Colonel Theodósio Constantino de Chermont to João Pereira Caldas, Santo Antônio de Maripí, August 16, 1782 (attachment), AHU, Rio Negro Avulsos, Cx. 5, Doc. 250. See also Sweet, "Native Resistance," 64.

107. Karasch, *Before Brasília*, 119.

108. Lieutenant Colonel João Batista Mardel to João Pereira Caldas, Nogueira, July 26, 1785, AHI, Cod. 340-4-6.

109. Director António Correia da Maia to governor, Serpa, July 21, 1785, APEP, Cod. 421, Doc. 17.

110. Alexandre Rodrigues Ferreira, "Memória sobre o gentio Mura, que voluntariamente descerão para as povoacões dos Rios Negro, Solimões, Amazonas, e Madeira, segundo a faz desenhar, e remetter para o Real Gabinete da História Natural o Doutor Naturalista Alexandre Rodrigues Ferreira," Barcelos, September 30, 1787, BNRJ, 21, 2, 17.

111. Director Domingos de Macedo Ferreira to Henrique João Wilkens[?], Alvelos, December 31, 1788, AHU, Rio Negro Avulsos, Cx. 15, Doc. 558 (attachment); emphasis mine. He was reporting on the Mura settlement at São Pedro de Mamiá.

112. Raúl Mandrini and Sara Ortelli, "Los 'Araucanos' en las Pampas (c. 1700–1850)," in *Colonización, Resistencia, y Mestizaje en las Américas (siglos XVI–XX)*, ed. Guillaume Boccara (Quito: Editorial Abya Yala, 2002), 237–57; Hämäläinen, *Comanche Empire*, 66, 172; Gary Clayton Anderson, *The Indian Southwest, 1580–1830* (Norman: University of Oklahoma Press, 1999), ch. 5.

113. "Supplement" to the letter of Lieutenant Colonel João Batista Mardel to João Pereira Caldas, Nogueira, June 1, 1785, AHI, Cod. 340-4-6; see also Sweet, "Native Resistance," 70.

114. See, for example, Henry Lister Maw, *Journal of a Passage from the Pacific to the Atlantic: Crossing the Andes in the Northern Provinces of Peru, and Descending the River Marañon or Amazon* (London: J. Murray, 1829), 317; Alfred Russel Wallace, *A Narrative of Travels on the Amazon and Rio Negro, with an Account of the Native Tribes, and Observations on the Climate, Geology, and Natural History of the Amazon Valley* (London: Reeve and Company, 1853), 511–12; João Barbosa Rodrigues, *Exploração dos Rios Urubú e Jatapú* (Rio de Janeiro: Typographia Nacional, 1875), 24.

115. Prado, *História dos índios cavaleiros*, 26–27.

116. Alexandre Rodrigues Ferreira, "Carta dirigida ao Governador e Capitão-General João de Albuquerque de Melo Pereira e Cáceres" (May 5, 1791), in *Viagem ao Brasil de Alexandre Rodrigues Ferreira: Coleção etnográfica*, ed. José Paulo Monteiro Soares and Cristina Ferrão (São Paulo: Kapa Editorial, 2005), 3:25–26. The sentiment was echoed by Félix de Azara, *Viajes por la América Meridional* (Buenos Aires: El Elefante Blanco, 1998), 2:60.

117. Sánchez Labrador, *El Paraguay católico*, 1:267; 2:311–12; Fernando Santos-Granero, *Vital Enemies: Slavery, Predation and the Amerindian Political Economy of Life* (Austin: University of Texas Press, 2009), 95–99, 121, 191.

118. Santos-Granero, *Vital Enemies*, 163–67, 189–90.

119. Serra, "Parecer," 210. For a synthesis of colonial descriptions of Guaikurú practices of infanticide, see Hemming, *Red Gold*, 390.

120. Sean F. McEnroe, "Sites of Diplomacy, Violence, and Refuge: Topography and Negotiation in the Mountains of New Spain," *The Americas* 69, no. 2 (2012): 188. See also Weber, *Bárbaros*, 228–29, 233.

121. Amoroso, "Guerra Mura," 133, quoting a footnote in Henrique João Wilkens's epic poem about the Mura, the *Muhuraida*. For another example from the Portuguese Amazon, one involving renegade Indians from the colonial village of Pinhel who made alliances with the Mawé and other Native groups in the Tapajós River region, see Roller, *Amazonian Routes*, 120–22.

122. Director Lucas José Espinosa de Brito Coelho Folqman to governor, Pombal, February 21, 1772, APEP, Cod. 241, Doc. 33.

123. James Axtell, "The White Indians of Colonial America," *William and Mary Quarterly* 32, no. 1 (1975): 55–56. See also Jill Lepore, *The Name of War: King Philip's War and the Origins of American Identity* (New York: Vintage Books, 1998), ch. 5.

124. Camelo, *Notícias práticas das minas do Cuiabá*, 25. The boy is described in "Notícia 8ª Prática," in *Relatos monçoeiros*, ed. Afonso de E. Taunay (Belo Horizonte/São Paulo: Itatiaia/Edusp, 1981), 190. Prado, *História dos índios cavaleiros*, 44, implied that this attack was a joint Guaikurú-Payaguá effort, which would correspond with the mocking phrase recorded in Camelo. Other contemporary accounts attributed it to the Payaguá alone. For a reconstruction of the 1730 attack, see also Thereza Martha Presotti, "Nas trilhas das águas: Índios e natureza na conquista colonial do centro da América do Sul, os sertões de Cuiabá e Mato Grosso (século XVIII)" (PhD diss., Universidade de Brasília, 2008), 214–21. The description of the chief's attire is in Domingos Lourenço de Araújo, "Notícia 3ª Prática," in Taunay, *Relatos monçoeiros*, 142.

125. Serra, "Continuação do parecer," 361–62.

126. Serra, "Continuação do parecer," 362.

127. Elisa Frühauf Garcia, *As diversas formas de ser índio: Políticas indígenas e Políticas indigenistas no extremo sul da América portuguesa* (Rio de Janeiro: Arquivo Nacional, 2009), 302; David Louis Mead, "Caiapó do Sul, an Ethnohistory (1610–1920)," (PhD diss., University of Florida, 2010), 219; and farther afield, in northern Mexico, Rafael Brewster Folsom, *The Yaquis and the Empire: Violence, Spanish Imperial Power, and Native Resilience in Colonial Mexico* (New Haven, CT: Yale University Press, 2014), 6.

128. Serra, "Continuação do parecer," 378–79. For echoes of these sentiments among other indigenous groups in Brazil, see Director Jeronimo Manoel de Carvalho to governor, Pinhel, November 29, 1762, APEP, Cod. 115, Doc. 52; Director Bernardo Gomes Pereira to governor, Souzel, January 28, 1773, APEP, Cod 257, Doc. 13.

129. Cesar Gordon, "Nossas utopias não são as deles: Os Mebengokre (Kayapó) e o mundo dos brancos," *Sexta-feira: Antropologia, Artes e Humanidades* 6 (2001): 134, citing Eduardo Viveiros de Castro.

Chapter 2

1. Most of these details have been compiled from Mary C. Karasch, "Rethinking the Conquest of Goiás, 1775–1819," *The Americas* 61, no. 3 (2005):

474–77; and Marta Rosa Amoroso, "Guerra e mercadorias: Os Kaingang nas cenas da 'Conquista de Guarapuava,'" in *Do contato ao confronto: A conquista de Guarapuava no século XVIII*, ed. Ana Maria de Moraes Belluzzo, Marta Rosa Amoroso, Nicolau Sevcenko, and Valéria Piccoli (São Paulo: BNB Paribas, 2003), 29–31.

2. Tamar Herzog, *Frontiers of Possession: Spain and Portugal in Europe and the Americas* (Cambridge, MA: Harvard University Press, 2015), 96. The most complete discussion of the advantages sought by Bourbon-era Spanish officials in their peace agreements with autonomous Indians can be found in David J. Weber, *Bárbaros: Spaniards and Their Savages in the Age of Enlightenment* (New Haven, CT: Yale University Press, 2005), especially 205–14. See also Carlos Lázaro Ávila, "Conquista, control y convicción: El papel de los parlamentos indígenas en México, El Chaco y Norteamérica," *Revista de Indias* 59, no. 217 (1999): 645–73. For Portuguese America, see Nádia Farage, *As muralhas dos sertões: Os povos indígenas no Rio Branco e a colonização* (Rio de Janeiro: AN-POCS, 1991); Ângela Domingues, *Quando os índios eram vassalos: colonização e relações de poder no Norte do Brasil na segunda metade do século XVIII* (Lisbon: Comissão Nacional para as Comemorações dos Descobrimentos Portugueses, 2000), ch. 4 and 292–94; Elisa Frühauf Garcia, *As diversas formas de ser índio: Políticas indígenas e políticas indigenistas no extremo sul da América portuguesa* (Rio de Janeiro: Arquivo Nacional, 2009); Francismar Alex Lopes de Carvalho, *Lealdades negociadas: Povos indígenas e a expansão dos impérios ibéricos nas regiões centrais da América do Sul (segunda metade do século XVIII)* (São Paulo: Alameda, 2014), especially ch. 6; Jeffrey Alan Erbig Jr., *Where Caciques and Mapmakers Met: Border Making in Eighteenth-Century South America* (Chapel Hill: University of North Carolina Press, 2020). As Erbig notes, however, these imperial initiatives in the border zone changed over time and diverged between regions, and colonial commitments to peacemaking might wane as frustrations with Native autonomy mounted (119).

3. Farage, *As muralhas dos sertões*, 75; Stuart B. Schwartz and Hal Langfur, "*Tapanhuns, Negros da Terra*, and *Curibocas*: Common Cause and Confrontation between Blacks and Natives in Colonial Brazil," in *Beyond Black and Red: African–Native Relations in Colonial Latin America*, ed. Matthew Restall (Albuquerque: University of New Mexico Press, 2005), 86. Some zones controlled by independent Indians were seen as places to cordon off from unauthorized access by people within colonial Brazilian society. In the forests of eastern Minas Gerais, for example, autonomous Indians proved to be "cooperative enemies," helping the state (if unwittingly) to prevent contraband and other illegal activities in that zone. Hal Langfur, *The Forbidden Lands: Colonial Identity, Frontier Violence, and the Persistence of Brazil's Eastern Indians, 1750–1830* (Stanford, CA: Stanford University Press, 2006), especially 200–204.

4. Carvalho, *Lealdades negociadas*, 142–43, 163–64; Weber, *Bárbaros*, 8–9, 50–51, 217. For an overview of *indigenista* policies during the period of the

Pombaline reforms in Brazil, see Maria Regina Celestino de Almeida, *Os índios na história do Brasil* (Rio de Janeiro: Editora FGV, 2010), ch. 5.

5. On continuing violence in this period in Brazil, see Hal Langfur, "The Return of the *Bandeira*: Economic Calamity, Historical Memory, and Armed Expeditions to the *Sertão* in Minas Gerais, Brazil, 1750–1808," *The Americas* 61, no. 3 (2005): 429–61. The quotation about the sertanistas comes from a governor's orders from the mid-1770s, transcribed by Francisco Rodrigues do Prado in his *História dos índios cavaleiros ou da Nação Guaycurú (1795)* (Campo Grande: Instituto Histórico e Geográfico do Mato Grosso do Sul, 2006), 52.

6. On fugitive communities, independent Indians, and places of refuge in the Amazonian borderlands, see Flávio dos Santos Gomes, "A 'Safe Haven': Runaway Slaves, *Mocambos*, and Borders in Colonial Amazonia, Brazil," *Hispanic American Historical Review* 82, no. 3 (2002): 469–98. An example of how such territories were described at the time can be found in Henrique João Wilkens, "Parecer," Barcelos, August 10, 1800, ANRJ, Cod. 807, vol. 13, 230–34, transcribed in Marta Rosa Amoroso, "Guerra Mura no século XVIII: Versos e versões, representações dos Mura no imaginário colonial" (MA thesis, Universidade Estadual de Campinas, São Paulo, 1991), 306–10.

7. As one expedition chronicler wrote of a friendly exchange with the Caripuna along the Madeira River in the early 1780s, "Humanity was not the only driving force behind the good reception we gave to these Indians; rather, the necessity of peace with them made us not mistreat them ... because there is no defense when one is in the middle of the rapids, if they were to attack us there like the Mura did in the river." Antônio Pires da Silva Pontes, "Diário histórico e físico da viagem dos oficiais da demarcação que partiram do quartel geral de Barcelos para a capital de Vila Bela da Capitania de Mato Grosso, em 1 de Setembro de 1781," *Revista do Instituto Histórico e Geográfico Brasileiro* 262 (1964): 363.

8. Amy Turner Bushnell, "'Gastos de indios': The Crown and the Chiefdom-Presidio Compact in Florida," in *El Gran Norte Mexicano: Indios, misioneros y pobladores entre el mito y la historia*, ed. Salvador Bernabéu Albert (Seville: Consejo Superior de Investigaciones Científicas, 2009), 137–63.

9. Governor João de Albuquerque de Melo Pereira e Cáceres to Martinho de Melo e Castro, Vila Bela, July 20, 1795, AHU, Mato Grosso Avulsos, Cx. 31, Doc. 1696. On Spanish trading relationships with autonomous Native groups in the context of Bourbon-era frontier policy, see Kristine L. Jones, "Comparative Raiding Economies, North and South," in *Contested Ground: Comparative Frontiers on the Northern and Southern Edges of the Spanish Empire*, ed. Donna J. Guy and Thomas E. Sheridan (Tucson: University of Arizona Press, 1998), 102–7; Weber, *Bárbaros*, 180–83.

10. See, for example, the accusations of the governor of Paraguay in his 1797 letter to the governor of Mato Grosso, quoted in Chiara Vangelista, "Los guaykurú, españoles y portugueses en una región de frontera: Mato Grosso,

1770–1830," *Boletín del Instituto de Historia Argentina y Americana Dr. Emilio Ravignani* 8, no. 39 (1993): 67.

11. Lieutenant Colonel João Batista Mardel to João Pereira Caldas, Nogueira, June 1, 1785, AHI, 340-4-6. Similar sentiments about the Mura can be found in "Illustração necessária e interessante, relativa ao gentio da nação Mura . . . feita por um anônimo em 1826," in Carlos de Araújo Moreira Neto, *Índios da Amazônia, de maioria a minoria* (Petrópolis: Vozes, 1988), 252. On the standard refrain in colonial Brazilian sources that Native peoples were concealing the riches of the backlands, see Hal Langfur, "Native Informants and the Limits of Portuguese Dominion in Late-Colonial Brazil," in *The Oxford Handbook of Borderlands of the Iberian World*, ed. Danna Levin Rojo and Cynthia Radding (Oxford: Oxford University Press, 2019), 215.

12. Pedro Puntoni, *A guerra dos bárbaros: Povos indígenas e a colonização do sertão nordeste do Brasil, 1650–1720* (São Paulo: Hucitec/Edusp/Fapesp, 2002); John M. Monteiro, *Blacks of the Land: Indian Slavery, Settler Society, and the Portuguese Colonial Enterprise in South America*, ed. and trans. James Woodard and Barbara Weinstein (Cambridge: Cambridge University Press, 2018).

13. Governor Tristão da Cunha Menezes to Martinho de Mello e Castro, Vila Boa, January 16, 1784, AIHGB, ARQ 1, 2, 7, fls. 278v–283.

14. General João Pereira Caldas to António Carlos da Fonseca Coutinho, Barcelos, June 28, 1786, AHU, Rio Negro Avulsos, Cx. 11, Doc. 435 (attachment). Though the Mura and Mundurukú are often described as historical enemies, this should not be taken at face value, since the construction of such oppositions might serve Portuguese colonial interests. I thank Mark Harris for reminding me to be skeptical on this point.

15. On these particular pairs, see Vangelista, "Los guaykurú, españoles y portugueses," 74; Carvalho, *Lealdades negociadas*, 238–40; David G. Sweet, "Native Resistance in Eighteenth-Century Amazonia: The 'Abominable Muras' in War and Peace," *Radical History Review* 53, no. 1 (1992): 72. On Portuguese aspirations for colonial village Indians to recruit independent Indigenous groups to settle in the colonial sphere, see Heather F. Roller, *Amazonian Routes: Indigenous Mobility and Colonial Communities in Northern Brazil* (Stanford, CA: Stanford University Press, 2014), 100–102.

16. See, for example, Odair Giraldin, *Cayapó e Panará: Luta e sobrevivência de um povo Jê no Brasil central* (Campinas: UNICAMP, 1997), 94; Domingues, *Quando os índios eram vassalos*, 290–91.

17. Garcia, *As diversas formas de ser índio*, 246–47, 262, 291.

18. This was the explanation offered by a large group of peacemaking Xavantes who refused to divide their group and have some resettle at the proposed site of Salinas on the Araguaia River; instead they all preferred to go to Carretão, a site closer to the colonial capital of Goiás, which also had a healthier climate and fewer mosquitoes in their estimation. José Rodrigues Freire, *Relação da conquista do gentio Xavante, conseguida pelo Illmo e Exmo Senhor*

Tristão da Cunha Menezes, Governador, e Capitão General da Capitania de Goiaz (Lisbon: Typografia Nunesianna, 1790), 21–22, Biblioteca Brasiliana Guita e José Mindlin, Digital Collection, https://digital.bbm.usp.br/handle/bbm/7425 (emphasis mine). On this episode, see also Karasch, "Rethinking the Conquest of Goiás," 483–84.

19. Historians writing about autonomous Native peoples in the Chaco, the Pampas, northern Patagonia, and northern Mexico have emphasized Indigenous agency in peace agreements with Spaniards. Lidia R. Nacuzzi and Carina Lucaioli, "'Y sobre las armas se concertaron las paces': Explorando las rutinas de los acuerdos diplomáticos coloniales," *Revista CUHSO (Cultura—Hombre—Sociedad)* 15, no. 2 (2008): 61–74; Lidia R. Nacuzzi, "Los cacicazgos del siglo XVIII en ámbitos de frontera de Pampa-Patagonia y el Chaco," in *De los cacicazgos a la ciudadanía: Sistemas políticos en la frontera, Rio de la Plata, siglos XVIII–XX*, ed. Mónica Quijada (Berlin: Gebr. Mann Verlag, 2011), 61–74; Carina P. Lucaioli, "Alianzas y estrategias de los líderes indígenas abipones en un espacio fronterizo colonial (Chaco, siglo XVIII)," *Revista Española de Antropología Americana* 39, no. 1 (2009): 77–96; Guillaume Boccara, "Etnogénesis mapuche: Resistencia y reestructuración entre los indígenas del centro-sur de Chile (siglos XVI–XVIII)," *Hispanic American Historical Review* 79, no. 3 (1999): especially 447–49; José Manuel Zavala, *Los mapuches del siglo XVIII: Dinámica interétnica y estrategias de resistencia* (Santiago: Editorial Universidad Bolivariana, 2008), especially 26; Juliana Barr, *Peace Came in the Form of a Woman: Indians and Spaniards in the Texas Borderlands* (Chapel Hill: University of North Carolina Press, 2007); Rafael Brewster Folsom, *The Yaquis and the Empire: Violence, Spanish Imperial Power, and Native Resilience in Colonial Mexico* (New Haven, CT: Yale University Press, 2014).

20. For evidence that these were among the goals of the Caiapó do Sul and Xavante—factions of whom made peace with the Portuguese in Central Brazil during the late eighteenth century—see Mary C. Karasch, "Inter-ethnic Conflict and Survival Strategies on the Tocantins-Araguaia Frontier, 1750–1890," in *Contested Ground: Comparative Frontiers on the Northern and Southern Edges of the Spanish Empire*, ed. Donna J. Guy and Thomas E. Sheridan (Tucson: University of Arizona Press, 1998), 129–32; David Louis Mead, "Caiapó do Sul, an Ethnohistory (1610–1920)" (PhD diss., University of Florida, 2010), 265–66.

21. Nacuzzi and Lucaioli, "'Y sobre las armas se concertaron las paces,'" 61–74.

22. On the formulaic nature of these peacemaking narratives in Brazil, and the ways in which narratives were modified in higher-level correspondence, see Herzog, *Frontiers of Possession*, 99–101. On the value of low-level sources for studying Native-Portuguese relations, see Langfur, *The Forbidden Lands*, 200.

23. Barr, *Peace Came in the Form of a Woman*, 13.

24. Florencia Roulet, "Con la pluma y la palabra: el lado oscuro de las negociaciones de paz entre españoles e indígenas," *Revista de Indias* 64, no. 231 (2004): 316, 337.

25. Freire, *Relação da conquista do gentio Xavante*, 26–27. On these contradictory images of the Xavante, see Karasch, "Rethinking the Conquest of Goiás," 465.

26. Governor Luís de Albuquerque de Melo Pereira e Cáceres to Governor Luís da Cunha Menezes, Vila Bela, November 22, 1782, APMT, Cod. 24, fl. 186v.

27. Roulet, "Con la pluma y la palabra," 321.

28. Mead, "Caiapó do Sul, an Ethnohistory," 196–97, citing an anonymous account of the episode.

29. For an analysis of the term, going back to its origins in Jesuit discourse in the sixteenth century, see Eduardo Viveiros de Castro, *The Inconstancy of the Indian Soul: The Encounter of Catholics and Cannibals in 16th-Century Brazil* (Chicago: Prickly Paradigm Press, 2011); see also Ferreira, "Conquista colonial," 114–15, 129.

30. Lieutenant Colonel João Batista Mardel to governor, Barcelos, July 1, 1786, APEP, Cod. 429, Doc. 5.

31. Garcia, *As diversas formas de ser índio*, 247; Herzog, *Frontiers of Possession*, 108.

32. Jeffrey A. Erbig, "Borderline Offerings: *Tolderías* and Mapmakers in the Eighteenth-Century Río de la Plata," *Hispanic American Historical Review* 96, no. 3 (2016): 473; Garcia, *As diversas formas de ser índio*, 303.

33. On royal funding for expeditions to contact independent Native groups, see Roller, *Amazonian Routes*, 93, 104.

34. Director António Gonçalves de Sousa to governor, Vila Franca, May 12, 1766, APEP, Cod. 167, Doc. 134; see also Roller, *Amazonian Routes*, 109–10. Another document, from nearly thirty years later, suggests that a small group of "Aretú" Indians came to settle at Monte Alegre, a colonial village on the Amazon River, in order to escape their enemies, the Mundurukú; they reportedly spoke the língua geral and joined a few of their group who already lived in the village. Vicar Domingos Caetano Lima to governor, Monte Alegre, November 23, 1792, APEP, Cod. 470, Doc. 56. I could not find any other documents relating to the Aritú/Aretú at APEP.

35. See, for example, Governor Luís de Albuquerque de Melo Pereira e Cáceres to Martinho de Melo e Castro, Vila Bela, June 8, 1775, AHU, Mato Grosso Avulsos, Cx. 17, Doc. 1102. Their long history of visits, peaceful and hostile, to Spanish cities, frontier outposts, and missions is described in the chronicle of the Jesuit who worked among them in the 1760s: José Sánchez Labrador, S.J., *El Paraguay católico* (Buenos Aires: Imprensa de Coni Hermanos, 1910), 1:255–59, 2:55–90.

36. For background on the shifting relationships between the Guaikurú, Spaniards, and Portuguese over the course of the eighteenth century, see Branislava Susnik, *El indio colonial del Paraguay: El Chaqueño*, vol. 3, part 1 (Asunción, Paraguay: Museo Etnográfico Andrés Barbero, 1971), 12–100; Sílvia Schmuziger Carvalho, "Chaco: Encruzilhada dos povos e 'melting pot' cultural, suas

relaões com a bacia do Paraná e o Sul mato-grossense," in *História dos índios do Brasil*, ed. Manuela Carneiro da Cunha (São Paulo: Companhia das Letras, 1992), 467–68; Vangelista, "Los guaykurú, españoles y portugueses," 60–69; Nidia Areces, "Paraguayos, portugueses y mbayás en Concepción, 1773–1840," *Memoria Americana* 8 (1999): 11–44; James Schofield Saeger, *The Chaco Mission Frontier: The Guaycuruan Experience* (Tucson: University of Arizona Press, 2000), 34–38; Francismar Alex Lopes de Carvalho, "Etnogênese mbayá-guaykuru: Notas sobre emergência identitária, expansão territorial e resistência de um grupo étnico no vale do rio paraguai (c. 1650–1800)," *Revista de História e Estudos Culturais* 3, no. 4 (2006): 1–20; Ana Lucia Herberts, "Panorama histórico dos mbayá-guaikuru entre os séculos XVI e XIX," in *Kadiwéu: Senhoras da arte, senhores da guerra*, ed. Giovani José da Silva (Curitiba: Editora CRV, 2011), 17–47.

37. Saeger, *The Chaco Mission Frontier*, 23–24.

38. The quotation is from Commander José António Pinto de Figueiredo to governor, Albuquerque, July 27, 1784, APMT, QM.TM.CA, Cx. 19, Doc. 1259.

39. Ricardo Franco de Almeida Serra, "Continuação do parecer sobre os índios Uaicurús e Guanás," *Revista do Instituto Histórico e Geográfico Brasileiro* 13 (1850): 391.

40. Darcy Ribeiro, *Os índios e a civilização: A integração das populações indígenas no Brasil moderno* (Rio de Janeiro: Editora Civilização Brasileira, 1970), 153. The quote is from an SPI functionary involved in the 1912 "pacification" of the Kaingang in São Paulo.

41. Commander José António Pinto de Figueiredo, quoted in Raul Silveira de Mello, *História do Forte de Coimbra* (Rio de Janeiro: Imprensa do Exército, 1959), 2:291, 292; Prado, *História dos índios cavaleiros*, 56. On Caimá's startling height, see Alexandre Rodrigues Ferreira, "Carta dirigida ao Governador e Capitão-General João de Albuquerque de Melo Pereira e Cáceres" (May 5, 1791), in *Viagem ao Brasil de Alexandre Rodrigues Ferreira: Coleção etnográfica*, ed. José Paulo Monteiro Soares and Cristina Ferrão (São Paulo: Kapa Editorial, 2005), 3:22.

42. Commander Joaquim José Ferreira to governor, Coimbra, March 10, 1791, APMT, FC.CA, Cx. 2, Doc. 126. Similar accounts of these events can be found in the account of a different Ferreira, the naturalist Alexandre Rodrigues Ferreira, "Carta dirigida ao Governador," 20; Prado, *História dos índios cavaleiros*, 56–57. Perhaps both had read the warnings of the Jesuit chronicler José Sánchez Labrador, who was convinced that the "greatest vigilance" was needed whenever the Guaikurú boasted of being honorable men of their word. *El Paraguay católico*, 2:306.

43. Commander Joaquim José Ferreira to governor, Coimbra, July 24, 1791, APMT, FC.CA, Cx. 2, Doc. 134. Barr notes that for Spaniards and Indians in Texas the absence of women often boded ill for peace negotiations; it "often brought an imbalance to these relations and meant that interactions remained only between sets of men." *Peace Came in the Form of a Woman*, 13.

44. Ferreira, "Carta dirigida ao Governador," 19, 24. Sánchez Labrador said that the Guaikurú looked upon the facial and body hair of whites with disdain; one old woman in the mission even surprised him by pulling suddenly at one of his eyebrows, "to remove this hair," she said, "that makes you ugly." *El Paraguay católico*, 1:246.

45. On the location of Caimá's village, see Commander Joaquim José Ferreira to governor, Coimbra, July 24, 1791, APMT, FC.CA, Cx. 2, Doc. 133. Details about Caimá's death can be found in Ricardo Francisco de Almeida Serra to unknown recipient, Coimbra, June 15, 1797, APMT, FC. CR, Cx. 5, Doc. 298.

46. Weber, *Bárbaros*, 201. Commander Serra also pointed out that the more southern Guaikurú groups sought to dominate the trade in Spanish tools and other goods that were at that time in short supply; the northern groups thus turned to Portuguese trade circuits. "Continuação do parecer," 383.

47. The 1791 peace treaty and the *carta patente* for the two Guaikurú chiefs have been reproduced in Prado, *História dos índios cavaleiros*, 58–60.

48. Commander Francisco Rodrigues do Prado to governor, Coimbra, January 8, 1795, APMT, FC.CA, Cx. 4, Doc. 197.

49. On the names and locations of each parcialidade, see ch. 1, note 61. Serra said that Emavidi Xané (Paulo) belonged to the Uatedeos subgroup (Guetiadegodis in Sánchez Labrador's account), situated on the western side of the Paraguay River and furthest to the north of any of the Guaikurú groups; indirect evidence suggests that Caimá (Queima) was from the Eyibegodegis (or Ejueos), on the eastern side, and that these two groups were linked by kinship ties. Ricardo Franco de Almeida Serra, "Parecer sobre o aldeamento dos índios Uaicurus e Guanás com a descripção dos seus usos, religião, estabilidade e costumes (1803)," *Revista do Instituto Histórico e Geográfico Brasileiro* 7 (1845): 207; Serra, "Continuação do parecer," 349–50. Over the next decade, chiefs of other Guaikurú parcialidades, as well as Guaná chiefs, went to Vila Bela to affirm peace with the Portuguese; see, for example, the documents from 1796 in AHU, Mato Grosso Avulsos, Cx. 31, Doc. 1722 (attachments 2 and 3). There were a few sporadic attacks in this period by Spanish-allied groups of Guaikurú—including one that occurred at the very moment that the two chiefs, Caimá and Emavidi Xané, were being hosted by the Portuguese governor in the capital. See Governor João de Albuquerque de Melo Pereira e Cáceres to Martinho de Melo e Castro, Vila Bela, July 2, 1792, AHU, Mato Grosso Avulsos, Cx. 29, Doc. 1644.

50. Commander Francisco Rodrigues do Prado to governor, Coimbra, January 29, 1797, APMT, FC.CA, Cx. 5, Doc. 241. By the following year, it was estimated that the Guaikurú had some 5,000–6,000 animals just in the vicinity of Albuquerque. Commander Ricardo Franco de Almeida Serra to governor, Coimbra, May 30, 1798, APMT, FC.CA, Cx. 6, Doc. 328.

51. Commander Francisco Rodrigues do Prado to governor, Coimbra, September 6, 1796, APMT, FC.CA, Cx. 4, Doc. 223. The Guaikurú were said to use

smoke signals to communicate with other parcialidades. Sánchez Labrador, *El Paraguay católico*, 1:261.

52. Commander Ricardo Franco de Almeida Serra to governor, Coimbra, May 4, 1802, APMT, FC.CA, Cx. 9, Doc. 475.

53. Carvalho, *Lealdades negociadas*, 238, 249.

54. On the importance of maintaining control over conduits of information in borderlands settings, see Pekka Hämäläinen, "The Shapes of Power: Indians, Europeans, and North American Worlds from the Seventeenth to the Nineteenth Century," in *Contested Spaces of Early America*, ed. Juliana Barr and Edward Countryman (Philadelphia: University of Pennsylvania Press, 2104), 49–50. Factionalism among the Guaikurú and the dividing line of the Fecho dos Morros are discussed in Prado, *História dos índios cavaleiros*, 63. The Guaikurú parcialidades to the south were likely the Apacachodegodegis and Lichagotegodis, among whom the Jesuit Sánchez Labrador had set up his short-lived mission of Belén.

55. Carvalho, *Lealdades negociadas*, 21.

56. On the commerce in stolen horses, see Benita Herreros Cleret de Langavant, "Portugueses, españoles y mbayá en el alto Paraguay: Dinámicas y estrategias de frontera en los márgenes de los imperios ibéricos (1791–1803)," *Nuevo Mundo—Mundos Nuevos* (2012), posted November 4, 2012, https://journals.openedition.org/nuevomundo/64467, paragraphs 19–21; Carvalho, *Lealdades negociadas*, 395. On the Guaikurú trying to sell old or infirm horses, see Commander Francisco Rodrigues do Prado to governor, Coimbra, October 20, 1795, APMT, FC.CA, Cx. 4, Doc. 207. On parallel Comanche strategies in the colonial horse trade, see Pekka Hämäläinen, "The Politics of Grass: European Expansion, Ecological Change, and Indigenous Power in the Southwest Borderlands," *William and Mary Quarterly* 67, no. 2 (2010): 198.

57. Portuguese reliance on Guaikurú spies and informants is made clear in Lieutenant Ignácio de Sousa Nogueira to Joaquim José Ferreira, Coimbra, October 31, 1791, APMT, FC.CA, Cx. 2, Doc. 142; Commander Ricardo Franco de Almeida Serra to governor, Coimbra, July 2, 1799, APMT, FC.CA, Cx. 7, Doc. 383; Governor Caetano Pinto de Miranda Montenegro to Francisco de Souza Coutinho, Vila Bela, September 17, 1801, AIHGB, Lata 762, Doc. 3.

58. Commander Francisco Rodrigues do Prado to governor, Coimbra, January 14, 1795, APMT, FC.CA, Cx. 4, Doc. 202. By the early nineteenth century, some parcialidades were being described as "*agregado*," or attached, to more powerful ones. Serra, "Parecer," 207. Erbig notes that Native tolderías/tolderias that lived closest to (or moved into) the imperial border area found opportunities to expand their authority, while groups that remained farther away found themselves weakened or more vulnerable, according to Erbig, *Where Caciques and Mapmakers Met*, 108.

59. Ferreira, "Carta dirigida ao Governador," 19.

60. Ávila, "Conquista, control y convicción," 666.

61. On the complex relationship between the Guaikurú and Guaná during the peacemaking years, see Ferreira, "Carta dirigida ao Governador," 19–27; Prado, *História dos índios cavaleiros*, 40; Serra, "Parecer," 210. For scholarly discussions, see Carvalho, *Lealdades negociadas*, 239–40; Fernando Santos-Granero, *Vital Enemies: Slavery, Predation and the Amerindian Political Economy of Life* (Austin: University of Texas Press, 2009), 92–99; John Hemming, *Red Gold: The Conquest of the Brazilian Indians* (Cambridge, MA: Harvard University Press, 1978), 394–95.

62. Serra, "Parecer," 209.

63. Commander Ricardo Franco de Almeida Serra to governor, Coimbra, December 29, 1798, APMT, FC.CA, Cx. 6, Doc. 352.

64. Commander Ricardo Franco de Almeida Serra to governor, Coimbra, May 30, 1798, APMT, FC.CA, Cx. 6, Doc. 328.

65. Serra, "Parecer," 204–5.

66. Andrey Cordeiro Ferreira, "Conquista colonial, resistência indígena e formação do estado-nação: Os índios Guaicuru e Guaná no Mato Grosso do século XIX," *Revista de Antropologia* 52, no. 1 (2009): 109, citing Hildebrando Campestrini and Acir Vaz Guimarães on Serra's marriage.

67. Serra, "Continuação do parecer," 380 (emphasis mine). For an analysis of Guaikurú "taming" strategies that draws heavily from Serra's reports, see Gilberto Brizolla Santos, "'Amansar os portugueses': Os índios Guaikurú nas representações portuguesas coloniais," in *Mato Grosso Português: Ensaios de antropologia histórica*, ed. Maria Fátima Roberto Machado (Cuiabá: UFMT, 2002), 67–119.

68. António de Morais Silva and Rafael Bluteau, *Diccionário da língua portugueza* (Lisbon: Oficina de S. T. Ferreira, 1789), 2:54. For an example of the Portuguese using the term *amansar* to refer to pacifying Indians (from a letter to the Spanish governor of Paraguay, offering reassurances that the Portuguese were focused on preventing the Guaikurú from launching raids across the border), see Governor Caetano Pinto de Miranda Montenegro to Lázaro de Ribera y Espinoza, Vila Bela, March 24, 1803, APMT, Cod. 40, fls. 202–3. The anthropologist Paola Colleoni describes the (Spanish) term *amansar* being used by the modern Waorani of Ecuadorian Amazon in reference to their historical process of becoming "civilized." In this case, the Waorani see themselves as being "tamed by the whites," but the way they speak about this process suggests that it is "the result of a conscious indigenous attempt to incorporate the Other into the sphere of indigenous social relations." Colleoni, "Becoming Tamed: The Meaning of 'Becoming Civilized' among the Waorani of Amazonian Ecuador," *Tipití: Journal of the Society for the Anthropology of Lowland South America* 14, no. 1 (2016): 95, http://digitalcommons.trinity.edu/tipiti/vol14/iss1/5.

69. Other examples can be found in Bruce Albert and Alcida Ramos, eds., *Pacificando o branco: Cosmologias do contato no Norte-Amazônico* (São Paulo:

UNESP, 2002); Ribeiro, *Os índios e a civilização*, 184–86; Luísa Tombini Wittmann, *O Vapor e o Botoque: Imigrantes alemães e índios Xokleng no Vale do Itajaí/SC (1850–1926)* (Florianópolis: Letras Contemporâneas, 2007), 161–63.

70. Commander Ricardo Franco de Almeida Serra to governor, Coimbra, May 30, 1798, APMT, FC.CA, Cx. 6, Doc. 328. On his suspicions that the Guaikurú used a secretive *"gíria particular,"* see Serra, "Continuação do parecer," 373.

71. "Observacções addicionaes a Illustração sobre o Gentio Mura, escripta por hum anônimo no anno de 1826," in Moreira Neto, *Índios da Amazônia*, 264. On the five speech channels in Pirahã, a dialect related to the now-extinct Mura language, see Daniel L. Everett, *Don't Sleep. There Are Snakes: Life and Language in the Amazonian Jungle* (New York: Pantheon Books, 2008), 185–88. For a summary of what is known about the Mura language, see Marta Amoroso, "Mura: Língua," Instituto Socioambiental, Povos Indígenas no Brasil, last modified August 1, 2018, https://pib.socioambiental.org/pt/Povo:Mura.

72. Serra, "Continuação do parecer," 374–75.

73. Commander António José Rodrigues to governor, Coimbra, November 15, 1813, APMT, FC.CA, Cx. 13, Doc. 816.

74. Sweet, "Native Resistance," 64. On the Mura peace as divine providence, see, for example, General João Pereira Caldas to João Batista Mardel, Barcelos, February 4, 1785, in Soares and Ferrão, *Viagem ao Brasil*, 3:41; "Observacções addicionaes," 264; and especially Sergeant Major Henrique João Wilkens's epic poem *Muhuraida, ou O Triumfo da Fé, 1785* (Manaus: Universidade Federal do Amazonas, 1993). Analyses of the poem can be found in Amoroso, "Guerra Mura," 112–18, 132–34; Neil Safier, "The Confines of the Colony: Boundaries, Ethnographic Landscapes, and Imperial Cartography in Iberoamerica," in *The Imperial Map: Cartography and the Mastery of Empire*, ed. James Akerman (Chicago: University of Chicago Press, 2009), 162–66.

75. On the Pombaline Crown reforms that led to the establishment of the Directorate villages on top of existing missions in Portuguese Amazonia, see Roller, *Amazonian Routes*. The Directorate was extended to the main Estado do Brasil in 1758. A study of the Directorate villages in Rio de Janeiro likewise emphasizes the security they represented to some Native peoples in a dangerous colonial world: Maria Regina Celestino de Almeida, *Metamorfoses indígenas: Identidade e cultura nas aldeias coloniais do Rio de Janeiro* (Rio de Janeiro: Arquivo Nacional, 2003), especially 102.

76. Mathias Fernandes to governor, Japurá, April 12, 1778, APEP, Cod. 340, Doc. 9.

77. Sergeant Major Henrique João Wilkens to João Pereira Caldas, Ega, July 5, 1782, AHU, Rio Negro Avulsos, Cx. 5, Doc. 245 (attachment).

78. Sweet, "Native Resistance," 64–65; Marta Rosa Amoroso, "Corsários no caminho fluvial: Os Mura do Rio Madeira," in *História dos índios no Brasil*, ed. Manuela Carneiro da Cunha (São Paulo: Companhia das Letras, 1992), 306;

General João Pereira Caldas to Martinho de Melo e Castro, Barcelos, November 13, 1782; letter from Director Mathias Fernandes, no recipient, July 25, 1782 (attachment); Lieutenant Colonel Theodósio Constantino de Chermont to João Pereira Caldas, Santo Antônio de Maripí, August 16, 1782 (attachment), all in AHU, Rio Negro Avulsos, Cx. 5, Doc. 250.

79. Commander Manoel José Valadão to João Pereira Caldas, Santo Antônio de Maripí, July 12, 1784, APEP, Cod. 407, Doc. 10; a published version (with minor differences) can be found in Soares and Ferrão, *Viagem ao Brasil*, 3:37–38. The visit is also described in Sweet, "Native Resistance," 65–66.

80. Commander Manoel José Valadão to João Pereira Caldas, Santo Antônio de Maripí, January 15, 1785, in Soares and Ferrão, *Viagem ao Brasil*, 3:39.

81. The importance of this particular riverine network for more efficient communication between colonial outposts on the two major tributaries is explained in Wilkens, "Parecer," in Amoroso, "Guerra Mura no século XVIII," 306–10.

82. The quotations about Ambrósio's appearance are from Lieutenant Colonel João Batista Mardel to governor, Ega, March 15, 1785, in Soares and Ferrão, *Viagem ao Brasil*, 3:41–42. The most complete version of his family's history is in the "supplement" to the letter of Lieutenant Colonel João Batista Mardel to João Pereira Caldas, Nogueira, June 1, 1785, AHI, Cod. 340-4-6. Further details can be found in Sweet, "Native Resistance," 70–71.

83. Sergeant Major Henrique João Wilkens to João Pereira Caldas, Ega, 25 February 1788, in Amoroso and Farage, *Relatos da Fronteira*, 57.

84. Lieutenant Colonel João Batista Mardel to General João Pereira Caldas, Ega, April 17, 1785, in Soares and Ferrão, *Viagem ao Brasil*, 3:45; Colonel João Batista Mardel to General João Pereira Caldas, Nogueira, June 24, 1785, AHI, Cod. 340-4-6. In his epic poem *Muhuraida*, Henrique João Wilkens portrayed the Muras' unexpected arrival in Nogueira during the festivals as a culmination of divine providence.

85. Lieutenant Colonel João Batista Mardel to General João Pereira Caldas, Barcelos, July 1, 1786, AHU, Rio Negro Avulsos, Cx. 11, Doc. 435 (attachment); General João Pereira Caldas to the Director of Moura, Barcelos, July 1, 1786, AHU, Rio Negro Avulsos, Cx. 11, Doc. 435 (attachment).

86. On the attraction of Mura women to churchgoing and the "old domestic Indian way of life," see Sweet, "Native Resistance," 71–72; Amoroso, "Corsários no caminho fluvial," 306–7.

87. Lieutenant Colonel João Batista Mardel to João Pereira Caldas, Nogueira, June 1, 1785, AHI, Cod. 340-4-6.

88. These successive visits (from April to June) are described in Commander António Carlos da Fonseca Coutinho to João Pereira Caldas, Borba, June 13, 1786, AHU, Rio Negro Avulsos, Cx. 11, Doc. 435 (attachment). The visitors were described as "Muras" by General João Pereira Caldas in his reply to António Carlos da Fonseca Coutinho, Barcelos, June 28, 1786, AHU, Rio Negro Avulsos, Cx. 11, Doc. 435 (attachment).

89. Marcy Norton, "Taming the Wild: Animal Familiarization in Greater Amazonia, 1492–1700" (lecture, Colgate University, Hamilton, NY, October 3, 2018); Philippe Erikson, "The Social Significance of Pet-Keeping among Amazonian Indians," in *Companion Animals and Us: Exploring the Relationships between People and Pets*, ed. Anthony L. Podberscek, Elizabeth Paul, and James A. Serpell (Cambridge: Cambridge University Press, 2000), 7–27.

90. Commander António Carlos da Fonseca Coutinho to João Pereira Caldas, Borba, June 13, 1786, AHU, Rio Negro Avulsos, Cx. 11, Doc. 435 (attachment).

91. Caetano Brandão, *Diários das visitas pastorais no Pará* (Porto: Instituto Nacional de Investigação Científica / Centro de História da Universidade do Porto, 1991), 118–20. The archbishop visited Borba in September 1788; mass baptisms of Mura children in Borba had occurred in 1787, according to Commander António Carlos da Fonseca Coutinho to João Pereira Caldas, August 17, 1787, Borba, AHU, Rio Negro Avulsos, Cx. 14, Doc. 526 (attachment). On the Mundurukú threat to the Muras who came to Borba, see General João Pereira Caldas to António Carlos da Fonseca Coutinho, Barcelos, June 28, 1786, AHU, Rio Negro Avulsos, Cx. 11, Doc. 435 (attachment); Commander António Carlos da Fonseca Coutinho to João Pereira Caldas, Borba, May 27, 1789, AHU, Rio Negro Avulsos, Cx. 15, Doc. 558 (attachment). The ambiguity of the ritual of baptism for Native peoples is discussed in Cristina Pompa, *Religião como tradução: Missionários, Tupi e "Tapuia" no Brasil colonial* (Bauru, São Paulo: EDUSC, 2003), 395.

92. Sweet, "Native Resistance," 77.

93. Commander Manoel José Valadão to João Batista Mardel, Santo António de Maripí, March 5, 1785, APEP, Cod. 420, Doc. 27.

94. Governor Luís da Cunha Menezes to Martinho de Melo e Castro, Vila Boa, July 20, 1781, AHU, Goiás Avulsos, Cx. 32, D. 2019. On this episode involving the old man, whom she identifies as Romexi, see Karasch, "Rethinking the Conquest of Goiás," 469–70.

95. Lieutenant Colonel João Batista Mardel to João Pereira Caldas, Ega, March 15, 1785, in Soares and Ferrão, *Viagem ao Brasil*, 3:42; Sweet, "Native Resistance," 72.

96. Lieutenant Colonel João Batista Mardel to João Pereira Caldas, Nogueira, June 1, 1785, AHI, Cod. 340-4-6.

97. Alexandre Rodrigues Ferreira, "Memória sobre o gentio Mura, que voluntariamente descerão para as povoações dos Rios Negro, Solimões, Amazonas, e Madeira, segundo a faz desenhar, e remetter para o Real Gabinete da História Natural o Doutor Naturalista Alexandre Rodrigues Ferreira," Barcelos, September 30, 1787, BNRJ, 21, 2, 17.

98. Sergeant Major Henrique João Wilkens to João Pereira Caldas, Ega, October 12, 1787, APEP, Cod. 443, Doc. 37. In SPI documents from Santa Catarina, Wittmann found descriptions of recently contacted Xokleng volunteering

for similar types of labor, which they approached as though they were sports or tests of strength (*O Vapor e o Botoque*, 171).

99. Fray José da Conceição to João Pereira Caldas, Airão, February 11, 1787, BNRJ, 21, 2, 23.

100. Alexandre Rodrigues Ferreira, "Memória sobre o gentio Mura."

101. Lieutenant Colonel João Batista Mardel to João Pereira Caldas, Barcelos, July 1, 1786, AHU, Rio Negro Avulsos, Cx. 11, Doc. 435 (attachment).

102. "Supplement" to the letter of Lieutenant Colonel João Batista Mardel to João Pereira Caldas, Nogueira, June 1, 1785, AHI, Cod. 340-4-6. Even as late as the 1840s, the southern Mura were described as being more integrated and forming larger kin groups than the dispersed Mura groups along the Solimões/Amazon River. "Observacções addicionaes," 259.

103. Director António [?] Correia da Maia to governor, Serpa, July 21, 1785, APEP, Cod. 421, Doc. 17; Lieutenant Colonel João Batista Mardel to João Pereira Caldas, Nogueira, July 26, 1785, AHI, Cod. 340-4-6; General João Pereira Caldas to Martinho de Souza e Albuquerque, Barcelos, April 15, 1786, APEP, Cod. 430, Doc. 37; José Manoel de Morais to Henrique João Wilkens, Mouth of the Içá River, November 4, 1787, APEP, Cod. 440, Doc. 41; Sergeant Major Henrique João Wilkens to João Pereira Caldas, Ega, March 4, 1789, AHU, Rio Negro Avulsos, Cx. 15, Doc. 558 (attachment).

104. Sergeant Major Henrique João Wilkens to João Pereira Caldas, Ega, November 22, 1787, AHU, Rio Negro Avulsos, Cx. 14, Doc. 526 (attachment).

105. Aparecida Vilaça, *Strange Enemies: Indigenous Agency and Scenes of Encounters in Amazonia* (Durham, NC: Duke University Press, 2010), 296–97; Aparecida Vilaça, *Morte na floresta* (São Paulo: Todavia, 2020), 20 (interview quotation).

106. On sleeping on the ground, rather than in hammocks, as a marker of poverty among Indians, see Claude Lévi-Strauss, *Tristes Tropiques*, trans. John Weightman and Doreen Weightman (New York: Penguin, 2012), 277. For an example of a Portuguese author referring to the Mura as a "herd of pigs," see Brandão, *Diários das visitas pastorais no Pará*, 115.

107. Sergeant Major Henrique João Wilkens to João Pereira Caldas, Ega, December 7, 1787, AHU, Rio Negro Avulsos, Cx. 14, Doc. 526 (attachment) (emphasis mine).

108. Sergeant Major Henrique João Wilkens to João Pereira Caldas, Ega, December 7, 1787, AHU, Rio Negro Avulsos, Cx. 14, Doc. 526 (attachment).

109. This is from a priest who supervised recently "pacified" Indians, likely Maxakalis, in Minas Gerais in the 1760s, quoted in Langfur, *The Forbidden Lands*, 213.

110. For colonial analysis of Mura motivations, see Governor Francisco de Souza Coutinho to Rodrigo de Souza Coutinho, "Informação sobre a civilização dos índios do Pará," Belém, August 2, 1797, AHU, Pará Avulsos, Cx. 109, Doc. 8610, paragraph 40. The governor claimed that, being at peace, the Mura

would soon become useful to the Portuguese state. For the argument that the Mundurukú were not a significant factor in the Mura decision to make peace, see Sweet, "Native Resistance," 77. On presumed Mundurukú motivations for peace, see Lieutenant Colonel José António Salgado to governor, Santarém, September 1, 1795, APEP, Cod. 470, Doc. 118. This process can be studied through the documents transcribed in Francisco Jorge dos Santos, ed., "Dossiê Munduruku: Uma contribuição para a história indígena da Amazônia colonial," *Boletim Informativo do Museu Amazônico* 5, no. 8 (1995): 1–103. See also Domingues, *Quando os índios eram vassalos*, 286–89.

111. Manoel António da Costa Soutto Maior to governor, Santarém, November 21, 1795, APEP, Cod. 517, Doc. 118.

Chapter 3

1. These refrains can be found in reports from the commanders of Coimbra Fort over the course of more than two decades of peacemaking with the Guaikurú and Guaná, beginning with the peace treaty of 1791.

2. For similar assessments coming out of North American contexts, see Juliana Barr, *Peace Came in the Form of a Woman: Indians and Spaniards in the Texas Borderlands* (Chapel Hill: University of North Carolina Press, 2007), especially 210–11, 280–83; Brian DeLay, *War of a Thousand Deserts: Indian Raids and the U.S.-Mexican War* (New Haven, CT: Yale University Press, 2008), 38; Pekka Hämäläinen, *Comanche Empire* (New Haven, CT: Yale University Press, 2008), 47; David L. Preston, *The Texture of Contact: European and Indian Settler Communities on the Frontiers of Iroquoia, 1667–1783* (Lincoln: University of Nebraska Press, 2009), 8. On these dynamics in South America, see Tamar Herzog, *Frontiers of Possession: Spain and Portugal in Europe and the Americas* (Cambridge, MA: Harvard University Press, 2015), 102, 106; Maria Regina Celestino de Almeida, *Metamorfoses indígenas: Identidade e cultura nas aldeias coloniais do Rio de Janeiro* (Rio de Janeiro: Arquivo Nacional, 2003), 99–101; Elisa Frühauf Garcia, *As diversas formas de ser índio: Políticas indígenas e políticas indigenistas no extremo sul da América portuguesa* (Rio de Janeiro: Arquivo Nacional, 2009), 235; Lidia R. Nacuzzi and Carina Lucaioli, "'Y sobre las armas se concertaron las paces': Explorando las rutinas de los acuerdos diplomáticos coloniales," *Revista CUHSO (Cultura—Hombre—Sociedad)* 15, no. 2 (2008): 71.

3. On patterns of frontier negotiation that involved symbolic and material exchanges between Native peoples and Spaniards who were otherwise at war, see David J. Weber, *Bárbaros: Spaniards and Their Savages in the Age of Enlightenment* (New Haven, CT: Yale University Press, 2005), 178–220; Luz María Méndez Beltrán, "La organización de los parlamentos de indios en el siglo XVIII," in *Relaciones fronterizas en la Araucanía*, ed. Sergio Villalobos, Carlos Aldunate, Horacio Zapater, Luz María Méndez, and Carlos Bascuñán (Santiago: Ediciones Universidad Católica de Chile, 1982), 107–74; Raúl Mandrini and Sara Ortelli, "Los 'Araucanos' en las Pampas (c. 1700–1850),"

in *Colonización, resistencia, y mestizaje en las Américas (siglos XVI–XX)*, ed. Guillaume Boccara (Quito: Editorial Abya Yala, 2002), 237–57; Cynthia Radding, *Landscapes of Power and Identity: Comparative Histories of the Sonoran Desert and the Forests of Amazonia from Colony to Republic* (Durham, NC: Duke University Press, 2005), 186–88; Cuauhtémoc Velasco Ávila, "Peace Agreements and War Signals: Negotiations with the Apaches and Comanches in the Interior Provinces of New Spain, 1784–1788," in *Negotiation within Domination: New Spain's Indian Pueblos Confront the Spanish State*, ed. Ethelia Ruiz Medrano and Susan Kellogg (Boulder: University Press of Colorado, 2010), 173–204. For written treaties that reveal some of these conventions and patterns of interaction, see the collection by Abelardo Levaggi, *Diplomacia hispano-indígena en las fronteras de América: Historia de los tratados entre la Monarquía española y las comunidades aborígenes* (Madrid: Centro de Estudios Constitucionales, 2002).

4. These dynamics were broadly shared across the hemisphere. José Manuel Zavala, *Los mapuches del siglo XVIII: Dinámica interétnica y estrategias de resistencia* (Santiago: Editorial Universidad Bolivariana, 2008), 159–87; Beltrán, "La organización de los parlamentos de indios," 173–74; Mary C. Karasch, "Rethinking the Conquest of Goiás, 1775–1819," *The Americas* 61, no. 3 (2005), especially 474–80; Colin Calloway, *Pen and Ink Witchcraft: Treaties and Treaty Making in American Indian History* (Oxford: Oxford University Press, 2013), ch. 1; Richard White, *The Middle Ground: Indians, Empires, and Republics in the Great Lakes Region, 1650–1815* (Cambridge: Cambridge University Press, 1991), 84, 93.

5. Governor José de Almeida Vasconcelos to Chief Abuênonâ, Vila Boa, May 4, 1775, AHU, Goiás Avulsos, Cx. 28, D. 1827 (attachment).

6. Chief Abuênonâ to José de Almeida Vasconcelos, Ilha de Santa Anna [Bananal Island], August 3, 1775, AHU, Goiás Avulsos, Cx. 28, D. 1827 (attachment). My translation draws on Karasch's version in "Rethinking the Conquest of Goiás," 479–80; see also the analysis of this episode in Juciene Ricarte Apolinário, "Os Akroá e outros povos indígenas nas fronteiras do sertão: As práticas das políticas indígena e indigenista no norte da Capitania de Goiás—século XVIII" (PhD diss., Universidade Federal de Pernambuco, 2005), 183–84; John Hemming, *Amazon Frontier: The Defeat of the Brazilian Indians* (Cambridge, MA: Harvard University Press, 1987), 68–70.

7. Florencia Roulet, "Con la pluma y la palabra: el lado oscuro de las negociaciones de paz entre españoles e indígenas," *Revista de Indias* 64, no. 231 (2004): 339; White, *The Middle Ground*, 84; Calloway, *Pen and Ink Witchcraft*, 24–25.

8. Weber, *Bárbaros*, 207–8. Transcriptions of capitulation accords, all from Northeastern Brazil in the 1690s, can be found in an appendix of Pedro Puntoni, *A Guerra dos Bárbaros: Povos indígenas e a colonização do sertão nordeste do Brasil, 1650–1720* (São Paulo: Hucitec/Edusp, 2002), 300–304; see also his analysis on 157–60.

9. Apolinário, "Os Akroá e outros povos indígenas," 189, 191–92; Karasch, "Rethinking the Conquest of Goiás," 476.

10. The treaty can be found in Francisco Rodrigues do Prado, *História dos índios cavaleiros ou da Nação Guaycurú (1795)* (Campo Grande: Instituto Histórico e Geográfico do Mato Grosso do Sul, 2006), 58–60.

11. On colonial gifts possibly being perceived as tribute by independent Indians, see Bushnell, "'Gastos de indios'" 146–47; Weber, *Bárbaros*, 192; Caroline A. Williams, "Living Between Empires: Diplomacy and Politics in the Late Eighteenth-Century Mosquitia," *The Americas* 70, no. 2 (2013), 248–49. Francismar Alex Lopes de Carvalho finds that both Portuguese and Spanish officials complained about this. Carvalho, *Lealdades negociadas: Povos indígenas e a expansão dos impérios ibéricos nas regiões centrais da América do Sul (segunda metade do século XVIII)* (São Paulo: Alameda, 2014), 220, 235.

12. Ricardo Franco de Almeida Serra, "Continuação do parecer sobre os índios Uaicurús e Guanás," *Revista do Instituto Histórico e Geográfico Brasileiro* 13 (1850): 349. See also the discussion of this passage in John Hemming, *Red Gold: The Conquest of the Brazilian Indians* (Cambridge: Harvard University Press, 1978), 392. I was struck by the resemblance of the demands made by a group of peacemaking Comanches about a decade later and a continent away: they wanted Spanish workers to build new houses for them, and the Spanish governor assented. See "Report on Comanche Affairs by the Governor of New Mexico, Joaquín Real Alencaster, Santa Fe, November 20, 1805, to the Commandante General of the Interior Provinces," in *Border Comanches: Seven Spanish Colonial Documents, 1785–1819*, ed. Marc Simmons (Santa Fe, NM: Stagecoach Press, 1967), 33–34. A similar demand was also made by a Mura group, discussed later in this chapter.

13. Barr, *Peace Came in the Form of a Woman*, 210.

14. Governor João de Albuquerque de Melo Pereira e Cáceres to Martinho de Melo e Castro, Vila Bela, September 9, 1791, AHU, Mato Grosso Avulsos, Cx. 28, Doc. 1617; see also Carvalho, *Lealdades negociadas*, 207–8. Not only the chiefs but also their attendants on these visits to Vila Bela received new, Portuguese names, even though they were not baptized (which would have been the more common route to receiving a new, Christian name); see the list "Names given to the two Guaikurú Captains" and their entourage in João de Albuquerque de Melo Pereira e Cáceres to Luís Pinto de Souza Coutinho, Vila Bela, January 4, 1796, AHU, Mato Grosso Avulsos, Cx. 31, Doc. 1722 (attachment). The Spanish, too, had been giving Christian names to the unbaptized Guaikurú with whom they made peace; see José Sánchez Labrador, *El Paraguay católico* (Buenos Aires: Imprensa de Coni Hermanos, 1910), 2:83, 104.

15. Commander Ricardo Franco de Almeida Serra to governor, Coimbra, December 29, 1798, APMT, FC.CA, Cx. 6, Doc. 352.

16. Commander Ricardo Franco de Almeida Serra to governor, Coimbra, May 30, 1798, APMT, FC.CA, Cx. 6, Doc. 328.

17. Commander Ricardo Franco de Almeida Serra to governor, Coimbra, September 29, 1798, APMT, FC.CA, Cx. 6, Doc. 346. Perhaps this concern about the fates of the Bororo can be traced to the incorporation of Bororo captives into Guaikurú society. Prado (*História dos índios cavaleiros*, 40) noted that the Guaikurú at Coimbra included Indians from nine different nations, including the Bororo. The visit of Capitão Luiz Pinto (along with Capitão José de Siabra) to Vila Bela is described in João de Albuquerque de Melo Pereira e Cáceres to Luís Pinto de Souza Coutinho, Vila Bela, February 10, 1796, AHU, Mato Grosso Avulsos, Cx. 31, Doc. 1722. On the status of Capitão Paulo among the Guaikurú being linked to his patente, see Commander Francisco Rodrigues do Prado to governor, Coimbra, September 9, 1793, APMT, FC.CA, Cx. 3, Doc. 179. Chiefs reportedly aspired to visit the governor to receive patentes "equal to those of Paulo and Queima [Caimá]." Commander Francisco Rodrigues do Prado to governor, Coimbra, January 14, 1795, APMT, FC.CA, Cx. 4, Doc. 202.

18. Alexandre Rodrigues Ferreira to João de Albuquerque de Melo Pereira e Cáceres, Lagoa da Uberava, May 5, 1791, in *Viagem ao Brasil de Alexandre Rodrigues Ferreira: Coleção etnográfica*, ed. José Paulo Monteiro Soares and Cristina Ferrão (São Paulo: Kapa Editorial, 2005), 3:21.

19. Lieutenant Commander Ignácio de Sousa Nogueira to Commander Joaquim José Ferreira, Coimbra, October 31, 1791, APMT, FC.CA, Cx. 2, Doc. 142; Commander Joaquim José Ferreira to governor, Coimbra, March 10, 1791, APMT, FC.CA, Cx. 2, Doc. 126. See also Carvalho, *Lealdades negociadas*, 318.

20. Zavala, *Los mapuches*, 166; Alejandra Dubcovsky, *Informed Power: Communication in the Early American South* (Cambridge, MA: Harvard University Press, 2016), 31.

21. The quote is in Commander Ricardo Franco de Almeida Serra to governor, Coimbra, March 25, 1799, APMT, FC.CA, Cx. 7, Doc. 370. Numerous sources on Vitória can be found at APMT. Her role in the 1791 peace treaty negotiations is described in Governor João de Albuquerque de Melo Pereira e Cáceres to Martinho de Melo e Castro, Vila Bela, September 9, 1791, AHU, Mato Grosso Avulsos, Cx. 28, Doc. 1617. On her trajectory from slavery in Cuiabá to captivity under the Guaikurú, see Alexandre Rodrigues Ferreira to João de Albuquerque de Melo Pereira e Cáceres, Lagoa da Uberava, May 5, 1791, in Soares and Ferrão, *Viagem ao Brasil*, 3:27. On concerns about what she would tell the Guaikurú of Portuguese plans, see Commander Francisco Rodrigues do Prado to the Alferes da Companhia de Pedestres, Coimbra, December 30, 1793, APMT, FC.CA, Cx. 3, Doc. 186. Doubts about the motives of another important interpreter among the Guaná and Guaikurú, a Black captive named Francisco, can be found in Commander Ricardo Franco de Almeida Serra to governor, Coimbra, September 6, 1797, ACBM, Cx. 22, Doc. 1912, Pasta 80.

22. Pekka Hämäläinen, "Lost in Transitions: Suffering, Survival, and Belonging in the Early Modern Atlantic World," *William and Mary Quarterly* 68,

no. 2 (2011): 220. On the roles played by bicultural and bilingual intermediaries between Europeans and autonomous Indians, see Alida C. Metcalf, *Go-Betweens and the Colonization of Brazil, 1500–1600* (Austin: University of Texas Press, 2005); Weber, *Bárbaros*, ch. 6; Carvalho, *Lealdades negociadas*, 312–22; Apolinário, "Os Akroá e outros povos indígenas," 182–83, 185–86; Karasch, "Rethinking the Conquest of Goiás," 474–75.

23. "Supplement" to the letter of Lieutenant Colonel João Batista Mardel to João Pereira Caldas, Nogueira, June 1, 1785, AHI, Cod. 340-4-6.

24. Caetano Brandão, *Diários das visitas pastorais no Pará* (Porto: Instituto Nacional de Investigação Científica / Centro de História da Universidade do Porto, 1991), 120, see also 115.

25. Daniel L. Everett, *Don't Sleep. There Are Snakes: Life and Language in the Amazonian Jungle* (New York: Pantheon Books, 2008), 21, 28; Curt Nimuendajú, "The Mura and Pirahã," in *Handbook of South American Indians*, ed. Julian H. Steward (Washington, DC: Smithsonian Institution, 1948), 3:257–58. On language change in Amazonia more broadly, see José Ribamar Bessa Freire, *Rio Babel: A história das línguas na Amazônia* (Rio de Janeiro: Atlântica, 2004).

26. Lieutenant Colonel João Batista Mardel to João Pereira Caldas, Nogueira, June 1, 1785, AHI, Cod. 340-4-6. General Caldas agreed that the decision to return the boy to Ambrósio was "indispensable." See his letter to Mardel, Barcelos, July 16, 1785, AHI, Cod. 340-4-6.

27. Two letters from Sergeant Major Henrique João Wilkens to João Pereira Caldas, Ega, March 30, 1789, AHU, Rio Negro Avulsos, Cx. 15, Doc. 558 (attachments).

28. The quote is in "Illustração necessária e interessante, relativa ao gentio da nação Mura . . . feita por um anônimo em 1826," in Carlos de Araújo Moreira Neto, *Índios da Amazônia, de maioria a minoria* (Petrópolis: Vozes, 1988), 252. On the rapid dissemination of the news, see also David G. Sweet, "Native Resistance in Eighteenth-Century Amazonia: The 'Abominable Muras' in War and Peace," *Radical History Review* 53, no. 1 (1992): 69; Lieutenant Colonel João Batista Mardel to João Pereira Caldas, Ega, January 22, 1785, in Soares and Ferrão, *Viagem ao Brasil*, 3:40; Director Domingos de Macedo Ferreira to João Batista Mardel, Alvelos, March 18, 1785, in Soares and Ferrão, *Viagem ao Brasil*, 3:45.

29. These encounters included dignitaries and naturalists as they passed through. See Alexandre Rodrigues Ferreira to João Pereira Caldas, September 11, 1788, Mouth of the Rio Madeira, in *O Doutor Alexandre Rodrigues Ferreira: Documentos coligidos*, ed. Américo Pires Lima (Lisbon: Agencia Central de Ultramar, 1953), 275–76; and the pastoral diaries of Brandão, *Diários das visitas pastorais*, 115–17, 120, 124.

30. Administrator João Pedro da Costa to João Pereira Caldas, Royal Fishery of Puraquequara, July 10, 1787, AHU, Rio Negro Avulsos, Cx. 13, Doc. 499 (attachment).

31. Though he does not indicate his source or time period, Nimuendajú asserted that each Mura head of family had his own fishing ground, which he would defend against any and all poachers. This defensiveness may have been at its peak in the early twentieth century, when he did his fieldwork among relatively small groups of Mura who felt that their territories were being invaded. Nimuendajú, "The Mura and Pirahã," 3:261.

32. Mark Harris, "Peasant Riverine Economies and Their Impact in the Lower Amazon," in *Human Impacts on Amazonia: The Role of Traditional Ecological Knowledge in Conservation and Development*, ed. Darrell Addison Posey and Michael J. Balick (New York: Columbia University Press, 2006), 231.

33. António Rodrigues Cardoso to Henrique João Wilkens, Royal Fishery of Jauató, November 23, 1787, APEP, Cod. 443, Doc. 60 (attachment). On competition over turtles and their unsustainable consumption during the colonial period and nineteenth century, see John Hemming, *Amazon Frontier: The Defeat of the Brazilian Indians* (Cambridge, MA: Harvard University Press, 1987), 249–51.

34. Sergeant Major Henrique João Wilkens to João Pereira Caldas, Ega, November 26, 1787, AHU, Rio Negro Avulsos, Cx. 14, Doc. 526 (attachment). Another altercation between some Muras and a group of Indians working for the Spanish demarcation party occurred in 1789, near the Spanish fishery at the mouth of the Juruá River; this time, the two parties reportedly came to blows over the sharing of some wild honey that the Muras had stored in their canoe. Sergeant Major Henrique João Wilkens to João Pereira Caldas, Ega, March 4, 1789, AHU, Rio Negro Avulsos, Cx. 15, Doc. 558 (attachment).

35. Sergeant Major Henrique João Wilkens to João Pereira Caldas, Ega, December 7, 1787, AHU, Rio Negro Avulsos, Cx. 14, Doc. 526 (attachment). For a parallel case among the Karajá, in which access to aquatic resources like turtles and fish was key to Native territoriality, see Apolinário, "Os Akroá e outros povos indígenas," 184.

36. General João Pereira Caldas to João Pedro da Costa, Barcelos, July 23, 1787; and Costa's reply from the Royal Fishery of Puraquequara, August 20, 1787, both in AHU, Rio Negro Avulsos, Cx. 13, Doc. 499 (attachments). Similar instructions can be found in General João Pereira Caldas to the Commander at Borba, Barcelos, July 28, 1786, AHU, Rio Negro Avulsos, Cx. 11, Doc. 435; and to João Batista Mardel, Barcelos, March 24, 1786, APEP, Cod. 430, Doc. 37. In this last document, on moving the first Mura establishment at the Amaná Lake to a site near the mouth of the Rio Japurá, Caldas warned that "great prudence and caution will be needed, so that the Indians do not take offense and get suspicious; you should be very sure of this before attempting and ordering such a move." When it came time for the move, there should be "gardens and other necessary conveniences prepared in advance at the new site, so as to lessen the doubts and repugnance of those barbarians [*bárbaros*]."

37. Concerns about Rojas's contact with the Mura are expressed in Lieutenant Colonel João Batista Mardel to João Pereira Caldas, Nogueira, June 1, 1785, AHI, Cod. 340-4-6; General João Pereira Caldas to João Batista Mardel, Barcelos, July 16, 1785, in Ibid. For what is known about Rojas, see David G. Sweet, "Juan de Silva y Fernando Rojas: Baqueanos Africanos de la Selva Americana," in *Lucha por la supervivencia en la América colonial*, ed. David G. Sweet and Gary B. Nash (México: Fondo de Cultura Económica), 234–46; Ângela Domingues, *Quando os índios eram vassalos: Colonização e relações de poder no Norte do Brasil na segunda metade do século XVIII* (Lisbon: Comissão Nacional para as Comemorações dos Descobrimentos Portugueses, 2000), 244–45. On other possible Spanish overtures to the Mura, see the letter from Director Mathias Fernandes, Santo Antônio de Maripí, July 28, 1785, APEP, Cod. 425, unnumbered doc.; Sergeant Major Henrique João Wilkens to João Pereira Caldas, Ega, November 26, 1787, AHU, Rio Negro Avulsos, Cx. 14, Doc. 526 (attachment).

38. Domingues, *Quando os índios eram vassalos*, 243. Portuguese intentions to surveil the movements of Spaniards along the Solimões River near its junction with the Japurá are made clear in a map by Lieutenant João Baptista Mardel, c. 1785, John Carter Brown Library, Map Collection, Cabinet Gl780 / 3 Ms, https://jcb.lunaimaging.com/luna/servlet/s/1y27mn.

39. Lourenço da Silva Araújo e Amazonas, *Diccionario topographico, historico, descriptivo da Comarca do Alto Amazonas* (Recife: Typographia Comercial de Meira Henriques, 1852), 259. The disappearance of the marker at the Javari River was also attributed to the Mura, but this seems unlikely, given its distance from the area regularly traveled by the Mura; the Auati-Paraná canal, in contrast, was a waterway well known to the Muras of the Japurá-Solimões region.

40. Nimuendajú, "The Mura and Pirahã," 3:260. See also a similar description of underwater canoe storage among the Indians of the Madeira River in José Gonçalves da Fonseca, "Primeira exploração do rios Madeira e Guaporé feita por José Gonçalves da Fonseca em 1749," in *Memorias para a historia do extincto estado do Maranhão, cujo territorio comprehende hoje as provincias do Maranhão, Piauhy, Grão-Pará e Amazonas*, ed. Cândido Mendes (Rio de Janeiro: Typographia de J. Paulo Hildebrandt, 1874), 2:299.

41. The "band of gypsies" phrase comes from a fort commander's description of a group of Guaikurús who were traveling to Cuiabá to hawk their horses at inflated prices. Ricardo Franco de Almeida Serra to governor, Coimbra, June 14, 1805, APMT, FC.CA, Cx. 10, Doc. 583.

42. On the Mura (including Ambrósio and his people) fleeing epidemics along the Rio Japurá, see Interim Director Manoel Antônio Furtado to unnamed recipient (probably Henrique João Wilkens), Santo Antônio de Maripí, December 31, 1788, AHU, Rio Negro Avulsos, Cx. 15, Doc. 558 (attachment).

43. Administrator Sebastião Pereira de Castro to João Pereira Caldas, Royal Fishery of Caldeirão, July 3, 1786, APEP, Cod. 431, Doc. 47; Sweet, "Native Resistance," 73–74.

44. João Pereira Caldas to João Batista Mardel, Barcelos, February 4, 1785, in *Viagem ao Brasil*, 3:41; Sweet, "Native Resistance," 68.

45. Lieutenant Colonel João Batista Mardel to João Pereira Caldas, Barcelos, July 1, 1786, AHU, Rio Negro Avulsos, Cx. 11, Doc. 435 (attachment).

46. As one friar complained to General Caldas in 1787, there was not a single gun in his village capable of firing, nor any gunpowder "for our defense, since we are here in the middle of so many heathens"—about a hundred Muras in all. He heard that all the other towns hosting Muras had received these supplies, so he hoped that Caldas would attend to his request (which he did). Fray José da Conceição to João Pereira Caldas, Airão, August 5, 1787; and Caldas's reply, Barcelos, August 12, 1787, both in AHU, Rio Negro Avulsos, Cx. 13, Doc. 499 (attachments). Similar concerns about lack of weapons to defend against the Guaikurú in case of an uprising can be found in Commander António José Pinto de Figueiredo to governor, Albuquerque, February 25, 1800, APMT, QM.TM.CA, Cx. 36, Doc. 2423.

47. Lieutenant Colonel João Batista Mardel to João Pereira Caldas, location unknown, c. 1786, AHU, Rio Negro Avulsos, Cx. 11, Doc. 435 (attachment).

48. General João Pereira Caldas to the Comandante do Registo da Vila de Borba, Barcelos, July 28, 1786, AHU, Rio Negro Avulsos, Cx. 11, Doc. 435 (attachment).

49. Governor Francisco de Souza Coutinho to Martinho de Mello e Castro, Belém, January 15, 1795," in Francisco Jorge dos Santos, ed., "Dossiê Munduruku: Uma contribuição para a história indígena da Amazônia colonial," *Boletim Informativo do Museu Amazônico* 5, no. 8 (1995): 72.

50. Brandão, *Diários das visitas pastorais*, 122, and a similar episode on 119.

51. Canon André Fernandes de Souza, "Notícias geográficas da Província do Rio Negro" (c. 1821), BNRJ, I-31, 17, 5; see also "Illustração necessária e interessante," 253.

52. Sweet, "Native Resistance," 69, 73–74.

53. Manoel de Jesus da Piedade to governor, Óbidos, June 29, 1791, APEP, Cod. 467, Doc. 8; I am very grateful to Mark Harris for sharing his transcription and photographs of this document. The governor's reply is in Governor Francisco de Souza Coutinho to Manoel de Jesus da Piedade, Belém, October 16, 1791, APEP, Cod. 466, Doc. 350. On allegations of continuing Mura depredations in the Lower Amazon during the early 1790s, see Harris, *Rebellion on the Amazon: The Cabanagem, Race, and Popular Culture in the North of Brazil, 1798–1840* (Cambridge: Cambridge University Press, 2010), 151–52.

54. Vicar Pedro José Ribeiro Pinto to governor, Óbidos, March 21, 1791, APEP, Cod. 478, Doc. 7. Again, I thank Mark Harris for sharing a copy and transcription of this document with me.

55. Garcia, *As diversas formas de ser índio*, 241, notes that Indians often refused to view the peace agreements as exclusive; they could still ally with other Native groups that were hostile to the Portuguese, for example, or negotiate with Spaniards when it suited their interests.

56. Failed or futile efforts to control Guaikurú mobility (especially border crossings) are described in Commander Francisco Rodrigues do Prado to governor, Coimbra, January 8, 1795, APMT, FC.CA, Cx. 4, Doc. 197; Prado to governor, Coimbra, November 22, 1795, APMT, FC.CA, Cx. 4, Doc. 209; Commander Ricardo Franco de Almeida Serra to governor, Coimbra, December 29, 1798, APMT, FC.CA, Cx. 6, Doc. 352; Serra to governor, Coimbra, January 10, 1799, APMT, FC.CA, Cx. 7, Doc. 365; Serra to governor, Coimbra, February 5, 1801, APMT, FC.CA, Cx. 8, Doc. 416; Serra to governor, Coimbra, March 26, 1803, APMT, FC.CA, Cx. 10, Doc. 540. In general, the only thing preventing the Guaikurú from traveling were high floodwaters, as several officials acknowledged (see Serra to governor, Coimbra, May 9, 1801, APMT, FC.CA, Cx. 8, Doc. 431. On the opportunities that autonomous Native groups found in the similarly fluid border zone of the Río de la Plata in this same period, see Jeffrey Alan Erbig Jr., *Where Caciques and Mapmakers Met: Border Making in Eighteenth-Century South America* (Chapel Hill: University of North Carolina Press, 2020).

57. This is what happened with a Guaikurú raid that was supposedly going to target the Bororo, but ended up being against the Guató: Serra, "Continuação do Parecer," 78; Serra to governor, Coimbra, April 1, 1801, APMT, FC.CA, Cx. 8, Doc. 426.

58. Governor João de Albuquerque de Melo Pereira e Cáceres to Francisco Rodrigues do Prado(?), Vila Bela, March 15, 1794, APMT, FC.CA, Cx. 2, Doc. 143, fls. 23v–25v.

59. Commander Ricardo Franco de Almeida Serra to governor, Coimbra, February 5, 1801, APMT, FC.CA, Cx. 8, Doc. 417.

60. Commander Ricardo Franco de Almeida Serra to governor, Coimbra, December 29, 1798, APMT, FC.CA, Cx. 6, Doc. 352.

61. The phrase "practices of peace" comes from Barr, *Peace Came in the Form of a Woman*.

62. Ricardo Franco de Almeida Serra, "Parecer sobre o aldeamento dos índios Uaicurus e Guanás com a descripção dos seus usos, religião, estabilidade e costumes (1803)," *Revista do Instituto Histórico e Geográfico Brasileiro* 7 (1845): 212–13. On Guaikurú encampments described as "volantes" or "ambulantes," see Commander Ricardo Franco de Almeida Serra to governor, Coimbra, February 5, 1801, APMT, FC.CA, Cx. 8, Doc. 416; Commander Francisco Rodrigues do Prado to governor, Coimbra, June 22, 1796, APMT, FC.CA, Cx. 4, Doc. 218.

63. Serra, "Continuação do parecer," 393 (emphasis mine). The governor begged to differ, saying that the Guaikurú would settle and become useful citizens sooner or later. Governor Caetano Pinto de Miranda Montenegro to Serra, Cuiabá, April 5, 1803, reproduced in Serra, "Parecer," 214.

64. Commander Francisco Rodrigues do Prado to governor, Coimbra, September 8, 1796, APMT, FC.CA, Cx. 4, Doc. 224; on these negotiations, see also Governor Caetano Pinto de Miranda Montenegro to Luís Pinto de Souza

Coutinho, Vila Bela, April 17, 1797, APMT, Cod. 41, fls. 9–11v. The Guaikurú parcialidades that historically lived on the western side of the Paraguay River were the Uatedeos (Guetiadegodis in Sánchez Labrador's account) and the Kadiwéus (Cadiguegodis); at this point in 1796, Prado was likely referring to negotiations with the Uatedeos.

65. Commander Ricardo Franco de Almeida Serra to governor, Coimbra, December 2, 1801, APMT, FC.CA, Cx. 8, Doc. 446.

66. Commander Ricardo Franco de Almeida Serra to governor, Coimbra, Dec. 22, 1802, APMT, FC.CA, Cx. 9, Doc. 515.

67. Commander Ricardo Franco de Almeida Serra to governor, Coimbra, July 2, 1799, APMT, FC.CA, Cx. 7, Doc. 383.

68. David Murray, *Indian Giving: Economies of Power in Indian-White Exchanges* (Amherst: University of Massachusetts Press, 2000), 27–29—"a very craving people" is on 27, from the English explorer John Lawson; "an ironic imitation of white expectations" is on 29.

69. Weber, *Bárbaros*, 191.

70. Commander Ricardo Franco de Almeida Serra to governor, Coimbra, May 30, 1798, APMT, FC.CA, Cx. 6, Doc. 328; see also Serra to governor, Coimbra, May 5, 1803, APMT, FC.CA, Cx. 10, Doc. 552.

71. Governor Caetano Pinto de Miranda Montenegro to Ricardo Franco de Almeida Serra, Cuiabá, April 5, 1803, reproduced in Serra, "Parecer," 217. See also Commander Ricardo Franco de Almeida Serra to governor, Coimbra, February 5, 1801, APMT, FC.CA, Cx. 8, Doc. 417; Serra to governor, Coimbra, October 30, 1802, APMT, FC.CA, Cx. 9, Doc. 501. Garcia, *As diversas formas de ser índio*, 49–50, points out that the manipulation went in both directions: the Portuguese used offers of gifts to manipulate Indians, and Indians manipulated the Portuguese into giving more than they received.

72. The demographic numbers are found in Serra, "Parecer," 206. The total of 1,400 Guaikurú and Guaná increased over four years (c. 1799–1803) to about 2,600. For the estimate of funds spent, see Serra, "Continuação do parecer," 384.

73. Commodity prices are for Southern Brazil in the late 1770s and can be found in Appendix V in Dauril Alden, *Royal Government in Colonial Brazil, With Special Reference to the Administration of the Marquis of Lavradio, Viceroy, 1769–1779* (Berkeley: University of California Press, 1968), 509–11. I have used the equivalency of one silver cruzado = 480 réis.

74. Robert Southey, *History of Brazil* (London: Longman, Hurst, Rees, Orme, and Brown, 1819), 3:800.

75. Governor Caetano Pinto de Miranda Montenegro to Ricardo Franco de Almeida Serra, Vila Bela, September 5, 1798, APMT, Cod. 37, fls. 145v–146. On the (Spanish-gathered) evidence that the Guaikurú were being armed and possibly trained by the Portuguese, see the discussion in Carvalho, *Lealdades negociadas*, 395–97.

76. Commander Francisco Rodrigues do Prado to governor, Coimbra, January 2(?), 1794, APMT, Cod. 35, fls. 125v–126; Prado to governor, Coimbra, October 20, 1795, APMT, FC.CA, Cx. 4, Doc. 207 (on red cloth and new tools); Prado to governor, Coimbra, January 8, 1795, APMT, FC.CA, Cx. 4, Doc. 197 (on aguardente, salt, and fat). On how Spanish officials similarly sought to abide by Native expectations and preferences for gifts—such as those designating personal status and social differentiation—see Beltrán, "La organización de los parlamentos," 167–68; Weber, *Bárbaros*, 186. The influence of Native American color symbolism on intercultural trade is discussed in Christopher L. Miller and George R. Hamell, "A New Perspective on Indian-White Contact: Cultural Symbols and Colonial Trade," *Journal of American History* 73, no. 2 (1986): 325–27.

77. Antônio Pires da Silva Pontes, "Diário histórico e físico da viagem dos oficiais da demarcação que partiram do quartel geral de Barcelos para a capital de Vila Bela da Capitania de Mato Grosso, em 1 de Setembro de 1781," *Revista do Instituto Histórico e Geográfico Brasileiro* 262 (1964): 362; Darcy Ribeiro, *Os índios e a civilização: A integração das populações indígenas no Brasil moderno* (Rio de Janeiro: Editora Civilização Brasileira, 1970), 154.

78. Claude Lévi-Strauss, *Tristes Tropiques*, trans. John Weightman and Doreen Weightman (New York: Penguin, 2012), 249.

79. The goods were given to visiting Guaikurú, Guaná, and Guató Indians at Coimbra between 1800 and 1802; the list can be found in APMT, PRFIO. MP, Cx. 8, Doc. 426. I have used these conversions: 1 *alqueire* = 8.17 US dry gallons, or 36 liters; 1 *arroba* = 32.4 US pounds.

80. Serra, "Continuação do parecer," 377.

81. The quote is from Commander Ricardo Franco de Almeida Serra to governor, Coimbra, May 30, 1798, APMT, FC.CA, Cx. 6, Doc. 328. On showing the Guaikurú the empty warehouses, see Serra, "Continuação do parecer," 394.

82. Commander Francisco Rodrigues do Prado to the Succession Government, Coimbra, May 23, 1796, APMT, Cod. 25, fls. 80–81. See also Serra's statement that "the Indians have the greatest passion for this liquor, and it is the only thing that keeps them in this friendship" in Commander Ricardo Franco de Almeida Serra to governor, Coimbra, January 10, 1799, APMT, FC.CA, Cx. 7, Doc. 366.

83. Officials in Vila Bela regularly discouraged Indigenous *capitães* from visiting; see, for example, the letter from the Succession Government to Francisco Rodrigues do Prado, Vila Bela, July 18, 1796, APMT, Cod. 25, fls. 81v–82; and correspondence between the governor in Vila Bela and Commander Serra in APMT, FC.CC, Cx. 2, Doc. 143. On why visits to the capital were so expensive, see the explanation of Governor Caetano Pinto de Miranda Montenegro to Rodrigo de Souza Coutinho, Vila Bela, April 28, 1800, APMT, Cod. 41, fls. 173–175v.

84. Fray José da Conceição to João Pereira Caldas, Airão, August 5, 1787, AHU, Rio Negro Avulsos, Cx. 13, Doc. 499 (attachment); this letter

acknowledged General Caldas's order not to send any Muras to Barcelos until the manioc meal supply had been replenished.

85. Commander António Carlos da Fonseca Coutinho to João Pereira Caldas, Borba, June 29, 1787, and Caldas's reply, Barcelos, July 19, 1787, both in AHU, Rio Negro Avulsos, Cx. 13, Doc. 499 (attachments).

86. Commander Francisco Rodrigues do Prado to governor, Coimbra, June 22, 1793, APMT, FC.CA, Cx. 3, Doc. 176. Precedent was seen as inescapable here: one governor noted that his predecessor established the custom of outfitting the visiting Guaikurú in officers' uniforms, and their warriors as foot soldiers; he therefore felt compelled to continue the practice, despite the expense, so as not to make a "disagreeable and dangerous impression" on the Indians. Governor Caetano Pinto de Miranda Montenegro to Rodrigo de Souza Coutinho, Vila Bela, April 28, 1800, APMT, Cod. 41, fls. 173–175v.

87. Commander Francisco Rodrigues do Prado to governor, Coimbra, November 22, 1795, APMT, FC.CA, Cx. 4, Doc. 209.

88. On demand sharing, see Nicolas Peterson, "Demand Sharing: Reciprocity and the Pressure for Generosity among Foragers," *American Anthropologist*, new series, 95, no. 4 (1993): 860–74; Elizabeth Ewart, "Demanding, Giving, Sharing, and Keeping: Panará Ideas of Economy," *Journal of Latin American and Caribbean Anthropology*, 18 (2013): 31–50; William H. Fisher, *Rainforest Exchanges: Industry and Community on an Amazonian Frontier* (Washington, DC: Smithsonian Institution Press, 2000), 135; Laura M. Rival, *Trekking Through History: The Huaorani of Amazonian Ecuador* (New York: Columbia University Press, 2002), 104–5. On "hyperactive soliciting" as a form of testing whites, see Eduardo Viveiros de Castro, *From the Enemy's Point of View: Humanity and Divinity in an Amazonian Society* (Chicago: University of Chicago Press, 1992), 20.

89. Ewart, "Demanding, Giving, Sharing, and Keeping," 37–38. Stephen Hugh-Jones suggests that descriptions like this are a standard feature of books about Amazonian anthropological fieldwork. Hugh-Jones, "Yesterday's Luxuries, Tomorrow's Necessities: Business and Barter in Northwest Amazonia," in *Barter, Exchange, and Value: An Anthropological Approach*, ed. Caroline Humphrey and Stephen Hugh-Jones (Cambridge: Cambridge University Press, 1992), 42–43. There are exceptions, however, as in Peter Gow, *An Amazonian Myth and Its History* (Oxford: Oxford University Press, 2001), 50n20.

90. Ewart, "Demanding, Giving, Sharing, and Keeping," 40; Beth Conklin, "For Love or Money? Indigenous Materialism and Humanitarian Agendas," in *Editing Eden: A Reconsideration of Identity, Politics, and Place in Amazonia*, ed. Frank Hutchison and Patrick C. Wilson (Lincoln: University of Nebraska Press, 2010), 148 (quote). See also Elizabeth Ewart, *Space and Society in Central Brazil: A Panará Ethnography* (London: Bloomsbury, 2013), 110–12.

91. Commander Ricardo Franco de Almeida Serra to governor, Coimbra, September 29, 1798, APMT, FC.CA, Cx. 6, Doc. 346. On the Guaikurú sending

gifts to the governor, see Commander Joaquim José Ferreira to governor, Coimbra, January 18, 1792, APMT, FC.CA, Cx. 3, Doc. 148.

92. Lieutenant Colonel José António Salgado to governor, Santarém, September 1, 1795, APEP, Cod. 470, Doc. 118.

93. Commander Francisco Rodrigues do Prado to governor, Coimbra, May 22, 1794, APMT, FC.CA, Cx. 4, Doc. 191. See also Prado, *História dos índios cavaleiros*, 61. Various epidemics afflicted the Guaikurú during their visits to Coimbra, some of which were said to be imported by the cargo canoes from Cuiabá. see, for example, Prado to governor, Coimbra, May 18, 1795, APMT, FC.CA, Cx. 4, Doc. 204.

94. Serra, "Continuação do parecer," 362.

95. Commander Ricardo Franco de Almeida Serra to governor, Coimbra, September 29, 1798, APMT, FC.CA, Cx. 6, Doc. 346 (on how 27 Guaikurú elites, including eleven "*capitães*," were eating at the commander's table every day). Troop levels at Coimbra varied, ranging from several hundred in the early 1790s (on the eve of the peace agreement) to around sixty or seventy in the mid to late 1790s and early 1800s.

96. Commander Ricardo Franco de Almeida Serra to governor, Coimbra, September 29, 1798, APMT, FC.CA, Cx. 6, Doc. 346. On the customary distribution of alcohol to independent Indians in eighteenth-century Spanish America, see Weber, *Bárbaros*, 184–85. On the centrality of shared food and drink between peacemaking Spaniards and Indians, see Beltrán, "La organización de los parlamentos de indios," 145–62.

97. Governor Caetano Pinto de Miranda Montenegro to Ricardo Franco de Almeida Serra, Vila Bela, November 22, 1798, APMT, Cod. 37, fls. 181–181v. See also Garcia, *As diversas formas de ser índio*, 242, where she notes that the quantity of gifts may not have been as important in cementing alliances as the mode of giving—that is, whether gifts were transferred according to Native rituals of giving.

98. See, for example, the list of metal tools and alcohol exchanged with the Mura in Ega, August 28, 1786, APEP, Cod. 435, Doc. 50. On trading tools for horses of the Guaikurú, see Commander Joaquim José Ferreira to governor, Coimbra, June 8, 1791, APMT, FC.CA, Cx. 2, Doc. 131; Governor Caetano Pinto de Miranda Montenegro to Rodrigo de Souza Coutinho, Vila Bela, April 28, 1800, APMT, Cod. 41, fls. 173–175v.

99. Sergeant Major Henrique João Wilkens to João Pereira Caldas, Ega, February 25, 1788, in *Relatos da fronteira Amazônica no século XVIII: Alexandre Rodrigues Ferreira e Henrique João Wilckens*, ed. Marta Rosa Amoroso and Nádia Farage (São Paulo: Universidade de São Paulo / Núcleo de História Indígena e do Indigenismo, 1994), 57.

100. Murray, *Indian Giving*, 18–19.

101. Catherine V. Howard, "A domesticação das mercadorias: Estratégias Waiwai," in *Pacificando o branco: Cosmologias do contato no Norte-Amazônico*, ed.

Bruce Albert and Alcida Ramos (São Paulo: UNESP, 2002), 44; Márcio Couto Henrique, "Presente de branco: A perspectiva indígena dos brindes da civilização (Amazônia, século XIX)," *Revista Brasileira de História* 37, no. 75 (2017): 7. The ideal of perpetual indebtedness comes across clearly in missionary chronicles from eighteenth-century Brazil and Paraguay, with examples meant to prove Native "ingratitude," stinginess, and unwillingness to pay back debts; see João Daniel, *Tesouro descoberto no máximo rio Amazonas* (Rio de Janeiro: Contraponto, 2004), 1:295–97; 2:124–25; José Sánchez Labrador, *El Paraguay católico* (Buenos Aires: Imprensa de Coni Hermanos, 1910), 1:251–52.

102. Examples of the Mura giving children (likely captives) can be found in Lieutenant Colonel João Batista Mardel to João Pereira Caldas, Nogueira, June 1, 1785, AHI, 340-4-6; Commander António Carlos da Fonseca Coutinho to João Pereira Caldas, Borba, June 13, 1786, AHU, Rio Negro Avulsos, Cx. 11, Doc. 435 (attachment). On possible Indigenous motivations behind trading children with whites, see David Louis Mead, "Caiapó do Sul, an Ethnohistory (1610–1920)" (PhD diss, University of Florida, 2010), 265–66.

103. Henrique João Wilkens, "Diário da viagem ao Japurá," in *Relatos da fronteira*, 27, 29 (giving gifts to the Tatuoca), 42–43 (Wilkens's refusal of the children).

104. Nádia Farage, *As muralhas dos sertões: Os povos indígenas no Rio Branco e a colonização* (Rio de Janeiro: ANPOCS, 1991), 115–16; Hugh-Jones, "Yesterday's Luxuries," 58; Marta Rosa Amoroso, "Guerra e mercadorias: Os Kaingang nas cenas da 'Conquista de Guarapuava,'" in *Do contato ao confronto: A conquista de Guarapuava no século XVIII*, ed. Ana Maria de Moraes Belluzzo, Marta Rosa Amoroso, Nicolau Sevcenko, and Valéria Piccoli (São Paulo: BNB Paribas, 2003), 28; Henrique, "Presente de branco," 15–16. See also Cornelius J. Jaenen, "Amerindian Views of French Culture in the Seventeenth Century," *Canadian Historical Review* 55, no. 3 (1974): 266–67; White, *The Middle Ground*, 99–100; Miller and Hamell, "A New Perspective on Indian-White Contact," 318; Laurier Turgeon, "The Tale of the Kettle: Odyssey of an Intercultural Object," *Ethnohistory* 44, no. 1 (1997): 9–18.

105. Lieutenant Colonel João Batista Mardel to João Pereira Caldas, Nogueira, June 1, 1785, AHI, 340-4-6. This group of Muras had also left a boy with an official in the village, "saying that it was for him to become civilized."

106. Howard, "A domesticação das mercadorias," 50. See also Cesar Gordon, "Nossas utopias não são as deles: Os Mebengokre (Kayapó) e o mundo dos brancos," *Sexta-feira: Antropologia, Artes e Humanidades* 6 (2001): 123–36; Conklin, "For Love or Money?" 127–50; Els Lagrou, "No caminho das miçangas: Arte, alteridade e relação entre os ameríndios," *Enfoques—Revista dos Alunos do PPGSA-UFRJ* 12 (2013): 18–49; Ewart, *Space and Society*, chs. 4 and 5; Hal Langfur, *The Forbidden Lands: Colonial Identity, Frontier Violence, and the Persistence of Brazil's Eastern Indians, 1750–1830* (Stanford, CA: Stanford University Press, 2006), 237–38.

107. The idea of material objects as "avatars" of the whites comes from Farage, *As muralhas dos sertões*, 76; I originally saw this discussed in Henrique, "Presente de branco," 4, 20. On symbolic transformations of "foreign" objects, with a focus on the missionary context, see Cristina Pompa, *Religião como tradução: Missionários, Tupi e "Tapuia" no Brasil colonial* (Bauru, São Paulo: EDUSC, 2003).

108. "Peace by deceit" tactics—as formulated by Bernardo de Gálvez, Viceroy of New Spain, in 1786—are described in David J. Weber, *The Spanish Frontier in North America* (New Haven, CT: Yale University Press, 1992), 229–30. On Indian-Iberian treaties as part of broader state efforts to extend hegemonic control over Native polities in the eighteenth-century borderlands, see Carvalho, *Lealdades negociadas*, ch. 6. On the Spanish American "pax colonial"— the facade of peace that overlay a society suffused by violence, especially at its edges and against those least likely to document it—see Murdo J. MacLeod, "Some Thoughts on the Pax Colonial, Colonial Violence, and Perceptions of Both," in *Native Resistance and the Pax Colonial in New Spain*, ed. Susan Schroder (Lincoln: University of Nebraska Press, 1998), 129–42.

109. Governor Caetano Pinto de Miranda Montenegro to José Teixeira Cabral, Vila Bela, January 16, 1797, APMT, Cod. 37, fls. 10–11v.

110. Lieutenant Colonel João Batista Mardel to João Pereira Caldas, Nogueira, June 1, 1785, AHI, 340-4-6.

Chapter 4

1. Lacking Indigenous-authored sources for autonomous groups in the nineteenth century, I have based these opening paragraphs in part on the experiences of twentieth-century Native Amazonian groups during periods of intensifying, threatening contact with outsiders, as described in firsthand narratives like that of Davi Kopenawa (with Bruce Albert), *The Falling Sky: Words of a Yanomami Shaman*, trans. Nicholas Elliott and Alison Dundy (Cambridge, MA: Harvard University Press, 2013).

2. Carlos de Araújo Moreira Neto, *Índios da Amazônia, de maioria a minoria* (Petrópolis: Vozes, 1988); Emilia Viotti da Costa, *The Brazilian Empire: Myths and Histories* (Chapel Hill: University of North Carolina Press, 2000); Kenneth Maxwell, "Why Was Brazil Different? The Contexts of Independence," in *Naked Tropics: Essays on Empire and Other Rogues* (New York: Routledge, 2003), 145–68; Patrícia Melo Sampaio, "Política indigenista no Brasil imperial," in *O Brasil Imperial*, ed. Keila Grinberg and Ricardo Salles (Rio de Janeiro: Civilização Brasileira, 2009), 1:175–206.

3. Cândido Xavier de Almeida e Souza, "Descrição diária dos progressos da expedição destinada à capitania de São Paulo para fronteiras do Paraguai, em 9 de outubro de 1800," *Revista do Instituto Histórico e Geográfico Brasileiro* 202 (1949): 76.

4. Almeida e Souza, "Descrição diária," 84.

5. See, for example, Ricardo Franco de Almeida Serra, "Continuação do parecer sobre os índios Uaicurús e Guanás," *Revista do Instituto Histórico e Geográfico Brasileiro* 13 (1850): 393. On some local officials' dissenting views in the context of the royal authorization of war against the Botocudo of eastern Brazil, see Hal Langfur, "Cannibalism and the Body Politic: Independent Indians in the Era of Brazilian Independence," *Ethnohistory* 65, no. 4 (Oct. 2018): 549–73.

6. On the changing Spanish American rhetoric about independent Indians in this period, see David J. Weber, *Bárbaros: Spaniards and Their Savages in the Age of Enlightenment* (New Haven, CT: Yale University Press, 2005), especially 275–77 (quoted phrase on 276). For Brazilian authors lamenting what they saw as the higher level of "civilization" achieved by Indians in Spanish America, see, for example, a report from Minas Gerais in 1827: "The state in which [our Indians] presently find themselves, compared to that of the Spanish Indians, should fill us with shame: the latter are good artists, good farmers, dexterous in all types of work; ours remain in a state of stupidity." Town Council of Barbacena to the Ouvidor Geral Francisco de Paula de Almedia Albuquerque, Barbacena, January 29, 1827, in *Documentos sobre o índio brasileiro (1500–1822): Arquivo histórico*, ed. Leda Maria Cardoso Naud (Brasília: Serviço Gráfico do Senado Federal, 1971), 89.

7. Governor Francisco de Souza Coutinho to Manoel da Gama Lobo D'Almada, Belém, March 13, 1795, in "Dossiê Munduruku: Uma contribuição para a história indígena da Amazônia colonial," ed. Francisco Jorge dos Santos, *Boletim Informativo do Museu Amazônico* 5, no. 8 (1995): 74.

8. Governor Manoel da Gama Lobo D'Almada to Francisco de Souza Coutinho, Barra do Rio Negro, July 15, 1795, in "Dossiê Munduruku," 80.

9. Lieutenant Colonel João Batista Mardel to João Pereira Caldas, Nogueira, June 1, 1785, AHI, Cod. 340-4-6.

10. Interim Commander José Craveiro de Sá to governor, Miranda, May 1, 1816, APMT, PM.CA, Cx. 3, Doc. 174.

11. Carta Régia of May 12, 1798, in Patrícia Melo Sampaio, "Espelhos partidos: Etnia, legislação e desigualdade na colônia sertões do Grão-Pará, c. 1755–1823" (PhD diss., Universidade Federal Fluminense, 2001), 333. On the Carta's condoning of forced labor for the Mura, Mundurukú, and Karajá, see Marta Rosa Amoroso, "Corsários no caminho fluvial: Os Mura do Rio Madeira," in *História dos índios no Brasil*, ed. Manuela Carneiro da Cunha (São Paulo: Companhia das Letras, 1992), 306, 308; Moreira Neto, *Índios da Amazônia*, 119.

12. Indian slavery had been made illegal back in 1755, though many loopholes remained. On increasing bellicosity against independent Native groups after 1798, see Patrícia Melo Sampaio, "Entre a tutela e a liberdade dos índios: Relendo a Carta Régia de 1798," in *Meandros da história: Trabalho e poder no Pará e Maranhão, séculos XVIII e XIX*, ed. Mauro Cezar Coelho, Flávio dos

Santos Gomes, Jonas Marçal Queiroz, Rosa E. Acevedo Marin, and Geraldo Prado (Belém: UNAMAZ, 2005), 68–84; Moreira Neto, *Índios da Amazônia*, 30–36; Caio Prado Júnior, *The Colonial Background of Modern Brazil* (Berkeley: University of California Press, 1967), 107–9.

13. Hal Langfur, *The Forbidden Lands: Colonial Identity, Frontier Violence, and the Persistence of Brazil's Eastern Indians, 1750–1830* (Stanford, CA: Stanford University Press, 2006), 272–78; a "war of extermination" is from Prince Maximilian of Wied-Neuwied, quoted on 277. Langfur notes on 243–44 that the evidence for Botocudo cannibalism is ambiguous, and accusations of the practice almost always grew louder in periods of military mobilization against Indians. On the resurgence of offensive war against the Botocudo, see also Izabel Missagia de Mattos, *Civilização e revolta: Os Botocudos e a catequese na Província de Minas* (Bauru, SP: EDUSC, 2004); Judy Bieber, "Catechism and Capitalism: Imperial Indigenous Policy on a Brazilian Frontier, 1808–1845," in *Native Brazil: Beyond the Convert and the Cannibal, 1500–1900*, ed. Hal Langfur (Albuquerque: University of New Mexico Press, 2014), 138–60.

14. Carta Régia to the Governor of Minas Gerais, Rio de Janeiro, May 13, 1808, reproduced in Manuela Carneiro da Cunha, ed., *Legislação indigenista no século XIX: Uma compilação, 1808–1889* (São Paulo: EDUSP, 1992), 57–60.

15. Yuko Miki, *Frontiers of Citizenship: A Black and Indigenous History of Postcolonial Brazil* (Cambridge: Cambridge University Press, 2018), 150.

16. See, for example, Álvaro José Xavier to Rodrigo de Souza Coutinho, Rio de Janeiro, July 7, 1808, AHI, Lata 265, Maço 11, Pasta 1.

17. Carta Régia to the Governor of Goiás, Rio de Janeiro, September 5, 1811, reproduced in Carneiro da Cunha, *Legislação indigenista*, 79–80.

18. Carneiro da Cunha, *Legislação indigenista*, 6–7n2, quoting Francisco de Paula Ribeiro.

19. David Louis Mead, "Caiapó do Sul, an Ethnohistory (1610–1920)," (PhD diss, University of Florida, 2010), 341–42, 347–48.

20. Miki, *Frontiers of Citizenship*, 62. Mary Karasch points out that many of the offensive war parties were organized and led by "adventurers" to whom local settlers would contribute cattle as a reward for what usually turned into a profitable slave-raiding enterprise. "Catequese e cativeiro: Política indigenista em Goiás, 1780–1889," in *História dos índios no Brasil*, ed. Manuela Carneiro da Cunha (São Paulo: Companhia das Letras, 1992), 403.

21. Indeed, the transatlantic slave trade ended in 1850. The quotations are from decrees of the provincial president, São Paulo, April 10, 1826, and April 1, 1827 [1826?], both in Naud, *Documentos sobre o índio brasileiro*, 111. For analysis of these documents, see John M. Monteiro, "Tupis, tapuias e historiadores: Estudos de história indígena a do indigenismo" (Tese de Livre Docência, Universidade Estadual de Campinas, 2001), 141–42. On the trafficking of Indigenous children, see Maria Hilda Baqueiro Paraíso, "As crianças indígenas e a formação de agentes transculturais: O comércio de kurukas na Bahia, Espírito

Santo e Minas Gerais," *Revista de Estudos e Pesquisas (Fundação Nacional do Índio)* 3 (2006): 41–106; Luísa Tombini Wittmann, *O Vapor e o Botoque: Imigrantes alemães e índios Xokleng no Vale do Itajaí/SC (1850–1926)* (Florianópolis: Letras Contemporâneas, 2007), ch. 3; Miki, *Frontiers of Citizenship*, 55–59.

22. See, for example, Henry Lister Maw, *Journal of a Passage from the Pacific to the Atlantic: Crossing the Andes in the Northern Provinces of Peru, and Descending the River Marañon or Amazon* (London: John Murray, 1829), 267–73.

23. Prado, *The Colonial Background of Modern Brazil*, 108.

24. Hercules Florence, *Viagem fluvial do Tietê ao Amazonas de 1825–1829* (São Paulo: Cultrix / Universidade de São Paulo, 1977), 197–98; Renate Brigitte Viertler, *A duras penas: Um histórico das relações entre índios Bororo e "civilizados" no Mato Grosso* (São Paulo: Universidade de São Paulo, 1990), 47–48. The commander of Vila Maria, João Pereira Leite, was said to have received his authorization from King João VI, so this must have been in the late 1810s or early 1820s. Florence met with these Bororos in 1827. On the later history of Bororo relations with settlers, missionaries, and the state, see Hal Langfur, "Myths of Pacification: Brazilian Frontier Settlement and the Subjugation of the Bororo Indians," *Journal of Social History* 32, no. 4 (1999): 879–905.

25. Salvador Monteiro and Leonel Kaz, eds., *Expedição Langsdorff ao Brasil, 1821–1829: Rugendas, Taunay, Florence* (Rio de Janeiro: Alumbramento, 1998), 266.

26. Johann Baptist von Spix and Carl Friendrich Phillipp von Martius, *Viagem pelo Brasil (1817–1820)*, trans. Lúcia Furquim Lahmeyer (Belo Horizonte: Editora Itatiaia, 1981), 3:149. Zany's three hundred Indians were mentioned in Maw, *Journal of a Passage from the Pacific to the Atlantic*, 302. For background on Zany, see John Hemming, *Amazon Frontier: The Defeat of the Brazilian Indians* (Cambridge, MA: Harvard University Press, 1987), 216–17; Sampaio, "Espelhos partidos," 102–4.

27. On support for private initiatives in bringing independent Indians out of the forest after 1798, which was when Directorate-village-sponsored expeditions came to end with the Directorate itself, see Sampaio, "Entre a tutela e a liberdade dos índios"; Heather F. Roller, *Amazonian Routes: Indigenous Mobility and Colonial Communities in Northern Brazil* (Stanford, CA: Stanford University Press, 2014), 197–200.

28. André Fernandes de Souza, "Notícias Geográphicas da Capitania do Rio Negro no Grande Rio Amazonas," *Revista do Instituto Histórico e Geográfico Brasileiro* 10 (1848): 489.

29. On Zany's proposal, see André Roberto de A. Machado, "O Conselho Geral da Província do Pará e a definição da política indigenista no Império do Brasil (1829–31)," *Almanack* 10 (2015): 439, 447. The proposal itself can be found in the the Portuguese parliament's "Sessão de 26 de Agosto," 1822, in *Diário das Cortes Geraes e Extraordinarias da Nação Portugueza*, 239–42, Assembleia da República, Debates Parlamentares, http://debates.parlamento.

pt/catalogo/mc/c1821/01/01/01/020/1822-08-26/. The quote on bringing Indians into "civil society" is on 240.

30. Spix and Martius, *Viagem pelo Brasil* 3:245.

31. That Martius intentionally purchased the captives (rather than receiving them as gifts or taking them on as charity cases) is based on a report by Martius and Spix in 1821, written before the travelers had returned to Munich. See Klaus Schönitzer, "From the New to the Old World: Two Indigenous Children Brought Back to Germany by Johann Baptist Spix and Carl Friedrich Martius," *Journal Fünf Kontinente* 1 (2015): 85–87, 94–96. Schönitzer notes that Martius's accounts of how he came to obtain Isabella were rife with contradictions; Martius once even claimed (via an inscription on Isabella's portrait) that she had been given to him by the governor of the Rio Negro Captaincy. Of the four remaining child captives, two died on the voyage downriver and two were deposited with a military commander in the town of Ega, on the Solimões River.

32. Spix and Martius, *Viagem pelo Brasil* 3:230–31. The Miranha had long been involved in interethnic warfare and captive-taking; what was new in this period was likely the regular commerce with white buyers. See Alexandre Rodrigues Ferreira's description from the 1780s, "Miranhas," in *Viagem ao Brasil de Alexandre Rodrigues Ferreira: Coleção etnográfica*, ed. José Paulo Monteiro Soares and Cristina Ferrão (São Paulo: Kapa Editorial, 2005), 3:35.

33. Spix and Martius, *Viagem pelo Brasil* 3:218. The 1787 diplomatic mission is mentioned in Alexandre Rodrigues Ferreira, "Memória sobre a explicação de ambos os desenhos da planta e do alçado em perspectiva de cada uma das malocas dos gentios curutus situados no rio Apaporis," in *Viagem filosófica pelas capitanias do Grão-Pará, Rio Negro, Mato Grosso e Cuiabá: Memórias, Antropologia* (Rio de Janeiro: Conselho Federal de Cultura, 1974), 24–25.

34. Maw, *Journal of a Passage from the Pacific to the Atlantic*, 268, 270.

35. Manuela Carneiro da Cunha, "Política indigenista no século XIX," in *História dos índios no Brasil*, ed. Manuela Carneiro da Cunha (São Paulo: Companhia das Letras, 1992), 150, quoting Saint-Hilaire. The Frenchman's acquisition of a Botocudo girl, whom he then exchanged for a boy, is described in Miki, *Frontiers of Citizenship*, 56n93.

36. Prince Maximilian of Wied-Neuwied, *Viagem ao Brasil nos anos de 1815 a 1817*, trans. Edgard Süsskind de Mendonça and Flávio Poppe de Figueiredo (São Paulo: Editora Nacional, 1942), 111–12. For analysis of this episode, see Vânia Maria Losada Moreira, "Índios no Brasil: Marginalização social e exclusão historiográfica," *Diálogos Latinoamericanos* 3 (2001): 102–3. The 1819 land grant to Freyreiss and several other immigrants, which would lead to the establishment of Colônia Leopoldina in southern Bahia, is mentioned in Miki, *Frontiers of Citizenship*, 37.

37. Jeffrey Alan Erbig Jr., *Where Caciques and Mapmakers Met: Border Making in Eighteenth-Century South America* (Chapel Hill: University of North Carolina

Press, 2020), 151–52; Elisa Frühauf Garcia, *As diversas formas de ser índio: Políticas indígenas e políticas indigenistas no extremo sul da América portuguesa* (Rio de Janeiro: Arquivo Nacional, 2009), 295.

38. Schönitzer, "From the New to the Old World," 87.

39. Raul Silveira de Mello, *História do Forte de Coimbra* (Rio de Janeiro: Imprensa do Exército, 1961), 4:241.

40. Erbig, *Where Caciques and Mapmakers Met*, 159–61.

41. António Maria da Silva Torres to governor, Vila Bela, August 24, 1812, ANRJ, Série Guerra, IG1-226. The Portuguese investigation of the attack on Fort Borbón, based on Kadiwéu and Paraguayan informants, determined that the Kadiwéu had not burned the fort to the ground, as had been alleged; rather, the Paraguayan soldiers had set it ablaze upon their retreat, so that they could plausibly claim to have been attacked within the fort's walls. The Kadiwéu were determined to set the record straight on that point, as well as the original provocation for the theft of the cattle and siege of the fort, which had involved the kidnapping of two Indian women (possibly captives of the Kadiwéu). The Portuguese briefly occupied the fort, during which time they convinced the Kadiwéu to return some of the stolen weapons; Borbón was then returned to the Paraguayans.

42. Nora Bouvet, "La política indígena del dictador supremo en la frontera norte paraguaya," *Suplemento Antropológico* 27 (1992): 93–124. For a contemporary account of these conflicts between Guaikurú and Paraguayans, see Johann Rudolph Rengger, *Viaje al Paraguay en los años 1816 a 1826* (Asunción: Editorial Tiempo de Historia, 2010), especially 255–57.

43. Spix and Martius, *Viagem pelo Brasil* 3:120, 163. Around this same time, the Mura were singled out as being a principal cause of the diminished population of turtles in the region, especially after they began using iron points on their arrows, which killed the turtles more efficiently when they were hunted for food. José de Brito Inglês, miscellaneous writings, c. 1820, BNRJ, II-32, 13, 014.

44. The Muras who worked for Zany were described at length by Spix and Martius, *Viagem pelo Brasil* 3:120, 149–50. The travelers also told of how Zany traveled with a Mundurukú man whose presence clearly intimidated the Mura community they visited (119–20), a scene captured in one of the engravings from the expedition; and Zany's formal proposal to the Portuguese parliament contained detailed plans for using the intimidating power of the Mundurukú to subdue independent Indigenous groups. "Sessão de 26 de Agosto," 1822, *Diário das Cortes Geraes e Extraordinarias da Nação Portugueza*, 241, Assembleia da República, Debates Parlamentares, http://debates.parlamento.pt/catalogo/mc/c1821/01/01/01/020/1822-08-26/.

45. Karasch, "Catequese e cativeiro," 401–2.

46. Maria Regina Celestino de Almeida, "Os índios na história do Brasil no século XIX: Da invisibilidade ao protagonismo," *Revista História Hoje* 1,

no. 2 (2012): 29; Miki, *Frontiers of Citizenship*, 13, 30–34. As Miki explains, the Constituent Assembly had been dissolved the year before the promulgation of the Constitution, which likely explains the omission of Assembly-generated language on the issue of Indigenous citizenship.

47. Manuela Carneiro da Cunha, "Pensar os índios: Apontamentos sobre José Bonifácio," in *Antropologia do Brasil: Mito, história, etnicidade* (São Paulo: Brasiliense / EDUSP, 1986), 165–73; the quote about the legislation of the period is on 166. The philanthropic approach is often linked to the proposal of José Bonifácio de Andrada e Silva, entitled *Apontamentos para a civilização dos Índios bravos do Império do Brasil* (1823). On regional diversity in Indian policies and ideas about Indians in the nineteenth century, see Monteiro, "Tupis, tapuias e historiadores," 131–42.

48. Weber, *Bárbaros*, 268–69.

49. Vânia Maria Losada Moreira, "Os índios na história política do Império: Avanços, resistências e tropeços," *Revista História Hoje—ANPUH/Brasil* 1, no. 2 (2012): 271.

50. On Indian labor control as central to the political and military struggles of the 1820s and on Native peoples as active participants in these struggles, see André Roberto de A. Machado, *A quebra da mola real das sociedades: A crise política do Antigo Regime Português na província do Grão-Pará (1821–25)* (São Paulo: Hucitec / Fapesp, 2010), 238–41; Miguel Menéndez, "A área Madeira-Tapajós: Situação de contato e relações entre colonizador e indígenas," in *História dos índios no Brasil*, ed. Manuela Carneiro da Cunha (São Paulo: Companhia das Letras, 1992), 291–92; Mark Harris, *Rebellion on the Amazon: The Cabanagem, Race, and Popular Culture in the North of Brazil, 1798–1840* (Cambridge: Cambridge University Press, 2010), 201; the radical priest, Antônio Manoel Sanches de Brito, is discussed on 196.

51. José de Brito Inglês, miscellaneous writings, c. 1820, BNRJ, II-32, 13, 014.

52. The attacks of 1824 are described in Harris, *Rebellion on the Amazon*, 190–93 (quotation on 191).

53. On crossing into different provinces, see Lieutenant Colonel and General Director of Indians Guido Marliére to president of Minas Gerais, Retiro, December 14, 1825, in Naud, *Documentos sobre o índio brasileiro*, 96; Governor Francisco de Paula Magessi Tavares de Carvalho to Tomás António de Vila Nova Portugal, Cuiabá, December 12, 1820, AHU, Mato Grosso Avulsos, Cx. 44, Doc. 2209.

54. Damiana da Cunha's life and work are profiled in Suelen Siqueira Julio, *Damiana da Cunha: Uma índia entre a "sombra da cruz" e os caiapós do sertão (Goiás, c. 1780–1831)* (Niterói, Brazil: EDUFF, 2016); Mead, "Caiapó do Sul," ch. 7; Mary C. Karasch, "Damiana da Cunha: Catechist and Sertanista," in *Struggle and Survival in Colonial America*, ed. David G. Sweet and Gary B. Nash (Berkeley: University of California Press, 1981), 102–20.

55. Mary C. Karasch, "Índios aldeados: Um perfil demográfico da Capitania de Goiás, 1755–1835," *Habitus: Goiânia* 15, no. 1 (2017): 36, quoting Raimundo José da Cunha Mattos on the Xavante and other groups. See also the analysis of Bishop José de Santíssima Trinidade, Mariana, August 28, 1826, in Naud, *Documentos sobre o índio brasileiro*, 103.

56. "Illustração necessária e interessante, relativa ao gentio da nação Mura . . . feita por um anônimo em 1826," in Moreira Neto, *Índios da Amazônia*, 253.

57. Florence, *Viagem fluvial do Tietê ao Amazonas*, 88. Florence went on to credit the shift to their "love of pillage."

58. For case studies that emphasize this dynamic, focusing on the Indigenous peoples of Central Brazil in the late eighteenth and early nineteenth century, see Mary C. Karasch, *Before Brasília: Frontier Life in Central Brazil* (Albuquerque: University of New Mexico Press, 2016), ch. 4.

59. Chiara Vangelista, "Los guaykurú, españoles y portugueses en una región de frontera: Mato Grosso, 1770–1830," *Boletín del Instituto de Historia Argentina y Americana Dr. Emilio Ravignani* 8, no. 39 (1993): 71–73.

60. Johann Rudolph Rengger and Marcelin Longchamp, *The Reign of Doctor Joseph Gaspard Roderick de Francia, in Paraguay: Being An Account of Six Years' Residence in That Republic, from July, 1819 to May, 1825* (London: T. Hurst, E. Chance & Company, 1827), 52–53.

61. The quote is in President José Saturnino de Costa Pereira to the Secretaria do Estado dos Negócios Estrangeiros, Cuiabá, August 9, 1826, AHI, 308-2-08. See also Manuel Ignacio Fernandes to the Secretaria do Estado dos Negócios Estrangeiros Luis José de Carvalho e Melo, Asunción, November 25, 1826, AHI, 308-2-08.

62. Alfredo d'Escragnolle Taunay, *Scenas de viagem: Exploração entre os rios Taquary e Aquidauana no districto de Miranda* (Rio de Janeiro: Typographia Americana, 1868), footnote on 127. This was not only a phenomenon of the borderlands; Teófilo Otoni described similar usage among a Botocudo subgroup in Minas Gerais. "Noticia sobre os selvagens do Mucuri em uma carta dirigida pelo Sr. Teofilo Benedito Otoni ao Sr. Dr. Joaquim Manuel de Macedo" (1858), in *Notícia sobre os selvagens do Mucuri*, ed. Regina Horta Duarte (Belo Horizonte: Editora UFMG, 2002), 51.

63. Mello, *História do Forte de Coimbra*, 4:5–6; Nidia Areces, "Paraguayos, portugueses y Mbayás en Concepción, 1773–1840," *Memoria Americana* 8 (1999): 33.

64. Commander Jerônimo Joaquim Nunes to provincial president, Coimbra, May 1, 1827, ANRJ, Série Guerra, IG1-228.

65. Commander Joaquim António Rodrigues to provincial president, Coimbra, November 15, 1826, AHI, 308-2-08. The Guaikurú chiefs Beque de Ayona (also called Joaquim Nunes) and Muchacho (otherwise known as José de Siabra) were described as wearing an officer's hat and cap in Lieutenant

Joaquim José de Góes to Commander Jerônimo Joaquim Nunes, Coimbra, January 20, 1827, ANRJ, Série Guerra, IG1-228.

66. Report from the Council of War, Cuiabá, December 5, 1826, ANRJ, Série Guerra, IG1-227.

67. Luiz D'Alincourt, "Reflexões sobre o systema que se deve adoptar na fronteira do Paraguay, em consequencia da revolta e dos insultos praticados ultimamente pela nação dos Índios Guaicurus ou cavalleiros (1826)," *Revista do Instituto Histórico e Geográfico Brasileiro* 20 (1857): 364.

68. Governor of Arms António Joaquim da Costa Gavião to unknown recipient, Cuiabá, December 19, 1826, ANRJ, Série Guerra, IG1-228.

69. D'Alincourt, "Reflexões sobre o systema," 365.

70. D'Alincourt, "Reflexões sobre o systema," 362.

71. On Beque de Ayona and generational cleavages among the Guaikurú, see Commander Jerônimo Joaquim Nunes to provincial president, Coimbra, October 31, 1827, ANRJ, Série Guerra, IG1-228; and on the controversies provoked by Ayona's murder, Nunes to António Joaquim da Costa Gavião, Coimbra, October 30, 1827, ANRJ, Série Guerra, IG1-228. For a list of chiefs who had made peace by mid-1827, see Nunes, "Rellação dos Caciques Aycurús, que se me tem apresentado de páz com as suas famílias," Coimbra, September 22, 1827, ANRJ, Série Guerra, IG1-228 (attachment). The list identified Beque de Ayona as belonging to the "Pacanodeo" subgroup, likely a spelling variant of the people Sánchez Labrador called the Apacachodegodegis and with whom the missionary had worked at Belén back in the 1760s. If this is correct, Beque de Ayona would have been the leader of a subgroup that moved quite late into the Luso-Brazilian sphere. On the process of bringing Guaikurú chiefs back into the fold, see Nunes to provincial president, January 27, 1827, Coimbra, ANRJ, Série Guerra, IG1-228; Nunes to António Joaquim da Costa Gavião, Coimbra, May 1, 1827, ANRJ, Série Guerra, IG1-228.

72. D'Alincourt, "Reflexões sobre o systema," 361.

73. Commander Jerônimo Joaquim Nunes to provincial president, January 27, 1827, Coimbra, ANRJ, Série Guerra, IG1-228. The new patente is mentioned in Nunes to provincial president, Coimbra, May 2, 1827, ANRJ, Série Guerra, IG1-228

74. D'Alincourt, "Reflexões sobre o systema," 361, 363.

75. Commander Jerônimo Joaquim Nunes to provincial president, Coimbra, January 27, 1827, ANRJ, Série Guerra, IG1-228. At least one military expedition against a group of Guaikurú raiders was successful. See Commander Joaquim Duarte Pinheiro to Jerônimo Joaquim Nunes, Miranda, June 28, 1827, ANRJ, Série Guerra, IG1-228.

76. Governor of Arms António Joaquim da Costa Gavião to the Ministro e Secretário do Estado dos Negócios da Guerra, Cuiabá, November 4, 1827, ANRJ, Série Guerra, IG1-228.

77. On gifts, see Commander Jerônimo Joaquim Nunes to provincial president, Coimbra, May 2, 1827, ANRJ, Série Guerra, IG1–228; President José Saturnino de Costa Pereira to Capitão Muchacho [also known as José de Siabra], Cuiabá, November 27, 1827, ANRJ, Série Guerra, IG1–228. The French traveler Hercules Florence, who passed through the frontier region in late 1826 and early 1827, recounted that fear of the Guaikurú was at that time widespread. Florence, *Viagem fluvial do Tietê ao Amazonas*, 87–88, 93, 99.

78. Carneiro da Cunha, *Legislação indigenista*, 29.

79. "Illustração necessária e interessante," 252–53. This 1826 text was probably written by Canon André Fernandes de Souza, as some of his other writings replicate passages almost word for word.

80. Canon André Fernandes de Souza, "Notícias geográficas da Província do Rio Negro," c. 1821, BNRJ, I-31, 17, 5, paragraph 32. This text was written for Archbishop Romualdo Antonio de Seixas. A somewhat less detailed version of this text, addressed to Pedro I instead of the archbishop, was published in the *Revista do Instituto Histórico e Geográfico Brasileiro*.

81. Spix and Martius, *Viagem pelo Brasil* 3:121; Alfred Russel Wallace, *A Narrative of Travels on the Amazon and Rio Negro, with an Account of the Native Tribes, and Observations on the Climate, Geology, and Natural History of the Amazon Valley* (London: Reeve, 1853), 480, 512.

82. The quote is in "Illustração necessária e interessante," 252. Mura territories and routes of access in the 1820s are described in Souza, "Notícias geográficas da Província do Rio Negro," paragraphs 22–24, 31, 44, 46.

83. "Observacções addicionaes a Illustração sobre o Gentio Mura, escripta por hum anônimo no anno de 1826," in Moreira Neto, *Índios da Amazônia*, 264 (quotation), 259. This account is probably from around the mid-1840s; it explicitly elaborates upon the earlier account of the Mura, cited in note 82, from 1826.

84. Spix and Martius, *Viagem pelo Brasil* 3:119.

85. On these episodes, see Harris, *Rebellion on the Amazon*, 209–10. The Mura attacks in and around Borba in 1833 are documented in APEP, Cod. 947; I thank Mark Harris for sharing a copy of this codex and some of his transcriptions. See also "Relatório" of President José Joaquim Machado de Oliveira, December 3, 1833, CRL, Provincial Presidential Reports: Pará, 3.

86. Souza, "Notícias geográficas da Província do Rio Negro," paragraph 23.

87. Spix and Martius, *Viagem pelo Brasil* 3:121. Trade and temporary work for settlers in the 1820s are also described in Souza, "Notícias geográficas da Província do Rio Negro," paragraphs 31–32.

88. Márcia Leila de Castro Pereira, "Rios de história: Guerra, tempo e espaço entre os Mura do baixo Madeira" (PhD diss., Universidade de Brasília, 2009).

89. The best recent study of the Cabanagem is Harris, *Rebellion on the Amazon*.

90. "Documents of repression" is how Harris described the vast majority of sources on the Cabanagem Rebellion (personal communication, July 2005).

91. On racial classification during the rebellion, see David Cleary, "'Lost Altogether to the Civilised World': Race and the Cabanagem in Northern Brazil, 1750–1850," *Comparative Studies in Society and History* 40, no. 1 (1998): 109–35. On the participation of residents from the former colonial Indian villages, the *povoações de índios*, see Roller, *Amazonian Routes*, 203–4.

92. João Henrique de Mattos, "Relatório do estado de decadência em que se encontra o Alto Amazonas (1845)," *Revista do Instituto Histórico e Geográfico Brasileiro* 325 (1979): 173 ("wicked people," or *malvados*); Henry Walter Bates, *A Record of Adventures, Habits of Animals, Sketches of Brazilian and Indian Life, and Aspects of Nature Under the Equator, During Eleven Years of Travel* (London: John Murray, 1864), 189 ("aroused the stupid and brutal animosity . . ."). On this as a refrain among elite commentators, see Magda Ricci and Luciano Demetrius Barbosa, "Letrados da Amazônia Imperial e saberes das populações analfabetas durante a Revolução Cabana (1835–1840)," *Revista Brasileira de Educação* 20 (2015): 856; Monteiro, "Tupis, tapuias e historiadores," 135.

93. Pereira, "Rios de história," 179–81, 219. In the 1920s, the French missionary Constantin Tastevin described these barriers in the region (and settlers' futile efforts to remove them) but had trouble explaining their origins or purpose. R. Verneau, "Introdução: Os índios Mura da região do Autaz," in *Tastevin e a etnografia indígena: Coletânea de traduções de textos produzidos em Tefé*, ed. Priscila Faulhaber and Ruth Monserrat (Rio de Janeiro: Museu do Índio/FUNAI, 2008), 58–59. On the many ways that Amazonians have modified their local waterways over time, see Hugh Raffles and Antoinette WinklerPrins, "Further Reflections on Amazonian Environmental History: Transformations of Rivers and Streams," *Latin American Research Review* 38, no. 3 (2003): 165–87.

94. Pereira, "Rios de história," 165, quoting an interview with Maria Adélia, Lago da Josefa.

95. President of Pará Francisco José de Souza Soares de Andréa to the Ministro e Secretário do Estado dos Negócios da Guerra, Belém, October 23, 1838, ANRJ, Série Guerra, IG1-10 (quote); Moreira Neto, *Índios da Amazônia*, 108–10; Harris, *Rebellion on the Amazon*, 273–74.

96. President of Pará Francisco José de Souza Soares de Andréa to the Ministro e Secretário do Estado dos Negócios da Guerra, Belém, May 2, 1838, ANRJ, Série Guerra, IG1-10. Harris, *Rebellion on the Amazon*, 248–49, notes that some groups of Mundurukús joined the rebels instead, though their participation was unreliable.

97. Commander José António Miranda to the Ministro e Secretário do Estado dos Negócios da Guerra, Belém, May 8, 1840, ANRJ, Série Guerra, IG1-10.

98. The workers' corps legislation can be found in Patrícia de Melo Sampaio and Regina de Carvalho Erthal, eds. *Rastros da memória: Histórias e trajetórias das populações indígenas na Amazônia* (Manaus: Editora da Universidade Federal

do Amazonas, 2006), 294–85; see also Harris, *Rebellion on the Amazon*, 272; Cleary, "'Lost Altogether to the Civilised World,'" 134. Mura memories of the "Pega-Pega" are in Pereira, "Rios de história," 136–37.

99. On such episodes, see, for example, "Relatório" of President João Baptista de Figueiredo Tenreiro Aranha, April 30, 1852, CRL, Provincial Presidential Reports: Amazonas, 7; "Exposição" of Manoel Gomes Corrêa de Miranda, January 28, 1857, CRL, Provincial Presidential Reports: Amazonas, 8; "Relatório" of President João Wilkens de Mattos, March 25, 1870, CRL, Provincial Presidential Reports: Amazonas, 10; Carlos Moreira Neto, *Os índios e a ordem imperial* (Brasília: Ministério da Justiça/FUNAI 2005), 75, 87.

100. William Henry Edwards, *A Voyage Up the River Amazon, Including a Residence at Pará* (London: John Murray, 1855), 82 (quote), 103–5, 124.

101. Bates, *The Naturalist on the River Amazons*, 192–93. On the Mura as the worst, most degraded, or laziest of all Indians, see also Franz Keller-Leuzinger, *The Amazon and Madeira Rivers: Sketches and Descriptions from the Note-Book of an Explorer* (London: Chapman and Hall, 1874), 159; William L. Herndon, *Exploration of the Valley of the Amazon* (Washington: Armstrong, 1853), 1:328; João Barbosa Rodrigues, *Exploração dos Rios Urubú e Jatapú* (Rio de Janeiro: Typographia Nacional, 1875), 22–23.

102. Wallace, *A Narrative of Travels on the Amazon and Rio Negro*, 512. He was describing the Muras of the Purús River region, which they inhabited from its juncture with the Solimões to about sixteen days' travel upriver.

103. President of Pará Francisco José de Souza Soares de Andréa to the Ministro e Secretário do Estado dos Negócios da Guerra, Belém, May 2, 1838, ANRJ, Série Guerra, IG1-10 (the Mundurukú chiefs were said to be from the Abacaxi and Canumã Rivers); the number of warriors is mentioned in Lieutenant Colonel João Henrique de Mattos to President of Pará, Santarém, June 15, 1837, APEP, Cod. 888, Doc. 123. "Hated Muras" is from Bates, *The Naturalist on the River Amazons*, 273. On the militarization of Indigenous populations after 1808, when many Native men were enlisted in auxiliary troops to fight Indian wars, see Vânia Maria Losada Moreira, "Os índios e Império: História, direitos sociais e agenciamento indígena" (paper presented at the XXV Simpósio Nacional de História, Fortaleza, July 13–17, 2009), 11–12.

104. Bates, *The Naturalist on the River Amazons*, 270–74 (quotation on 273).

105. Bates, *The Naturalist on the River Amazons*, 273. See also Harris, *Rebellion on the Amazon*, 238–39, 270.

106. As recorded by the French engineer Alphonse Maugin de Lincourt in the 1840s, quoted in Hemming, *Amazon Frontier*, 236.

107. Bates, *The Naturalist on the River Amazons*, 273–74.

108. The 1845 decree, the "Regulamento acerca das Missões de catechese e civilização dos Índios," can be found in Sampaio and Erthal, *Rastros da memória*, 298–309.

109. Fernanda Sposito, *Nem cidadãos, nem brasileiros: Indígenas na formação*

do Estado nacional brasileiro e conflitos na província de São Paulo (1822–1845) (São Paulo: Alameda, 2012), 18.

110. In Pará, for example, the first General Director of the Indians was Colonel João Henrique de Mattos, who had commanded legalist troops during the Cabanagem; he was also the grandson of the military engineer profiled in chapter 2 of this book, Henrique João Wilkens, who had helped broker the late-eighteenth-century peace with the Mura and had married a Native woman. Harris, *Rebellion on the Amazon*, 82.

111. The directors of aldeamentos tended to be men with stakes in the extractive economy. Davi Avelino Leal, "Direitos e processos diferenciados de territorialização: Os conflitos pelo uso dos recursos naturais no rio Madeira (1861–1932)" (PhD diss., Universidade Federal do Amazonas, 2013), 129, 132, 162. Carmelite and Capuchin missionaries had been active in parts of Brazil before 1845, but the new legislation put them in the service of the state, subordinate to the civil directors. Sampaio, "Política indigenista no Brasil imperial," 179–80.

112. On the nineteenth-century aldeamentos in Brazil, see Moreira Neto, *Os índios e a ordem imperial*; Marta Rosa Amoroso, *Terra de índio: Imagens em aldeamentos do Império* (São Paulo: Editora Terceiro Nome, 2014). On how a set of complementary laws (including the Regulation of 1845 and the Land Law of 1850) enabled the expropriation of Native village lands during the second half of the century, see Vânia Maria Losada Moreira, "Terras indígenas do Espírito Santo sob o regime territorial de 1850," *Revista Brasileira de História* 22, no. 43 (2002), 153–69.

113. Francis de Castelnau, *Expedição às regiões centrais da América do Sul* (Rio de Janeiro: Itatiaia, 2000), 365, 366.

114. Castelnau, *Expedição*, 386 (quote), 388. Portuguese reliance on Guaikurú spies and informants after the peace agreement of 1791 is made clear in Ignácio de Souza Nogueira to Joaquim José Ferreira, Coimbra, October 31, 1791, APMT, FC.CA, Cx. 2, Doc. 142. The Kadiwéu would continue to serve in this role during the Paraguayan War, as described in Alfredo d'Escragnolle Taunay, *A Retirada da Laguna* (Rio de Janeiro: Typografia Americana, 1874), 34, 47, 62.

115. Augusto Leverger, "Roteiro da navegação do rio Paraguay desde a foz do São Lourenço até o Paraná," *Revista Trimestral do Instituto Histórico, Geográfico e Etnográfico do Brasil* 25 (1862): 227–28. Leverger said that he explored these streams (*riachos*) in 1846. Emphasis mine.

116. Augusto Leverger, "Notas sobre diversos pontos do Rio Paraguay," c. 1841, AIHGB, Lata 168, Doc. 5.

117. João Henrique Elliott, "Itinerário das viagens exploradoras emprehendidas pelo Sr. Barão de Antonina para descobrir uma via de communicação entre o porto da villa de Antonina e o Baixo-Paraguay na província de Mato-Grosso: feitas nos annos de 1844 a 1847 pelo sertanista o Sr. Joaquim Francisco

Lopes, e descriptas pelo Sr. João Henrique Elliott," *Revista do Instituto Histórico e Geográfico Brasileiro* 10 (1848): 169–70.

118. General Director of Indians Joaquim Alves Ferreira to the Minister and Secretary of State for Imperial Affairs, Cuiabá, December 2, 1848, APMT, Livro 101. I am grateful to Vanda da Silva for sharing the transcription of these documents (Livros 101 and 191, the Registro da Correspondência Oficial da Diretoria Geral dos Índios com a Presidência da Província, 1848–1872), which was done by Luzinete Xavier de Lima. On this same episode, see also "Discurso" of President Ricardo José Gomes Jardim, June 10, 1846, CRL, Provincial Presidential Reports: Mato Grosso, 33.

119. General Director of Indians Joaquim Alves Ferreira to the Minister and Secretary of State for Imperial Affairs, Cuiabá, December 2, 1848, APMT, Livro 101. By 1858, no Guaikurús were included in the report on existing aldeamentos in the province. General Director of Indians João Batista de Oliveira to the President of Mato Grosso, Cuiabá, December 31, 1858, APMT, Livro 101. They appeared again in a report from 1872, but that report is highly suspect, because it appears to have been copied, nearly verbatim, from the 1848 report cited above. General Director of Indians António Luís Brandão to the President of Mato Grosso, Cuiabá, March 13, 1872, APMT, Livro 191.

120. Márcio Couto Henrique, "Presente de branco: A perspectiva indígena dos brindes da civilização (Amazônia, século XIX)," *Revista Brasileira de História* 37, no. 75 (2017): 8 ("savage lifestyle"), 9 ("deceiving the government").

121. Carlos Moreira Neto, *Os índios e a ordem imperial*, 194, quoting the provincial president of Goiás.

122. On not granting Native requests for guns, see, for example, General Director of Indians Henrique José Vieira to the President of Mato Grosso, Cuiabá, January 30, 1855, APMT, Livro 101.

123. Amoroso, *Terra do índio*, 79–80.

124. Miki, *Frontiers of Citizenship*, 79.

125. "Discurso" of President Manoel Paranhos da Silva Velloso, August 15, 1844, CRL, Provincial Presidential Reports: Pará, 16.

126. General Director of the Indians João Henrique de Mattos, August 25, 1858, attachment to the "Relatório" of President Francisco José Furtado, September 7, 1858, CRL, Provincial Presidential Reports: Amazonas, AM-2; "Relatório" of President João Capistrano Bandeira de Mello Filho, March 9, 1878, CRL, Provincial Presidential Reports: Pará, 104.

127. Vânia Maria Losada Moreira, "Entre as vilas e os sertões: Trânsitos indígenas e transculturações nas fronteiras do Espírito Santo (1798–1840)," *Nuevo Mundo—Mundos Nuevos* (2011), paragraph 13, posted January 31, 2011, http://journals.openedition.org/nuevomundo/60746; Márcio Couto Henrique, "A perspectiva indígena das missões religiosas na Amazônia (século XIX)," *História Social* 25 (2013), 141–42. For parallels in the Bolivian Amazon

during the same period, see Gary Van Valen, *Indigenous Agency in the Amazon: The Mojos in Liberal and Rubber-Boom Bolivia, 1842–1932* (Tucson: University of Arizona Press, 2013), ch. 3.

128. General Director of the Indians João Henrique de Mattos, August 25, 1858, attachment to the "Relatório" of President Francisco José Furtado, September 7, 1858, CRL, Provincial Presidential Reports: Amazonas, AM-8; Francisco Bernardino de Souza, *Lembranças e curiosidades do vale do Amazonas* (Manaus: Associação Comercial do Amazonas / Fundo Editorial, 1988 [1873]), 151. Both of these sources identified the Murified leader as being from the Juma nation.

129. The British naval officer, Henry Lister Maw, visited Matari in the late 1820s, when the elderly Carmelite missionary José das Chagas had just begun building the mission. Maw, *Journal of a Passage from the Pacific to the Atlantic*, 316–17. On the sly, the Mura successfully traded turtles and fowl for aguardente (317–18). In Canon André Fernandes de Souza's account from the early 1820s, Matari was still described as an independent Mura village squeezed between the properties of settlers from Barra and those from Serpa. Souza, "Notícias Geográphicas da Capitania do Rio Negro," 431.

130. The destruction of Matari during the Cabanagem was recounted in the 1840s account of Italian traveler Gaetano Osculati, *Exploraciones de las regiones ecuatoriales a lo largo del Napo y del Río de la Amazonas*, trans. Alberto Guaraldo (Iquitos, Peru: CETA, 2003), 298.

131. Bates, *The Naturalist on the River Amazons*, 191–92; Edwards, *A Voyage Up the River Amazon*, 131–32.

132. Roller, *Amazonian Routes*, 206–9.

133. Such problems fill the reports of provincial presidents from the 1840s through the 1880s: CRL, Provincial Presidential Reports: Pará, Amazonas, and Mato Grosso; for a synthesis, see Sampaio, "Política indigenista no Brasil imperial," 197–200. On the impact of epidemics in Central Brazil, especially smallpox and measles, see Karasch, *Before Brasília*, 28–31. The possibility that some diseases were intentionally transmitted to Native groups is mentioned in Karasch, *Before Brasília*, 29, 105; a particular episode is described at length for the Canela of southern Maranhão in Francisco de Paula Ribeiro, "Roteiro da viagem que fez o Capitão Francisco de Paula Ribeiro às fronteiras da Capitania do Maranhão e da de Goiás no ano de 1815 em serviço de S.M. Fidelíssima," in *Francisco de Paula Ribeiro, desbravador dos sertões de Pastos Bons: A base geográfica e humana do Sul do Maranhão*, ed. Adalberto Franklin and João Renôr F. de Carvalho (Imperatriz, Brazil: Ética, 2005), 99. Decades later, Claude Lévi-Strauss alleged that a favorite pastime of Brazilian elites in the early twentieth century was to hang clothing infected by smallpox along with gifts on Native pathways in the interior of São Paulo state. Lévi-Strauss, *Tristes Tropiques*, trans. John Weightman and Doreen Weightman (New York: Penguin, 2012), 49.

134. "Observacções addicionaes a Illustração sobre o Gentio Mura," 261; Director Geral S. Orlando de Araujo Costa, "Directoria Geral dos Indios no Amazonas em Manáos," January 27, 1866, CRL, Provincial Presidential Reports: Amazonas, A-334.

135. Edwards, *A Voyage Up the River Amazon*, 82, 109–10, 112, 123–24, 131–33. Edwards passed through Matari around 1846.

136. Rodrigues, *Exploração dos Rios Urubú e Jatapú*, 27.

137. Herndon, *Exploration of the Valley of the Amazon*, 278. See also Antonio Alexandre Isidio Cardoso, "O Eldorado dos deserdados: Indígenas, escravos, migrantes, regatões e o avanço rumo ao oeste amazônico (1830–1880)" (PhD diss., Universidade de São Paulo, 2018), 204–5.

138. Miki, *Frontiers of Citizenship*, 58 (on Bahia and Espírito Santo); Sposito, *Nem cidadãos, nem brasileiros*, 19–20 (on São Paulo).

139. Henrique, "A perspectiva indígena das missões religiosas na Amazônia," 142–43, summarizing a bishop's account from Itaituba, a town on the Tapajós River in Pará, in 1847.

140. Miki, *Frontiers of Citizenship*, 58. This episode, which involved the Brazilian statesman and businessman Teófilo Otoni, occurred in the Mucuri River Valley in 1847.

141. Florence described how a group of Mundurukús had come right up to the travelers' canoes when they stopped for supper on the bank of the Tapajós, and how the Indians had traded two large baskets of foodstuffs for two "worthless knives." One of these Mundurukús likely sat for the portrait. Florence, *Viagem fluvial*, 287.

142. On famous warriors living in missions in Paraná, see Marta Rosa Amoroso, "Guerra e mercadorias: Os Kaingang nas cenas da 'Conquista de Guarapuava,'" in *Do contato ao confronto: A conquista de Guarapuava no século XVIII*, ed. Ana Maria de Moraes Belluzzo, Marta Rosa Amoroso, Nicolau Sevcenko, and Valéria Piccoli (São Paulo: BNB Paribas, 2003), 34–35.

143. Manoel Nicolau de Mello to president of Amazonas, Aiapuiá, January 16, 1854, quoted in Cardoso, "O Eldorado dos deserdados," 83.

144. False rumors of Indian attacks were common—and were often used to justify armed expeditions into Native territories. Moreira Neto, *Os índios e a ordem imperial*, 90.

145. Cardoso, "O Eldorado dos deserdados."

146. Taunay, *A Retirada da Laguna*, 34, 47, 62; on Taunay's deep ambivalence about Guaikurú allies in the war, see Tracy Devine Guzmán, *Native and National in Brazil: Indigeneity after Independence* (Chapel Hill: University of North Carolina Press, 2013), 86–87.

147. Maria de Fátima Costa, "Indigenous Peoples of Brazil and the War of the Triple Alliance, 1864–1870," in *Military Struggle and Identity Formation in Latin America: Race, Nation, and Community During the Liberal Period*, ed. Nicola Foote and René D. Harder Horst (Gainesville: University Press of Florida, 2010), 168 (quotation), 170–72.

148. On Mura memories of the "Pega-Pega," see Pereira, "Rios de história," 136–37. Mura fears of conscription for the Paraguayan War are mentioned in Leal, "Direitos e processos diferenciados de territorialização," 161, 157.

149. Cardoso, "O Eldorado dos deserdados." 239–40, quoting the account of Ernesto Mattoso Maia Forte. Mura men had been depicted in this arrow shooting pose since the eighteenth century; see, for example, figure 2.2.

150. Barbara Weinstein speculates that the Mundurukú may have assisted rubber bosses in the coercion of rival groups, such as the Apiacá, who were drafted as rubber tappers. Weinstein, *The Amazon Rubber Boom, 1850–1920* (Stanford, CA: Stanford University Press, 1983), 189.

151. On rubber-boom Amazonia as a place of startling diversity and cosmopolitanism, as well as extreme violence and treachery, see Susanna B. Hecht, *The Scramble for the Amazon and the Lost Paradise of Euclides da Cunha* (Chicago: University of Chicago Press, 2013), especially ch. 15.

152. On Indianist literature and romanticism, see David Treece, *Exiles, Allies, Rebels: Brazil's Indianist Movement, Indigenist Politics, and the Imperial Nation-State* (Westport, CT: Greenwood Press, 2000); Guzmán, *Native and National in Brazil.*

Chapter 5

1. In her essay against dependency perspectives on the history of neocolonial enclaves, Catherine LeGrand writes that Colombians in the banana-producing region of Magdalena saw their history as a "time of bananas and much more besides." As one informant says, "We must pass down what we have lived in all its richness to our children and the generations to come as our legacy to constructing the future in ways we don't yet know." LeGrand, "Living in Macondo: Economy and Culture in a United Fruit Company Banana Enclave (Santa Marta, Colombia, 1890–1930)," in *Close Encounters of the Imperial Kind: Writing the Cultural History of U.S.–Latin American Relations*, ed. Gilbert Joseph, Ricardo Salvatore, and Catherine LeGrand (Durham, NC: Duke University Press, 1998), 352. On "topographic writing" and the ways in which Native Amazonian peoples imbue features of the landscape with historical meaning, see Fernando Santos-Granero, "Writing History into the Landscape: Space, Myth, and Ritual in Contemporary Amazonia," *American Ethnologist* 25, no. 2 (1998): 128–48.

2. This paragraph was inspired, in part, by the fieldwork letters of Curt Nimuendajú, *Cartas do sertão, de Curt Nimuendajú para Carlos Estevão de Oliveira*, ed. Thekla Hartmann (Lisbon: Museu Nacional de Etnologia / Assírio & Alvim, 2000), though Nimuendajú would not have accepted settlers' accounts at face value. It also draws on narratives about "so-called Indians" that were popular among local officials in the Indian Protection Service (SPI); an example can be found in Joaquim Melo, *SPI—A Política Indigenista no Amazonas* (Manaus: Edições do Governo do Estado, 2009), 103.

3. John M. Monteiro, "Redescobrindo os índios da América portuguesa: Antropologia e história," in *Olhares contemporâneos: Cenas do mundo em discussão na universidade*, ed. Odílio Alves Aguiar, José Élcio Batista, and Jocely Pinheiro (Fortaleza, Edições Demócrito Rocha, 2001), 136–37; Mariana Albuquerque Dantas, "Estratégias indígenas: Dinâmica social e relações interétnicas no aldeamento do Ipanema no final do século XIX," in *A presença indígena no Nordeste: Processos de territorialização, modos de reconhecimento e regimes de memória*, ed. João Pacheco de Oliveira (Rio de Janeiro: Contra Capa, 2011), 413–45; Maria Regina Celestino de Almeida, "Os índios na história do Brasil no século XIX: Da invisibilidade ao protagonismo," *Revista História Hoje* 1, no. 2 (2012): 21–39; Soraia Sales Dornelles, "A produção da invisibilidade indígena: Sobre construção de dados demográficos, apropriação de terras e o apagamento de identidades indígenas na segunda metade do XIX a partir da experiência paulista," *Revista Brasileira de História & Ciências Sociais* 10, no. 20 (2018): 62–80.

4. On salvage ethnography, see the classic essay by Jacob W. Gruber, "Ethnographic Salvage and the Shaping of Anthropology," *American Anthropologist* 72, no. 6 (1970): 1289–99; Elizabeth Edwards, "Surveying Culture: Photography and the Collection of Culture, British New Guinea, 1898," in *Hunting the Gatherers: Ethnographic Collectors, Agents and Agency in Melanesia, 1870s–1930s*, ed. Michael O'Hanlon and Robert L. Welsch (Oxford: Berghahn, 2000), 103–26. A call to reinterpret these sources in collaboration with Native scholars and activists can be found in Stephen Warren and Ben Barnes, "Salvaging the Salvage Anthropologists: Erminie Wheeler-Voegelin, Carl Voegelin, and the Future of Ethnohistory," *Ethnohistory* 65, no. 2 (2018): 189–214.

5. For Brazil, see John M. Monteiro, "Tupis, tapuias e historiadores: Estudos de história indígena a do indigenismo" (Tese de Livre Docência, Universidade Estadual de Campinas, 2001), especially chs. 6–8; Tracy Devine Guzmán, *Native and National in Brazil: Indigeneity after Independence* (Chapel Hill: University of North Carolina Press, 2013), ch. 2; Yuko Miki, *Frontiers of Citizenship: A Black and Indigenous History of Postcolonial Brazil* (Cambridge University Press, 2018), especially ch. 3. For North America, see Philip J. Deloria, *Playing Indian* (New Haven, CT: Yale University Press, 1998); Sherry Smith, *Reimagining Indians: Native Americans Through Anglo Eyes, 1880–1940* (Oxford: Oxford University Press, 2000); Jean M. O'Brien, *Firsting and Lasting: Writing Indians out of Existence in New England* (Minneapolis: University of Minnesota Press, 2010).

6. Henri Coudreau, *Viagem ao Tapajós (28 de julho de 1895 a 7 de janeiro de 1896)*, trans. A. de Miranda Bastos (São Paulo: Companhia Editora Nacional, 1941), 211.

7. Charles Hartt, quoted in Miki, *Frontiers of Citizenship*, 129.

8. Vânia Maria Losada Moreira, "Terras indígenas do Espírito Santo sob o regime territorial de 1850," *Revista Brasileira de História* 22, no. 43 (2002), 167. On the ways this argument was levelled against the Mura in the early decades

of the twentieth century, see Adriana Romano Athila, "Índios de verdade: Territorialidade, história e diferença entre os Mura da Amazônia Meridional" (MA thesis, Universidade Federal do Rio de Janeiro, 1998), 96–97.

9. Neil L. Whitehead, "Ethnic Transformation and Historical Discontinuity in Native Amazonia and Guayana, 1500–1900," *L'Homme* 33, no. 126/128 (1993): 297–98; Andrey Cordeiro Ferreira, "Conquista colonial, resistência indígena e formação do estado-nação: Os índios Guaicuru e Guaná no Mato Grosso do século XIX," *Revista de Antropologia* 52, no. 1 (2009): 124–25.

10. Pavel Frič and Yvonna Fričová, *Guido Boggiani: Fotograf = Photographer* (Prague: Titanic, 1997), 30–35.

11. Guido Boggiani, "Viajes de un artista por la América Meridional: Los Caduveos. Expedición al Río Nabileque, en la región de las grandes cacerías de venados, Matto Grosso (Brasil)," *Revista del Instituto de Etnología de la Universidad Nacional de Tucumán* 1, no. 3 (1930): 531, 533, 537–38.

12. Guido Boggiani, *Os Caduveos* (Belo Horizonte: Editora Itatiaia, 1975), 118, 243. This diary recounts his first stay among the Kadiwéu, in 1892.

13. Boggiani, "Viajes," 542.

14. Patrícia Melo Sampaio, "Política indigenista no Brasil imperial," in *O Brasil Imperial*, ed. Keila Grinberg and Ricardo Salles (Rio de Janeiro: Civilização Brasileira, 2009), 1:199.

15. General Director of Indians António Luís Brandão to the President of Mato Grosso, Cuiabá, March 13, 1872, APMT, Livro 191. It is nearly the same as a report from 1848.

16. Some of the quoted terms are from Maria Regina Celestino de Almeida, *Os índios na história do Brasil* (Rio de Janeiro: Editora FGV, 2010), 157–58. Yuko Miki, *Frontiers of Citizenship*, 115, argues that this had been the goal of the 1845 regulation all along, in its program of state-sponsored "civilization and catechism." See also Dornelles, "A produção da invisibilidade indígena," 70–74.

17. Boggiani, *Os Caduveos*; Boggiani, "Viajes de un artista," 495–556; Emilio Rivasseau, *A vida dos indios Guaycurús: Quinze dias nas suas aldeias (sul de Matto-Grosso)* (São Paulo: Companhia Editora Nacional, 1936).

18. Mariana Giordano, "Las múltiples facetas de Guido Boggiani," in *Boggiani y el Chaco: Una aventura del siglo XIX*, ed. Pavel Frič and Yvonna Fričová (Buenos Aires: Museo Fernández Blanco, 2002), 25–35.

19. R. Verneau, "Introdução: Os índios Mura da região do Autaz," in *Tastevin e a etnografia indígena: Coletânea de traduções de textos produzidos em Tefé*, ed. Priscila Faulhaber and Ruth Monserrat (Rio de Janeiro: Museu do Índio/FUNAI, 2008), 56; Constantin Tastevin, "Os índios Mura da região do Autaz," in Faulhaber and Monserrat, *Tastevin e a etnografia indígena*, 59 (quotation).

20. Nimuendajú to Carlos Estevão de Oliveira, Manaus, June 14, 1926, in *Cartas do sertão*, 94.

21. Nimuendajú to Carlos Estevão de Oliveira, Borba, April 10, 1926, in *Cartas do sertão*, 93.

22. Nimuendajú to Carlos Estevão de Oliveira, Manaus, June 14, 1926, in *Cartas do sertão*, 94. On his sales to museums, see Priscila Faulhaber, "Etnografia na Amazônia e tradução cultural: Comparando Constant Tastevin e Curt Nimuendaju," *Boletim do Museu Paraense Emílio Goeldi—Ciências Humanas* 3, no. 1 (2008): 25–26.

23. Nimuendajú, *Cartas do sertão*; Curt Nimuendajú, "The Mura and Pirahã," in *Handbook of South American Indians*, ed. Julian H. Steward (Washington, DC: Smithsonian Institution, 1948), 3:255–68; Curt Nimuendajú, "As Tribus do Alto Madeira," *Journal de la Société des Américanistes* 17 (1925): 137–72. Some of the photographs can be found in the virtual museum of the Coleção Carlos Estevão de Oliveira, Museu do Estado de Pernambuco, http://www3.ufpe.br/carlosestevao/museu-virtual-fotoetno.php.

24. I first saw this photograph in a blog post by Renato Athias, "Coleção Fotoetnográfica Indígena Carlos Estevão de Oliveira II," June 18, 2007, http://renatoathias.blogspot.com/2007/06/#1686193191423646085. I thank Dr. Athias for offering to help me obtain a high-resolution copy.

25. See, for example, Nimuendajú to Carlos Estevão de Oliveira, Boa Vista (Goiás), June 18, 1937, in *Cartas do sertão*, 264; Rivasseau, *A vida dos indios Guaycurús*, 85–86, 108.

26. Coudreau, *Viagem ao Tapajós*, 170–71, drawing on an account by Gonçalves Tocantins.

27. Curt Nimuendajú, *Reconhecimento dos rios Içána, Ayarí e Uaupés: Apontamentos linguísticos e ensaio fotográfico*, ed. Renato Athias (Rio de Janeiro: Museu do Índio, 2015), 65.

28. The original name was the Serviço de Proteção ao Índio e Localização dos Trabalhadores Nacionais (SPILTN). On the SPI in Amazonas, see Melo, *SPI*; Davi Avelino Leal, "Direitos e processos diferenciados de territorialização: Os conflitos pelo uso dos recursos naturais no rio Madeira (1861–1932)" (PhD diss., Universidade Federal do Amazonas, 2013), ch. 4. The classic scholarly critique of the agency is Antonio Carlos de Souza Lima, *Um grande cerco de paz: Poder tutelar, indianidade e formação do estado no Brasil* (Petrópolis: Vozes, 1995). On the SPI archives, see Carlos Augusto da Rocha Freire, ed., *Memória do SPI: Textos, imagens e documentos sobre o Serviço de Proteção aos Índios (1910–1967)* (Rio de Janeiro: Museu do Índio/FUNAI, 2011).

29. José Bezerra Cavalcante, Director of the SPI in Amazonas, 1911, quoted in Melo, *SPI*, 83.

30. Nimuendajú to Carlos Estevão de Oliveira, Manaus, June 14, 1926, in *Cartas do sertão*, 94.

31. The Comissão de Inquérito de 1931 is described in Athila, "Índios de verdade," 96–97. The municipalities said to be without Indians were Manaus, Itacoatiara, Borba, and Manicoré.

32. Ricardo Franco de Almeida Serra, "Parecer sobre o aldeamento dos índios Uaicurus e Guanás com a descripção dos seus usos, religião, estabilidade

e costumes (1803)," *Revista do Instituto Histórico e Geográfico Brasileiro* 7 (1845): 207. On these subgroups in the late colonial period, see chapter 1, note 61.

33. On Guaikurú subgroups in the 1840s, see Francis de Castelnau, *Expedição às regiões centrais da América do Sul* (Rio de Janeiro: Itatiaia, 2000), 403; in the 1860s, Alfredo d'Escragnolle Taunay, *Scenas de viagem: Exploração entre os rios Taquary e Aquidauana no districto de Miranda* (Rio de Janeiro: Typographia Americana, 1868), 111.

34. Mônica Thereza Soares Pechincha, "Memória e história entre índios brasileiros: Os Kadiwéu e seus etnógrafos Darcy Ribeiro e Guido Boggiani," *História Revista (UFG)* 5 (2000): 161.

35. See, for example, Robert H. Lowie, "The Southern Cayapó," in *Handbook of South American Indians*, ed. Julian H. Steward (Washington, DC: Smithsonian Institution, 1946), 1:519–20.

36. Elizabeth Ewart, "Coisas com as quais os antropólogos se preocupam: Grupos de descendência espacial entre os Panará," *Revista de Antropologia* 58, no. 1 (2015): 199–221; Odair Giraldin, *Cayapó e Panará: luta e sobrevivência de um povo Jê no Brasil central* (Campinas: Editora da UNICAMP, 1997); Eduardo Alves Vasconcelos, "Investigando a hipótese Cayapó do Sul-Panará" (PhD diss., Universidade de Campinas, 2013); David Louis Mead, "Caiapó do Sul, an Ethnohistory (1610–1920)," (PhD diss., University of Florida, 2010). On Panará oral histories, see "Panará: Histórico do contato," Instituto Socioambiental, Povos Indígenas no Brasil, https://pib.socioambiental.org/pt/Povo:Panará.

37. Peter Gow, "'Who Are These Wild Indians': On the Foreign Policies of Some Voluntarily Isolated Peoples in Amazonia," *Tipití: Journal of the Society for the Anthropology of Lowland South America* 16, no. 1 (2018): 13.

38. Rivasseau, *A vida dos indios Guaycurús*, 51, describes the rifles. On later displays of these items, see G. A. Colini, "Notícia histórica e etnográfica sobre os Guaicuru e os Mbayá," in Boggiani, *Os Caduveos*, 267; Carvalho, "Chaco," 468–70 (the last page features a photograph of two Terena elders wearing their wartime uniforms).

39. Castelnau, *Expedição*, 390.

40. Giovani José da Silva, *A Reserva Indígena Kadiwéu (1899–1984): Memória, identidade e história* (Dourados: Editora UFGD, 2014), 109–12.

41. Rivasseau, *A vida dos indios Guaycurús*, 69 (on the alliance that led to the demarcation), 181–83 (on other advantageous relationships with government officials).

42. Jaime Garcia Siqueira Jr., "Esse campo custou o sangue dos nossos avós: A construção do tempo e espaço Kadiwéu," in *Kadiwéu: Senhoras da arte, senhores da guerra*, ed. Giovani José da Silva (Curitiba: Editora CRV, 2011), 83–84 (quote).

43. Rivasseau, *A vida dos indios Guaycurús*, 50–51, 53. See also Carvalho, "Chaco," 469–70; Herbert Baldus, "Introdução," in Boggiani, *Os Caduveos*, 36–46.

44. Boggiani, *Os Caduveos*, 87; Boggiani, "Viajes de un artista," p. 548–49. This account is contradicted by at least one other version of the story, as noted in Baldus, "Introdução," 42–43. On Kadiwéu factionalism as a product of the alliances with ranchers, see Siqueira, "Esse campo custou o sangue dos nossos avós," 85–86. Rivasseau, *A vida dos índios Guaycurús*, 53–54, 66–69, describes what were probably escalating conflicts between the Kadiwéu and Malheiros during the process of demarcating the reserve. The history went deeper, though: Malheiros had served as director of the Kadiwéu village of Nalique beginning in the 1870s, a post he used to extract Kadiwéu labor and to gain control over their land. Baldus, "Introdução," 36–37.

45. Boggiani, "Viajes de un artista," 543–44, 554–55. It is worth noting that some of the details on the assassination plot came from a dubious source: Malheiros himself, whom Boggiani encountered in 1898 at Fort Olimpo (formerly Borbón).

46. Pechincha, "Memória e história," 154, 159, 161; Boggiani, *Os Caduveos*, 128, 136, 142–44, 149–50. On Boggiani's drawing and photography as another form of "entanglement" with his Kadiwéu hosts, see Luciana Martins, "'Resemblances to Archaeological Finds': Guido Boggiani, Claude Lévi-Strauss and Caduveo Body Painting," *Journal of Latin American Cultural Studies* 26, no. 2 (2017): 187–219. His drawings, in particular, "were produced in a setting of reciprocity, in a context of daily exchanges of experiences between the Kadiwéu artists and Boggiani." Chiara Vangelista, "Textos, dibujos, fotografías: La construcción de la imagen de los kadiwéu en los diarios de viaje de Guido Boggiani (1892 y 1897)," in *El mundo latinoamericano como representación, siglos XIX–XX*, ed. Pilar García Jordán (Barcelona: Publicacions i Edicions UB/ TEIAA/ IFEA, 2015), 193.

47. Boggiani, *Os Caduveos*, 177, 183 (quote), 185–86.

48. Curt Nimuendajú, "Excursões pela Amazônia," trans. Thekla Hartmann, *Revista de Antropologia* 44, no. 2 (2001): 196. Nimuendajú noted that he dutifully submitted these complaints to the SPI Inspector in Manaus.

49. Nimuendajú to Carlos Estevão de Oliveira, Borba, April 10, 1926, in *Cartas do sertão*, 92. In this same letter, Nimuendajú recounts how a group of Mundurukú on the Paracuni River also appealed to him for counsel and protection against a group of predatory river traders; one of the traders had been appointed by the SPI to serve as the "*delegado*," or representative, of the Mundurukú (91).

50. These cases from the Autazes region are discussed in the 1911 account of an engineer named João Augusto Zany, quoted in Melo, *SPI*, 100; and in the 1912 report by Domingos Theóphilo de Carvalho Leal, in Melo, *SPI*, 105. See also Athila, "Índios de verdade," ch. 2.

51. Marta Rosa Amoroso, "Nimuendajú às voltas com a história," *Revista de Antropologia* 44, no. 2 (2001): 175.

52. Lieutenant Colonel João Batista Mardel to João Pereira Caldas, Nogueira, July 26, 1785, AHI, Cod. 340-4-6.

53. João Barbosa Rodrigues, *Exploração dos Rios Urubú e Jatapú* (Rio de Janeiro: Typographia Nacional, 1875), 24.

54. Tastevin, "Os índios Mura da região do Autaz," 63–68 (quotation is on 67).

55. Tastevin, "Os índios Mura da região do Autaz," 72–73.

56. Robert Stewart Clough, quoted and analyzed in Antonio Alexandre Isidio Cardoso, "O Eldorado dos deserdados: Indígenas, escravos, migrantes, regatões e o avanço rumo ao oeste amazônico (1830–1880)" (PhD diss., Universidade de São Paulo, 2018), 264–65. On the rise of new modes of Native leadership in the context of economic and political disruption, see Whitehead, "Ethnic Transformation and Historical Discontinuity," 297–98.

57. Report by Domingos Theóphilo de Carvalho Leal, quoted in Melo, *SPI*, 103.

58. Tastevin, "Os índios Mura da região do Autaz," 60. See also Marta Rosa Amoroso, "O nascimento da aldeia mura: Sentidos e modos de habitar a beira," in *Paisagens Ameríndias: Lugares, circuitos e modos de vida na Amazônia*, ed. Marta Rosa Amoroso and Gilton Mendes dos Santos (São Paulo: Editora Terceiro Nome, 2013), 100; Márcia Leila de Castro Pereira, "Território e mobilidade Mura no Baixo Rio Madeira (AM)," *Habitus: Goiânia* 14, no. 2 (2016), 274. For a call to decolonize the concept of *mestiçagem* (mixing) by considering its indigenous forms and purposes, see Guillaume Boccara, "Poder colonial e etnicidade no Chile: Territorialização e reestruturação entre os Mapuche da época colonial." *Tempo* 12, no. 23 (2007): 59.

59. On alcohol as a force of cultural corruption, see, for example, Baldus, "Introdução," 41. Anthropologists have found parallels in Indigenous alcohol use across countries and regions; see, for example, Sherry Saggers and Dennis Gray, *Dealing with Alcohol: Indigenous Usage in Australia, New Zealand, and Canada* (Cambridge: Cambridge University Press, 1998); Gretchen Pierce and Áurea Toxqui, eds., *Alcohol in Latin America: A Social and Cultural History* (Tucson: University of Arizona Press, 2014).

60. Castelnau, *Expedição*, 407.

61. Boggiani, *Os Caduveos*, 111 (quotation), 162, 171, 172, 176, 209, 220.

62. Boggiani, *Os Caduveos*, 164–66, 188, 230 (quotation). For a similar assessment by another nineteenth-century traveler in the Amazon, see Henry Walter Bates, *A Record of Adventures, Habits of Animals, Sketches of Brazilian and Indian Life, and Aspects of Nature Under the Equator, During Eleven Years of Travel* (London: John Murray, 1864), 276.

63. Rivasseau, *A vida dos indios Guaycurús*, 105–6 (quotation), 110–11. See also the description of low-stakes trading of horses for aguardente by the Kadiwéu in the 1840s in João Henrique Elliot, "Itinerário das viagens exploradoras emprehendidas pelo Sr. Barão de Antonina para descobrir uma via de communicação entre o porto da villa de Antonina e o Baixo-Paraguay na província de Mato-Grosso: feitas nos annos de 1844 a 1847 pelo sertanistas

o Sr. Joaquim Francisco Lopes, e descriptas pelo Sr. João Henrique Elliott," *Revista do Instituto Histórico e Geográfico Brasileiro* 10 (1848): 169–70.

64. Boggiani, *Os Caduveos*, 111. In Pierre Clastres' classic description of the South American Indian chieftainship, the leader is under a strict obligation to be generous; his power and authority rest upon his ability to continue giving. Clastres, *Society Against the State: Essays in Political Anthropology*, trans. Robert Hurley (New York: Urizen Books, 1977). Contemporary parallels can be found in Beth Conklin, "For Love or Money? Indigenous Materialism and Humanitarian Agendas," in *Editing Eden: A Reconsideration of Identity, Politics, and Place in Amazonia*, ed. Frank Hutchison and Patrick C. Wilson (Lincoln: University of Nebraska Press, 2010), 134.

65. Commander Francisco Rodrigues do Prado to governor, Coimbra, January 2(?), 1794, APMT, Cód. 35, fls. 125v–126; Prado to governor, Coimbra, January 8, 1795, APMT, FC.CA, Cx. 4, Doc. 197; Commander Ricardo Franco de Almeida Serra to governor, Coimbra, May 30, 1798, APMT, FC.CA, Cx. 6, Doc. 328.

66. Darcy Ribeiro, *Kadiwéu: Ensaios etnológicos sobre o saber, o azar e a beleza* (Petrópolis: Vozes, 1980), 24. An anthropologist who visited the reserve in the late 1940s noted that the Kadiwéu had only one or two horses per family. Kalervo Oberg, *The Terena and the Caduveo of Southern Mato Grosso, Brazil* (Washington, DC: Smithsonian Institution, 1949), 60.

67. Cristiane Lasmar, *De volta ao lago de leite: Gênero e transformação no Alto Rio Negro* (São Paulo: Edusp/ISA, 2005), 257. On the pacification of whites/outsiders/others via material exchange and acquisition, through the lens of modern Brazilian ethnography, see Bruce Albert and Alcida Ramos, eds., *Pacificando o branco: Cosmologias do contato no Norte-Amazônico* (São Paulo: UNESP, 2002); Pechincha, "Memória e história," 157–61; Lisiane Koller Lecznieski, "Objetos relacionais Ameríndios: Sobre a (in)visibilidade da arte Kadiwéu na novela Alma Gêmea da Rede Globo," *Espaço Ameríndio (UFRGS)* 4 (2010): 44–61; Cesar Gordon, "Nossas utopias não são as deles: Os Mebengokre (Kayapó) e o mundo dos brancos," *Sexta-feira: Antropologia, Artes e Humanidades* 6 (2001): 123–36; Aparecida Vilaça, *Strange Enemies: Indigenous Agency and Scenes of Encounters in Amazonia* (Durham, NC: Duke University Press, 2010), conclusion; Conklin, "For Love or Money?" 127–50; Els Lagrou, "No caminho das miçangas: Arte, alteridade e relação entre os ameríndios," *Enfoques—Revista dos Alunos do PPGSA-UFRJ* 12 (2013): 18–49; Elizabeth Ewart, *Space and Society in Central Brazil: A Panará Ethnography* (London: Bloomsbury, 2013), chs. 4 and 5. On rejecting that which causes damage: the Ka'apor of eastern Amazonia recently banned alcohol within their communities, having identified its role in ill health and in the exploitive agreements made with outsiders. See Piero Locatelli, "Após expulsarem de madeireiros a médicos, índios defendem autonomia total no Maranhão," *Uol: Notícias*, January 9, 2018, https://noticias.uol.com.br/cotidiano/ultimas-noticias/2018/01/09/apos-expulsarem-de-madeireiros-a-professores-indios-defendem-autonomia-total-no-maranhao.htm.

68. Vilaça, *Strange Enemies*, 13. See also Márcio Couto Henrique, "Presente de branco: A perspectiva indígena dos brindes da civilização (Amazônia, século XIX)," *Revista Brasileira de História* 37, no. 75 (2017): 10–14; Luísa Tombini Wittmann, *O Vapor e o Botoque: Imigrantes alemães e índios Xokleng no Vale do Itajaí/SC (1850–1926)* (Florianópolis: Letras Contemporâneas, 2007), 164–87.

69. Fray Luís Cemitile, quoted in Monteiro, "Tupis, tapuias e historiadores," 166.

70. Marta Rosa Amoroso, "Guerra e mercadorias: Os Kaingang nas cenas da 'Conquista de Guarapuava,'" in *Do contato ao confronto: A conquista de Guarapuava no século XVIII*, ed. Ana Maria de Moraes Belluzzo, Marta Rosa Amoroso, Nicolau Sevcenko, and Valéria Piccoli (São Paulo: BNB Paribas, 2003), 35.

71. Monteiro, "Tupis, tapuias e historiadores," 145–46, citing Marta Rosa Amoroso.

72. Tastevin, "Os índios Mura da região do Autaz," 62.

73. Nimuendajú to Carlos Estevão de Oliveira, Manaus, June 14, 1926, in *Cartas do sertão*, 94–95.

74. João Azevedo Fernandes, "Liquid Fire: Alcohol, Identity, and Social Hierarchy in Colonial Brazil," in Pierce and Toxqui, *Alcohol in Latin America*, 53, 55 (quotations), 57. On the use of intoxicants and narcotics among the Mura, see Nimuendajú, "The Mura and Pirahã," 3:263.

75. Cornelius J. Jaenen, "Amerindian Views of French Culture in the Seventeenth Century," *Canadian Historical Review* 55, no. 3 (1974): 268.

76. Tastevin, "Os índios Mura da região do Autaz," 63.

77. Boggiani, "Viajes," 544.

78. Rivasseau, *A vida dos indios Guaycurús*, 309–10.

79. Rivasseau, *A vida dos indios Guaycurús*, 121–32, 230–31; Boggiani, *Os Caduveos*, 133, 170–71, 191–92. Mock fights back in the 1840s are also described in Castelnau, *Expedição*, 371–72, 390.

80. Boggiani, *Os Caduveos*, 85–86 (quotation), 102.

81. Boggiani, *Os Caduveos*, 119.

82. Boggiani, *Os Caduveos*, 216–18. The settler was an employee of Malheiros and had borrowed money from the Kadiwéus, which he had not repaid. See also Boggiani, "Viajes de un artista," 548, on a ranch that was abandoned after the Kadiwéu threatened its owner.

83. Rivasseau, *A vida dos indios Guaycurús*, 64–65, see also 54–55.

84. Quoted in Marta Rosa Amoroso, "Crânios e cachaça: Coleções ameríndias e exposições no século XIX," *Revista de História*, São Paulo, 154, no. 1 (2006): 140.

85. Vânia Maria Losada Moreira, "Terras indígenas do Espírito Santo sob o regime territorial de 1850," *Revista Brasileira de História* 22, no. 43 (2002): 166–67.

86. Seth Garfield, personal communication, April 4, 2016; Siqueira, "Esse campo custou o sangue dos nossos avós," 81–87; Eduardo Viveiros de Castro, *From the Enemy's Point of View: Humanity and Divinity in an Amazonian Society* (Chicago: University of Chicago Press, 1992), 33; Conrad Feather, "The Restless Life of the Nahua: Shaping People and Places in the Peruvian Amazon," in *Mobility and Migration in Indigenous Amazonia: Contemporary Ethnoecological Perspectives*, ed. Miguel N. Alexiades (New York: Berghahn Books, 2009), 74–75; João Pacheco Oliveira Filho, ed., *Indigenismo e territorialização: Poderes, rotinas e saberes coloniais no Brasil contemporâneo* (Rio de Janeiro: Contra Capa, 1998).

87. Oberg, *The Terena and the Caduveo*, 56.

88. On memories of Malheiros as late as the 1990s, see Pechincha, "Memória e história," 159.

89. Silva, *A Reserva Indígena Kadiwéu*, 74–75.

90. Interview with João Matexua, age 70, Bodoquena (MS), by Mônica Thereza Soares Pechincha, "Histórias de admirar: Mito, rito e história Kadiwéu" (MA thesis, University of Brasília, 1994), 116–17.

91. Paul Marcoy, *Travels in South America, from the Pacific Ocean to the Atlantic Ocean* (New York: Scribner, Armstrong, 1875), 2:389–90.

92. Márcia Leila de Castro Pereira, "Rios de história: Guerra, tempo e espaço entre os Mura do baixo Madeira" (PhD diss., Universidade de Brasília, 2009), 24, 26 (quotation).

93. Richard B. Lee and Richard Daly, "Introduction: Foragers and Others," in *Cambridge Encyclopedia of Hunter-Gatherers* (1999), ed. Richard B. Lee and Richard Daly (Cambridge: Cambridge University Press, 1999), 6.

94. Tastevin, "Os índios Mura da região do Autaz," 61. See also the vivid assessment of Canon André Fernandes de Souza, "Notícias geográficas da Província do Rio Negro," c. 1821, BNRJ, I-31, 17, 5, paragraph 31.

95. Melo, *SPI*, 39. The "time of the bosses" is described by Ondino Casimiro (Ticuna) in the documentary film *Caminho de Mutum*, dir. Edson Tosta Matarezio Filho and Marília Senlle (Laboratório de Imagem e Som em Antropologia—Universidade de São Paulo, 2018).

96. Athila, "Índios de verdade," 93.

97. Athila, "Índios de verdade," 89, 96–98; Leal, "Direitos e processos," 179. The status of Indians as legal minors or people in need of state tutelage was reaffirmed by later legislation in Brazil, most recently by the Statute of the Indian (1973), which has never been repealed or rewritten. For analysis of these legal ambiguities and the ways in which they have been used to deprive contemporary Indigenous peoples of their rights, see Ana Valéria Araújo, *Povos indígenas e a lei dos brancos: O direito à diferença* (Brasília: Ministério da Educação, Secretaria de Educação Continuada, Alfabetização e Diversidade; LACED/Museu Nacional, 2006).

98. Leal, "Direitos e processos," 179.

99. Tastevin, "Os índios Mura da região do Autaz," 60.

100. Leal, "Direitos e processos," 79. On the parallel privatizations of Brazil nut groves in the Lower Amazon between 1910 and 1930 in the territories of free Black peasants, see Oscar de la Torre, *The People of the River: Nature and Identity in Black Amazonia, 1835–1945* (Chapel Hill: University of North Carolina Press, 2018), ch. 4.

101. Marta Rosa Amoroso, "Mura: Localização," Instituto Socioambiental, Povos Indígenas no Brasil, https://pib.socioambiental.org/pt/Povo:Mura; Athila, "Índios de verdade," 102.

102. Nimuendajú to Carlos Estevão de Oliveira, Borba, April 10, 1926, in *Cartas do sertão*, 92–93.

103. João Augusto Zany, quoted in Melo, *SPI*, 102.

104. Izabel Cavalcanti Ibiapina Parente, "O amazonismo e as representações sobre os seringueiros e a natureza amazônica" (PhD diss., Universidade de Brasília, 2018), 122, citing Arthur Cézar Ferreira Reis. Accounts of how the Englishman collected the hevea seeds, including Wickham's own, are ambiguous and contradictory, but he apparently obtained them from the Tapajós River region, collecting some with the help of native assistants and purchasing others from local tappers. Warren Dean, *Brazil and the Struggle for Rubber: A Study in Environmental History* (Cambridge: Cambridge University Press, 1987), 16–17 (accounts of seed gathering), 18 ("most fateful cargo").

105. The excavation of an urn from a *terra preta* (plot of anthropogenic black earth) in the Sampaio Lake area is mentioned in Nimuendajú to Carlos Estevão de Oliveira, Borba, April 10, 1926, in *Cartas do sertão*, 92.

106. Carlos de Araújo Moreira Neto, *Índios da Amazônia, de maioria a minoria* (Petrópolis: Vozes, 1988), 109; João Augusto Zany, quoted in Melo, *SPI*, 99.

107. Nimuendajú to Carlos Estevão de Oliveira, Borba, April 10, 1926, in *Cartas do sertão*, 91.

108. Director Domingos de Macedo Ferreira to Henrique João Wilkens[?], Alvelos, December 31, 1788, AHU, Rio Negro Avulsos, Cx. 15, Doc. 558 (attachment). The settlement was called São Pedro de Mamiá and was located near the mouth of the Japurá River.

109. Michael L. Cepek, *Life in Oil: Cofán Survival in the Petroleum Fields of Amazonia* (Austin: University of Texas Press, 2018), 47.

110. Boggiani, *Os Caduveos*, 243.

111. Claude Lévi-Strauss, *Tristes Tropiques*, trans. John Weightman and Doreen Weightman (New York: Penguin, 2012), 173 (on population and decadence), 176–77, 185–87 (on perceiving continuities).

112. Ribeiro, *Kadiwéu*, 11–12; Pechincha, "Memória e história," 159–61. Pechincha's Kadiwéu informants gave particular emphasis to the long trips that both Boggiani and Ribeiro made around their territory, getting to know its boundaries and place names.

113. Lévi-Strauss, *Tristes Tropiques*, 176.

114. Carlos Fausto and Michael Heckenberger, "Introduction: Indigenous

History and the History of the 'Indians,'" in *Time and Memory in Indigenous Amazonia: Anthropological Perspectives*, ed. Fausto and Heckenberger (Gainesville: University Press of Florida, 2007), 4–5, 10.

115. Monteiro, "Tupis, tapuias e historiadores," 128.

Conclusion

1. Seth Garfield, *Indigenous Struggle at the Heart of Brazil: State Policy, Frontier Expansion, and the Xavante Indians, 1937–1988* (Durham, NC: Duke University Press, 2001), 64, characterizing the views of Chico Meireles, contracted by the SPI to "pacify" the Xavante in the 1940s. The same rhetoric is heard today among politicians on the right and members of the general public in Brazil and elsewhere in the Americas.

2. Interview with Jair Bolsonaro during his electoral campaign for the presidency, *GloboNews*, August 3, 2018, accessed June 18, 2019, https://www.youtube.com/watch?v=zykvBACFzGg (1:23:55–1:26:00).

3. Aparecida Vilaça, *Strange Enemies: Indigenous Agency and Scenes of Encounters in Amazonia* (Durham, NC: Duke University Press, 2010), 13.

4. In affirming these things, I have been inspired by Laura Zanotti's discussion of contemporary Kayapó perspectives (during her visit to Colgate University on November 6, 2018); by Michael Cepek's nuanced portrait of the Cofán people of the Ecuadorian Amazon (*Life in Oil: Cofán Survival in the Petroleum Fields of Amazonia* [Austin: University of Texas Press, 2018]); by the words of Guarani-Kaiowá participants in a documentary film about their land reclamations in Mato Grosso do Sul (*Martírio*, dir. Vincent Carelli, Tatiana Almeida, and Ernesto de Carvalho [Pragda, 2016]); and by the work of Joseph Weiss among the Haida people of western Canada (*Shaping the Future on Haida Gwaii: Life Beyond Settler Colonialism* [Vancouver: University of British Columbia Press, 2018]). In a similar vein, Aleut scholar Eve Tuck has called for a moratorium on "damage-centered research"—research that seeks to document pain and loss in the past, with the aim of explaining the brokenness of Native communities in the present. Tuck, "Suspending Damage: A Letter to Communities," *Harvard Educational Review* 79, no. 3 (2009), 409–27.

5. These allegations were leveled against the Guarani-Kaiowá, among other groups, by members of the ruralist faction in Congress. Carelli, Almeida, and Carvalho, *Martírio*. For an excellent analysis of the rhetoric promoted by landowners and the local media about Tupinambá groups involved in land reclamations in southern Bahia, see Daniela Fernandes Alarcón, "O retorno da terra: As retomadas na aldeia Tupinambá da Serra do Padeiro, sul da Bahia" (MA thesis, Universidade de Brasília, 2013), ch. 2. On the billboards, see, for example, "Vídeo denuncia atentados e campanha de ódio contra indígenas na Bahia," *Revista Forum*, September 6, 2013, https://revistaforum.com.br/noticias/video-denuncia-atentados-e-campanha-de-odio-contra-indigenas-na-bahia/.

6. Fabiano Maisonnave, "Brazil's First Indigenous Congresswoman Defends Her People's Rights from Bolsonaro," *Climate Change News*, February 19, 2019, https://www.climatechangenews.com/2019/02/19/brazils-first-indigenous-congresswoman-defends-peoples-rights-bolsonaro/.

7. Tracy Devine Guzmán, *Native and National in Brazil: Indigeneity after Independence* (Chapel Hill: University of North Carolina Press, 2013), 200, quoting an open letter presented at the Indigenous Social Forum in 2012; Intergovernmental Science-Policy Platform on Biodiversity and Ecosystem Services (IPBES), "Global Assessment Report on Biodiversity and Ecosystem Services, 2019," as summarized in "UN Report: Nature's Dangerous Decline 'Unprecedented'; Species Extinction Rates 'Accelerating'," *Sustainable Development Goals* (blog), https://www.un.org/sustainabledevelopment/blog/2019/05/nature-decline-unprecedented-report/. See also the recent book by Indigenous leader Ailton Krenak, *Idéias para adiar o fim do mundo* (São Paulo: Companhia das Letras, 2019).

8. On these developments among the Kayapó, see Terence Turner, "Representing, Resisting, Rethinking: Historical Transformation of Kayapo Culture and Anthropological Consciousness," in *Colonial Situations: Essays on the Contextualization of Ethnographic Knowledge*, ed. George W. Stocking (Madison: University of Wisconsin Press, 1991), 302. See also Cesar Gordon, "Nossas utopias não são as deles: Os Mebengokre (Kayapó) e o mundo dos brancos," *Sexta-feira: Antropologia, Artes e Humanidades* 6 (2001): 123–36. Xavante NGOs are discussed in Laura R. Graham, "Fluid Subjectivity: Reflections on Self and Alternative Futures in the Autobiographical Narrative of Hiparidi Top'tiro, a Xavante Transcultural Leader," in *Fluent Selves: Autobiography, Person, and History in Lowland South America*, ed. Suzanne Oakdale and Magnus Course (Lincoln: University of Nebraska Press, 2014), 238–39.

9. Fany Ricardo and Majoí Fávero Gongora, eds., *Enclosures and Resistance: Isolated Indigenous Peoples in Brazilian Amazonia* (São Paulo: Instituto Socioambiental, 2019).

10. Joênia Wapichana, for example, recently co-authored an op-ed in the *Washington Post* with Deb Haaland (Laguna Pueblo)—one of the first two Indigenous women to be elected to the US Congress—to denounce recent efforts in both countries to undermine the territorial sovereignty and human rights of Indigenous peoples. Joênia Wapichana, "Protecting Indigenous Lands Protects the Environment; Trump and Bolsonaro Threaten Both," *Washington Post*, March 18, 2019, https://www.washingtonpost.com/opinions/2019/03/18/protecting-indigenous-lands-protects-environment-trump-bolsonaro-threaten-both.

11. See, for example, the film *Tupinambá: O Retorno da Terra*, dir. Daniela Fernandes Alarcón (Reportér do Brasil, 2015).

12. Carelli, Almeida, and Carvalho, *Martírio*.

13. Official Facebook page of APIB—Articulação dos Povos Indígenas do Brasil, https://www.facebook.com/apiboficial/; Glenn H. Shepard, "Voluntary

Isolation in the Time of Coronavirus," *Chacruna*, March 24, 2020, https://chacruna.net/voluntary-isolation-in-the-age-of-coronavirus/; Mateus Parreiras, "Índios Pataxó de São Joaquim de Bicas alegam desamparo e fecham tribo," *Estado de Minas Gerais*, April 3, 2020, https://www.em.com.br/app/noticia/gerais/2020/04/03/interna_gerais,1135141/indios-pataxo-de-sao-joaquim-de-bicas-alegam-desamparo-e-fecham-tribo.shtml; Vasconcelo Quadros, "Dois mil garimpeiros buscam ouro em Raposa Serra do Sol," *Pública*, May 22, 2020, https://apublica.org/2020/05/dois-mil-garimpeiros-buscam-ouro-em-raposa-serra-do-sol/; Laura R. Graham, "Brazil Fails to Prevent COVID-19 Spread in Indigenous Communities: The Xavante Example," *Cultural Survival*, May 31, 2020, https://www.culturalsurvival.org/news/brazil-fails-prevent-covid-19-spread-indigenous-communities-xavante-example.

14. Aparecida Vilaça, *Morte na floresta* (São Paulo: Todavia, 2020); Bruce Albert, "Covid-19: Lessons from the Yanomami," *New York Times*, April 27, 2020; Laura R. Graham with collaboration from Edson Krenak Naknanuk, "A'uwẽ-Xavante Leaders Denounce Bogus Consultations Regarding 3 Hydroelectric Dams, Demand Halt to Commercial Transport on Federal Highways During COVID," *Cultural Survival*, May 13, 2020, https://www.culturalsurvival.org/news/auwe-xavante-leaders-denounce-bogus-consultations-regarding-3-hydroelectric-dams-demand-halt; Carlos Fausto, "'Vamos fazer lockdown na aldeia': governança indígena e desgoverno," *Nexo*, June 11, 2020, https://www.nexojornal.com.br/ensaio/debate/2020/'Vamos-fazer-lockdown-na-aldeia'-governança-indígena-e-desgoverno.

15. Jonilda Gouveia, "Pandemias e 'brancos': relatos de como sobreviver," in *Reflexões ameríndias em tempos de pandemia*, Núcleo de Estudos da Amazônia Indígena (NEAI), Social Anthropology Program, Universidade Federal do Amazonas, https://neai.ufam.edu.br/mapa-da-pandemia-local/94-reflexoes-ameri.html

16. Kate Brown, "The Pandemic Is Not a Natural Disaster," *New Yorker*, April 13, 2020; Kyle Powys Whyte, "Our Ancestors' Dystopia Now: Indigenous Conservation and the Anthropocene," in *The Routledge Companion to the Environmental Humanities*, ed. Ursula K. Heise, Jon Christensen, and Michelle Niemann (London: Routledge, 2017), 206–18. I thank Coll Thrush for recommending the latter essay to me.

17. Andrej Grubacic and Denis O'Hearn, eds., *Living at the Edges of Capitalism: Adventures in Exile and Mutual Aid* (Berkeley: University of California Press, 2016). I am grateful to Sean Burns for recommending this book on contemporary forms of autonomy.

18. Giovani José da Silva, *A Reserva Indígena Kadiwéu (1899–1984): Memória, identidade e história* (Dourados: Editora UFGD, 2014), 84–93; Lisiane Koller Lecznieski, "Estranhos laços: Predação e cuidado entre os Kadiwéu" (PhD diss., Universidade Federal de Santa Catarina, 2005), ch. 4; Sílvia Schmuziger Carvalho, "Chaco: Encruzilhada dos povos e 'melting pot' cultural, suas

relaões com a bacia do Paraná e o Sul mato-grossense," in *História dos índios do Brasil*, ed. Manuela Carneiro da Cunha (São Paulo: Companhia das Letras, 1992), 470; Jaime Garcia Siqueira Jr., "Esse campo custou o sangue dos nossos avós: A construção do tempo e espaço Kadiwéu," in *Kadiwéu: Senhoras da arte, senhores da guerra*, ed. Giovani José da Silva (Curitiba: Editora CRV, 2011), 89; João Flores, "Muita terra para pouco índio? A formação de fazendas em território Kadiwéu (1950–1984)" (MA thesis, Universidade Federal da Grande Dourados—Dourados, 2009).

19. Interview with Capitão Amadeus Kadiwéu in Ruy Sposati, "Kadiwéu: Com fim da greve da PF, indígenas podem ser despejados de terra homologada," *CIMI*, October 16, 2012, https://cimi.org.br/2012/10/34128/.

20. Lúcia Murat, dir., *Brava Gente Brasileira* (Taiga Filmes e Vídeo, 2000).

21. Lúcia Murat and Rodrigo Hinrichsen, dirs., *A nação que não esperou por Deus* (Taiga Filmes e Vídeo, 2015). On Kadiwéu living in cities, see the annual reports of the Conselho Indigenista Missionário (CIMI), *Relatório: Violência contra os povos indígenas no Brasil*, https://cimi.org.br/observatorio-da-violencia/edicoes-anteriores/.

22. Renata Domingues Sampaio, "Para além da excepcionalidade: A patrimonialização do Monumento Indígena Marco Zero Kadiwéu" (MA thesis, Instituto do Patrimônio Histórico e Artístico Nacional, Rio de Janeiro, 2018).

23. Mônica Thereza Soares Pechincha, "Histórias de admirar: Mito, rito e história Kadiwéu" (MA thesis, Universidade de Brasília, 1994), 73–80.

24. Renato Santana and Tiago Miotto, "Focos de incêndio em terras indígenas aumentaram 88% em 2019," *CIMI*, September 10, 2019, https://cimi.org.br/2019/09/focos-incendio-terras-indigenas-aumentaram-88-2019/; Clara Roman, "Brigadas indígenas na linha de frente contra o fogo," *ISA: Notícias*, November 1, 2019, https://www.socioambiental.org/pt-br/noticias-socio ambientais/brigadas-indigenas-na-linha-de-frente-contra-o-fogo.

25. *Projeto Noleedi: Efeito do fogo na biota do Pantanal sul-mato-grossense e sua interação com os diferentes regimes de inundação* (blog), https://noleedi.blogspot.com.

26. Vinicius Lemos, "Por que Pantanal vive 'maior tragédia ambiental' em décadas," *BBC News Brazil*, August 5, 2020, https://www.bbc.com/portuguese/brasil-53662968; Instituto Socioambiental, "Como amansar o fogo," *Medium.com*, December 14, 2017, https://medium.com/historias-socioambientais/fogo-do-indio-65df77094096.

27. Marta Rosa Amoroso, "Os Mura tentam recuperar terras loteadas e reduzidas no passado," in *Povos indígenas no Brasil, 1996–2000*, ed. Carlos Alberto Ricardo (São Paulo: Instituto Socioambiental, 2000), 467–68; Marta Rosa Amoroso, "O nascimento da aldeia mura: Sentidos e modos de habitar a beira," in *Paisagens Ameríndias: Lugares, circuitos e modos de vida na Amazônia*, ed. Marta Rosa Amoroso and Gilton Mendes dos Santos (São Paulo: Editora Terceiro Nome, 2013), 93–114; Marta Rosa Amoroso, "Mura,"

Instituto Socioambiental, Povos Indígenas no Brasil, https://pib.socioambiental.org/pt/Povo:Mura; Adriana Romano Athila, "Índios de verdade: Territorialidade, história e diferença entre os Mura da Amazônia Meridional" (MA thesis, Universidade Federal do Rio de Janeiro, 1998); CIMI, *Relatório: Violência contra os povos indígenas no Brasil—Dados de 2017*, 107–8, https://cimi.org.br/wp-content/uploads/2018/09/Relatorio-violencia-contra-povos-indigenas_2017-Cimi.pdf; CIMI, *Relatório: Violência contra os povos indígenas no Brasil—Dados de 2018*, 92, https://cimi.org.br/wp-content/uploads/2019/09/relatorio-violencia-contra-os-povos-indigenas-brasil-2018.pdf. As Ana Mariella Bacigalupo writes of the Mapuche, their "notions of tradition are less about preservation than about transformative practice and selective symbolization of continuity. Like most other indigenous peoples, Mapuche use their historical consciousness to create themselves in history rather than simply inheriting static traditions from the past." Bacigalupo, *Shamans of the Foye Tree: Gender, Power, and Healing among Chilean Mapuche* (Austin: University of Texas Press, 2007), 155.

28. Marta Rosa Amoroso, "Pajé e Piwara: A construção dos coletivos Mura (Amazônia, Brasil)" (paper presented at the Latin American Studies Association Congress, Barcelona, May 24, 2018). These convictions run through many of the interviews gathered by Márcia Nunes Maciel (Márcia Mura), "Tecendo tradições indígenas" (PhD diss., Universidade de São Paulo, 2016), vol. 1. See also the oral history project *Yandé Anama Mura—Documentação audiovisual e recuperação do patrimônio imaterial dos pajés e pearas Mura, Amazônia-Brasil*, spearheaded by a Mura teachers' organization in the Autazes region, the Organização dos Professores Indígenas Mura (OPIM) and the documentary filmmaker Raoni Valle (Manaus: Instituto Nacional de Pesquisas da Amazônia (INPA)/Núcleo de Pesquisas em Ciências Humanas e Sociais (NPCHS), 2008. It features dozens of interviews with elders, most of them over age seventy, on topics such as shamanism, language, and the presence of enchanted beings in the landscape.

29. CIMI, *Relatório: Violência contra os povos indígenas no Brasil—Dados de 2017*, 71, 99, 107–8. On the resistance mounted against potassium mining in Mura territories, especially in the undemarcated lands of Soares Lake and Urucurituba village in Autazes municipality, see Renildo Viana Azevedo, "Território dos 'Flutuantes': Resistência, terra indígena Mura e mineração de potássio em Autazes (AM)" (PhD diss., Universidade Federal do Amazonas, 2019); Thais Borges, Sue Branford, and Mauricio Torres, "Amazon's Mura Indigenous Group Demands Input over Giant Mining Project," *Mongabay*, December 27, 2019, https://news.mongabay.com/2019/12/amazons-mura-indigenous-group-demands-input-over-giant-mining-project/.

30. Márcia Leila de Castro Pereira, "Território e mobilidade Mura no Baixo Rio Madeira (AM)," *Habitus: Goiânia* 14, no. 2 (2016), 270–71.

31. Amoroso, "Pajé e Piwara."

32. Adriana Romano Athila, *Relatório circunstanciado de identificação e delimitação da Terra Indígena Lago do Limão* (Brasília: FUNAI, 2011), 67–72 (quotation is on 72).

33. Ana Mary Azevedo, Mura, reports of April 15 and April 23, 2020, "Pandemia local," Núcleo de Estudos da Amazônia Indígena (NEAI), Social Anthropology Program, Universidade Federal do Amazonas, https://neai.ufam.edu.br/mapa-da-pandemia-local/95-sobrevivendo-na-pandemia-relatos-indigenas-sobre-a-situacao-do-covid-19-no-amazonas.html

34. Márcia Leila de Castro Pereira, "Rios de história: Guerra, tempo e espaço entre os Mura do baixo Madeira" (PhD diss., Universidade de Brasília, 2009), 163–84; R. Verneau, "Introdução: Os índios Mura da região do Autaz," in *Tastevin e a etnografia indígena: Coletânea de traduções de textos produzidos em Tefé*, ed. Priscila Faulhaber and Ruth Monserrat (Rio de Janeiro: Museu do Índio/FUNAI, 2008), 58–59.

35. Alyssa Battistoni, "The Green and the Red," in *The Future We Want: Radical Ideas for a New Century*, ed. Sarah Leonard and Bhaskar Sunkara (New York: Metropolitan Books, 2016), 80. See also the critique of the concept of resilience in Brad Evans and Julian Reid, *Resilient Life: The Art of Living Dangerously* (Cambridge, UK: Polity Press, 2014).

36. For a recent denunciation of personnel and policy changes at FUNAI that would threaten the right to voluntary isolation, see Instituto Socioambiental, "O contato da morte," *ISA: Notícias*, February 5, 2020, https://www.socioambiental.org/pt-br/noticias-socioambientais/o-contato-da-morte. On reconceptualizing development, see Guzmán, *Native and National in Brazil*, 27. For the manifesto of the 2019 Acampamento Terra Livre—the fifteenth annual gathering of Indigenous groups from across the country and the largest Indigenous mobilization to date, with some four thousand participants coming to Brasília—see "Documento Final do XV Acampamento Terra Livre," April 26, 2019, https://mobilizacaonacionalindigena.wordpress.com/2019/04/26/documento-final-do-xv-acampamento-terra-livre/. In 2020, the Acampamento Terra Livre occurred virtually for the first time, due to the pandemic. "Acampamento Terra Livre 2020—Documento Final," April 30, 2020, http://apib.info/2020/05/01/acampamento-terra-livre-2020-documento-final/.

Bibliography

Archives
Arquivo da Casa Barão de Melgaço (Cuiabá, Brazil)
Arquivo do Instituto Histórico e Geográfico Brasileiro (Rio de Janeiro, Brazil)
Arquivo Histórico Estadual de Goiás (Goiânia, Brazil)
Arquivo Histórico do Exército (Rio de Janeiro, Brazil)
Arquivo Histórico do Itamaraty (Rio de Janeiro, Brazil)
Arquivo Histórico Ultramarino (Lisbon, Portugal)
Arquivo Nacional (Rio de Janeiro, Brazil)
Arquivo Público do Estado de Mato Grosso (Cuiabá, Brazil)
Arquivo Público do Estado do Pará (Belém, Brazil)
Biblioteca Nacional (Rio de Janeiro, Brazil)
Biblioteca Pública de Évora (Évora, Portugal)

Digital and Online Primary Sources
Acampamento Terra Livre. "Acampamento Terra Livre 2020—Documento Final," April 30, 2020. http://apib.info/2020/05/01/acampamento-terra-livre-2020-documento-final/.
———. "Documento Final do XV Acampamento Terra Livre," April 26, 2019. https://mobilizacaonacionalindigena.wordpress.com/2019/04/26/documento-final-do-xv-acampamento-terra-livre/.
Arquivo Histórico Ultramarino (Lisbon). *Projeto Resgate de Documentação Histórica "Barão do Rio Branco": Documentos Manuscritos Avulsos da Capitania de Goiás (1731–1822)*. Conselho Ultramarino/Brasil, Arquivo Histórico Ultramarino. Rio de Janeiro: Montreal Informática, 2003. CD-ROM.
———. *Projeto Resgate de Documentação Histórica "Barão do Rio Branco":*

Documentos Manuscritos Avulsos da Capitania de Mato Grosso (1720–1827). Conselho Ultramarino/Brasil, Arquivo Histórico Ultramarino. Rio de Janeiro: Montreal Informática, 2003. CD-ROM.

———. *Projeto Resgate de Documentação Histórica "Barão do Rio Branco": Documentos Manuscritos Avulsos da Capitania do Pará (1616–1833)*. Conselho Ultramarino/Brasil, Arquivo Histórico Ultramarino. Rio de Janeiro: Montreal Informática, 2003. CD-ROM.

———. *Projeto Resgate de Documentação Histórica "Barão do Rio Branco": Documentos Manuscritos Avulsos da Capitania do Rio Negro (1723–1825)*. Conselho Ultramarino/Brasil, Arquivo Histórico Ultramarino. Rio de Janeiro: Montreal Informática, 2003. CD-ROM.

Articulação dos Povos Indígenas do Brasil (APIB). Facebook. https://www.facebook.com/apiboficial.

Assembleia da República, Debates Parlamentares. http://debates.parlamento.pt/catalogo/mc.

Athias, Renato. *Imagens & Palavras* (blog). "Coleção Fotoetnográfica Indígena Carlos Estevão e Oliveira II." Posted June 18, 2007. http://renatoathias.blogspot.com/2007/06/#1686193191423646085.

Biblioteca Brasiliana Guita e José Mindlin, Digital Collection. https://digital.bbm.usp.br/.

Center for Research Libraries (CRL), Brazilian Government Documents Collection. Provincial Presidential Reports, 1830–1930. http://ddsnext.crl.edu/brazil.

Conselho Indigenista Missionário (CIMI). *Relatório: Violência contra os povos indígenas no Brasil—Dados de 2017*. https://cimi.org.br/wp-content/uploads/2018/09/Relatorio-violencia-contra-povos-indigenas_2017-Cimi.pdf.

———. *Relatório: Violência contra os povos indígenas no Brasil—Dados de 2018*. https://cimi.org.br/wp-content/uploads/2019/09/relatorio-violencia-contra-os-povos-indigenas-brasil-2018.pdf.

John Carter Brown Library, Portugal and Brazil Collection. Internet Archive. https://archive.org/details/jcbportugalbrazil.

Krenak, Ailton. "O eterno retorno do encontro." Instituto Socioambiental. Povos Indígenas no Brasil. Last modified April 27, 2018. https://pib.socioambiental.org/pt/O_eterno_retorno_do_encontro.

Museu do Estado de Pernambuco, Coleção Carlos Estevão de Oliveira, Museu Virtual. http://www3.ufpe.br/carlosestevao/museu-virtual-fotoetno.php.

Pandemia local. Núcleo de Estudos da Amazônia Indígena (NEAI), Social Anthropology Program, Universidade Federal do Amazonas. https://neai.ufam.edu.br/mapa-da-pandemia-local/95-sobrevivendo-na-pandemia-relatos-indigenas-sobre-a-situacao-do-covid-19-no-amazonas.html.

Projeto Noleedi: Efeito do fogo na biota do Pantanal sul-mato-grossense e sua interação com os diferentes regimes de inundação (blog). https://noleedi.blogspot.com.

Reflexões ameríndias em tempos de pandemia. Núcleo de Estudos da Amazônia

Indígena (NEAI), Social Anthropology Program, Universidade Federal do Amazonas. https://neai.ufam.edu.br/mapa-da-pandemia-local/94-reflexoes-ameri.html.

Sustainable Development Goals (blog). "UN Report: Nature's Dangerous Decline 'Unprecedented'; Species Extinction Rates 'Accelerating.'" Posted May 6, 2019. https://www.un.org/sustainabledevelopment/blog/2019/05/nature-decline-unprecedented-report/.

Xavante, Paulo Cipassé. "Histórias de um líder Xavante." Interview by Tereza Ruiz. Museu da Pessoa, November 25, 2014. http://www.museudapessoa.net/pt/destaque/historias-de-um-lider-xavante.

Published Primary Sources

Amazonas, Lourenço da Silva Araújo e. *Diccionario topographico, historico, descriptivo da Comarca do Alto Amazonas.* Recife: Typographia Comercial de Meira Henriques, 1852.

Amoroso, Marta Rosa and Nádia Farage, eds. *Relatos da fronteira Amazônica no século XVIII: Alexandre Rodrigues Ferreira e Henrique João Wilckens.* São Paulo: Universidade de São Paulo / Núcleo de História Indígena e do Indigenismo, 1994.

Annaes do Sennado da Câmara de Cuyabá, 1719–1830. Transcription by Yumiko Takamoto Suzuki. Cuiabá: Entrelinhas / APMT, 2007.

Azara, Félix de. "Correspondencia oficial e inédita sobre la demarcación de límites entre el Paraguay y el Brasil." In *Colección de obras y documentos relativos a la historia antigua y moderna de las provincias del Río,* edited by Pedro de Angelis. Vol. 4. Buenos Aires: Imprenta del Estado, 1836.

———, *Viajes por la América Meridional.* Vol. 2. Buenos Aires: El Elefante Blanco, 1998.

Bates, Henry Walter. *The Naturalist on the River Amazons: A Record of Adventures, Habits of Animals, Sketches of Brazilian and Indian Life, and Aspects of Nature Under the Equator, During Eleven Years of Travel.* London: John Murray, 1864.

Boggiani, Guido. *Os Caduveos.* Belo Horizonte: Editora Itatiaia, 1975.

———. "Viajes de un artista por la América Meridional: Los Caduveos. Expedición al Río Nabileque, en la región de las grandes cacerías de venados, Matto Grosso (Brasil)." *Revista del Instituto de Etnología de la Universidad Nacional de Tucumán* 1, no. 3 (1930): 495–556.

Brandão, Caetano. *Diários das visitas pastorais no Pará.* Porto: Instituto Nacional de Investigação Científica / Centro de História da Universidade do Porto, 1991.

Cáceres, Luís de Albuquerque de Melo Pereira e. "Exploração do Rio Paraguay e primeiras práticas com os índios Guaikurús." *Revista Trimensal do Instituto Histórico Geográfico e Ethnographico do Brasil* 28 (1865): 70–88.

Camelo, João Antônio Cabral. *Notícias práticas das minas do Cuiabá.* Cuiabá: IHGMT, 2002.

Castelnau, Francis de. *Expedição às regiões centrais da América do Sul*. Rio de Janeiro: Itatiaia, 2000.

———. *Expédition dans les parties centrales de l'Amérique du Sud, de Rio de Janeiro à Lima et de Lima au Para*. Vol. 2, *Vues et Scènes*. Paris: P. Bertrand, 1852.

Chermont, Teodósio Constantino de. "Memória dos mais temíveis contágios de bexigas e sarampo d'este Estado desde o ano de 1720 por diante." *Revista Trimensal do Instituto Histórico e Geográfico do Brasil* 48 (1885): 28–30.

Coudreau, Henri. *Viagem ao Tapajós (28 de julho de 1895 a 7 de janeiro de 1896)*. Translated by A. de Miranda Bastos. São Paulo: Companhia Editora Nacional, 1941.

D'Alincourt, Luiz. "Reflexões sobre o systema que se deve adoptar na fronteira do Paraguay, em consequencia da revolta e dos insultos praticados ultimamente pela nação dos Índios Guaicurus ou cavalleiros (1826)." *Revista do Instituto Histórico e Geográfico Brasileiro* 20 (1857), 360–65.

Daniel, João. *Tesouro descoberto no máximo rio Amazonas*. 2 vols. Rio de Janeiro: Contraponto, 2004.

Edwards, William Henry. *A Voyage Up the River Amazon, Including a Residence at Pará*. London: John Murray, 1855.

Elliott, João Henrique. "Itinerário das viagens exploradoras emprehendidas pelo Sr. Barão de Antonina para descobrir uma via de communicação entre o porto da villa de Antonina e o Baixo-Paraguay na província de Mato-Grosso: feitas nos annos de 1844 a 1847 pelo sertanista o Sr. Joaquim Francisco Lopes, e descriptas pelo Sr. João Henrique Elliott." *Revista do Instituto Histórico e Geográfico Brasileiro* 10 (1848): 153–77.

Ferreira, Alexandre Rodrigues. *Viagem filosófica pelas capitanias do Grão-Pará, Rio Negro, Mato Grosso e Cuiabá: Memórias, Anthropologia*. Rio de Janeiro: Conselho Federal de Cultura, 1974.

Florence, Hercules. *Viagem fluvial do Tietê ao Amazonas de 1825–1829*. São Paulo: Cultrix / Universidade de São Paulo, 1977.

Fonseca, José Gonçalves da. "Primeira exploração do rios Madeira e Guaporé feita por José Gonçalves da Fonseca em 1749." In *Memorias para a historia do extincto estado do Maranhão, cujo territorio comprehende hoje as provincias do Maranhão, Piauhy, Grão-Pará e Amazonas*, edited by Cândido Mendes, 296–314. Vol. 2. Rio de Janeiro: Typographia de J. Paulo Hildebrandt, 1874.

Freire, Carlos Augusto da Rocha, ed. *Memória do SPI: Textos, imagens e documentos sobre o Serviço de Proteção aos Índios (1910–1967)*. Rio de Janeiro: Museu do Índio/FUNAI, 2011.

Herndon, William L. *Exploration of the Valley of the Amazon*. Washington, DC: Armstrong, 1853.

"Illustração necessária e interessante, relativa ao gentio da nação Mura, habitador dos Rios Madeira, Trombeta, Guatazes, Cadajazes, Purus, Mamiá, Coarí, Paruá e Copacá, na Capitania do Rio Negro, feita por um

anônimo em 1826." In Carlos de Araújo Moreira Neto, *Índios da Amazônia, de maioria a minoria*, 249–57. Petrópolis: Vozes, 1988.
Keller-Leuzinger, Franz. *The Amazon and Madeira Rivers: Sketches and Descriptions from the Note-Book of an Explorer*. London: Chapman and Hall, 1874.
Kopenawa, Davi, and Bruce Albert. *The Falling Sky: Words of a Yanomami Shaman*. Translated by Nicholas Elliott and Alison Dundy. Cambridge, MA: Harvard University Press, 2013.
Krenak, Ailton. *Idéias para adiar o fim do mundo*. São Paulo: Companhia das Letras, 2019.
Lehmann-Nitsche, Robert. *Colección Boggiani de tipos indígenas de la Sudamérica Central*. Buenos Aires: Casa Rosauer, 1904.
Léry, Jean de. *History of a Voyage to the Land of Brazil, Otherwise Called America*. Translated by Janet Whatley. Berkeley: University of California Press, 1990.
Leverger, Augusto. "Roteiro da navegação do rio Paraguay desde a foz do São Lourenço até o Paraná." *Revista Trimestral do Instituto Histórico, Geográfico e Etnográfico do Brasil* 25 (1862): 211–84.
Lévi-Strauss, Claude. *Tristes Tropiques*. Translated by John Weightman and Doreen Weightman. New York: Penguin, 2012.
Lima, Américo Pires, ed. *O Doutor Alexandre Rodrigues Ferreira: Documentos coligidos*. Lisbon: Agencia Central de Ultramar, 1953.
Marcoy, Paul. *Travels in South America, from the Pacific Ocean to the Atlantic Ocean*. Vol. 2. New York: Scribner, Armstrong, 1875.
Mattos, João Henrique de. "Relatório do estado de decadência em que se encontra o Alto Amazonas (1845)." *Revista do Instituto Histórico e Geográfico Brasileiro* 325 (1979): 143–80.
Maw, Henry Lister. *Journal of a Passage from the Pacific to the Atlantic: Crossing the Andes in the Northern Provinces of Peru, and Descending the River Marañon or Amazon*. London: J. Murray, 1829.
Maximilian, Prince of Wied-Neuwied. *Viagem ao Brasil nos anos de 1815 a 1817*. Translated by Edgard Süssekind de Mendonça and Flávio Poppe de Figueiredo. São Paulo: Editora Nacional, 1942.
Mendes, Francisco. "Carta . . . sobre las costumbres, religion, terreno y tradiciones de los Yndios Mbayás, Guanás y demas naciones que ocupan la region boreal del Rio Paraguay (1772)." In *Do Tratado de Madri à conquista do Sete Povos*, edited by Jaime Cortesão, 53–69. Rio de Janeiro: Biblioteca Nacional, 1969.
Monteiro, Salvador, and Leonel Kaz, eds. *Expedição Langsdorff ao Brasil, 1821–1829: Rugendas, Taunay, Florence*. Rio de Janeiro: Alumbramento, 1998.
Naud, Leda Maria Cardoso, ed. *Documentos sobre o índio brasileiro (1500–1822): Arquivo histórico*. Brasília: Serviço Gráfico do Senado Federal, 1971.
Nimuendajú, Curt. *Cartas do sertão, de Curt Nimuendajú para Carlos Estevão de Oliveira*. Edited by Thekla Hartmann. Lisbon: Museu Nacional de Etnologia / Assírio & Alvim, 2000.

———. "Excursões pela Amazônia." Translated by Thekla Hartmann. *Revista de Antropologia* 44, no. 2 (2001): 189–200.

———. *Reconhecimento dos rios Içána, Ayarí e Uaupés: Apontamentos linguísticos e ensaio fotográfico*. Edited by Renato Athias. Rio de Janeiro: Museu do Índio, 2015.

Oberg, Kalervo. *The Terena and the Caduveo of Southern Mato Grosso, Brazil*. Washington, DC: Smithsonian Institution, 1949.

"Observacções addicionaes a Illustração sobre o Gentio Mura, escripta por hum anônimo no anno de 1826." In Carlos de Araújo Moreira Neto, *Índios da Amazônia, de maioria a minoria*, 258–266. Petrópolis: Vozes, 1988.

Osculati, Gaetano. *Exploraciones de las regiones ecuatoriales a lo largo del Napo y del Río de la Amazonas*. Translated by Alberto Guaraldo. Iquitos, Peru: CETA, 2003.

Otoni, Teófilo. "Noticia sobre os selvagens do Mucuri em uma carta dirigida pelo Sr. Teofilo Benedito Otoni ao Sr. Dr. Joaquim Manuel de Macedo." In *Notícia sobre os selvagens do Mucuri*, edited by Regina Horta Duarte, 39–94. Belo Horizonte: Editora UFMG, 2002.

Porro, Antonio. "Uma crônica ignorada: Anselm Eckart e a Amazônia setecentista." *Boletim do Museu Paraense Emílio Goeldi—Ciências Humanas* 6, no. 3 (2011): 575–92.

Prado, Francisco Rodrigues do. *História dos índios cavaleiros ou da Nação Guaycurú (1795)*. Campo Grande: Instituto Histórico e Geográfico do Mato Grosso do Sul, 2006.

Rengger, Johann Rudolph. *Viaje al Paraguay en los años 1816 a 1826*. Asunción: Editorial Tiempo de Historia, 2010.

Rengger, Johann Rudolph, and Marcelin Longchamp. *The Reign of Doctor Joseph Gaspard Roderick de Francia, in Paraguay: Being an Account of Six Years' Residence in That Republic, from July, 1819 to May, 1825*. London: T. Hurst, E. Chance, 1827.

Ribeiro, Francisco de Paula. "Roteiro da viagem que fez o Capitão Francisco de Paula Ribeiro às fronteiras da Capitania do Maranhão e da de Goiás no ano de 1815 em serviço de S. M. Fidelíssima." In *Francisco de Paula Ribeiro, desbravador dos sertões de Pastos Bons: A base geográfica e humana do Sul do Maranhão*, edited by Adalberto Franklin and João Renôr F. de Carvalho, 55–129. Imperatriz, Brazil: Ética, 2005.

Rivasseau, Emilio. *A vida dos indios guaycurús: Quinze dias nas suas aldeias (sul de Matto-Grosso)*. São Paulo: Companhia Editora Nacional, 1936.

Rodrigues, Bartolomeu. "Carta do Padre Bartholomeu Rodrigues, ao Provincial Jacintho de Carvalho, datada de Guaicurupá dos Tupinambaranas a 2 de Maio de 1714." In *Corografia histórica, cronográfica, genealógica, nobiliária e política do Império do Brasil*, edited by Alexandre J. e Mello Moraes, 361–72. Vol. 4. Rio de Janeiro: Tipografia Brasileira, 1872.

Rodrigues, João Barbosa. *Exploração dos Rios Urubú e Jatapú*. Rio de Janeiro: Typographia Nacional, 1875.
Salvador, Vicente do. *História do Brasil*. Curitiba: Juruá, 2007 (1627).
Sampaio, Francisco Xavier Ribeiro de. *Diário da viagem que em visita, e correição das povoações da Capitania de S. Jozé do Rio Negro fez o Ouvidor, e Intendente Geral da mesma . . . no anno de 1774 e 1775*. Lisbon: Typografia da Academia, 1825.
Sánchez Labrador, José. *El Paraguay católico*. 2 vols. Buenos Aires: Imprensa de Coni Hermanos, 1910.
Santos, Francisco Jorge dos, ed. "Dossiê Munduruku: Uma contribuição para a história indígena da Amazônia colonial." *Boletim Informativo do Museu Amazônico* 5, no. 8 (1995): 1–103.
Serra, Ricardo Franco de Almeida. "Continuação do parecer sobre os índios Uaicurús e Guanás." *Revista do Instituto Histórico e Geográfico Brasileiro* 13 (1850): 348–95.
———. "Parecer sobre o aldeamento dos índios Uaicurus e Guanás com a descripção dos seus usos, religião, estabilidade e costumes (1803)." *Revista do Instituto Histórico e Geográfico Brasileiro* 7 (1845): 204–18.
Silva, António de Morais, and Rafael Bluteau, *Diccionário da língua portugueza*. Lisbon: Oficina de S. T. Ferreira, 1789.
Silva, Ignacio Accioli de Cerqueira e. *Corografia Paraense, ou, descripção física, histórica, e política da província do Gram-Pará*. Bahia: Typologia do Diário, 1833.
Silva Pontes, Antônio Pires da. "Diário histórico e físico da viagem dos oficiais da demarcação que partiram do quartel geral de Barcelos para a capital de Vila Bela da Capitania de Mato Grosso, em 1 de Setembro de 1781." *Revista do Instituto Histórico e Geográfico Brasileiro* 262 (1964): 344–406.
Simmons, Marc, ed. *Border Comanches: Seven Spanish Colonial Documents, 1785–1819*. Santa Fe, NM: Stagecoach Press, 1967.
Soares, José Paulo Monteiro, and Cristina Ferrão, eds. *Viagem ao Brasil de Alexandre Rodrigues Ferreira: Coleção Etnográfica*. Vol. 3. São Paulo: Kapa Editorial, 2005.
Southey, Robert. *History of Brazil*. Vol. 3. London: Longman, Hurst, Rees, Orme, and Brown, 1819.
Souza, André Fernandes de. "Notícias Geográphicas da Capitania do Rio Negro no Grande Rio Amazonas." *Revista Trimensal do Instituto Histórico e Geográfico Brasileiro* 10 (1848): 410–504.
Souza, Cândido Xavier de Almeida. "Descrição diária dos progressos da expedição destinada à capitania de São Paulo para fronteiras do Paraguai, em 9 de outubro de 1800." *Revista do Instituto Histórico e Geográfico Brasileiro* 202 (1949): 6–132.
Souza, Francisco Bernardino de. *Lembranças e curiosidades do vale do Amazonas*. Manaus: Associação Comercial do Amazonas / Fundo Editorial, 1988.

Spix, Johann Baptist von, and Carl Friedrich Phillipp von Martius. *Viagem pelo Brasil (1817–1820)*. Translated by Lúcia Furquim Lahmeyer. Vol. 3. Belo Horizonte: Editora Itatiaia, 1981.

Tastevin, Constantin. *Tastevin e a etnografia indígena: Coletânea de traduções de textos produzidos em Tefé*. Edited by Priscila Faulhaber and Ruth Monserrat. Rio de Janeiro: Museu do Índio/FUNAI, 2008.

Taunay, Afonso de E., ed. *Relatos monçoeiros*. Belo Horizonte/São Paulo: Itatiaia/Edusp, 1981.

Taunay, Alfredo d'Escragnolle. *A Retirada da Laguna*. Rio de Janeiro: Typografia Americana, 1874.

———. *Scenas de viagem: Exploração entre os rios Taquary e Aquidauana no districto de Miranda*. Rio de Janeiro: Typografia Americana, 1868.

Universidade do Amazonas. *Autos da devassa contra os índios Mura do Rio Madeira e nações do Rio Tocantins, 1738–1739*. Manaus: CEDEAM, 1986.

Valle, Raoni, and Organização dos Professores Indígenas Mura (Opim-AM). *Yandé Anama Mura—Documentação audiovisual e recuperação do patrimônio imaterial dos pajés e pearas Mura, Amazônia-Brasil*. Manaus: Instituto Nacional de Pesquisas da Amazônia (INPA)/Núcleo de Pesquisas em Ciências Humanas e Sociais (NPCHS), 2008.

Velloso, José Mariano da Conceição. *O Fazendeiro do Brasil*. Vol. 2, Part 1, *Tinturaria*. Lisbon: Impressam Régia, 1806.

Wallace, Alfred Russel. *A Narrative of Travels on the Amazon and Rio Negro, with an Account of the Native Tribes, and Observations on the Climate, Geology, and Natural History of the Amazon Valley*. London: Reeve, 1853.

Wilkens, Henrique João. *Muhuraida, ou O Triumfo da Fe, 1785*. Manaus: Universidade Federal do Amazonas, 1993.

Secondary Sources

Adelman, Jeremy, and Stephen Aron. "From Borderlands to Borders: Empires, Nation-States, and the Peoples in Between in North American History." *American Historical Review* 104, no. 3 (June 1999): 814–41.

Alarcón, Daniela Fernandes. "O retorno da terra: As retomadas na aldeia Tupinambá da Serra do Padeiro, sul da Bahia." MA thesis, Universidade de Brasília, 2013.

Albert, Bruce. "A fumaça do metal: História e representações do contato entre os Yanomami." *Anuário Antropológico* 89 (1992): 151–89.

Albert, Bruce, and Alcida Ramos, eds. *Pacificando o branco: Cosmologias do contato no Norte-Amazônico*. São Paulo: UNESP, 2002.

Alden, Dauril. *Royal Government in Colonial Brazil, With Special Reference to the Administration of the Marquis of Lavradio, Viceroy, 1769–1779*. Berkeley: University of California Press, 1968.

Almeida, Maria Regina Celestino de. *Os índios na história do Brasil*. Rio de Janeiro: Editora FGV, 2010.

———. "Os índios na história do Brasil no século XIX: Da invisibilidade ao protagonismo." *Revista História Hoje* 1, no. 2 (2012): 21–39.
———. *Metamorfoses indígenas: Identidade e cultura nas aldeias coloniais do Rio de Janeiro*. Rio de Janeiro: Arquivo Nacional, 2003.
Amoroso, Marta Rosa. "Corsários no caminho fluvial: Os Mura do Rio Madeira." In *História dos índios no Brasil*, edited by Manuela Carneiro da Cunha, 297–310. São Paulo: Companhia das Letras, 1992.
———. "Crânios e cachaça: Coleções ameríndias e exposições no século XIX." *Revista de História*, São Paulo, 154, no. 1 (2006): 119–50.
———. "Guerra e mercadorias: Os Kaingang nas cenas da 'Conquista de Guarapuava.'" In *Do contato ao confronto: A conquista de Guarapuava no século XVIII*, edited by Ana Maria de Moraes Belluzzo, Marta Rosa Amoroso, Nicolau Sevcenko, and Valéria Piccoli, 26–41. São Paulo: BNB Paribas, 2003.
———. "Guerra Mura no século XVIII: Versos e versões, representações dos Mura no imaginário colonial." MA thesis, Universidade Estadual de Campinas, São Paulo, 1991.
———. "Mura: Localização." Instituto Socioambiental. Povos Indígenas no Brasil. Last modified August 1, 2018. https://pib.socioambiental.org/pt/Povo:Mura.
———. "Os Mura tentam recuperar terras loteadas e reduzidas no passado." In *Povos indígenas no Brasil, 1996-2000*, edited by Carlos Alberto Ricardo, 465–68. São Paulo: Instituto Socioambiental, 2000.
———. "O nascimento da aldeia mura: Sentidos e modos de habitar a beira." In *Paisagens Ameríndias: Lugares, circuitos e modos de vida na Amazônia*, edited by Marta Rosa Amoroso and Gilton Mendes dos Santos, 93–114. São Paulo: Editora Terceiro Nome, 2013.
———. "Nimuendajú às voltas com a história." *Revista de Antropologia* 44, no. 2 (2001): 173–86.
———."Pajé e Piwara: A construção dos coletivos Mura (Amazônia, Brasil)." Paper presented at the Latin American Studies Association Congress, Barcelona, May 24, 2018.
———. *Terra de índio: Imagens em aldeamentos do Império*. São Paulo: Editora Terceiro Nome, 2014.
Anderson, Gary Clayton. *The Indian Southwest, 1580–1830*. Norman: University of Oklahoma Press, 1999.
Apolinário, Juciene Ricarte. "Os Akroá e outros povos indígenas nas fronteiras do sertão: As práticas das políticas indígena e indigenista no norte da Capitania de Goiás—século XVIII." PhD diss., Universidade Federal de Pernambuco, 2005.
Araújo, Ana Valéria. *Povos indígenas e a lei dos brancos: O direito à diferença*. Brasília: Ministério da Educação, Secretaria de Educação Continuada, Alfabetização e Diversidade; LACED/Museu Nacional, 2006.

Areces, Nidia. "Paraguayos, portugueses y mbayás en Concepción, 1773–1840." *Memoria Americana 8* (1999): 11–44.

Arruti, José Maurício Andio. "A emergência dos 'remanescentes': Notas para o diálogo entre indígenas e quilombolas." *Mana* 3, no. 2 (1997): 7–38.

Athila, Adriana Romano. "Índios de verdade: Territorialidade, história e diferença entre os Mura da Amazônia Meridional." MA thesis, Universidade Federal do Rio de Janeiro, 1998.

———. *Relatório circunstanciado de identificação e delimitação da Terra Indígena Lago do Limão*. Brasília: FUNAI, 2011.

Ávila, Carlos Lázaro. "Conquista, control y convicción: El papel de los parlamentos indígenas en México, El Chaco y Norteamérica." *Revista de Indias* 59, no. 217 (1999): 645–73.

Ávila, Cuauhtémoc Velasco. "Peace Agreements and War Signals: Negotiations with the Apaches and Comanches in the Interior Provinces of New Spain, 1784–1788." In *Negotiation within Domination: New Spain's Indian Pueblos Confront the Spanish State*, edited by Ethelia Ruiz Medrano and Susan Kellogg, 173–204. Boulder: University Press of Colorado, 2010.

Axtell, James. "Prologue: The Ethnohistory of Native America." In *Natives and Newcomers: The Cultural Origins of North America*, 1–12. Oxford: Oxford University Press, 2001.

———. "The White Indians of Colonial America." *William and Mary Quarterly* 32, no. 1 (1975): 55–88.

Azevedo, Renildo Viana. "Território dos 'Flutuantes': Resistência, terra indígena Mura e mineração de potássio em Autazes (AM)." PhD diss., Universidade Federal do Amazonas, 2019.

Bacigalupo, Ana Mariella. *Shamans of the Foye Tree: Gender, Power, and Healing among Chilean Mapuche*. Austin: University of Texas Press, 2007.

Baldus, Herbert. "Introdução." In *Os Caduveos*, by Guido Boggiani, 11–46. Belo Horizonte: Editora Itatiaia, 1975.

Barr, Juliana. "Geographies of Power: Mapping Indian Borders in the 'Borderlands' of the Early Southwest." *William and Mary Quarterly* 68, no. 1 (2011): 5–46.

———. *Peace Came in the Form of a Woman: Indians and Spaniards in the Texas Borderlands*. Chapel Hill: University of North Carolina Press, 2007.

Bastos, Uacury Ribeiro de A. *Expansão territorial do Brasil Colônia no Vale do Paraguai (1767–1801)*. São Paulo: Universidade de São Paulo, 1978.

Battistoni, Alyssa. "The Green and the Red." In *The Future We Want: Radical Ideas for a New Century*, edited by Sarah Leonard and Bhaskar Sunkara, 64–81. New York: Metropolitan Books, 2016.

Beltrán, Luz María Méndez. "La organización de los parlamentos de indios en el siglo XVIII." In *Relaciones fronterizas en la Araucanía*, edited by Sergio Villalobos, Carlos Aldunate, Horacio Zapater, Luz María Méndez, and

Carlos Bascuñán, 107–74. Santiago: Ediciones Universidad Católica de Chile, 1982.

Benton, Lauren. *A Search for Sovereignty: Law and Geography in European Empires, 1400–1900.* Cambridge: Cambridge University Press, 2010.

Bieber, Judy. "Catechism and Capitalism: Imperial Indigenous Policy on a Brazilian Frontier, 1808–1845." In *Native Brazil: Beyond the Convert and the Cannibal, 1500–1900*, edited by Hal Langfur, 138–60. Albuquerque: University of New Mexico Press, 2014.

Boccara, Guillaume. "Etnogénesis mapuche: Resistencia y reestructuración entre los indígenas del centro-sur de Chile (siglos XVI–XVIII)." *Hispanic American Historical Review* 79, no. 3 (1999): 425–61.

———. "Poder colonial e etnicidade no Chile: Territorialização e reestruturação entre os Mapuche da época colonial." *Tempo* 12, no. 23 (2007): 56–72.

———. *Los vencedores: Los Mapuche en la época colonial.* San Pedro de Atacama/Santiago, Chile: Línea Editorial IIAM, 2007.

Bouvet, Nora. "La política indígena del dictador supremo en la frontera norte paraguaya." *Suplemento Antropológico* 27 (1992): 93–124.

Bushnell, Amy Turner. "'Gastos de indios': The Crown and the Chiefdom-Presidio Compact in Florida." In *El Gran Norte Mexicano: Indios, misioneros y pobladores entre el mito y la historia*, edited by Salvador Bernabéu Albert, 137–63. Seville: Consejo Superior de Investigaciones Científicas, 2009.

———. "Indigenous America and the Limits of the Atlantic World, 1493–1825." In *Atlantic History: A Critical Appraisal*, edited by Jack P. Greene and Philip Morgan, 191–221. Oxford: Oxford University Press, 2009.

Calloway, Colin. *Pen and Ink Witchcraft: Treaties and Treaty Making in American Indian History.* Oxford: Oxford University Press, 2013.

Cardoso, Antonio Alexandre Isidio. "O Eldorado dos deserdados: Indígenas, escravos, migrantes, regatões e o avanço rumo ao oeste amazônico (1830–1880)." PhD diss., Universidade de São Paulo, 2018.

Carneiro da Cunha, Manuela, ed. *História dos índios no Brasil.* São Paulo, Companhia das Letras, 1992.

———, ed. *Legislação indigenista no século XIX: Uma compilação, 1808–1889.* São Paulo: EDUSP, 1992.

———. "Pensar os índios: Apontamentos sobre José Bonifácio." In *Antropologia do Brasil: Mito, história, etnicidade*, 165–173. São Paulo: Brasiliense / EDUSP, 1986.

———. "Política indigenista no século XIX." In *História dos índios no Brasil*, edited by Manuela Carneiro da Cunha, 133–154. São Paulo: Companhia das Letras, 1992.

Carvalho, Francismar Alex Lopes de. "Etnogênese mbayá-guaykuru: Notas sobre emergência identitária, expansão territorial e resistência de um grupo étnico no vale do rio paraguai (c. 1650–1800)." *Revista de História e Estudos Culturais* 3, no. 4 (2006): 1–20.

———. *Lealdades negociadas: Povos indígenas e a expansão dos impérios ibéricos nas regiões centrais da América do Sul (segunda metade do século XVIII)*. São Paulo: Alameda, 2014.

Carvalho, Sílvia Schmuziger. "Chaco: Encruzilhada dos povos e 'melting pot' cultural, suas relações com a bacia do Paraná e o Sul mato-grossense." In *História dos índios do Brasil*, edited by Manuela Carneiro da Cunha, 457–474. São Paulo: Companhia das Letras, 1992.

Castro, Eduardo Viveiros de. *The Inconstancy of the Indian Soul: The Encounter of Catholics and Cannibals in 16th-Century Brazil*. Chicago: Prickly Paradigm Press, 2011.

———. *From the Enemy's Point of View: Humanity and Divinity in an Amazonian Society*. Chicago: University of Chicago Press, 1992.

Cepek, Michael L. "Indigenous Difference: Rethinking Particularity in the Anthropology of Amazonia." *Journal of Latin American and Caribbean Anthropology* 18 (2013): 359–370.

———. *Life in Oil: Cofán Survival in the Petroleum Fields of Amazonia*. Austin, TX: University of Texas Press, 2018.

Chambouleyron, Rafael, Benedito Costa Barbosa, Fernanda Aires Bombardi, and Claudia Rocha de Sousa. "'Formidable Contagion': Epidemics, Work and Recruitment in Colonial Amazonia (1660–1750)." *História, Ciências, Saúde—Manguinhos* 18, no. 4 (2011): 987–1004.

Chernela, Janet M. "Directions of Existence: Indigenous Women Domestics in the Paris of the Tropics." *Journal of Latin American and Caribbean Anthropology* 20, no. 1 (2015): 201–229.

Clastres, Pierre. *Society Against the State: Essays in Political Anthropology*. Translated by Robert Hurley. New York: Urizen Books, 1977.

Cleary, David. "'Lost Altogether to the Civilised World': Race and the Cabanagem in Northern Brazil, 1750–1850." *Comparative Studies in Society and History* 40, no. 1 (1998): 109–135.

Cohen, Paul. "Was There an Amerindian Atlantic? Reflections on the Limits of a Historiographical Concept." *History of European Ideas* 34, no. 4 (2008), 388–410.

Colini, G. A. "Notícia histórica e etnográfica sôbre os Guaicuru e os Mbayá." In *Os Caduveos* by Guido Boggiani, 249–307. Belo Horizonte: Editora Itatiaia, 1975.

Colleoni, Paola. "Becoming Tamed: The Meaning of 'Becoming Civilized' among the Waorani of Amazonian Ecuador." *Tipití: Journal of the Society for the Anthropology of Lowland South America* 14, no. 1 (2016): 72–101. http://digitalcommons.trinity.edu/tipiti/vol14/iss1/5.

Conklin, Beth. "For Love or Money? Indigenous Materialism and Humanitarian Agendas." In *Editing Eden: A Reconsideration of Identity, Politics, and*

Place in Amazonia, edited by Frank Hutchison and Patrick C. Wilson, 127–150. Lincoln: University of Nebraska Press, 2010.

Costa, Emilia Viotti da. *The Brazilian Empire: Myths and Histories*. Chapel Hill: University of North Carolina Press, 2000.

Costa, Maria de Fátima. *História de um país inexistente: O Pantanal entre os séculos XVI e XVIII*. São Paulo: Estação Liberdade/Kosmos, 1999.

———. "Indigenous Peoples of Brazil and the War of the Triple Alliance, 1864–1870." In *Military Struggle and Identity Formation in Latin America: Race, Nation, and Community During the Liberal Period*, edited by Nicola Foote and René D. Harder Horst, 159–174. Gainesville: University Press of Florida, 2010.

Dantas, Mariana Albuquerque. "Estratégias indígenas: Dinâmica social e relações interétnicas no aldeamento do Ipanema no final do século XIX." In *A presença indígena no Nordeste: Processos de territorialização, modos de reconhecimento e regimes de memória*, edited by João Pacheco de Oliveira, 413–445. Rio de Janeiro: Contra Capa, 2011.

De la Torre, Oscar. *The People of the River: Nature and Identity in Black Amazonia, 1835–1945*. Chapel Hill, NC: University of North Carolina Press, 2018.

Dean, Warren. *Brazil and the Struggle for Rubber: A Study in Environmental History*. Cambridge: Cambridge University Press, 1987.

DeLay, Brian. *War of a Thousand Deserts: Indian Raids and the U.S.-Mexican War*. New Haven, CT: Yale University Press, 2008.

Deloria, Philip J. *Playing Indian*. New Haven, CT: Yale University Press, 1998.

Domingues, Ângela. *Quando os índios eram vassalos: colonização e relações de poder no Norte do Brasil na segunda metade do século XVIII*. Lisbon: Comissão Nacional para as Comemorações dos Descobrimentos Portugueses, 2000.

Dornelles, Soraia Sales. "A produção da invisibilidade indígena: Sobre construção de dados demográficos, apropriação de terras e o apagamento de identidades indígenas na segunda metade do XIX a partir da experiência paulista." *Revista Brasileira de História & Ciências Sociais* 10, no. 20 (2018): 62–80.

Dubcovsky, Alejandra. *Informed Power: Communication in the Early American South*. Cambridge, MA: Harvard University Press, 2016.

DuVal, Kathleen. *The Native Ground: Indians and Colonists in the Heart of the Continent*. Philadelphia: University of Pennsylvania Press, 2006.

Edwards, Elizabeth. "Surveying Culture: Photography and the Collection of Culture, British New Guinea, 1898." In *Hunting the Gatherers: Ethnographic Collectors, Agents and Agency in Melanesia, 1870s-1930s*, edited by Michael O'Hanlon and Robert L. Welsch, 103–126. Oxford: Berghahn, 2000.

Erbig, Jeffrey Alan, Jr. "Borderline Offerings: *Tolderías* and Mapmakers in the Eighteenth-Century Río de la Plata." *Hispanic American Historical Review* 96, no. 3 (2016): 443–80.

———. "Forging Frontiers: Félix de Azara and the Making of the Virreinato del Río de La Plata." MA Thesis, University of North Carolina, Chapel Hill, 2010.

———. *Where Caciques and Mapmakers Met: Border Making in Eighteenth-Century South America*. Chapel Hill: University of North Carolina Press, 2020.

Erbig, Jeffrey A., and Sergio Latini. "Across Archival Limits: Colonial Records, Changing Ethnonyms, and Geographies of Knowledge." *Ethnohistory* 66, no. 2 (2019): 249–273.

Erikson, Philippe. "The Social Significance of Pet-Keeping among Amazonian Indians." In *Companion Animals and Us: Exploring the Relationships between People and Pets*, edited by Anthony L. Podberscek, Elizabeth Paul, and James A. Serpell, 7–27. Cambridge: Cambridge University Press, 2000.

Espelt-Bombin, Silvia. "Makers and Keepers of Networks: Amerindian Spaces, Migrations, and Exchanges in the Brazilian Amazon and French Guiana, 1600–1730." *Ethnohistory* 65, no. 4 (2018): 597–620.

Evans, Brad, and Julian Reid. *Resilient Life: The Art of Living Dangerously*. Cambridge, England: Polity Press, 2014.

Everett, Daniel L. *Don't Sleep. There Are Snakes: Life and Language in the Amazonian Jungle*. New York: Pantheon Books, 2008.

Ewart, Elizabeth. "Coisas com as quais os antropólogos se preocupam: Grupos de descendência espacial entre os Panará." *Revista de Antropologia* 58, no. 1 (2015): 199–221.

———. "Demanding, Giving, Sharing, and Keeping: Panará Ideas of Economy." *Journal of Latin American and Caribbean Anthropology*, 18 (2013): 31–50.

———. *Space and Society in Central Brazil: A Panará Ethnography*. London: Bloomsbury, 2013.

Farage, Nádia. *As muralhas dos sertões: Os povos indígenas no Rio Branco e a colonização*. Rio de Janeiro: ANPOCS, 1991.

Faulhaber, Priscila. "Etnografia na Amazônia e tradução cultural: Comparando Constant Tastevin e Curt Nimuendaju." *Boletim do Museu Paraense Emílio Goeldi—Ciências Humanas* 3, no.1 (2008): 15–29.

Fausto, Carlos. "If God Were a Jaguar: Cannibalism and Christianity among the Guaraní (16th-20th Centuries)." In *Time and Memory in Indigenous Amazonia: Anthropological Perspectives*, edited by Carlos Fausto and Michael Heckenberger, 74–105. Gainesville: University Press of Florida, 2007.

———. *Warfare and Shamanism in Amazonia*. Cambridge: Cambridge University Press, 2012.

Fausto, Carlos, and Michael Heckenberger. "Introduction: Indigenous History and the History of the 'Indians." In *Time and Memory in Indigenous Amazonia: Anthropological Perspectives*, edited by Carlos Fausto and Michael Heckenberger, 1–43. Gainesville: University Press of Florida, 2007.

———, eds. *Time and Memory in Indigenous Amazonia: Anthropological Perspectives*. Gainesville: University Press of Florida, 2007.

Feather, Conrad. "The Restless Life of the Nahua: Shaping People and Places in the Peruvian Amazon," in *Mobility and Migration in Indigenous Amazonia: Contemporary Ethnoecological Perspectives*, edited by Miguel N. Alexiades, 69–85. New York: Berghahn Books, 2009.

Fenn, Elizabeth A. "Biological Warfare in Eighteenth-Century North America: Beyond Jeffery Amherst." *Journal of American History* 86, no. 4 (2000): 1552–80.

Ferguson, R. Brian. "Blood of the Leviathan: Western Contact and Warfare in Amazonia." *American Ethnologist* 17 (1990): 237–57.

Ferguson, R. Brian, and Neil L. Whitehead. "The Violent Edge of Empire." In *War in the Tribal Zone: Expanding States and Indigenous Warfare*, edited by R. Brian Ferguson and Neil L. Whitehead, 1–30. Santa Fe, NM: School of American Research Press, 1992.

———. *War in the Tribal Zone: Expanding States and Indigenous Warfare*. Santa Fe, NM: School of American Research Press, 1992.

Fernandes, João Azevedo. "Liquid Fire: Alcohol, Identity, and Social Hierarchy in Colonial Brazil." In *Alcohol in Latin America: A Social and Cultural History*, edited by Gretchen Pierce and Áurea Toxqui, 46–66. Tucson: University of Arizona Press, 2014.

Ferreira, Andrey Cordeiro. "Conquista colonial, resistência indígena e formação do estado-nação: Os índios Guaicuru e Guaná no Mato Grosso do século XIX." *Revista de Antropologia* 52, no. 1 (2009): 97–136.

Fisher, William H. *Rainforest Exchanges: Industry and Community on an Amazonian Frontier*. Washington, DC: Smithsonian Institution Press, 2000.

Flores, João. "Muita terra para pouco índio? A formação de fazendas em território Kadiwéu (1950–1984)." MA thesis, Universidade Federal da Grande Dourados—Dourados, 2009.

Folsom, Rafael Brewster. *The Yaquis and the Empire: Violence, Spanish Imperial Power, and Native Resilience in Colonial Mexico*. New Haven, CT: Yale University Press, 2014.

Freire, José Ribamar Bessa. *Rio Babel: A história das línguas na Amazônia*. Rio de Janeiro: Atlântica, 2004.

French, Jan Hoffman. *Legalizing Identities: Becoming Black or Indian in Brazil's Northeast*. Chapel Hill: University of North Carolina Press, 2009.

Frič, Pavel, and Yvonna Fričová. *Guido Boggiani: Fotograf = Photographer*. Prague: Titanic, 1997.

Fullagar, Kate, and Michael A. McDonnell, eds. *Facing Empire: Indigenous Experiences in a Revolutionary Age*. Baltimore: Johns Hopkins University Press, 2018.

Ganson, Barbara. "The Evueví of Paraguay: Adaptive Strategies and Responses to Colonialism, 1528–1811." *The Americas* 45, no. 4 (1989): 461–88.

García, Claudia. *Etnogénesis, hibridación y consolidación de la identidad del pueblo Miskitu*. Madrid: Consejo Superior de Investigaciones Científicas, 2007.

Garcia, Elisa Frühauf. *As diversas formas de ser índio: Políticas indígenas e políticas indigenistas no extremo sul da América portuguesa*. Rio de Janeiro: Arquivo Nacional, 2009.

Garfield, Seth. *Indigenous Struggle at the Heart of Brazil: State Policy, Frontier Expansion, and the Xavante Indians, 1937–1988*. Durham, NC: Duke University Press, 2001.

Giordano, Mariana. "Las múltiples facetas de Guido Boggiani." In *Boggiani y el Chaco: Una aventura del siglo XIX*, edited by Pavel Frič and Yvonna Fričová, 25–35. Buenos Aires: Museo Fernández Blanco, 2002.

Giraldin, Odair. *Cayapó e Panará: Luta e sobrevivência de um povo Jê no Brasil central*. Campinas: Editora da UNICAMP, 1997.

Giudicelli, Christophe, ed. *Luchas de clasificación: Las sociedades indígenas entre taxonomía, memoria y reapropiación*. Rosario, Argentina: Prohistoia, 2018.

Giudicelli, Christophe. "'Identidades' rebeldes: Soberanía colonial y poder de clasificación: sobre la categoría calchaquí (Tucumán, Santa Fe, siglos XVI-XVII)." In *América colonial: Denominaciones, clasificaciones e identidades*, edited by Alejandra Araya Espinoza and Jaime Valenzuela Márquez, 137–72. Santiago de Chile: RIL Editores, 2010.

Gomes, Flávio dos Santos. "A 'Safe Haven': Runaway Slaves, *Mocambos*, and Borders in Colonial Amazonia, Brazil." *Hispanic American Historical Review* 82, no. 3 (2002): 469–98.

Gordon, Cesar. "Nossas utopias não são as deles: Os Mebengokre (Kayapó) e o mundo dos brancos." *Sexta-feira: Antropologia, Artes e Humanidades* 6 (2001): 123–36.

———. "The Objects of the Whites: Commodities and Consumerism among the Xikrin-Kayapó (Mebengokre) of Amazonia." *Tipití: Journal of the Society for the Anthropology of Lowland South America* 8, no. 2 (2010): 1–20.

Gow, Peter. "'Who Are These Wild Indians': On the Foreign Policies of Some Voluntarily Isolated Peoples in Amazonia." *Tipití: Journal of the Society for the Anthropology of Lowland South America* 16, no. 1 (2018): 6–20.

Guzmán, Tracy Devine. *Native and National in Brazil: Indigeneity after Independence*. Chapel Hill: University of North Carolina Press, 2013.

Graham, Laura R. "Fluid Subjectivity: Reflections on Self and Alternative Futures in the Autobiographical Narrative of Hiparidi Top'tiro, a Xavante Transcultural Leader." In *Fluent Selves: Autobiography, Person, and History in Lowland South America*, edited by Suzanne Oakdale and Magnus Course, 235–70. Lincoln: University of Nebraska Press, 2014.

Grubacic, Andrej, and Denis O'Hearn, eds. *Living at the Edges of Capitalism: Adventures in Exile and Mutual Aid*. Berkeley: University of California Press, 2016.

Gruber, Jacob W. "Ethnographic Salvage and the Shaping of Anthropology." *American Anthropologist* 72, no. 6 (1970): 1289–99.

Hämäläinen, Pekka. *Comanche Empire.* New Haven, CT: Yale University Press, 2008.
———. "Lost in Transitions: Suffering, Survival, and Belonging in the Early Modern Atlantic World." *William and Mary Quarterly* 68, no. 2 (2011): 219–23.
———. "The Politics of Grass: European Expansion, Ecological Change, and Indigenous Power in the Southwest Borderlands." *William and Mary Quarterly* 67, no. 2 (2010): 173–208.
———. "The Shapes of Power: Indians, Europeans, and North American Worlds from the Seventeenth to the Nineteenth Century." In *Contested Spaces of Early America*, edited by Juliana Barr and Edward Countryman. Philadelphia: University of Pennsylvania Press, 2104.
Hämäläinen, Pekka, and Samuel Truett. "On Borderlands." *Journal of American History* 98, no. 2 (2011): 338–61.
Harris, Mark. "The Making of Regional Systems: The Tapajós/Madeira and Trombetas/Nhamundá Regions in the Lower Brazilian Amazon, Seventeenth and Eighteenth Centuries." *Ethnohistory* 65, no. 4 (2018): 621–45.
———. "Peasant Riverine Economies and Their Impact in the Lower Amazon." In *Human Impacts on Amazonia: The Role of Traditional Ecological Knowledge in Conservation and Development*, edited by Darrell Addison Posey and Michael J. Balick, 222–37. New York: Columbia University Press, 2006.
———. *Rebellion on the Amazon: The Cabanagem, Race, and Popular Culture in the North of Brazil, 1798–1840.* Cambridge: Cambridge University Press, 2010.
Harris, Olivia. "'The Coming of the White People': Reflections on the Mythologisation of History in Latin America." *Bulletin of Latin American Research* 14, no. 1 (1995): 9–24.
Hecht, Susanna B. *The Scramble for the Amazon and the Lost Paradise of Euclides da Cunha.* Chicago: University of Chicago Press, 2013.
Hemming, John. *Red Gold: The Conquest of the Brazilian Indians.* Cambridge, MA: Harvard University Press, 1978.
Henrique, Márcio Couto. "A perspectiva indígena das missões religiosas na Amazônia (século XIX)." *História Social* 25 (2013): 133–55.
———. "Presente de branco: A perspectiva indígena dos brindes da civilização (Amazônia, século XIX)." *Revista Brasileira de História* 37, no. 75 (2017): 1–22.
Herberts, Ana Lucia. "Panorama histórico dos mbayá-guaikuru entre os séculos XVI e XIX." In *Kadiwéu: Senhoras da arte, senhores da guerra*, edited by Giovani José da Silva, 17–47. Curitiba: Editora CRV, 2011.
Herzog, Tamar. *Frontiers of Possession: Spain and Portugal in Europe and the Americas.* Cambridge, MA: Harvard University Press, 2015.
Hill, Jonathan, ed. *History, Power, and Identity: Ethnogenesis in the Americas, 1492–1992.* Iowa City: University of Iowa Press, 1996.

Howard, Catherine V. "A domesticação das mercadorias: Estratégias Waiwai." In *Pacificando o branco: Cosmologias do contato no Norte-Amazônico*, edited by Bruce Albert and Alcida Ramos, 25–60. São Paulo: UNESP, 2002.

Hugh-Jones, Stephen. "Yesterday's Luxuries, Tomorrow's Necessities: Business and Barter in Northwest Amazonia." In *Barter, Exchange, and Value: An Anthropological Approach*, edited by Caroline Humphrey and Stephen Hugh-Jones, 42–74. Cambridge: Cambridge University Press, 1992.

Instituto Socioambiental. "Panará: Histórico do contato." Povos Indígenas no Brasil. Last modified October 7, 2019. https://pib.socioambiental.org/pt/Povo:Panará.

———. Povos Indígenas no Brasil. https://pib.socioambiental.org/pt/página_principal.

Jaenen, Cornelius J. "Amerindian Views of French Culture in the Seventeenth Century." *Canadian Historical Review* 55, no. 3 (1974): 261–91.

Jones, Kristine L. "Comparative Raiding Economies, North and South." In *Contested Ground: Comparative Frontiers on the Northern and Southern Edges of the Spanish Empire*, edited by Donna J. Guy and Thomas E. Sheridan, 97–114. Tucson: University of Arizona Press, 1998.

Julio, Suelen Siqueira. *Damiana da Cunha: Uma índia entre a "sombra da cruz" e os caiapós do sertão (Goiás, c. 1780–1831)*. Niterói, Brazil: EDUFF, 2016.

Karasch, Mary C. *Before Brasília: Frontier Life in Central Brazil*. Albuquerque: University of New Mexico Press, 2016.

———. "Catequese e cativeiro: Política indigenista em Goiás, 1780–1889." In *História dos índios no Brasil*, edited by Manuela Carneiro da Cunha, 397–412. São Paulo : Companhia das Letras, 1992.

———. "Damiana da Cunha: Catechist and Sertanista." In *Struggle and Survival in Colonial America*, edited by David G. Sweet and Gary B. Nash, 102–20. Berkeley: University of California Press, 1981.

———. "Índios aldeados: Um perfil demográfico da Capitania de Goiás, 1755–1835." *Habitus* 15, no. 1 (2017): 21–38.

———. "Inter-ethnic Conflict and Survival Strategies on the Tocantins-Araguaia Frontier, 1750–1890." In *Contested Ground: Comparative Frontiers on the Northern and Southern Edges of the Spanish Empire*, edited by Donna J. Guy and Thomas E. Sheridan, 115–34. Tucson: University of Arizona Press, 1998.

———. "Rethinking the Conquest of Goiás, 1775–1819." *The Americas* 61, no. 3 (2005): 463–92.

Lagrou, Els. "No caminho das miçangas: Arte, alteridade e relação entre os ameríndios." *Enfoques—Revista dos Alunos do PPGSA-UFRJ* 12 (2013): 18–49.

Lamaison, Pierre, and Pierre Bourdieu. "From Rules to Strategies: An Interview with Pierre Bourdieu." *Cultural Anthropology* 1, no. 1 (1986): 110–20.

Langavant, Benita Herreros Cleret de. "Portugueses, españoles y mbayá en el alto Paraguay. Dinámicas y estrategias de frontera en los márgenes de los imperios ibéricos (1791–1803)." *Nuevo Mundo—Mundos Nuevos*, Debates, posted November 4, 2012. https://journals.openedition.org/nuevomundo/64467.

Langfur, Hal, ed. *Native Brazil: Beyond the Convert and the Cannibal, 1500–1900*. Albuquerque: University of New Mexico Press, 2014.

Langfur, Hal. "Cannibalism and the Body Politic: Independent Indians in the Era of Brazilian Independence." *Ethnohistory* 65, no. 4 (2018): 549–73.

———. *The Forbidden Lands: Colonial Identity, Frontier Violence, and the Persistence of Brazil's Eastern Indians, 1750–1830*. Stanford, CA: Stanford University Press, 2006.

———. "Myths of Pacification: Brazilian Frontier Settlement and the Subjugation of the Bororo Indians." *Journal of Social History* 32, no. 4 (1999): 879–905.

———. "The Return of the *Bandeira*: Economic Calamity, Historical Memory, and Armed Expeditions to the *Sertão* in Minas Gerais, Brazil, 1750–1808." *The Americas* 61, no. 3 (2005): 429–61.

Lasmar, Cristiane. *De volta ao lago de leite: Gênero e transformação no Alto Rio Negro*. São Paulo: Edusp/ISA, 2005.

Leal, Davi Avelino. "Direitos e processos diferenciados de territorialização: Os conflitos pelo uso dos recursos naturais no rio Madeira (1861–1932)." PhD diss., Universidade Federal do Amazonas, 2013.

Lecznieski, Lisiane Koller. "Objetos relacionais Ameríndios: Sobre a (in)visibilidade da arte Kadiwéu na novela Alma Gêmea da Rede Globo." *Espaço Ameríndio (UFRGS)* 4 (2010): 44–61.

Lee, Richard B., and Richard Daly. "Introduction: Foragers and Others." In *Cambridge Encyclopedia of Hunter-Gatherers* (1999), edited by Richard B. Lee and Richard Daly, 1–19. Cambridge: Cambridge University Press, 1999.

LeGrand, Catherine. "Living in Macondo: Economy and Culture in a United Fruit Company Banana Enclave (Santa Marta, Colombia, 1890–1930)." In *Close Encounters of the Imperial Kind: Writing the Cultural History of U.S.–Latin American Relations*, edited by Gilbert Joseph, Ricardo Salvatore, and Catherine LeGrand, 333–68. Durham, NC: Duke University Press, 1998.

Lehmann, Johannes, Dirse C. Kern, Bruno Glaser, and William I. Woods, eds. *Amazonian Dark Earths: Origins, Properties, Management*. Boston: Kluwer Academic, 2003.

Lennox, Jeffers. *Homelands and Empires: Indigenous Spaces, Imperial Fictions, and Competition for Territory in Northeastern North America, 1690–1763*. Toronto: University of Toronto Press, 2017.

Lepore, Jill. *The Name of War: King Philip's War and the Origins of American Identity*. New York: Vintage Books, 1998.

Levaggi, Abelardo. *Diplomacia hispano-indígena en las fronteras de América: Historia de los tratados entre la Monarquía española y las comunidades aborígenes*. Madrid: Centro de Estudios Constitucionales, 2002.

Levin Rojo, Danna A., and Cynthia Radding, eds. *The Oxford Handbook of Borderlands of the Iberian World*. Oxford: Oxford University Press, 2019.

Lima, Antonio Carlos de Souza. *Um grande cerco de paz: Poder tutelar, indianidade e formação do estado no Brasil*. Petrópolis: Vozes, 1995.

Lowie, Robert H. "The Southern Cayapó." In *Handbook of South American Indians*, edited by Julian H. Steward, 519–20. Vol. 1. Washington, DC: Smithsonian Institution, 1946.

Lucaioli, Carina P. "Alianzas y estrategias de los líderes indígenas abipones en un espacio fronterizo colonial (Chaco, siglo XVIII)." *Revista Española de Antropología Americana* 39, no. 1 (2009): 77–96.

Machado, André Roberto de A. "O Conselho Geral da Província do Pará e a definição da política indigenista no Império do Brasil (1829–31)." *Almanack* 10 (2015): 409–64.

———. *A quebra da mola real das sociedades: A crise política do Antigo Regime Português na província do Grão-Pará (1821–25)*. São Paulo: Hucitec / Fapesp, 2010.

Maciel, Márcia Nunes (Márcia Mura). "Tecendo tradições indígenas." Vol. 1. PhD diss., Universidade de São Paulo, 2016.

MacLeod, Murdo J. "Some Thoughts on the Pax Colonial, Colonial Violence, and Perceptions of Both." In *Native Resistance and the Pax Colonial in New Spain*, edited by Susan Schroder, 129–42. Lincoln: University of Nebraska Press, 1998.

Mandrini, Raúl, and Sara Ortelli. "Los 'Araucanos' en las Pampas (c. 1700–1850)." In *Colonización, resistencia, y mestizaje en las Américas (siglos XVI–XX)*, edited by Guillaume Boccara, 237–57. Quito: Editorial Abya Yala, 2002.

Martins, Luciana. "'Resemblances to Archaeological Finds': Guido Boggiani, Claude Lévi-Strauss and Caduveo Body Painting." *Journal of Latin American Cultural Studies* 26, no. 2 (2017): 187–219.

Matthew, Laura E., and Michel R. Oudijk, eds. *Indian Conquistadors: Indigenous Allies in the Conquest of Mesoamerica*. Norman: University of Oklahoma Press, 2007.

Mattos, Izabel Missagia de. *Civilização e revolta: Os Botocudos e a catequese na Província de Minas*. Bauru, São Paulo: EDUSC, 2004.

Maxwell, Kenneth. "Why Was Brazil Different? The Contexts of Independence." In *Naked Tropics: Essays on Empire and Other Rogues*, 145–68. New York: Routledge, 2003.

McEnroe, Sean F. "Sites of Diplomacy, Violence, and Refuge: Topography and Negotiation in the Mountains of New Spain." *The Americas* 69, no. 2 (2012): 179–202.

Mead, David Louis. "Caiapó do Sul, an Ethnohistory (1610–1920)." PhD diss., University of Florida, 2010.

Mello, Raul Silveira de. *História do Forte de Coimbra*, 4 vols. Rio de Janeiro: Imprensa do Exército, 1958–1961.

Melo, Joaquim. *SPI—A Política Indigenista no Amazonas*. Manaus: Edições do Governo do Estado, 2009.

Menéndez, Miguel. "A área Madeira-Tapajós: Situação de contato e relações entre colonizador e indígenas." In *História dos índios no Brasil*, edited by Manuela Carneiro da Cunha, 281–96. São Paulo: Companhia das Letras, 1992.

Metcalf, Alida C. *Go-Betweens and the Colonization of Brazil, 1500–1600*. Austin: University of Texas Press, 2005.

Métraux, Alfred. "Ethnography of the Chaco." In *Handbook of South American Indians*, edited by Julian H. Steward, 197–370. Vol. 1, part 2. Washington DC: Smithsonian Institution, 1946.

Miki, Yuko. *Frontiers of Citizenship: A Black and Indigenous History of Postcolonial Brazil*. Cambridge: Cambridge University Press, 2018.

Miller, Christopher L., and George R. Hamell. "A New Perspective on Indian-White Contact: Cultural Symbols and Colonial Trade." *Journal of American History* 73, no. 2 (1986): 311–28.

Mitchell, Peter. *Horse Nations: The Worldwide Impact of the Horse on Indigenous Societies Post-1492*. Oxford: Oxford University Press, 2015.

Monteiro, John M. *Blacks of the Land: Indian Slavery, Settler Society, and the Portuguese Colonial Enterprise in South America*. Edited and translated by James Woodard and Barbara Weinstein. Cambridge: Cambridge University Press, 2018.

———. "The Heathen Castes of Sixteenth-Century Portuguese America: Unity, Diversity, and the Invention of the Brazilian Indians." *Hispanic American Historical Review* 80, no. 4 (2000): 697–719.

———. "Redescobrindo os índios da América portuguesa: Antropologia e história." In *Olhares contemporâneos: Cenas do mundo em discussão na universidade*, edited by Odílio Alves Aguiar, José Élcio Batista, and Joceny Pinheiro, 135–42. Fortaleza, Edições Demócrito Rocha, 2001.

———. "Rethinking Amerindian Resistance and Persistence in Colonial Portuguese America." In *New Approaches to Resistance in Brazil and Mexico*, edited by John Gledhill and Patience A. Schell. Durham, NC: Duke University Press, 2012.

———. "Tupis, tapuias e historiadores: Estudos de história indígena a do indigenismo." Tese de Livre Docência, Universidade Estadual de Campinas, 2001.

Moreira Neto, Carlos de Araújo. *Índios da Amazônia, de maioria a minoria*. Petrópolis: Vozes, 1988.

———. *Os índios e a ordem imperial*. Brasília: Ministério da Justiça/FUNAI, 2005.

Moreira, Vânia Maria Losada. "Entre as vilas e os sertões: Trânsitos indígenas e transculturações nas fronteiras do Espírito Santo (1798–1840)." *Nuevo Mundo—Mundos Nuevos* (2011). http://journals.openedition.org/nuevomundo/60746.

———. "Os índios e Império: História, direitos sociais e agenciamento indígena." Paper presented at the XXV Simpósio Nacional de História da ANPUH, Fortaleza, 2009.

———. "Os índios na história política do Império: Avanços, resistências e tropeços." *Revista História Hoje—ANPUH/Brasil* 1, no. 2 (2012): 269–74.

———. "Índios no Brasil: Marginalização social e exclusão historiográfica." *Diálogos Latinoamericanos* 3 (2001): 87–113.

———. "Terras indígenas do Espírito Santo sob o regime territorial de 1850." *Revista Brasileira de História* 22, no. 43 (2002): 153–69.

Murray, David. *Indian Giving: Economies of Power in Indian-White Exchanges.* Amherst: University of Massachusetts Press, 2000.

Nacuzzi, Lidia R. "Los cacicazgos del siglo XVIII en ámbitos de frontera de Pampa-Patagonia y el Chaco." In *De los cacicazgos a la ciudadanía: Sistemas políticos en la frontera, Rio de la Plata, siglos XVIII-XX,* edited by Mónica Quijada, 23–77. Berlin: Gebr. Mann Verlag, 2011.

Nacuzzi, Lidia R., and Carina Lucaioli. "'Y sobre las armas se concertaron las paces': Explorando las rutinas de los acuerdos diplomáticos coloniales." *Revista CUHSO (Cultura—Hombre—Sociedad)* 15, no. 2 (2008): 61–74.

Nimuendajú, Curt. *Mapa etno-histórico do Brasil e regiões adjacentes.* Rio de Janeiro: IBGE, 1981 [1944].

———. "The Mura and Pirahã." *The Handbook of South American Indians,* edited by Julian H. Steward, 255–68. Vol. 3. Washington, DC: Smithsonian Institution, 1948.

———. "As Tribus do Alto Madeira." *Journal de la Société des Américanistes* 17 (1925): 137–72.

O'Brien, Jean M. *Firsting and Lasting: Writing Indians Out of Existence in New England.* Minneapolis: University of Minnesota Press, 2010.

Oliveira, João Pacheco de, ed. "Uma etnologia dos 'índios misturados'? Situação colonial, territorialização e fluxos culturais." *Mana* 4, no. 1 (1998): 47–77.

———. "Pacificação e tutela militar na gestão de populações e territórios." *Mana* 20, no. 1 (2014): 125–61.

———. *A viagem da volta: Etnicidade, política e reelaboração cultural no Nordeste indígena.* Rio de Janeiro: Contracapa, 1999.

Ortelli, Sara. *Trama de una guerra conveniente: Nueva Vizcaya y la sombra de los apaches (1748–1790).* Mexico City: El Colegio de México, Centro de Estudios Históricos, 2007.

Paraíso, Maria Hilda Baqueiro. "As crianças indígenas e a formação de agentes transculturais: O comércio de kurukas na Bahia, Espírito Santo e Minas Gerais." *Revista de Estudos e Pesquisas (Fundação Nacional do Índio)* 3 (2006): 41–106.

Parente, Izabel Cavalcanti Ibiapina. "O amazonismo e as representações sobre os seringueiros e a natureza amazônica." PhD diss., Universidade de Brasília, 2018.

Pechincha, Mônica Thereza Soares. "Histórias de admirar: Mito, rito e história Kadiwéu." MA thesis, Universidade de Brasília, 1994.

———. "Memória e história entre índios brasileiros: Os Kadiwéu e seus etnógrafos Darcy Ribeiro e Guido Boggiani." *História Revista (UFG)* 5 (2000): 151–63.

Pereira, Márcia Leila de Castro. "Rios de história: Guerra, tempo e espaço entre os Mura do baixo Madeira." PhD diss., Universidade de Brasília, 2009.

———. "Território e mobilidade Mura no Baixo Rio Madeira (AM)." *Habitus: Goiânia* 14, no. 2 (2016): 263–75.

Perrone-Moisés, Beatriz. "Índios livres e índios escravos: Os princípios da legislação indigenista do período colonial (séculos XVI a XVIII)." In *História dos índios no Brasil*, edited by Manuela Carneiro da Cunha, 115–32. São Paulo: Schwarcz, 1992.

Perrone-Moisés, Beatriz, and Renato Sztutman. "Notícias de uma certa confederação Tamoio." *Mana* 16, no. 2 (2010): 401–33.

Peterson, Nicolas. "Demand Sharing: Reciprocity and the Pressure for Generosity among Foragers." *American Anthropologist*, new series, 95, no. 4 (1993): 860–74.

Pierce, Gretchen, and Áurea Toxqui, eds. *Alcohol in Latin America: A Social and Cultural History.* Tucson: University of Arizona Press, 2014.

Pompa, Cristina. *Religião como tradução: Missionários, Tupi e "Tapuia" no Brasil colonial.* Bauru, São Paulo: EDUSC, 2003.

Porro, Antonio. "Os povos indígenas da Amazônia à chegada dos europeus." In *História da Igreja na Amazônia*, edited by Eduardo Hoornaert, 11–48. Petrópolis: Vozes, 1992.

Prado, Caio, Júnior. *The Colonial Background of Modern Brazil.* Berkeley: University of California Press, 1967.

Presotti, Thereza Martha. "*Nas trilhas das águas: Índios e natureza na conquista colonial do centro da América do Sul, os sertões de Cuiabá e Mato Grosso (século XVIII).*" PhD diss., Universidade de Brasília, 2008.

Preston, David L. *The Texture of Contact: European and Indian Settler Communities on the Frontiers of Iroquoia, 1667–1783.* Lincoln: University of Nebraska Press, 2009.

Puntoni, Pedro. *A guerra dos bárbaros: Povos indígenas e a colonização do sertão nordeste do Brasil, 1650–1720.* São Paulo: Hucitec/Edusp/Fapesp, 2002

Radding, Cynthia. *Landscapes of Power and Identity: Comparative Histories of the Sonoran Desert and the Forests of Amazonia from Colony to Republic.* Durham, NC: Duke University Press, 2005.

Raffles, Hugh, and Antoinette WinklerPrins. "Further Reflections on Amazonian Environmental History: Transformations of Rivers and Streams." *Latin American Research Review* 38, no. 3 (2003): 165–87.

Ramos, Alcida Rita. "Indian Voices: Contact Experienced and Expressed." In *Rethinking History and Myth: Indigenous South American Perspectives on the*

Past, edited by Jonathan D. Hill, 214–34. Chicago: University of Illinois Press, 1988.

———. *Indigenism: Ethnic Politics in Brazil*. Madison, WI: University of Wisconsin Press, 1998.

Restall, Matthew. *Seven Myths of the Spanish Conquest*. Oxford: Oxford University Press, 2003.

Ribeiro, Darcy. *Os índios e a civilização: A integração das populações indígenas no Brasil moderno*. Rio de Janeiro: Editora Civilização Brasileira, 1970.

———. *Kadiwéu: Ensaios etnológicos sobre o saber, o azar e a beleza*. Petrópolis: Vozes, 1980.

Ricci, Magda. "O fim do Grão-Pará e o nascimento do Brasil: Movimentos sociais, levantes e deserções no alvorecer do novo império, 1808–1840." In *Os Senhores dos Rios: Amazônia, Margens e Histórias*, edited by Mary Del Priore and Flávio dos Santos Gomes, 165–93. Rio de Janeiro: Elsevier, 2003.

Ricci, Magda, and Luciano Demetrius Barbosa. "Letrados da Amazônia Imperial e saberes das populações analfabetas durante a Revolução Cabana (1835–1840)." *Revista Brasileira de Educação* 20 (2015): 845–67.

Ricardo, Fany, and Majoí Fávero Gongora, eds. *Enclosures and Resistance: Isolated Indigenous Peoples in Brazilian Amazonia*. São Paulo: Instituto Socioambiental, 2019.

Richter, Daniel K. *Facing East from Indian Country: A Native History of Early America*. Cambridge, MA: Harvard University Press, 2001.

Rival, Laura M. *Trekking Through History: The Huaorani of Amazonian Ecuador*. New York: Columbia University Press, 2002.

Roller, Heather F. *Amazonian Routes: Indigenous Mobility and Colonial Communities in Northern Brazil*. Stanford, CA: Stanford University Press, 2014.

———. "River Guides, Geographical Informants, and Colonial Field Agents in the Portuguese Amazon." *Colonial Latin American Review* 21, no. 1 (2012): 101–26.

Roulet, Florencia. "Con la pluma y la palabra: el lado oscuro de las negociaciones de paz entre españoles e indígenas." *Revista de Indias* 64, no. 231 (2004): 313–48.

Saeger, James Schofield. *The Chaco Mission Frontier: The Guaycuruan Experience*. Tucson: University of Arizona Press, 2000.

Safier, Neil. "The Confines of the Colony: Boundaries, Ethnographic Landscapes, and Imperial Cartography in Iberoamerica." In *The Imperial Map: Cartography and the Mastery of Empire*, edited by James Akerman, 133–83. Chicago: University of Chicago Press, 2009.

Saggers, Sherry, and Dennis Gray. *Dealing with Alcohol: Indigenous Usage in Australia, New Zealand, and Canada*. Cambridge: Cambridge University Press, 1998.

Salomon, Frank. "Testimonies: The Making and Reading of Native South American Historical Sources." In *South America*, vol. 3, pt. 1 of *The Cambridge*

History of the Native Peoples of the Americas, edited by Frank Salomon and Stuart B. Schwartz, 19–95. Cambridge: Cambridge University Press, 1999.

Salomon, Frank, and Stuart B. Schwartz. "Introduction." In *South America*, vol. 3, pt. 1 of *The Cambridge History of the Native Peoples of the Americas*, edited by Frank Salomon and Stuart B. Schwartz, 1–18. Cambridge: Cambridge University Press, 1999

Sampaio, Patrícia Maria Melo. "Entre a tutela e a liberdade dos índios: Relendo a Carta Régia de 1798." In *Meandros da história: Trabalho e poder no Pará e Maranhão, séculos XVIII e XIX*, edited by Mauro Cezar Coelho, Flávio dos Santos Gomes, Jonas Marçal Queiroz, Rosa E. Acevedo Marin, and Geraldo Prado, 68–84. Belém: UNAMAZ, 2005.

———. "Espelhos partidos: Etnia, legislação e desigualdade na colônia sertões do Grão-Pará, c. 1755-1823." PhD diss., Universidade Federal Fluminense, 2001.

———. "Política indigenista no Brasil imperial." In *O Brasil Imperial*, edited by Keila Grinberg and Ricardo Salles, 175–206. Vol. 1. Rio de Janeiro: Civilização Brasileira, 2009.

Sampaio, Patrícia Melo, and Regina de Carvalho Erthal, eds. *Rastros da memória: Histórias e trajetórias das populações indígenas na Amazônia*. Manaus: Editora da Universidade Federal do Amazonas, 2006.

Sampaio, Renata Domingues. "Para além da excepcionalidade: A patrimonialização do Monumento Indígena Marco Zero Kadiwéu." MA thesis, Instituto do Patrimônio Histórico e Artístico Nacional, Rio de Janeiro, 2018.

Santos, Gilberto Brizolla. "'Amansar os portugueses': Os índios Guaikurú nas representações portuguesas coloniais." In *Mato Grosso Português: Ensaios de antropologia histórica*, edited by Maria Fátima Roberto Machado, 67–119. Cuiabá: UFMT, 2002.

Santos, Maria Cristina dos, and Guilherme Galhegos Felippe. "Apropriações possíveis de um protagonismo outro." *Revista Brasileira de História* 37, no. 76 (2017): 115–36.

Santos-Granero, Fernando. *Vital Enemies: Slavery, Predation and the Amerindian Political Economy of Life*. Austin: University of Texas Press, 2009.

———. "Writing History into the Landscape: Space, Myth, and Ritual in Contemporary Amazonia." *American Ethnologist* 25, no. 2 (1998): 128–48.

Schaub, Jean-Frédéric. "Is the 'Colonial Studies' Category Indispensable?" *Annales. Histoire, Sciences Sociales* 63, no. 3 (2008): 625–46.

Schönitzer, Klaus. "From the New to the Old World: Two Indigenous Children Brought Back to Germany by Johann Baptist Spix and Carl Friedrich Martius." *Journal Fünf Kontinente* 1 (2015): 78–105.

Schwartz, Stuart B., and Hal Langfur. "*Tapanhuns, Negros da Terra*, and *Curibocas*: Common Cause and Confrontation between Blacks and Natives in Colonial Brazil." In *Beyond Black and Red: African–Native Relations in*

Colonial Latin America, edited by Matthew Restall, 81–114. Albuquerque: University of New Mexico Press, 2005.

Schwartz, Stuart B., and Frank Salomon. "New Peoples and New Kinds of People: Adaptation, Readjustment, and Ethnogenesis in South American Indigenous Societies (Colonial Era)." In *South America*, vol. 3, pt. 2 of *The Cambridge History of the Native Peoples of the Americas*, edited by Frank Salomon and Stuart B. Schwartz, 443–501. Cambridge: Cambridge University Press, 1999.

Scott, James C. *The Art of Not Being Governed: An Anarchist History of Upland Southeast Asia*. New Haven, CT: Yale University Press, 2009.

Shepard, Glenn H. Jr. "Ceci N'est Pas un Contacte: The Fetishization of Isolated Indigenous People Along the Peru-Brazil Border." *Tipití: Journal of the Society for the Anthropology of Lowland South America* 14, no. 1 (2016): 135–37.

Sheridan, Cecilia. "Social Control and Native Territoriality in Northeastern New Spain." In *Choice, Persuasion, and Coercion: Social Control on Spain's North American Frontiers*, edited by Jesús F. de la Teja and Ross Frank, 121–48. Albuquerque: University of New Mexico Press, 2005.

Shoemaker, Nancy. "Categories." In *Clearing a Path: Theorizing the Past in Native American Cultures*, edited by Nancy Shoemaker, 51–74. New York: Routledge, 2002.

Sider, Gerald. *Living Indian Histories: Lumbee and Tuscarora People in North Carolina*. 2nd ed. Chapel Hill: University of North Carolina Press, 2003.

Silva, Aracy Lopes da. "Dois séculos e meio de história Xavante." In *História dos índios no Brasil*, edited by Manuela Carneiro da Cunha, 357–78. São Paulo: Companhia das Letras, 1992.

Silva, Giovani José da. "Os Kadiwéu e seus etnógrafos: De além do Atlântico, história e antropologia nos séculos XIX e XX." Paper presented at the XXVI Simpósio Nacional de História da ANPUH, São Paulo, 2011. http://www.ifch.unicamp.br/ihb/SNH2011/TextoGiovaniJS.pdf.

———. "A Reserva Indígena Kadiwéu (1899–1984): Demarcações e conflitos pela posse da terra." In *Kadiwéu: Senhoras da arte, senhores da guerra*, edited by Giovani José da Silva, 49–72. Curitiba: Editora CRV, 2011.

———. *A Reserva Indígena Kadiwéu (1899–1984): Memória, identidade e história*. Dourados: Editora UFGD, 2014.

Siqueira, Jaime Garcia, Jr. "Esse campo custou o sangue dos nossos avós: A construção do tempo e espaço Kadiwéu." In *Kadiwéu: Senhoras da arte, senhores da guerra*, edited by Giovani José da Silva, 75–91. Curitiba: Editora CRV, 2011.

Smith, Sherry. *Reimagining Indians: Native Americans Through Anglo Eyes, 1880–1940*. Oxford: Oxford University Press, 2000.

Soares, Marília Facó. "Ticuna." Instituto Socioambiental. Povos Indígenas no Brasil. Last modified August 20, 2018. https://pib.socioambiental.org/pt/Povo:Ticuna.

Sommer, Barbara A. "Colony of the Sertão: Amazonian Expeditions and the Indian Slave Trade." *The Americas* 61, no. 3 (2005): 401–28.

———. "Cracking Down on the Cunhamenas: Renegade Amazonian Traders under Pombaline Reform." *Journal of Latin American Studies* 38, no. 4 (2006): 767–91.

Souza, Eliane da Silva, Pequeno. "Mura, guardiães do caminho fluvial." *Revista de Estudos e Pesquisas (FUNAI)* 3, no. 1/2 (2006), 133–55.

Sposito, Fernanda. *Nem cidadãos, nem brasileiros: Indígenas na formação do estado nacional brasileiro e conflitos na província de São Paulo (1822–1845)*. São Paulo: Alameda, 2012.

Susnik, Branislava. *El indio colonial del Paraguay: El Chaqueño*. Vol. 3, no. 1. Asunción, Paraguay: Museo Etnográfico Andrés Barbero, 1971.

Sweet, David G. "Juan de Silva y Fernando Rojas: Baqueanos Africanos de la Selva Americana." In *Lucha por la supervivencia en la América colonial*, edited by David G. Sweet and Gary B. Nash, 234–46. México: Fondo de Cultura Económica, 1987.

———. "Native Resistance in Eighteenth-Century Amazonia: The 'Abominable Muras' in War and Peace." *Radical History Review* 53, no. 1 (1992): 49–80.

———. "A Rich Realm of Nature Destroyed: The Middle Amazon Valley, 1640–1750." PhD diss., University of Wisconsin, 1974.

Sweet, James H. "The Quiet Violence of Ethnogenesis." *William and Mary Quarterly* 68, no. 2 (2011): 209–14.

Taylor, Anne-Christine. "Sick of History: Contrasting Regimes of Historicity in the Upper Amazon." In *Time and Memory in Indigenous Amazonia: Anthropological Perspectives*, edited by Carlos Fausto and Michael Heckenberger, 133–68. Gainesville: University Press of Florida, 2007.

Tuck, Eve. "Suspending Damage: A Letter to Communities." *Harvard Educational Review* 79, no. 3 (2009): 409–27.

Turgeon, Laurier. "The Tale of the Kettle: Odyssey of an Intercultural Object." *Ethnohistory* 44, no. 1 (1997): 1–29.

Turner, Terence. "Representing, Resisting, Rethinking: Historical Transformation of Kayapo Culture and Anthropological Consciousness." In *Colonial Situations: Essays on the Contextualization of Ethnographic Knowledge*, edited by George W. Stocking, 285–313. Madison: University of Wisconsin Press, 1991.

Van Valen, Gary. *Indigenous Agency in the Amazon: The Mojos in Liberal and Rubber-Boom Bolivia, 1842–1932*. Tucson: University of Arizona Press, 2013.

Vangelista, Chiara. "Los guaykurú, españoles y portugueses en una región de frontera: Mato Grosso, 1770–1830." *Boletín del Instituto de Historia Argentina y Americana Dr. Emilio Ravignani* 8, no. 39 (1993): 55–76.

———. "Textos, dibujos, fotografías: La construcción de la imagen de los kadiwéu en los diarios de viaje de Guido Boggiani (1892 y 1897)." In *El mundo latinoamericano como representación, siglos XIX–XX*, edited by Pilar García Jordán, 177–98. Barcelona: Publicacions i Edicions UB/ TEIAA/ IFEA, 2015.

Vasconcelos, Eduardo Alves. "Investigando a hipótese Cayapó do Sul-Panará." PhD diss., Universidade de Campinas, 2013.

Viertler, Renate Brigitte. *A duras penas: Um histórico das relações entre índios Bororo e "civilizados" no Mato Grosso*. São Paulo: Universidade de São Paulo, 1990.

Vilaça, Aparecida. *Morte na floresta*. São Paulo: Todavia, 2020.

———. *Strange Enemies: Indigenous Agency and Scenes of Encounters in Amazonia*. Durham, NC: Duke University Press, 2010.

Warren, Stephen. *The Worlds the Shawnees Made: Migration and Violence in Early America*. Chapel Hill: University of North Carolina Press, 2014.

Warren, Stephen, and Ben Barnes. "Salvaging the Salvage Anthropologists: Erminie Wheeler-Voegelin, Carl Voegelin, and the Future of Ethnohistory." *Ethnohistory* 65, no. 2 (2018): 189–214.

Weber, David J. *Bárbaros: Spaniards and Their Savages in the Age of Enlightenment*. New Haven, CT: Yale University Press, 2005.

———. *The Spanish Frontier in North America*. New Haven, CT: Yale University Press, 1992.

Weinstein, Barbara. *The Amazon Rubber Boom, 1850–1920*. Stanford, CA: Stanford University Press, 1983.

Weiss, Joseph. *Shaping the Future on Haida Gwaii: Life Beyond Settler Colonialism*. Vancouver: University of British Columbia Press, 2018.

White, Richard. *The Middle Ground: Indians, Empires, and Republics in the Great Lakes Region, 1650–1815*. Cambridge: Cambridge University Press, 1991.

Whitehead, Neil. "Ethnic Transformation and Historical Discontinuity in Native Amazonia and Guayana, 1500–1900." *L'Homme* 33, no. 126/128 (1993): 285–305.

———. "Native Peoples Confront Colonial Regimes in Northeastern South America (c. 1500–1900)." In *South America*, vol. 3, pt. 2 of *The Cambridge History of the Native Peoples of the Americas*, edited by Frank Salomon and Stuart B. Schwartz, 382–442. Cambridge: Cambridge University Press, 1999.

Whyte, Kyle Powys. "Our Ancestors' Dystopia Now: Indigenous Conservation and the Anthropocene." In *The Routledge Companion to the Environmental Humanities*, edited by Ursula K. Heise, Jon Christensen, and Michelle Niemann, 206–18. London: Routledge, 2017.

Williams, Caroline A. "Living Between Empires: Diplomacy and Politics in the Late Eighteenth-Century Mosquitia." *The Americas* 70, no. 2 (2013): 237–68.

Witgen, Michael. *An Infinity of Nations: How the Native New World Shaped Early North America*. Philadelphia: University of Pennsylvania Press, 2011.

Wittmann, Luísa Tombini. *O Vapor e o Botoque: Imigrantes alemães e índios Xokleng no Vale do Itajaí/SC (1850–1926)*. Florianópolis: Letras Contemporâneas, 2007.

Zavala, José Manuel. *Los mapuches del siglo XVIII: Dinámica interétnica y estrategias de resistencia*. Santiago: Editorial Universidad Bolivariana, 2008.

Media Articles

Albert, Bruce. "Covid-19: Lessons From the Yanomami." *New York Times*, April 27, 2020.

Borges, Thais, Sue Branford, and Mauricio Torres. "Amazon's Mura Indigenous Group Demands Input Over Giant Mining Project." *Mongabay*, December 27, 2019. https://news.mongabay.com/2019/12/amazons-mura-indigenous-group-demands-input-over-giant-mining-project/.

Brown, Kate. "The Pandemic Is Not a Natural Disaster." *New Yorker*, April 13, 2020.

Fausto, Carlos. "'Vamos fazer lockdown na aldeia': governança indígena e desgoverno." *Nexo*, June 11, 2020. https://www.nexojornal.com.br/ensaio/debate/2020/'Vamos-fazer-lockdown-na-aldeia'-governança-indígena-e-desgoverno.

Graham, Laura R. "Brazil Fails to Prevent COVID-19 Spread in Indigenous Communities: The Xavante Example." *Cultural Survival*, May 31, 2020. https://www.culturalsurvival.org/news/brazil-fails-prevent-covid-19-spread-indigenous-communities-xavante-example.

Graham, Laura R., with collaboration from Edson Krenak Naknanuk. "A'uwẽ-Xavante Leaders Denounce Bogus Consultations Regarding 3 Hydroelectric Dams, Demand Halt to Commercial Transport on Federal Highways During COVID." *Cultural Survival*, May 13, 2020. https://www.culturalsurvival.org/news/auwe-xavante-leaders-denounce-bogus-consultations-regarding-3-hydroelectric-dams-demand-halt.

Instituto Socioambiental. "Como amansar o fogo." *Medium.com*, December 14, 2017. https://medium.com/historias-socioambientais/fogo-do-indio-65df77094096.

———. "O contato da morte." *ISA: Notícias*, February 5, 2020. https://www.socioambiental.org/pt-br/noticias-socioambientais/o-contato-da-morte.

Lemos, Vinicius. "Por que Pantanal vive 'maior tragédia ambiental' em décadas." *BBC News Brazil*, August 5, 2020. https://www.bbc.com/portuguese/brasil-53662968.

Locatelli, Piero. "Após expulsarem de madeireiros a médicos, índios defendem autonomia total no Maranhão." *Uol: Notícias*, January 9, 2018. https://noticias.uol.com.br/cotidiano/ultimas-noticias/2018/01/09/apos-expulsarem-de-madeireiros-a-professores-indios-defendem-autonomia-total-no-maranhao.htm.

Maisonnave, Fabiano. "Brazil's First Indigenous Congresswoman Defends

Her People's Rights from Bolsonaro." *Climate Change News*, February 19, 2019. https://www.climatechangenews.com/2019/02/19/brazils-first-indigenous-congresswoman-defends-peoples-rights-bolsonaro/.

Parreiras, Mateus. "Índios Pataxó de São Joaquim de Bicas alegam desamparo e fecham tribo." *Estado de Minas Gerais*, April 3, 2020. https://www.em.com.br/app/noticia/gerais/2020/04/03/interna_gerais,1135141/indios-pataxo-de-sao-joaquim-de-bicas-alegam-desamparo-e-fecham-tribo.shtml.

Quadros, Vasconcelos. "Dois mil garimpeiros buscam ouro em Raposa Serra do Sol." *Pública*, May 22, 2020. https://apublica.org/2020/05/dois-mil-garimpeiros-buscam-ouro-em-raposa-serra-do-sol/.

Rocha, Bruna, and Rosamaria Loures. "In Amazonia, Libraries are Being Set Alight." *OpenDemocracy*, July 20, 2020. https://www.opendemocracy.net/en/amazonia-libraries-are-being-set-alight/.

Rohter, Larry. "Language Born of Colonialism Thrives Again in Amazon." *New York Times*, August 28, 2005.

Roman, Clara. "Brigadas indígenas na linha de frente contra o fogo." *ISA: Notícias*, November 1, 2019. https://www.socioambiental.org/pt-br/noticias-socioambientais/brigadas-indigenas-na-linha-de-frente-contra-o-fogo.

Santana, Renato, and Tiago Miotto. "Focos de incêndio em terras indígenas aumentaram 88% em 2019." *CIMI*, September 10, 2019. https://cimi.org.br/2019/09/focos-incendio-terras-indigenas-aumentaram-88-2019/.

Shepard, Glenn H., Jr. "Voluntary Isolation in the Time of Coronavirus." *Chacruna*, March 24, 2020. https://chacruna.net/voluntary-isolation-in-the-age-of-coronavirus/.

Sposati, Ruy. "Kadiwéu: Com fim da greve da PF, indígenas podem ser despejados de terra homologada." *CIMI*, October 16, 2012. https://cimi.org.br/2012/10/34128/.

"Vídeo denuncia atentados e campanha de ódio contra indígenas na Bahia." *Revista Forum*, September 6, 2013. https://revistaforum.com.br/noticias/video-denuncia-atentados-e-campanha-de-odio-contra-indigenas-na-bahia/.

Wapichana, Joênia, and Deb Haaland. "Protecting Indigenous Lands Protects the Environment; Trump and Bolsonaro Threaten Both." *Washington Post*, March 18, 2019. https://www.washingtonpost.com/opinions/2019/03/18/protecting-indigenous-lands-protects-environment-trump-bolsonaro-threaten-both.

Films

Alarcón, Daniela Fernandes, dir. *Tupinambá: O Retorno da Terra*. Reportér do Brasil, 2015.

Carelli, Vincent, Tatiana Almeida, and Ernesto de Carvalho, dirs. *Martírio*. Pragda, 2016.

Franca, Belisário, dir. *Estratégia Xavante*. Giros and IDET, 2007.
Matarezio Filho, Edson Tosta, and Marília Senlle, dirs. *Caminho de Mutum*. Laboratório de Imagem e Som em Antropologia—Universidade de São Paulo, 2018.
Murat, Lúcia, dir. *Brava Gente Brasileira*. Taiga Filmes e Vídeo, 2000.
Murat, Lúcia, and Rodrigo Hinrichsen, dirs. *A nação que não esperou por Deus*. Taiga Filmes e Vídeo, 2015.

Index

Note: Page numbers followed by *f* indicate figures.

Abuênonâ (Karajá leader), 91–92
Afro-Brazilians: captured by Native groups, 53, 55–56, 95–96, 248n21; fugitives, 19, 24, 26, 27*f*; 50–51, 60, 103, 174; integrated into Native groups, 174; rebels, 133. *See also* Slaves, African
Agriculture: expansion of, 132–33, 191; Native attitudes toward, 93, 123; Native practices of, 14, 37, 138, 150
Airão, 78, 83–85
Aires Pinto (Guaná leader), 94–95, 138
Akroá, 34–36, 43, 62, 226n68
Albuquerque, 72, 74, 121–22, 135, 146, 149–50
Alcohol: gifts of, 95, 110–11, 116; social and ritual drinking, 178–79; trade in, 141, 145, 150, 153–54, 175–76; as vice product, 28, 118, 130, 138–39, 162, 175–78
Aldeamentos (state-sponsored villages), 64, 146, 150–54, 164
Alliances, 52–53, 61–63, 71–75, 134–39, 144–45, 169–74. *See also* Peacemaking
Amazon River, 37–38, 80, 82–83, 85, 153, 185. *See also* Solimões River
Ambrósio (Mura leader), 79–87, 97–103, 116, 119, 123
Ambushes. *See* Guerrilla warfare
Anthropologists, 7, 16, 113, 187, 190, 194
Apinajé, 46, 125
Apoena (Xavante leader), 1–2
Asunción, 24, 28–29, 33, 41, 67–68, 136
Attacks, Native: allegations of, 38, 41; fears of, 28, 68, 76, 180; motives for, 30–31, 43–55
Autazes (region), 19, 37, 41, 85, 140–42, 165–68, 173–75, 198, 223n41
Autonomous peoples: contemporary, 14–17, 194; depictions of, 5, 9–11, 51, 60,

122–24; repression of, 45, 123–25; territories, 3, 5, 8, 34–42, 60
Azevedo, Ana Mary, 198

Bananal Island, 90–92
Baptism: of children, 80–81, 104, 141, 155; Native fears of, 81; rejection of, 93, 122
Bararoá (Ambrósio Pedro Ayres), 142–43, 186
Barcelos, 87, 112–13, 129
Bates, Henry Walter, 144–45, 153–54
Belém, 141, 154
Belén, 28–29, 67, 219n15
Beque de Ayona (Guaikurú leader), 137–38, 266n65, 267n71
Big Catch (Pega-Pega), 143, 158
Biopiracy, 185
Blacks. *See* Afro-Brazilians
Bodoquena Mountains, 40, 70, 150, 182
Body painting, 7–8, 13, 20, 115, 134, 149, 152, 162–64, 186; patterns and motifs, 70*f*, 147*f*, 156*f*, 163*f*. *See also* Urucum
Boggiani, Guido, 162–65, 172–73, 175–80, 186–87, 280n46
Borba (Trocano), 32, 80–82, 140–41, 184–85, 196, 243n91
Borbón (Olimpo), Fort, 106, 131, 136, 148, 264n41
Borderlands, 3, 7–13, 19, 22, 25–43; changing conditions in, 130–31, 135–39
Borders: closing of, 15, 179; demarcation of, 22, 27*f*, 42–43, 59–60, 78, 82; disputes over, 18, 103, 106–7; markers, 103, 195*f*, 251n39; movements across, 67–68, 71–73, 90, 106–7, 109, 123, 146–51; opportunities near, 73, 106–107, 109, 239n58, 253n56. *See also* Demarcation

Bororo, 95, 118–19, 126, 127*f*, 261n13
Botocudo, 124–25, 155, 161
Brava Gente Brasileira (film), 195
Cabanagem Rebellion, 141–45, 153, 159, 185–86, 197
Cacao, 23–24, 31, 133
Caiapó do Sul: contact history, 125, 134, 168–69; peacemaking, 62, 65, 82; territory, 34
Caimá (Queima, Guaikurú leader), 69*f*, 70*f*, 75, 94, 221n31; kinship ties of, 228–29n94, 238n49
Calabá (Kadiwéu leader), 136
Caldas, João Pereira, 102–4, 113, 250n36, 252n46
Cannibalism, accusations of, 10, 124, 261n13; as metaphor, 16
Canoes: attacks on, 44–45, 86; colonial use, 23, 32; and communication, 75, 99–100; crews, 143, 154, 227n75; fabrication and maintenance, 104, 161; Native use, 6, 36–37, 41, 101*f*, 131, 158–59, 198
Capitãozinho (Kadiwéu leader), 169–72, 170*f*, 176, 179, 182
Captives: as cultural intermediaries, 24, 50–55, 58, 97–98, 117; raids for, 31, 41, 73, 106–8, 125–31; return of, 55–56, 80, 98; settler trade in, 11, 125–30, 261n20; status of, 116; women, 53, 55–56, 225n62. *See also* Slaves, Native; Children: trafficking of
Castelnau, Francis de, 146–48, 149*f*, 169–71, 175–76
Cattle: and expansion of ranching, 133, 191; feral, 40–41; Native possession of, 21, 180–81; raids for, 131, 136, 139
Chaco, 41, 57, 68, 146–50, 179–80

Index   327

Chamacoco, 53, 73, 109, 162, 172–73, 180
Chiefs: control of trade, 127–30, 150; and decision-making, 1–2, 25, 29, 42, 137–38; demands or complaints made by, 114–17, 173; and prestige, 73, 111–13, 129, 176–77, 248n17; role in peacemaking, 69–76, 78–79, 91–97, 144–45, 151, 238n49; violent encounters with, 30, 47–49, 55, 135–36. *See also specific Native leaders*
Children: incorporation of, 51–53, 78–79; as intermediaries, 1–2; protectiveness over, 105; role in peacemaking, 48, 80–81, 117, 155; trafficking in, 4, 53, 117, 125–28, 130–31, 263n31
Christianity: evangelization efforts, 97, 105, 177; rejection of, 54–56, 122–23, 177; rituals associated with, 33, 80–81, 87, 155, 221n31. *See also* Baptism
Citizenship, 132
Civilizing campaigns, 19, 105, 121, 127, 145–46, 151–52, 164, 188
Clothing: gifts of, 58, 89, 97, 114; symbolism, 55, 115, 129, 134; uniforms, 94–95, 136, 169–71, 256n86
Coimbra, Fort: attacks at, 48–49, 68, 136, 229n103; location, 47, 107; Native visitors to, 48, 68–76, 108–16; supply shortages at, 93, 111; symbolic importance of, 78
Colonization: by Europeans, 8–9, 24–34, 59–62; internal, 132–33; in modern period, 5, 189.
Concubines, 53, 74–75, 98, 172–73
Constitution, of Brazil, 132, 191
Contact: dangers associated with, 13–15, 47, 68–69, 78, 130, 189; efforts to control, 1–4, 14–15, 39, 63, 118, 128–30, 152, 189, 192–93; first or recent, 68–69, 77–78, 85, 110, 152, 199; historical patterns of, 7, 14, 189; Native perspectives on, 3, 13–17, 63, 86, 189, 240n68; state policies on, 60, 145–46, 152, 188–89
Conversion. *See* Christianity: evangelization efforts
Coronavirus, 15, 192–193. *See also* Epidemics
Crown, Portuguese: objectives, 8, 11, 59–62, 108–9, 118–19; reforms, 104–6
Cuiabá, 29–30, 113, 115
Cunha, Damiana da, 134

Daniel, João, 30–31
Deception: in peacemaking, 30–31, 66, 118–19; in war, 46–50
Demands, Native, 89–90, 108–119, 151–52
Demarcation, 22, 27f, 42–43, 59–60, 78, 82, 191–92, 199. *See also* Borders; Land; Reserves
Demography: depopulation, 39–40, 140; population counts, 38, 104, 109, 166–68, 186, 194, 196; predictions of collapse, 161–62, 166, 182–83
Descendant communities, 7, 17, 22, 194–98
Diplomacy. *See* Alliances; Peacemaking
Directorate. *See* Indian Directorate
Directors: of aldeamentos, 146, 153–54, 271n111, 280n44; of colonial Indian villages, 38, 50, 77
Diseases. *See* Epidemics
Domestication. *See* Taming

Ecological change, 8–9, 62, 68, 132–33, 159, 183–84, 191, 196–97

Economy: export sector, 132–33, 145, 173, 183–85; Native participation in, 14, 63, 158–59, 191–92. *See also* Extractive industries; Labor
Edwards, William Henry, 143–44, 153–54
Ega (Tefé), 45, 79, 82, 87, 102, 116, 165
Elliott, João Henrique, 149–50
Emavidi Xané (Paulo, Guaikurú leader), 71, 73–74, 76, 93–95; kinship ties of, 137, 228–29n94, 238n49
Emissaries. *See* Intermediaries
Empire, Brazilian, 5, 121, 139, 142
Epidemics: and contact strategies, 13–15, 62, 104, 192–93, 198; and depopulation, 166; settler weaponization of, 28, 154, 273n133
Ethnogenesis, 19–20
Ethnography, salvage, 13, 161–69, 174–75
Ethnonyms, 18–21, 42, 168–69, 208n14
Ewart, Elizabeth, 113
Extinction narratives, 5, 17, 161–69, 182–83
Extractive industries: expansion of, 5, 60–61, 145, 173, 183–84, 193; and land encroachment, 15, 132, 173, 183–84, 191, 196–97; and Native labor, 133, 158–59, 160, 166–68, 173, 183–86. *See also* Rubber

Factionalism, Native, 42, 66, 72–73, 82–87, 137–39, 172, 267n71; and warfare, 18–19, 62, 119
Families. *See* Kinship ties; Malocas
Farming. *See* Agriculture
Fecho dos Morros, 47, 72, 228–29n94
Fernandes, Mathias, 77–78, 99
Ferreira, Alexandre Rodrigues, 52–53, 69–70, 83–85, 209n16
Firearms. *See* Guns
Fires, 48, 196, 222n40
Fishing: conflicts over, 99–103, 250n31; Mura renowned for, 139, 144, 183; work in, 131, 141
Florence, Hercule, 155–57
Forests: destruction of, 2, 132–33, 196–97; as Native realm, 8–9, 44–45, 61, 191, 232n3; as refuge, 32, 39, 129, 133, 189
Forts: attacks on, 48–49, 68, 131, 136, 264n41; establishment of, 44, 47, 78, 106–7; Native visitors at, 48, 68–76, 89, 108–16; presence of women at, 69, 74. *See also specific forts*
Freyreiss, Georg Wilhelm, 130
Frontiers, 8, 44, 60, 76–78, 125–31, 135–39, 146–48, 157. *See also* Borderlands; Borders
Fugitives: Native peoples harboring, 19, 24, 50–51, 60, 79, 174; runaways from colonial settlements, 24, 26, 44, 67, 103
FUNAI. *See* National Indian Foundation

General Director of Indians, 145–46, 164, 271n110
Gifts: of children, 117; decline in, 123, 130–31; expenditures on, 61, 110–12, 112*f*; Native demands for, 89–90, 108–119, 151–52; Native preferences for, 109–10, 255n76; and peacemaking, 108–118; and prestige, 89, 115–16, 177; shortages of, 93, 111. *See also* Alcohol; Clothing; Guns
Goiás (captaincy or province), 34–36, 35*f*, 43, 62, 134, 151
Gold, 32, 41, 193

Gouveia, Jonilda, 193
Guaikurú: alliance and peacemaking, 16, 57, 67–76, 92–96, 106–7, 121–22, 134–35, 171; depictions of, 10, 69–70, 70*f*, 108, 122, 147*f*, 149*f*; ethnonyms, 208n14; and gifting, 33, 93, 108–116; horses, 6, 40, 61, 72, 75, 148–50; identity, 19; interethnic relations, 52–53, 135, 138–39; language, 75; leaders, 48–49, 69–73, 76, 93–95, 114–16, 137, 267n71; mobility, 39–40, 106–7, 148–51; in Paraguayan War, 158, 170–71; raids, 41, 53, 61, 73, 106–7, 131, 136, 146–48; social hierarchy, 52–53, 74, 93–94, 115–16; Spanish relations with, 6, 27–29, 33, 70–72, 108–9; subgroups, 19, 41–42, 71–72, 168, 219n15, 224n59, 228–29n94, 238n49, 267n71, 239n54; territory, 6, 19, 21, 39–41, 107, 148, 171; trade goods, 33–34, 43, 109–111, 176, 238n46; and violence, 30, 46–49, 55, 67–68, 131, 136–39, 146–48, 158, 229n103; women, 69–70, 74, 238n44. *See also* Kadiwéu

Guaná: in aldeamentos, 150; alliances and peacemaking, 95, 109, 115–16; relationship with Guaikurú, 53, 62, 73–74, 116, 135, 138–39; seeking refuge, 123; women, 74

Guarani-Kaiowá, 152, 192, 286n5
Guató, 73, 138
Guerrilla warfare, 32, 44–46, 49, 68, 227n77
Guides, 18, 25, 40, 138, 148
Guns: Native use of, 43–44, 110, 122, 169; prohibitions on trade, 43, 109–10, 135, 152, 226n72; shortages of, 252n46; symbolic importance of, 48–50, 91

Handbook of South American Indians (Steward), 165
Harris, Mark, 100
Headmen. *See* Chiefs
Hierarchies: gift exchanges and, 115–16; in Native society, 52–53, 73–74, 85, 93–94, 169
Horses: and territoriality, 21, 40, 180–81; taken in raids, 43, 61, 71–72, 136; as trade item, 61, 72, 116, 149–50, 175–76; use in warfare, 6, 19, 43
Hunting, 40, 68, 99–102, 101*f*, 106

Identity: claims about, 18, 20–21, 51–52, 66, 80, 181, 196–98; and erasure, 17–18, 141–42, 182–83, 188–89; territory and, 19, 181; transformation of, 19–20, 183, 190–91, 196
Inconstancy, Native reputation for, 66, 69, 75, 86, 104, 151
Independence, of Brazil, 5, 19, 121, 127, 133–34
Indian Directorate, 77, 105, 146, 222n41, 223n48, 241n75, 262n27
Indian Protection Service (SPI), 68, 111, 166–68, 173–75, 178, 183–85, 275n2
Informants. *See* Spies, Native
Information gathering, 24–25, 47, 63, 75–76
Intermediaries, 14, 25–27, 50–55, 95–98, 117, 173
Interpreters, 12, 55, 58, 85, 91, 95–98, 102–3
Intoxication, 178–79
Isolated peoples, 14–15, 36, 192–93, 199
Itinerant villages, 107, 198. *See also* Mobility

Japurá River, 77–80, 87, 103, 127–29, 182, 251n42
Jesuits, 9–10, 27–33, 43, 67. *See also* Missionaries
Joana (mother of Ambrósio), 79–82, 97
João Manoel (Miranha leader), 128–29
Joaquina (wife of Caimá), 69–71, 70*f*, 228–29n94
Juruá River, 38, 83, 250n34
Juruna, 44, 50, 54

Kadiwéu: alliances and peacemaking, 72, 108–9, 170–73, 187, 194; artistry of, 13, 162, 186–87; depictions of, 147*f*, 149–51, 162–65, 163*f*, 170*f*, 186–87; and drinking, 175–79; firefighting role of, 196; as Guaikurú subgroup, 19, 168, 219n15, 225n61, 253–54n64; and gifting, 108, 110–11; identity, 13, 19, 21; leaders, 135–36, 149–50, 169, 179; mobility, 72, 146–51, 182; in Paraguayan War, 169–70, 271n114; population, 186; present-day, 194–96; raids, 131, 139, 146–50, 179; social hierarchy, 196; territorial reserve, 171, 181–82, 194–96, 195*f*; and violence, 131, 135–36, 172, 179–80, 264n41; women, 13, 162, 163*f*, 187. *See also* Guaikurú
Kaingang, 177, 181
Karajá, 90–92, 99, 124–25, 226n71, 250n35
Kayapó, 191–92
Kin groups. *See* Malocas
Kinship ties, 42, 53, 64, 71, 81, 117, 157, 228–29n94, 238n49, 244n102
Kopenawa, Davi, 17
Krenak, Ailton, 13

Kueretú, 129

Labor: coerced, 124–27, 133–34, 139, 143, 157–59, 166–68, 173; Native evasion of, 93, 105, 122, 128, 139, 145, 186, 189; for private parties, 105–6, 126–27, 131–32, 172; temporary or seasonal, 65, 122, 154–55, 160, 172. *See also* Slaves, Native
Land: defense of, 179–85; demarcation, 17, 22, 27*f*, 42–43, 59–60, 78, 82, 191–92, 199; reclamation of, 2, 192, 198; and territorialization, 19, 181, 216n71; rights, 17, 20, 181, 194. *See also* Borderlands; Reserves
Language: interpreters, 12, 55, 91, 96–97; loss of, 97; reclamation of, 20; secret, 75. *See also* Língua geral
Leaders. *See* Chiefs
Lévi-Strauss, Claude, 16, 110, 186–87
Língua geral, 20, 67, 78, 96–97, 139, 174
Livestock. *See* Cattle; Horses
Logging. *See* Extractive industries
Lourenço (Guaikurú leader), 47–48

Madeira River, 31–32, 37–38, 85, 140–43, 158, 168, 223n42
Malheiros, Antônio Joaquim, 172, 180–82, 280n44
Malocas (extended kin groups), 64, 85, 88, 140, 153
Manacapurú, 102–3, 157
Manaus (Barra), 140, 154–55, 173, 184, 196
Manoel Aropquimbe (Kaingang leader), 177
Maps, 8, 34–36, 35*f*, 191, 251n38
Mardel, João Batista, 80, 98, 117–18, 119, 123

Maripí, Santo Antônio de, 45, 50–51, 77–79, 99
Marmelos River, 37, 222n38
Marriage, 53, 71, 93, 177, 196, 228–29n94. *See also* Mixing, racial and ethnic
Martius, Carl von, 126–29, 139–41, 263n31
Massacres: of Native groups, 28, 45, 123; of whites, 48–49, 68–69, 146, 229n103
Matari, São José do, 153–54, 273n129
Mato Grosso (captaincy, province, or state), 32, 41, 126, 136–39, 150, 169, 171
Mato Grosso do Sul (state), 73, 194
Mawé. *See* Sateré-Mawé
Mbayá-Guaikurú. *See* Guaikurú
Military: punitive expeditions, 29–30, 39, 44–45, 60, 88, 124–25, 172; strategy, 46–49, 69, 78–79, 107, 270n103; titles and commissions, 94–95, 138, 144. *See also* Forts; Soldiers
Minas Gerais (province), 124, 130, 152, 155, 232n3
Mining. *See* Extractive industries
Miranda, Fort, 72, 74, 123, 135–36
Miranha, 127–29, 263n32
Missionaries: aims of, 25–26, 60, 153; as chroniclers, 9–10, 30–31, 44, 165, 174–75, 177; interactions with Native groups, 27–31, 33. *See also* Jesuits
Missions, 28–33, 37, 41, 43, 67, 145–46, 152
Mixing, racial and ethnic, 26, 53, 93, 175, 196
Mobility: attempts to restrict, 106, 131, 143, 184; depictions of, 10–11; seasonal, 36–40, 63, 71–72, 104–6, 146–51, 166, 176, 182–83, 192; and social networks, 82–83, 175, 198
Monteiro, John, 187
Muhuraida (poem by Wilkens), 15, 76, 242n84
Mundurukú: alliances and peacemaking, 88, 114, 144–45, 158; attacks, 82; depictions of, 156*f*, 274n141; expansion, 62, 85, 88; and gifting, 114; interethnic strife, 62, 132, 143–44, 234n14, 264n44, 275n150; and labor negotiation, 133, 145, 280n49
Mura: alliances and peacemaking, 15, 76–88, 97–106, 141; canoes, 6, 61, 104, 131, 142; depictions of, 9–10, 30, 83, 84*f*, 101*f*, 104, 123, 143–44, 158, 165, 167*f*, 186, 197*f*; enslavement, 30–32, 134, 139; and ethnic incorporation, 19, 50–52, 54, 77–80, 82–83, 97, 173–75, 196; forced labor, 143, 158, 173; and gifting, 113, 116; identity, 20–21, 51–52, 77–80, 174–75, 186, 196–98; interethnic strife, 62, 78, 119, 132, 143–44, 234n14, 264n44, 275n150; intoxication, 178–79; language, 20, 75, 97; leaders, 15, 78–87, 112; mobility, 36–39, 82–83, 104–6, 131–32, 183–84; population, 168, 196; present-day, 7, 15, 196–98; 197*f*; raids, 37–39, 77, 106, 140; resettlement plans for, 98, 102–5, 105–6, 250n36; rubber, 158–59, 183–86; Spanish relations with, 102–3, 250n34; subgroups, 85–86, 140, 222n38; territory, 6, 19, 32, 37–39, 85, 140, 182–86, 198, 250n31; trade goods, 117–18, 139, 153, 178; and violence, 30–32, 37–39, 45, 77, 140–44, 157, 184–85; women, 79–82, 97–98, 105
Mura, Barreto, 15

Mura, Márcia, 20
Murat, Lúcia, 195

Nalique, 172, 175, 180
Names, Christian or honorific, 94, 247n14
National Indian Foundation (FUNAI), 189, 191
Nations, Indigenous, 18, 21, 51, 64, 66, 74, 86, 174, 181. *See also specific ethnic groups*
Nauvilla (Kadiwéu leader), 172
Negro, Rio, 37, 45, 78–80, 83, 112, 166
Nheengatu. *See* Língua geral
Nimuendajú, Curt, 165–68, 173, 178, 184–86
Nogueira, 79–80, 98

Oral histories, Native, 3, 7, 24, 141–42, 158, 160, 169, 183, 193

Pachico (Kueretú leader), 129–30
Pacificando o branco (Albert and Ramos), 16
Pacification. *See* Peacemaking; Taming
Panará, 113, 169. *See also* Caiapó do Sul
Pandemics. *See* Epidemics
Pantanal, 40–41, 40*f*, 136, 148, 165, 182, 194–196; definition, 224n54
Paraguay, 67, 131, 135–39, 146–48, 158, 194
Paraguay River: attacks along, 30, 55; exploration of, 47; and Guaikurú territory, 19, 39–41, 70–72, 176, 225n61, 238n49; Portuguese outposts on, 68, 107
Paraguayan War, 158, 169–71, 194
Payaguá, 30, 41, 44, 55
Peacemaking: deception in, 30–31, 66, 118–19; gifts and, 47, 69–75, 108–19, 138–39; Guaikurú process of, 67–76, 92–96, 106–7; intermediaries in, 95–98; Mura process of, 76–87, 97–106; Native perspectives on, 59, 63, 75–76, 80–88; rituals of, 58, 90–94, 257n97; role of chiefs in, 69–76, 78–79, 91–97, 144–45, 151, 238n49; role of children in, 48, 80–81, 117, 155; state objectives, 59–62, 118, 233n7, 238n49; symbols of, 64, 90, 94–95, 155, 171; role of women in, 64, 69–70, 237n43; written records of, 63–67
Photography, 162–67, 187
Pirahã, 75, 97, 222n38
Population. *See* Demography
Purí, 130
Purús River, 157, 174, 270n102

Raids: for captives, 31–32, 53, 73, 124–129; for cattle or horses, 43, 61, 71–72, 131, 136, 139; efforts to prevent, 106–7, 179; fears of, 148, 180; purposes, 11, 37–38, 41–42, 45, 61, 65, 77–78. *See also* Violence; Warfare
Railroads, 158, 182
Ranches: expansion of, 1–2, 21, 62, 67–68, 133, 191; and Native labor, 126, 133, 171–72; Native occupations of, 180–81, 194; raiding of, 41, 61, 71–73, 136. *See also* Cattle
Reforms. *See* Crown: reforms
Regulation Concerning the Missions of Indian Catechism and Civilization, 145–46, 151, 153, 271n112
Religion. *See* Christianity; Rituals
Reserves: demarcation of, 16–17, 181; Kadiwéu, 171, 181–82, 194–96,

195*f*; Mura, 196–98
Resettlement, 31, 63, 93, 98, 102–7, 234n18, 250n36
Resistance: histories of, 15, 20, 197; knowledge and, 43–56; and organized rebellion, 135–39, 141–44, 157; protest, 197*f*; and refusal, 20–21, 55–56, 105, 122–23, 139, 154, 234n18. *See also* Cabanagem
Ribeiro, Darcy, 186–87
Rituals: of Christianity, 33, 80–81, 87, 155, 221n31; Native, 10, 13, 20, 108, 178–79; of peacemaking, 58, 90–94, 257n97
Rivasseau, Émile, 164, 171, 176, 179, 182
Rojas, Fernando, 27*f*, 103
Romexi (Caiapó leader), 82
Rubber, 14, 133, 145, 158–59, 160, 173, 183–86, 285n104

Sampaio Lake, 142–43, 185–86, 285n105
Sánchez Labrador, José, 27–29, 33, 41, 219n15, 237n42, 238n44
São Paulo (captaincy, province, or state), 1–2, 41, 152, 182
Sateré-Mawé, 44, 226n72
Scouts. *See* Spies, Native
Seasonality: of movements, 17, 39–40, 63, 71–72, 104, 166, 176, 192; of natural resources, 36–40, 104, 107, 196; of residence, 29, 63, 107, 148–54;
Serra, Ricardo Franco de Almeida, 74–75, 93–96, 108, 111, 114, 209n16
Sertanistas (backwoodsmen), 60, 188
Sertão (wilderness), 8, 10, 34, 60
Settlers. *See* Whites
Severino (Mura leader), 141

Shepard, Glenn, 14–15
Silva, António Batista da, 96
Slaves, African: 38, 133; fugitives, 19, 24, 60, 96, 103, 133; killing of, 55, 106, 126; Native attitudes toward, 74, 93
Slaves, Native: expansion or revival of trade in, 8, 26, 31–32, 123–30, 159; fears of becoming, 44, 134, 139–40. *See also* Children: trafficking of
Soldiers: as deserters or rebels, 19, 60, 140, 174; interactions with Native peoples, 30, 43, 48–49, 74, 89, 102; as intermediaries, 96; recruitment of, 39, 142, 144, 257n95, 270n103
Solimões River, 37–38, 45, 78–80, 85, 103, 157. *See also* Amazon River
Sovereignty: European, 8–9, 34–35; Native, 92, 181, 192
Spanish: Guaikurú relations with, 27–29, 39–42, 46–47, 70–73, 106–7; Mura encounters with, 102–3; Native alliances with, 67, 71–72, 90, 103, 122; rivalry with Portuguese, 6, 25, 59–63, 76, 78, 103, 108–9. *See also* Borderlands; Borders
SPI. *See* Indian Protection Service
Spies, Native, 23–24, 32, 68, 76, 131, 148, 158
Spix, Johann Baptist von, 126–27, 139–41

Taming: of animals, 75, 81; of fire, 196; of people, 1–2, 16, 74–75, 155, 240n68
Tapajós River, 144, 156*f*, 161, 274n141, 285n104
Tastevin, Constantin, 165, 174–75, 178–79, 183–84, 269n93
Terra preta (anthropogenic black

soil), 37, 185, 285n105
Territorialization, 19, 181, 216n71
Ticuna, 18
Torá, 80–83
Trade: ambiguous intentions in, 3, 48–49, 68–69, 74, 88, 180; and manipulation, 118, 177–78; Native control of, 4, 41, 43, 116–18, 153–54, 174, 238n46; and raiding, 61, 71, 106–7, 125–131; restrictions on, 43, 109–10, 135, 226n72. *See also* Alcohol; Gifts; Horses
Travelers, Euro-American: 13, 126–30, 143–48, 153–55, 162–65, 182–83, 186–87. *See also* Ethnography, salvage; *individual traveler names*
Treaties: between Spain and Portugal, 59; of Native capitulation, 92; Native sovereignty recognized by, 92; written, 63–65
Trickery. *See* Deception
Turtles: competition over, 31, 99–102, 101*f*, 131, 264n43; in trade, 78, 116, 141, 174

Uniforms. *See* Clothing: uniforms
Uprisings. S*ee* Resistance; Cabanagem Rebellion
Urucum (Annatto), 7–8, 13, 70*f*, 115, 134, 149, 160, 209n23

Vieira, António, 44–45
Vila Bela da Santíssima Trindade, 71–73, 94, 113, 238n49
Vilaça, Aparecida, 86
Violence: and extermination, 124–25, 131; by Guaikurú, 30, 46–49, 55, 68, 136–39; in labor recruitment, 124–25, 133–34, 139, 143; against landowners, 133; by Mura, 37–38, 45, 85, 140–44, 184–85; state-sponsored, 28–32, 39, 44–45, 60, 88, 124–25. *See also* Warfare; Massacres
Visitors: to capital cities, 71–73, 94, 113, 151, 238n49; to forts, 48, 61, 68–76, 89, 108–16, 114; to plantations, 12*f*; seeking gifts, 111–14
Vitória (Black interpreter), 56, 95–96

Wapichana, Joênia, 191
Warfare: biological, 28, 154, 273n133; deception in, 46–50; of extermination, 124–25, 131; guerrilla warfare, 32, 44–46, 49, 68, 227n77; interethnic, 18–19, 62, 119, 263n32; against Native peoples, 28, 39, 42, 44–45, 60, 88, 124–26, 131; psychological, 53–56; return to, 121, 136–39, 141–43, 157–58; threats of, 42–43. *See also* Paraguayan War; Raids; Violence
Wari', 86, 190
Whites: as captives, 55; drawing closer to, 1–2, 4, 62–63, 82, 86–87, 177, 189; Native views of, 15–16, 25–34, 56–57, 129, 135, 145, 238n44; taming of, 1–2, 16, 74–75, 155, 240n68; violence committed by, 28–32, 39, 44–45, 60, 88, 124–26, 142–43, 172; withdrawal from, 4, 129–130, 139. *See also* Missionaries; Soldiers; Travelers, Euro-American
Wickham, Henry, 185, 285n104
Wilkens, Henrique João, 76, 85–87, 117, 271n110
Women, Native: agency of, 29, 81–82, 105, 130, 162, 187, 192–93, 197; artistry of, 13; captives, 53, 79–80, 225n62; as concubines, 53, 74–75, 98, 172–73; as enticements, 46, 48–49, 74; images of, 70*f*, 122, 162–63*f*, 166–67*f*; leadership roles of, 191;

role in peacemaking, 58, 64, 69–70, 79–80, 91, 237n43; social connections and, 79–82
Workers' corps, 143, 154, 159

Xavante, 1–2, 34–36, 35f, 65, 91, 192, 234n18

Xerente, 151–52
Xumana, 51–52, 62, 83, 98, 103

Yurí, 126–28

Zany, Francisco Ricardo, 126–28, 131–32, 141, 185, 264n44

The authorized representative in the EU for product safety and compliance is:
Mare Nostrum Group
B.V Doelen 72
4831 GR Breda
The Netherlands

www.ingramcontent.com/pod-product-compliance
Lightning Source LLC
Chambersburg PA
CBHW031754220426
43662CB00007B/395